REFERENCE BOOKS BULLETIN 2003 2004

A Compilation of Evaluations
September 2003 through August 2004

Prepared by American Library Association Reference Books Bulletin Editorial Board

Edited by Mary Ellen Quinn
Compiled by Keir Graff

Booklist Publications
Chicago, 2004

Copyright 1996, 2005 by the American Library Association.

Permission to quote any review in full or in part must be obtained from the Office of Rights and Permissions of the American Library Association. Permission to quote a review in full will be granted only to the publisher of the work reviewed.

Library of Congress Catalog Card Number 73-159565

International Standard Book Number 0-8389-8333-2

International Standard Serial Number 8755-0962

Printed in the United States of America

Cover design by Jim Lange

Contents

iv	Preface
v	Reference Books Bulletin Editorial Board
vi	Contributing Reviewers
1	Encyclopedia Update, 2003
5	Special Features
15	Reference on the Web
	Reviews
21	Generalities
24	Philosophy, Psychology, Religion
29	Sociology, Anthropology, Political Science
37	Business, Economics, Resources
40	Law, Public Administration, Social Problems and Services
45	Education, Commerce, Customs
48	Language
48	Science
54	Medicine, Health Technology, Management
60	Fine Arts, Decorative Arts, Music
63	Performing Arts, Recreation
69	Literature
77	Geography, Biography
82	History
	Indexes
91	Subject Index
94	Title Index

Preface

Guided by the steady hand of Mary Ellen Quinn, *Reference Books Bulletin* has weathered another year of reference publishing and brought in a fine catch of reviews to serve reference and collection development librarians. This thirty-sixth annual compilation consists of the reviews and feature articles appearing in *RBB* from September, 2003 through August, 2004. The *RBB* Editorial Board and contributing reviewers continue to provide the careful and thoughtful reviews needed for wise collection decisions in these tough fiscal times. Their contribution to the profession is invaluable. I am very pleased and proud to be associated with such a knowledgeable and dedicated group of individuals.

I would like to extend my thanks to Mary Ellen Quinn, editor, and Keir Graff, editorial assistant, for their patience and assistance. I would also like to thank the staffs of *Booklist* and ALA Publishing. Finally, I would like to thank my colleagues at the Chicago Public Library for their continued support.

Carolyn M. Mulac,
Chair

Reference Books Bulletin Editorial Board
2004-2005

Reference Books Bulletin Editorial Board, 2003–2004

Jack O'Gorman, Reference Librarian, Roesch Library, University of Dayton, Dayton, Ohio, Chair.

Donald Altschiller, History Bibliographer, Mugar Memorial Library, Boston University, Boston, Massachusetts.

Barbara Bibel, Reference Librarian, Oakland Public Library, Oakland, California.

Christine Bulson, Assistant Director for Reference and Circulation Services, Milne Library, SUNY Oneonta, Oneonta, New York.

Susan Gardner, Reference/Instruction Librarian, Leavey Library, University of Southern California, Los Angeles, California.

Dona Helmer, Librarian, Anchorage School District, Alaska.

Merle Jacob, Director of Library Collection Development, Chicago Public Library, Chicago, Illinois.

Deborah Rollins, Head, Collection Services Department, Fogler Library, University of Maine, Orono, Maine.

Linda Loos Scarth, Reference Librarian, Busse Center Library, Mount Mercy College, Cedar Rapids, Iowa.

Shauna Yusko, Children's Librarian, Bellevue Regional Library, Bellevue, Washington.

Reference Books Bulletin Contributing Reviewers, 2003–2004

James D. Anderson, Professor, School of Communication, Information and Library Studies, Rutgers University, New Brunswick, New Jersey.

Susan Awe, Director, Business and Economics, Parish Memorial Library, University of New Mexico, Albuquerque, New Mexico.

John-Leonard Berg, Coordinator of Public Services, Karrmann Library, Platteville, Wisconsin.

Ken Black, Director of Teaching and Learning Technology, Dominican University, River Forest, Illinois.

Craig Bunch, Librarian, Coldspring-Oakhurst High School Library, Coldspring, Texas.

Susan Burks, Public Services Librarian, University of Central Arkansas, Conway, Arkansas.

Nancy Cannon, Reference Librarian, Milne Library, SUNY Oneonta, Oneonta, New York.

Jerry Carbone, Director, Brooks Memorial Library, Brattleboro, Vermont.

Ann E. Cohen, Assistant Division Head, Information Center, Rochester Public Library, Rochester, New York.

Sharon E. Cohen, Boynton Beach, Florida.

Harold V. Cordry, Independent scholar, Baldwin, Kansas.

Jennifer Dawson, Electronic Resources Librarian, Kanawha County Public Library, Charleston, West Virginia.

Charlotte Decker, Librarian, Children's Learning Center, Public Library of Cincinnati and Hamilton County, Cincinnati, Ohio.

Carole C. Deily, Reference Librarian, Plano Public Library System, Plano, Texas.

John Doherty, Librarian, Arts and Humanities, Cline Library, Northern Arizona University, Flagstaff, Arizona.

Marie Ellis, Librarian IV Emeritus, University of Georgia Libraries, Athens, Georgia.

Susanna Eng, Reference/Instruction Librarian, University of Southern California, Los Angeles, California.

Stephen Fadel, Public Services Librarian, Everett Community College, Everett, Washington.

Lesley S. J. Farmer, Professor, CSU Long Beach, Long Beach, California.

Jack Forman, Public Services Librarian, San Diego Mesa College Library/LRC, San Diego, California.

Rochelle Glantz, Reviews Editor, Linworth Publishing, Santa Fe, New Mexico.

Susan Gooden, Librarian, Concord High School, Wilmington, Delaware.

Carol Sue Harless, Stone Mountain High School, Dekalb County School System, Stone Mountain, Georgia.

Nora Harris, Harris Indexing Service, Novato, California.

Michelle Hendley, Reference/Instruction Librarian, Milne Library, SUNY Oneonta, Oneonta, New York.

Robin Hoelle, Cybrarian, Live Oaks Career Development Center, Milford, Ohio.

Patricia M. Hogan, Administrative Librarian, Poplar Creek Public Library District, Streamwood, Illinois.

Danise Hoover, Associate Librarian for Public Services, Hunter College Library, New York, New York.

Jennifer L. Jack, Senior Librarian, U.S. News & World Report Library, Washington, D.C.

Sally Sartain Jane, former Head of Adult Collection Development, Lee County Library System, Fort Myers, Florida.

Cynthia Jasper-Parisey, Upper School Library, Cincinnati Country Day School, Cincinnati, Ohio.

Lisa N. Johnston, Associate Director/Head of Public Services, Sweet Briar College Libraries, Sweet Briar, Virginia.

Sean Kinder, Humanities/Social Sciences Librarian, Helm Library, Western Kentucky University, Bowling Green, Kentucky.

Jeff Kosokoff, Head of Reference Services, Lamont Library, Harvard University, Cambridge, Massachusetts.

Marlene M. Kuhl, Catonsville Library, Catonsville, Maryland.

Abbie Vestal Landry, Head of Reference Division, Watson Library, Northwestern State University, Natchitoches, Louisiana.

Jan Lewis, Interim Head of Reference, Joyner Library, East Carolina University, Greenville, North Carolina.

Art A. Lichtenstein, Director of Library, University of Central Arkansas, Conway, Arkansas.

Marilyn L. Long, Carmel Valley, California.

Kathleen M. McBroom, Resource Teacher for Library Media and Automation, Dearborn Public Schools, Dearborn, Michigan.

Christopher McConnell, Librarian, Protein Design Labs, Inc., Fremont, California.

H. Robert Malinowsky, Professor and Manager of Collection Development, University of Illinois at Chicago Library, Chicago, Illinois.

Arthur S. Meyers, Library Director, Russell Library, Middletown, Connecticut.

Carolyn M. Mulac, Information Center, Chicago Public Library, Chicago, Illinois.

Clark Nall, Reference/Instruction Librarian, Joyner Library, East Carolina University, Greenville, North Carolina.

Kathryn C. O'Gorman, Director, Johnnie Mae Berry Library, Cincinnati State, Cincinnati, Ohio.

Maren C. Ostergard, Children's Librarian, Bellevue Regional Library, Bellevue, Washington.

Deborah Carter Peoples, Science Library Manager, Ohio Wesleyan University Libraries, Delaware, Ohio.

Sue Polanka, Coordinator, Reference and Instruction, Roesch Library, University of Dayton, Dayton, Ohio.

Margaret Power, Reference Services Coordinator, DePaul University Library, Chicago, Illinois.

James Rettig, University Librarian, Boatwright Memorial Library, University of Richmond, Richmond, Virginia.

Diana Donner Shonrock, Science Librarian/Family and Consumer Sciences Bibliographer, Parks Library, Iowa State University, Ames, Iowa.

Esther Sinofsky, Coordinating Field Librarian, Library Services, Los Angeles Unified School District, Los Angeles, California.

Mary Ellen Snodgrass, Independent Scholar, Hickory, North Carolina.

Kathleen Stipek, Adult Services Librarian, Alachua County Library District, Gainesville, Florida.

Stephen E. Stratton, Head, Collections and Technical Services, California State University, Channel Islands, Camarillo, California.

Martin D. Sugden, Reference Librarian, Florida/Genealogy Department, Jacksonville Public Library, Jacksonville, Florida.

Kaye M. Talley, Coordinator of Technical Services, Torreyson Library, University of Central Arkansas, Conway, Arkansas.

William Joseph Thomas, Instruction/Reference Librarian, Joyner Library, East Carolina University, Greenville, North Carolina.

Michael Tosko, Information Literacy Coordinator, University of Akron, Akron, Ohio.

Scottie Wallace, Managing Librarian, Downtown Reno Library, Washoe County Library System, Reno, Nevada.

Cheryl Karp Ward, East Hartford High School, Library Media Center, East Hartford, Connecticut.

Sarah Barbara Watstein, Associate University Librarian for Public Services, VCU Libraries, Virginia Commonwealth University, Richmond, Virginia.

Ann Welton, Grant Center for the Expressive Arts, Tacoma, Washington.

Christine A. Whittington, Director of Library Services, Greensboro College, Greensboro, North Carolina.

Carolyn N. Willis, Reference Librarian, Joyner Library, East Carolina University, Greenville, North Carolina.

Encyclopedia Update, 2003

Encyclopaedia Britannica...1
Encyclopaedia Britannica Online..1
Encyclopedia American 2
Encyclopedia American Online 2
Grolier Multimedia Encyclopedia 3
The New Book of Knowledge 3
The New Book of Knowledge Online 3
World Book Encyclopedia 4
World Book Online Reference Center 4

This year's Encyclopedia Update features reviews of four print sets—*Encyclopaedia Britannica, Encyclopedia Americana, The New Book of Knowledge,* and *World Book Encyclopedia.* We also take a look at their online counterparts as well as *Grolier Multimedia Encyclopedia.*

From our perspective, the encyclopedia world has been fairly quiet over the past year. *Compton's Encyclopedia* reverted back to its previous owner, Britannica, and they supplied us with statistical data about the new edition, which we included in our "Encyclopedias in Print" chart, although the set itself was not available in time for us to review. We hope to include it in a future issue along with *New Standard Encyclopedia,* which also had a late publication date.

Online encyclopedia publishers have been taking a more global approach lately, bundling several different databases together to supplement and expand their encyclopedia offerings. Grolier Online has offered simultaneous searching of *Encyclopedia Americana, Grolier Multimedia Encyclopedia,* and *New Book of Knowledge,* along with several other databases, for several years. Britannica recently followed suit by adding *Britannica Student Encyclopedia* to *Encyclopedia Britannica Online.* This year, World Book has changed the name of *World Book Online* to *World Book Online Reference Center* to reflect a shift away from the stand-alone encyclopedia model.

For last year's update we paid particular attention to how encyclopedia publishers handled September 11, a challenge because it occurred relatively late in the year. This year we decided to focus on its aftermath, including events leading up the war in Iraq. We also took a look at the entries for some key players—Tony Blair, George W. Bush, and Hamid Karzai, among others. In addition, we checked the handling of some emerging diseases, severe acute respiratory syndrome (SARS) and West Nile virus.

—Susan Awe and Barbara Bibel

Encyclopaedia Britannica. 32v. 15th ed. 2003. Britannica, $1,395 (0-85229-961-3).

Encyclopaedia Britannica Online. [Internet database]. 2003. Britannica, pricing beginning at $195/year [http://www.eb.com/].

Encyclopaedia Britannica (EB) continues to be an authoritative resource. The 64,900 articles are signed by more than 4,300 contributors and have extensive bibliographies. The latest printing of the fifteenth edition retains the Micropaedia/Macropaedia/Propaedia structure that originated with great fanfare in 1974: short articles for quick reference in the Micropaedia, in-depth treatment of broad topics in the Macropaedia, and an "outline of knowledge" in the Propaedia.

New entries cover the September 11 attacks, al-Jazeera, and al- Qaeda, all in the Micropaedia. *September 11 attacks* includes a map showing the flight plans of the doomed planes and a picture of the World Trade Center in flames. Others among the 115 new entries include *Barbie, Botox, Designer drugs, Ecoterrorism, Ethnic cleansing,* and *Swiss Army Knife.* Among the 64 rewritten or revised articles are *Crusades, Geometry, Intelligence and counterintelligence,* and *Solar system.* Twelve new maps and 180 new illustrations make the material more current. There is no coverage of SARS (too new), but users will find West Nile virus. Unless attached to rewritten entries, the bibliographies have not been updated.

The Macropaedia article on Afghanistan is 12 pages long and has been updated in several places to reflect changes in 2002, although there is no mention of Hamid Karzai's election on June 13. The index misses the reference in the article to the September 11 attacks. The Micropaedia article on George W. Bush, which ends with the November 2002 elections, mentions his efforts during that year to focus world attention on Iraq. The Macropaedia article on Iraq ends in 2000, but users are referred to the *Britannica Book of the Year* for later developments.

We particularly like EB's coverage of non-U.S. topics. Macropaedia articles on other countries and on cities outside the U.S can be extensive. *United Kingdom* is 137 pages; *Vienna* and *Venice* are 6 and 8 pages, respectively; *West Indies* is almost 70 pages. We also like the extensive, scholarly Macropaedia bibliographies. The three-part structure can be cumbersome, so users should check the index first (in fact, the Micropaedia often prompts them to do so) in order to take fullest advantage of what EB has to offer.

Encyclopaedia Britannica Online (EB Online) has a clean, uncluttered home page with a single search box. Users may search with keywords, Boolean operators, and truncation. They may also browse alphabetically or by broad subject area. A spell-check option in the search engine will help them find what they need even if they are unsure of the correct letter combination. They have a choice of searching *Encyclopaedia Britannica, Britannica Student Encyclopedia* (geared toward middle-school students), *Britannica Internet Guide,* or video and media separately or in any combination. These tools offer more than 123,000 articles, 22,000 illustrations, 215,000 dictionary entries, and 167,000 Web links. In addition to the encyclopedia, users have access to the Merriam-Webster *Collegiate Dictionary* and *Collegiate Thesaurus* as well as a world atlas. Updates are monthly.

Britannica states that EB Online has 264 new and 2,565 replaced articles. Among the new entries are those for select U.S counties, absent from the print set. Some articles differ substantially from corresponding entries in the print set; the new one on Pope John Paul II, for example, is more current and much more detailed and also adds a list of further reading, which the Micropaedia article does not provide. Because of the option to search several databases, users also have access to 272 new and 589 replaced articles in *Britannica Student Encyclopedia* and 505 new articles in *Britannica Elementary Encyclopedia.* As with the print version, users must refer to the yearbook for more current information on Afghanistan; this is true for all of the articles about countries. The article on Iraq ends with the Persian Gulf War, although the *Britannica Student Encyclopedia* entry is somewhat more current. The George W. Bush entry is more up-to-date than that in the print set, with information from March 2003 about the launch of U.S. attacks on Iraq. The Saddam Hussein entry has been similarly updated. Oddly, among the Web links for the new *September 11 attacks* article, users will find sites for the Starr Report (issued on September 11, 1998) and *Apollo 11.* The video and media links are irrelevant, too. They include videos on heart attacks and plants ("defenses against attacks").

There is no information on SARS. Entering *severe acute respiratory syndrome* produces information about the respiratory system and links to articles on various syndromes. A brief article about West Nile virus has basic information and good Web links to the CDC and the Pennsylvania Department of Agriculture, but the video links are strange. There are videos on the Virginia Woolf–Vita Sackville-West relationship, the Notre Dame–West Virginia football game, and the Nile in ancient Egypt, among others.

Encyclopedias Online

Name	Number of Entries	Illustrations	Maps	Videos	Sounds	Web Links	Other Multimedia	Update Schedule	Base Annual Subscription Rate
Encyclopaedia Britannica Online	123,256	22,315	2,559	1,980	103	167,000	36 animations	Monthly	$195
Encyclopedia Americana Online	45,000	1,674	39	N/A	N/A	153,741		Quarterly (some features updated weekly)	$415
Grolier Multimedia Encyclopedia Online	40,000	7,500	896	13	786	114,000	33 animations, 151 panoramas, 28 interactive cutaways, 12 dynamic maps	Monthly	$415
New Book of Knowledge Online	9,000	5,200	630	N/A	N/A	8,276	Occasional animated cartoons, interactive games and puzzles	Monthly (some features updated weekly)	$415
World Book Online	38,000	10,000	1,500	70	10,000	14,000	45 animations, 114 panoramas	Monthly (some features updated daily)	$395

†The Grolier base price of $415 is for a bundled package, not an individual encyclopedia.

There are a number of special features available in EB Online. The Workspace button on the menu bar allows users to mark articles and store them for research projects. Britannica Heritage has articles from previous editions by notable contributors as well as galleries of maps and images so that users can learn about the "changing nature of human knowledge." Interactive time lines charts the development of the arts, sciences, technology, etc. The world atlas allows users to click on a part of the world to see regional maps or on index tabs to select political, physical, or economic maps. To see a map of an individual country, one must click on it to go to the article about the country and then click on the map.

The Annals of American History Online is a collection of primary source material from more than 1,500 authors. It includes speeches, landmark court decisions, and essays. Users may search alphabetically by author; by subject (discrimination and diversity, war and peace, American democracy, etc.); or by time period. This database requires a separate subscription. The *Britannica Online School Edition* [RBB N 1 02], for K–12 students, is also a special subscription. It includes the *Encyclopaedia Britannica, Britannica Student Encyclopedia,* and *Britannica Elementary Encyclopedia* as well as extra material for teachers to use in the classroom.

Conclusion: EB retains its position as an excellent scholarly reference source for public, academic, and secondary-school libraries. EB Online has current, authoritative information at several reading levels, an excellent selection of Web links, and links to magazine articles. Although it may not be as up-to-date as other online encyclopedias, EB Online is an excellent resource for academic, public, and high-school libraries.

Encyclopedia Americana. 30v. 2002. Grolier, $1,049 (0-7172-0136-8).
Encyclopedia Americana Online. [Internet database]. Grolier, pricing from $415 in combination with other Grolier Online products. Visit [http://go.grolier.com] for free 30-day trial.

Encyclopedia Americana (EA), known for thorough scholarly coverage since it was first published in 1829, had numerous changes for 2003—adding 50 distinguished new contributors, adding 135 new color photographs and 25 new black-and-white ones, and revising or adding 160 bibliographies—in addition to ongoing projects. There are 44 new entries, among them *Direct marketing; East Timor; Graves, Michael; Iguanadon;* and *Mississippian Culture. Aztecs, Eskimos, Microbiology,* and *Psychiatry* are among the 29 replacement entries, and *Adams, Abigail; China: Literature; Encyclopedia; Grasshopper; Hydroelectric power; and Powell, Colin* are among 193 entries that have been significantly revised. A focus on Islamic studies resulted in new entries for *Islamic philosophy and science* and *Islamic poetry* and revised entries for *Islam* and *Islamic art and architecture.* The *Space shuttle* article mentions the Columbia disaster in February 2003. There is no entry for West Nile virus.

Last year, EA created an index entry for *September 11 attacks,* under which one could find citations to *bin Laden, Osama; Bush, George Walker; disasters; hijacking; New York City; terrorism;* and *United States.* The 2003 edition adds citations to *New York Stock Exchange, Pentagon,* and *Port Authority of N.Y. and N.J.* There is a new index entry for *Qaeda, al.* The article on President Bush is current through the November 2002 elections and mentions possible confrontation with Iraq. *Afghanistan* has been updated through December 2001 and the installation of Hamid Karzai as interim leader. There is also a new biographical entry on Karzai. In last year's update we mentioned that many bibliographies have no books added since the 1980s, and this is still the case—*Clothing, Compact Disc,* and *Consumer protection* are just a few examples. The most current title in the bibliography for *Computers and computer science: history of the computer* was published in 1993. *Air traffic control* has no titles more recent than 1990; the same is true of *Interior design* (where the illustrations also need a serious facelift). On the other hand, the *Afghanistan* bibliography includes several titles published in 2002.

Encyclopedia Americana Online (EA Online) is well organized and frequently updated. The attractive splash page leads the user to four modules: Browse, *Americana Journal,* Editors' Picks, and Profiles. Browse is an

Encyclopedias in Print

Name	Number of Volumes	Number of Entries	Number of Pages	Number of Illustrations	Percent of Illustrations in Full Color	Price
Americana	30	45,000	26,800	23,000	20	$1,049
Britannica	32	64,900	32,000	24,400	32	$1,395
Compton's	26	37,000	11,000	22,500	NA	$699
New Book of Knowledge	21	9,243	10,576	27,850	93	$699
World Book	22	17,000	14,228	27,500	80+	$849

easy-to-use subject search; a more complex Query Builder, allowing highly refined searches, is available in the Advanced Search page. The expanded *Americana Journal* continues as EA Online's weekly update feature and is searchable by keyword as well as by country. Editors' Picks, also updated weekly, contains essays on particular topics, and Profiles assembles 1,500 frequently consulted biographies, classified by subject. An atlas and dictionary are available via the GO frame, which simultaneously searches all Grolier databases to which a library subscribes.

EA Online has added thousands of current Web links plus new maps and illustrations. Most of the articles now link directly to the OCLC WorldCat and EBSCO databases. Among the 222 new articles are *Bentonville; Bush-Gore Election 2000; Gorey, Edward; Industrial archaeology; Islamic philosophy and science; Mississippian culture; Process philosophy;* and *Silk Road;* the last four examples have also been added to the print set.

EA Online has many advantages over its print counterpart in terms of currency. Among the articles that have been replaced or significantly revised online but not in print are *Bonhoeffer, Dietrich; Caffeine; Carbohydrate; Ecology; Germany; Pacemaker;* and *Social sciences.* The online version of *Consumer protection* has an updated section relating to the European Union and a 2001 title in its bibliography. The online *Iraq* article is more current, adding a paragraph with information from late 2002. *Afghanistan* ends at the same point as the article in the print set—December 2001—but for both countries, the online version has a more extensive bibliography with several very current titles as well as links to magazine articles and *Americana Journal* entries. Periodical articles and *Journal* entries are also the sources for updated information on Tony Blair, whose encyclopedia entry ends in 1998. There is no entry for West Nile virus, but a full-text search leads to the article *Encephalitis,* where it is mentioned. A *Journal* search results in nine documents specific to West Nile. The *Journal* is the only place to find coverage of SARS.

Maps are a good size and readable and print quickly and easily. Most Web links are relevant and current. The fact that Article Titles Search is the default is still a drawback. Searching for George W. Bush results in no hits because George Walker Bush is the proper heading. Another annoying feature is that the search term must be retyped in order to try a full-text search instead.

Conclusion: EA offers in-depth treatment of many topics and is a good choice for academic, public, and high-school libraries, though the appearance of the print version makes it less inviting for students than other encyclopedias that use more color. For this reason, libraries might choose to skip the print set and opt for EA Online, which has made improvements in user-friendliness and is the first online encyclopedia to offer an ADA-compliant version.

Grolier Multimedia Encyclopedia. [Internet database]. Grolier, pricing from $415 in combination with other Grolier Online databases. Visit [http://go.grolier.com] for free 30-day trial.

Designed for students in grades five and up, *Grolier Multimedia Encyclopedia* (GME) launched a new version, 3.0, in May 2003, with a new design and an AD-compliant version. Among the new features are Today is . . . , which highlights birthdays of well-known people as well as historic events; new games and a Games Archive; and a How to Cite This Article link. Searches now retrieve media items as well as articles, listing each separately in the results. The weekly News feature now offers a link to "a selection of respected national and international news stories." Several enhancements have been made to GME's multimedia components. For example, videos, panoramas, and maps are now linked to other related material.

The encyclopedia can be searched by keyword or title or browsed by subject. In Advanced Search, users can employ Boolean operators and wild cards. Articles tend to be shorter than those in other encyclopedias, reflecting GME's roots as the short-entry *Academic American Encyclopedia,* which Grolier published in print form from 1980 to 1998. Entries are linked to media, to Web sites, and to full-text articles from 700 periodicals available through EBSCO Content Solutions. Among the nearly 600 new articles added since February 2002 are *African Union; Labor economics; Nanotechnology; Open source; School vouchers;* and *Superfund.* There are also entries for the space probes Aqua, Genesis, and Nozomi. Additional new articles cover topics in British, Irish, and Russian history; Christian contemporary music; and biographies of contemporaries like Michael Bloomberg and Annika Sorenstam. More than 90 articles have been rewritten or replaced, among them *Army, E-Commerce, Mars (planet),* and *United States education.* Additionally, 400 new photographs, pieces of art, and multimedia have been added.

The main Afghanistan article is current through March 2003. The article on September 11, 2001, mentions the sentencing of Moroccan Mounir al-Motassadek to 15 years in prison by a German court in February 2003. Both the George W. Bush and Iraq articles are current into June 2003. There is also an article on the Iraq War. We found biographical entries for Hamid Karzai and Tom Ridge. The article on SARS is current through May 2003, giving death rate and infection statistics as well as symptoms, though no periodical articles are listed under the Periodicals tab. There is no article on West Nile virus, but it is mentioned in *Encephalitis.*

The familiar Research Starter feature has more than 150 topics, many in the sciences. Brain Jam is the monthly feature highlighting a subject of current interest and often relates to the calendar month, such as Space Exploration and NASA for July 2003, with a picture of Buzz Aldrin walking on the moon July 20, 1969. Timelines consists of 24 main time-line screens covering world history events from 4,000 B.C.E. to the present. Printing with the Print/Email tab is easy and fast. An atlas and dictionary are available via the GO frame, which simultaneously searches all Grolier databases to which a library subscribes.

Conclusion: GME is an attractive, up-to-date resource for school and public libraries.

The New Book of Knowledge. 21v. 2003. Grolier, $699 (0-7172-0535-5).
The New Book of Knowledge Online. [Internet database]. Grolier, pricing from $415 in combination with other Grolier Online databases. Visit [http://go.grolier.com] for free 30-day trial.

The New Book of Knowledge (NBK) provides balanced, appropriate, and engaging coverage of a wide range of topics for students in grades four through six. Many appealing features, illustrations, and maps complement encyclopedia entries. For the 2003 edition, 51 completely new articles were added to the print set, among them *African Union; Chirac, Jacques; Grief; Giuliani, Rudolph; Mesopotamia; Snails and slugs;* and *Zoology.* Fifty-three articles were replaced, including *China, Conservation, Contact lenses, Medicine, Narcotics, Shanghai,* and *Sudan.* Another 38 articles, including *Arabs, Food supply, Koran, Olympic Games,* and *Postal Service,* received significant revisions. About 1,200 new images, photographs, and works of art were added, and now more than one-third of the space in NBK is devoted to illustrations. Approximately 1,500 bibliographies were added, bringing the total number of titles to nearly 8,000.

The replacement article on Afghanistan is current into June 2002 and Hamid Karzai's election as president of the Transitional Authority. *Terrorism, war on* is a new entry, and *Bush, George W.* and *Terrorism* were replaced. The Bush entry notes his address to the United Nations in September 2002, and the new entry on Tony Blair mentions the prime minister's support for Bush's plans to disarm Iraq. The postdeadline *Columbia* space shuttle disaster made it into the entries for *Space exploration and travel* and *Space shuttles.*

Each volume has its own index with blue pages, which makes it easy to locate, and there is a well-constructed comprehensive index volume for the set. Items such as pictures, maps, and diagrams are clearly identified in the index entries. Unfamiliar words are often defined briefly in the index, which is very helpful. All entries are signed, with a few words to identify the contributor; additionally, experts have reviewed some entries. Bibliographies appear in the "Home and School Reading and Study Guides," which accompanies the print set and is also available online.

Articles in *The New Book of Knowledge Online* often contain graphics, fact boxes, projects, and links to related NBK News stories (updated weekly), Web sites, articles in around 50 selected magazines appropriate for the elementary- and lower-middle-school level, and further reading lists. Longer articles have tables of contents allowing users to easily access the sections they want. Under NBK News, SummerScoops is a fun section that currently links to the Great Outdoors, Sightseeing.com, Rainy Day Fun, Summer Reading, and more. Other regular features, such as Wonder Questions, Literary Selections, and Projects and Experiments, are also found in the print set. These features, along with World History Time Line, Homework Help, and Bibliographies, are all accessible from every screen in the left frame. Encyclopedia Spotlight (a monthly topic) and Web Feat! (a fun-and-games approach to learning) are accessible only from the main page. Printing from all sections is easy to do and works quickly. An atlas and dictionary are available via the GO frame, which simultaneously searches all Grolier databases to which a library subscribes.

A Subject Browse, Alphabetical Browse, and Advanced Search are available in addition to a full-text Quick Search. A Quick Search for *September 11* yielded a useful collection of 143 encyclopedia articles and NBK News stories, while *Afghanistan* retrieved 78 articles and news stories. Being able to retrieve articles and updates in a single search is a great feature, making Quick Search very user-friendly. The George W. Bush article discusses the president's State of the Union speech and also the start of the U.S.-led invasion on March 19, 2003. The article on Iraq mentions the fall of Baghdad on April 9, and there is a separate entry for *Iraq War.* The entry for Saddam Hussein has been updated to record the fall of his regime. Users can links to information on both SARS and West Nile virus in NBK News and encyclopedia articles.

Conclusion: In both its print and online version NBK is well suited to its young audience, a group generally underserved by reference publishers. Its many appealing features encourage children to explore and to develop good research skills.

World Book Encyclopedia. 22v. World Book, $849 (0-7166-0103-6).
World Book Online Reference Center. [Internet database]. World Book, pricing from $395. Visit [http://www.worldbookonline.com] for free 30-day trial.

World Book (WB) continues to be a first choice for libraries, schools, and homes. The 2003 print edition has 114 new articles. They include *Blood doping, People for the Ethical Treatment of Animals, Hot spot,* and *Intellectual property.* John Ashcroft, Hugh Masekela, Marcia Muller, and Sara Paretsky are a few of the people covered in new biographical entries. Some 184 articles have been extensively revised or rewritten, among them *Cancer (disease), Basques, Element—chemical, Immigration and Naturalization Service, Khyber Pass,* and *Food additive.* More than 190 maps have been revised, and 350 new photographs have been added. The editors have revised 294 bibliographies. This year's special volume is *World Book Focus on Terrorism,* which contains encyclopedia articles and special reports on topics such as "The Attacks of September 11" and "Homeland Security: Fighting Terrorism at Home."

World Book is almost always up-to-date, although its early revision deadline—printing of the 2003 edition began in October—means that it misses events that some other encyclopedias are able to include. New entries cover the Department of Homeland Security, al-Qaeda, Tom Ridge, and the Taliban. The Afghanistan entry has been rewritten and is current through the establishment of the transitional government in April 2002. The article on terrorism covers new airport security procedures. The entries on Tony Blair and George W. Bush both make reference to the war in Afghanistan but have not yet been updated to reflect later events. Also not yet updated are the entries for Saddam Hussein and Iraq. There is no entry for Hamid Karzai. The index is detailed and easy to use, including page numbers for illustrations and maps.

In July the name *World Book Online* was changed to *World Book Online Reference Center* (WBORC) to reflect the fact that it offers access to multiple databases. The *World Book* database contains the complete text of the print edition and the *World Book Dictionary* as well as 8,000 articles created for the electronic version and 13,000 Back in Time articles from earlier annual supplements. Users may browse by broad subject area or media type or use the Basic or Advanced keyword search functions. The Advanced search mode allows Boolean operators, limits (article text, title word, atlas, media type, Back in Time, or special reports), and truncation.

The more than 800 new articles in WBORC include biographies of all Nobel Prize winners and all current U.S. senators; NBA teams; current news topics *(Department of Homeland Security, LASIK surgery, Obesity)*; and biographies of celebrities and political leaders (Mahmoud Abbas, Julia Child, Tommy Franks). *Angiogenesis, Chartres Cathedral,* and *Microelectromechanical systems* are among the revised articles. The article on Afghanistan has been rewritten with Web links to the Country Study and Background Notes from the State Department, the *CIA Factbook,* and the *Washington Post* as well as Canadian and British news sources, along with magazine articles from EBSCO Content Solutions. There is an article on the war in Iraq (here called "Persian Gulf War of 2003") as well as a special "War in Iraq" feature. The entries on Tony Blair and George W. Bush are both more current than those in the print set, noting the beginning of the war; *Hussein, Saddam* and *Iraq* both note the toppling of the former leader's regime. The article on AIDS has been extensively revised, with a map showing the worldwide incidence of the disease and a brief discussion of the cost of therapy and drug availability in the Third World. A search for information about SARS produces an article on the topic as well as a picture showing protection against the spread of the disease in Hong Kong.

Special features in WBORC include Surf the Ages, which is a set of simulated Web sites representing different historical periods. The Back in Time section allows users to see articles about important events in earlier *World Book* annuals. Today in History lists events that happened on that day with links to relevant articles. The feature of the month highlights an important event that occurred during that month—in July it was hurricanes. Behind the Headlines links users to articles that provide background for current events. Clicking on the More Resources box in the menu bar leads users to tools for parents, teachers, and students.

In addition to *World Book* and its suite of features, WBORC offers access to a Spanish-language encyclopedia and *World Book Research Libraries. World Book Research Libraries,* requiring a separate subscription, offers eight extensive collections of primary sources in broad subject areas—science, literature, history, and so on. Clicking on the Research Library link takes users out of the World Book site with no link to return, a minor inconvenience.

WBORC is very current. Features such as Behind the Headlines are revised daily, and new and revised articles are added monthly. Web links are validated on a continuous basis. The new site design is easier to navigate, and it makes all of the features available from anywhere in the site. Articles download faster, too. The print capability now allows users to print specific sections of an article, which saves ink and paper. These improvements plus the broad range of content at several different reading levels make *World Book* an excellent resource for school and public libraries.

Conclusion: World Book is recommended for its high-quality, current, and accurate information in attractive print and online packages.

Special Features

Another Look At . . . World Authors. 1995–2000 5
Atlas and Dictionary Update, 2004 5
Childern's Atlas Roundup 6
Reference Books in Spanish for Children and Adolescents 7
Top 10 Science Reference Sources for under $100 8
Twenty Best Bets for Student Researchers 9
Focus Reviews
    Ancient Europe, 8,000 B.C.–A.D. 1,000 10
    The Chicago Manual of Style. 15th ed. 10
    Dictionary of the Middle Ages 11
    Gale Virtual Reference Library 12
    Oxford Scholarship Online 12
    A History of Women in the United States 12
    Merrian-Webster's Collegiate Dictionary 13
    RX for Consumer Health Reference 13
    Spanish-Language Online Encyclopedias 14

Another Look At . . .

World Authors, 1995–2000. Ed. by Clifford Thompson and Mari Rich. 2003. 872p. bibliogs. illus. Wilson, $150 (0-8242-1032-8). 809.

In library school, many of us learned to refer to *Twentieth Century Authors* as "Kunitz and Haycraft" after its editors, Stanley J. Kunitz and Howard Haycraft. The review of *Twentieth Century Authors* in the January 1943 issue of *Subscription Books Bulletin* (as RBB was then called) contains this biographical nugget: "Mr. Kunitz began writing for the *Wilson Library Bulletin* in 1928 under the pseudonym 'Dilly Tante.' He was editor of that publication until he recently went into the service." For years, Kunitz and Haycraft and its supplement, published in 1955, were library staples. *World Authors, 1950–1970: A Companion to Twentieth Century Authors* was published in 1975 and followed by regular updates, beginning with *World Authors, 1970– 1975* (1980). In 1996, Wilson produced a much needed revision to the foundation set, the four-volume *World Authors, 1900–1950,* which profiles just over 2,500 individuals.

The recently released *World Authors, 1995–2000* treats 336 poets, dramatists, essayists, novelists, biographers, and other writers "who have published significant work within the time period." Articles, ranging in length from 1,000 to 3,000 words, contain a short overview of the author's work, the biographical article, suggested reading, and selected works. Some also have rather grainy photographs. Many of the entrants supplied brief autobiographical pieces specifically for this book. There is diversity in both the ethnic and writing backgrounds of the authors represented. Among the writers who appear here are journalist Hilton Als, historian Michael Beschloss, historical novelists Bernard Cornwell and Dorothy Dunnett, children's author Lemony Snicket, and Gao Xingjian, the first Chinese writer to win the Nobel Prize for Literature (2000). Some inclusions, such as Dave Eggers and Jhumpa Lahiri, are up-to-the-minute. Entries for fewer than 5 percent of the authors, among them Maya Angelou, John Irving, and Philip Roth, are revisions of material that appeared in previous volumes.

Work on *World Authors* is ongoing. Approximately 120 profiles are added to the database each year and appear in the online version (and also in the larger online *Biography Reference Bank*) before they appear in print. In electronic form, *World Authors* profiles are kept fresh by links to reviews, articles, obituaries, and other material that provides more current information.

Is *World Authors* still a necessary title? Kunitz and Haycraft was just about the only thing of its kind back when the first supplement appeared, but since then, and especially in the last few years, we have been swamped with reference sources that have a similar mission. These range from Gale's behemoth *Contemporary Authors* to more thinly sliced works on poets, or women, or African Americans, or lesbians, or all of the above. Still, the *World Authors* profiles are unique to it, and it remains a good choice for larger collections that need to offer multiple resources on authors as well as for smaller libraries that want broad coverage without investing space and dollars in either larger series or numerous specialized volumes.

—Mary Ellen Quinn

Atlas and Dictionary Update, 2004

The atlases and dictionaries listed here are ones we've seen since our last Atlas and Dictionary Update, in the May 15, 2003, issue. Some of the reviews are printed here for the first time; others are excerpts of reviews previously published in RBB or brief notes on new editions. This year, we've added children's atlases to the mix; turn to p.6 for our Children's Atlas Roundup. For our full list of current atlases and dictionaries, go to the *Booklist* Web site at http://www.ala.org/booklist. Click on Special Lists and Features and then on Reference.

How often should atlases and dictionaries be replaced? The atlas collection needs regular updating and weeding, since geographic changes make older editions inaccurate. Some atlases, such as the *Oxford Atlas of the World*, are revised every year. Changes to the language don't necessarily render older words and forms obsolete, so dictionaries don't become superannuated as quickly. At the adult level and at the upper levels of children's dictionaries, it's important to have at least one title on hand that contains newer words and reflects current usage.

Atlases

Atlas of the World. 2003. 412p. DK, $50 (0-7894-9672-0).
Compact Atlas of the World. 2003. 192p. DK, paper, $13 (0- 7894-9357-8).
Concise Atlas of the World. 2003. 350p. DK, $30 (0-7894- 9362-4).

DK updated three atlases in 2003. *Atlas of the World* has more than 450 maps, *Concise Atlas of the World* has around 400 maps, and *Compact Atlas of the World* has around 60. In the two larger atlases, maps are surrounded by plenty of facts and graphics. Among the revisions is the new name for the former Yugoslavia—Serbia and Montenegro.

HarperCollins New World Atlas. 2001. 336p. HarperCollins, $50 (0-06-052120-1).

The HarperCollins maps are from the Bartholomew database, which is also used by the Times Books, Reader's Digest, and World Book atlases. This *New World Atlas* was published first in the U.K. and released in the U.S. in 2003.

The introduction appears to set the tone, with small print that is very difficult to read. A section called "World" follows, with thematic maps of physical features, countries, land images, earthquakes and volcanoes, population, and more. The maps in many cases occupy a limited portion of the page, with a number of small photographs or charts and graphs filling the page. The major map section is by continent, beginning with *Europe* and ending with *Oceans*. Introductory material on the continents includes thematic maps, photographs, charts, and graphs similar to the section on the world. There are boxes for country information—flags, population, currency, etc. The print on maps is difficult to read, especially in high-density areas. The coverage of Asia is impressive, with 20 maps. "Connection" boxes accompany each map and refer the user to thematic information.

The index is the best part of the atlas, easy to read with dark print on pale green paper. It is consistent in size (80,000 place-names) with comparable atlases. This atlas would be appropriate for school, academic, and public libraries as a relatively current, supplemental resource in the medium size and price category.

Dictionaries

Merriam-Webster's Collegiate Dictionary. 11th ed. 2003. 1,623p. Merriam-Webster, $25.95 (0-87779-807-9).

For this edition, M-W lexicographers chose 10,000 new words for a total of 165,000 entries and 225,000 definitions. There are 100,000 "changes" from the tenth edition. Users asked for more usage examples and idioms and phrases, so there are now 40,000 examples and a "significant" increase in idioms. There are 91,000 pronunciations, 33,000 etymologies, 2,700 illustrative quotations, 650 foreign words and phrases, and 700 illustrations. Terms added to this edition include *Botox, comb-over, crunch-exercise, dead-cat bounce, dead presidents, def, exfoliant, identity theft, phat,* and *tweener*.

Webster's New Explorer College Dictionary. 2003. 1,098p. Federal Street, $14.98 (1-892859-42-4).

From the "value" division of Merriam-Webster comes this dictionary with more than 100,000 definitions. Definitions are less detailed and more simply written than those in *Merriam-Webster's Collegiate Dictionary*. An inexpensive supplement to a library's core dictionary collection.

Dictionaries for Grades K–12

The American Heritage Children's Dictionary. 2003. 856p. Houghton Mifflin, $17.95 (0-618-28002-2).

Some of the illustrations have been replaced, but the vocabulary, definitions, and boxed features appear to be unchanged from the 1998 edition. For grades three to six.

The American Heritage First Dictionary. By Kaethe Ellis. 2003. 377p. Houghton Mifflin, $16.95 (0-618-28007-3).

This attractive full-color dictionary for kindergarten to grade three mainly defines one- and two-syllable words. Some of the photographs have been replaced since the 1997 edition, and sections on homophones and parts of speech have been added to the back matter. Since this dictionary is mostly about basic concepts and vocabulary, you can probably still get by with the 1997 edition if your copy is in good shape.

The American Heritage Student Dictionary. 2003. 1,068p. Houghton Mifflin, $19.95 (0-618-25619-9).

The most noticeable change in this dictionary since the 1998 edition is that all the black-and-white illustrations have been replaced with full color. More than 3,000 new words and senses have been added, among them *dark matter, deep-dish pizza,* and *instant messaging*. Entries for people and places have been updated and expanded. For grades six to nine.

The Kingfisher Children's Illustrated Dictionary and Thesaurus. 2003. 320p. Kingfisher, $12.95 (0-7534-5653-2).

This version appears to be identical to *The Kingfisher Illustrated Junior Dictionary* (1997) for ages 7 to 10 except that most of the special features have been eliminated in favor of a thesaurus. The dictionary portion has approximately 4,000 entries and 600 illustrations; the thesaurus has more than 5,000 headwords.

The Kingfisher First Dictionary. 2004. 176p. Kingfisher, paper, $9.95 (0-7534-5807-1).

Designed for ages five through eight, this dictionary has approximately 1,500 words and 1,000 illustrations. Most definitions have inflected forms and italicized sample sentences. A few also include homophones, word origins, and pronunciations. There are "picture pages" illustrating such topics as dinosaurs and musical instruments. Though it's not essential to update the previous edition, this dictionary's price makes it worth considering for multiple circulating copies.

Children's Atlas Roundup

by Mary Ellen Quinn

The world changes rapidly; boundaries shift; countries take on new names. Libraries need a current collection of atlases for children, just as they do for adults. The atlases listed here are all 2003 editions or printings, the most current as we write. Typically, all have introductory sections providing information about planet Earth and its general features—climate, vegetation, people, and so forth. Arrangement of maps is by continent, with separate maps for regions or individual countries within each continent. Since their mission is not only to draw the interest of young users but to introduce them to basic map concepts, most of the atlases combine eye-catching graphics with standard atlas features such as longitude and latitude lines, scales, locator globes, and grids. Beyond these similarities, the atlases vary considerably in the approaches they take to demystifying maps.

Unless otherwise indicated, all of the atlases are intended by their publishers to be used by children ages 8 through 14. However, some are more appropriate for 8-year-olds, and others are better suited to the middle- or junior-high-school level. None of these items are costly, and a library should stock several, making sure to replace those that are out-of-date.

Children's World Atlas. 2003. 136p. DK, $24.99 (0-7894-5845-4).

This atlas has large-scale maps generated from satellite photography. There are six pages of introductory material. Regions, some individual countries, and oceans are represented on 50 different maps, each of which is surrounded by small color photographs and brief text delineating some aspects of life in the region. The U.S. is divided into five regions. Maps in this atlas are fairly complex and have more features than are found in the other atlases; it's the only atlas that shows airports or highways around the world, for example. The level of detail makes some of the maps quite dense. End papers contain a world map and country flags. Despite the fact that there are page-continuation guides referring readers to maps for neighboring regions, it can be difficult to get a sense in this atlas of where regions and countries are located and how they fit together. There are five maps for regions of Africa, for example, but no map of Africa as a whole. An index provides page references for topics discussed in the text; there is a separate gazetteer for map locations.

Facts On File Children's Atlas. 2003. 96p. Facts On File, $18.95 (0-8160-5581-5).

The 13-page opening section includes some thematic maps and an explanation of elevation and scale. Sections on the continents begin with physical and political maps of the areas covered, along with fact files (smallest country, largest lake, etc.). Each of 37 regional or country maps shows major cities as well as any city that is referred to in the text. Every map has insets that contain a locator map, the height of the landmass, and a scale legend. Additional material includes pictures of postage stamps and flags and sidebars highlighting aspects of history or culture. All maps appear on one page of a double-page spread, so there is no gutter loss, although some of the maps are quite small. Besides elevation, water features are the only physical features shown. The 4 U.S. maps include Alaska, eastern U.S., western U.S., and a simple U.S. map showing state capitals. Unlike most of the other atlases discussed here, the index does not indicate the country in which indexed places are located.

Gareth Stevens Atlas of the World. 2004. 200p. Gareth Stevens, $29.95 (0-8368-4091-7).

Mapquest provided the nearly 200 maps found in this atlas. Eight pages of introductory material, called "Portrait of the World in the 21st Century," contain mostly statistical information and are followed by a world map. Coverage of each continent begins with a continental map and maps showing GNP, vegetation, and population. There are also lists of major cities with population and graphs showing climate and population figures. More than in any of the other atlases, the focus is on maps for individual countries and, for Canada and the U.S., individual provinces and states. Countries may be grouped on a two-page spread, but each country has its own map with its own index as well as a fact box showing the flag and listing the capital, language, and monetary unit. Maps indicate main divisions and cities and towns, along with four water features. The U.S. is covered in a special, separately indexed section. Here, political and physical maps are followed by state maps, which are much more detailed than the maps for the rest of the world. Canadian province maps are also more detailed. The strengths of this atlas are its individual country maps and its treatment of the states. Of all the atlases in the group, this one most resembles an atlas for adults; younger children may find it heavy going.

Illustrated Atlas. 2003. 208p. World Book, $36 (0-7166-4042-2).

Intended for grades two through eight, this atlas has 100 maps, along with plenty of photographs and color illustrations. Everything about it is geared toward younger children. The 35 pages of introductory material introduce basic concepts, and maps are the least detailed of any of the atlases in the group, with no grids or scales. Countries and capitals are the only features on the political maps. Each section deals with a region (Western Europe) or a country (Japan) and begins with two pages of introduction that includes a locater map. This is followed by a simple political map for the region or country along with a fact box and pictures of the flag or flags. Following this is a succession of two-page spreads on plants and animals, people, and more; some of these spreads include uncluttered thematic maps. There are no maps dealing specifically with the U.S.; instead, it is treated as part of North America. This volume looks as much like a picture book as it does like an atlas, making it best suited for the younger range of its audience.

The Kingfisher Student Atlas. 2003. 128p. Kingfisher, $24.95 (0-7534-5580-7).

A 10-page introductory section is followed by physical and political world maps and maps of the poles. Except for a map legend, there is no explanation of atlas conventions or how to read maps. The atlas has maps for 41 regions or countries and four oceans. Regional and country maps have quite a bit of detail—major cities and towns and 12 physical features—but are nevertheless easy to read and do not bleed into the gutter even when they are spread across more than one page. Each map is accompanied by a few paragraphs of text, country flags, and a useful elevation (called "Land Height") legend. The U.S. section has four maps. Although this atlas does not have as many supplemental facts or graphics as some of the other atlases do, its clear maps are a plus. The foldout map of North America and the CD-ROM that come with the volume are better suited to home use. Kingfisher also has an atlas for ages 7 through 10, *The Kingfisher Children's Atlas*, which uses picture symbols; a new edition will be available in September.

National Geographic World Atlas for Young Explorers. 2003. 192p. National Geographic, $24.95 (0-7922-2870-0).

Introductory material is one of the strong points in this atlas. Twenty-five thematic maps show climate, vegetation, population density, endangered species, world economies, and more. There is also a good explanation of the types of maps and how to read a map. The section for each continent starts with a physical and a political map; sandwiched between are four pages of color photos. Regions or countries are divided into 32 separate maps that show 20 political and physical features plus icons for crops, industries, and other aspects of the economy. Maps are generally large and very easy to read, although in some cases—Western Europe, for example—18 countries are crowded onto a single map and some information is lost in the gutter. Each map is accompanied by flags and facts about each country's area, population, capital, and chief language. The 8 U.S. maps come with similar information for the states. An impressive 15-page section on oceans follows the sections on the continents.

The Reader's Digest Children's Atlas of the World. 3d ed. 2003. 128p. Reader's Digest, $24.99 (0-7944-0207-0).

Maps are preceded by 20 pages of introductory material. Sections on continents are introduced by political and physical maps and also by "records" (world's largest gorge, continent's highest mountain). This atlas divides the world into 30 countries and regions, with just two maps apiece for Africa and South America. There are eight pages of U.S. maps. Accompanying the maps are lists of country populations and capitals, "amazing facts," and hands-on projects ("Make a Mexican Piñata"). Maps are large and quite dense. Longitude and latitude are not indicated, and fewer political and geographic features are shown than in some of the other atlases. Instead, there is heavy reliance on pictures and symbols for wildlife, industries, and so on that sometimes overwhelm boundaries and names of cities and towns. A "World Fact File," which includes pronunciations for country names, follows the maps. This is a good choice for younger children, with lots of kid-friendly features not found in other atlases.

Scholastic Atlas of the World. 224p. 2001. Scholastic, $12.95 (0-439-52797-X).

Although the copyright is 2001, there was a new and updated printing of this atlas in 2003. The almost 30 pages of introductory material has information not found in other atlases, such as a section on how mountains are formed and the different kinds of rocks. There is also a good explanation of the types of maps. The map section is introduced by political and physical world maps. Each continental, country, and regional map is accompanied by fact boxes, a "Search and Find" key for locating geographic locations, time zone information, small color photographs, and more. This atlas is second only to *Gareth Stevens Atlas of the World* in the number of individual maps representing regions and countries—there are more than 70, including 9 for Africa and 10 for the U.S. Maps are not highly detailed and don't show latitude and longitude, although these are given for some locations. Following the maps is a list of dependencies and disputed territories.

Reference Books in Spanish for Children and Adolescents

by Isabel Schon

Dictionaries

Diccionario de Internet. (Dictionary of the Internet). By Igor Galo. 2001. 91p. Acento Editorial, paper, $8.95 (84-483-0579-5).

Gr. 7–adult. In a handy format, this dictionary provides definitions of more than 900 terms commonly used on the Internet and related technologies. It defines numerous acronyms, such as JPEG, ICQ, and HDSL, as well as English terms and other concepts used in cyberspace. Lists of commonly used emoticons and worldwide country code top-level domains are also included.

Gran diccionario de la pintura: Siglo XIX. (Great Dictionary of Painting: Nineteenth Century). 2001. 374p. Carroggio Ediciones, $150 (84-7254-381-1).

Gr. 9–adult. This enticing overview offers biographical sketches of the most influential artists of the nineteenth century with excellent, full-color reproductions of their work. It also includes brief essays on the artistic styles of the period: neoclassicism, realism, romanticism, and impressionism.

Gran diccionario de refranes. (Great Dictionary of Proverbs). Ed. by Regino Etxabe Díaz. 2001. 491p. Larousse/Spes, $29.95 (84-8016-544-8).

Gr. 8–adult. More than 4,500 proverbs, from well-known aphorisms of classic Spanish literature to colloquial expressions, are included in this dictionary. Readers will appreciate the details on the origin and development of these concise verbal expressions, which are widely used among Spanish speakers around the world. A concept index, classified according to subject and usage, assists users in finding the right proverb for a particular theme or purpose.

The University of Chicago Spanish Dictionary: Spanish-English, English- Spanish. 5th ed. Ed. by David Pharies. 2002. 586p. Univ. of Chicago, $27.50 (0-226-66688-3); paper, $11 (0-116-66689-1).

Gr. 8–adult. This revised bilingual dictionary, now with 80,000 entries, includes recent technical and cultural terms as well as parenthetical words that will greatly assist English speakers interested in learning Spanish and Spanish speakers interested in American English. Noteworthy features are the easy-to-use format, clear typography, Spanish and English grammar notes, and the stylistic markers that guide users to taboo or offensive words.

Encyclopedias

Enciclopedia de la ciencia y la tecnología. (Encyclopedia of Science and Technology). 3v. 2003. 1,350p. Editorial Oceano; dist. by Gale, $295 (84-494-2460-7).

Gr. 9–adult. Arranged in alphabetical order, this well-organized encyclopedia provides a wealth of information from the fields of science and technology. From *Abaco* (Abacus) to *Zooplancton* (Zooplankton), it explains words, terms, concepts, and theories from physics, health, mathematics, biology, psychology, engineering, technology, and the environment. Especially noteworthy are the informative sidebars that explain *palabras clave* (keywords) as well as the engaging text and numerous cross-references, color photographs, drawings, maps, and charts. An interactive CD- ROM version with more than 20,000 definitions is also included.

Enciclopedia Oxford de filosofía. (The Oxford Companion to Philosophy). Ed. by Ted Honderich. Tr. by Carmen García Trevijano. 2001. 1,141p. Tecnos/Grupo Anaya, $96.95 (84-309-3699-8).

Gr. 9–adult. The purpose of this encyclopedia is to offer the reader a complete guide to philosophy—its preeminent and lesser-known philosophers as well as its history, theories, doctrines, movements, and traditions. With approximately 2,000 entries written by 250 scholars and informative appendixes that explain symbols, doctrines and events, this encyclopedia will be of value to serious students or specialists in the field.

Primaria activa: Enciclopedia escolar. (Active Elementary: Student Encyclopedia). 3v. 2002. 1,056p. Editorial Oceano; dist. by Gale, $160 (84-494-2330-9).

Gr. 3–6. Designed for elementary-school students, this encyclopedia provides an overview of grammar, mathematics, astronomy, physics, biology, geography, technology, history, and other subjects studied in school. Students will appreciate the easy- to-read text and amusing color cartoons, photos, charts, and drawings. Unfortunately, with the exception of a brief name index, it does not contain an index or any cross-references; rather, it includes a table of contents incorrectly labeled *Indice general*.

Handbooks

Manual de educación física y departes: Técnicas y actividades prácticas. (Manual of Physical Education and Sports: Techniques and Practical Activities). 2002. 607p. Editorial Oceano; dist. by Gale, $85 (84-494-2270-1).

Gr. 9–adult. Designed for professionals in the field of physical education, this manual will appeal to all sports enthusiasts. It includes information on such topics as physical education in ancient Greece, hygiene and nutrition, sports injuries, recreational sports, and suggestions to teach the most popular sports. Clear color photos, charts and drawings, and well-done indexes add to its value.

El mundo de la pintura: Los grandes temas del arte universal. (The World of Painting: The Great Themes of Universal Art). 2002. 384p. Editorial Oceano; dist. by Gale, $95 (84-494-2330-7).

Gr. 9–adult. The purpose of this attractive, large-format publication is to invite readers to appreciate art with open spirits and inquisitive eyes. Beginning with a chapter on "Cómo mirar un cuadro" ("How to Look at a Painting"), it discusses the history, movement, and styles of the most important Western paintings. More than 300 exquisite full-page reproductions and an artist index complement this beautiful guide.

Style Manuals

Dígalo sin errores: Diccionario de dudas. (Say It Without Errors: Dictionary of Doubts). By Fernando Ávila. 2002. 212p. Grupo Editorial Norma, paper, $11 (958-04-7060-X).

Gr. 8–adult. Ávila provides guidance to readers who want to use Spanish correctly, clearly, and naturally. Based on the most recent interpretations of the 22 *Academias de la Lengua Española* and arranged alphabetically, the book explains troublesome words and phrases and shows correct and incorrect usages. In contrast to other Spanish style manuals, it gives clear indications regarding acceptable or unacceptable terms: for example, *chance* is now valid in Spanish; *chatear* does not exist in Spanish.

Manual de estilo de la lengua española. (Style Manual of the Spanish Language). Rev. ed. By José Martínez de Sousa. 2001. 671p. Ediciones Trea, paper, $15.95 (84- 9704-022-8).

Gr. 10–adult. Designed as a reference tool for writers, editors, translators, and proofreaders, this comprehensive style manual has now been revised and includes a useful subject index. It provides guidance on grammar, usage, punctuation, and spelling as well as Anglicisms, idiomatic expressions, abbreviations, and numerous other topics of concern to modern writers. Arranged alphabetically, each entry includes a definition followed by examples and illustrative quotations from published sources. The scarcity of style manuals of the Spanish language, particularly in scientific and technical disciplines, makes this a welcome resource.

Distributors

Lectorum Pub., Inc., call 800-345-5946.
Mariuccia Iaconi Book Imports, call 800- 955-9577.

Top 10 Science Reference Sources for under $100

by Mary Ellen Quinn

The massive *Grzimek's Animal Life Encyclopedia*, like *The McGraw-Hill Encyclopedia of Science and Technology* (9th ed., 2002), is a cornerstone of the science reference collection. For libraries whose budgets don't allow the purchase of such pricey items, or that want to build their sci tech collections around big core sets by adding some less expensive titles, we've selected the top ten science reference sources that were reviewed in RBB from December 1, 2002 through November 15, 2003 and cost less than $100. Unless otherwise indicated, all are appropriate for users at the high-school level and up.

American Heritage Student Science Dictionary. 2002. 376p. Houghton, $18 (0-618-18919-X).

Students who might be intimidated by larger scientific dictionaries will like this attractive volume, which was designed for grades seven and up. The 4,500 entries provide pronunciation, part of speech, and definition, with enough detail to explain the scientific meaning and relevance of each term. Some 300 of the entries are biographical.

American Horticultural Encyclopedia of Plants and Flowers. Rev. ed. Ed. by Christopher Brickell and Tyrevor Cole. 2002. 720p. DK, $60 (0- 7894-8993-7).

Tightly packed into a single volume is nearly everything that amateur landscapers and gardeners need to consider for outlining, designing, and planting their outdoor growing areas. In the main portion of the encyclopedia, "The Plant Catalog," plants are arranged by size, season of interest, and color.

Astronomy Encyclopedia: An A–Z Guide to the Universe. Ed. by Patrick Moore. 2002. 456p. Oxford, $50 (0-19-521833-7).

Moore's numerous publications are the "granddaddies" of books for the general reader that explain all that one needs to know about stars, planets, moons, and other heavenly bodies. In this revision of *The Astronomy Encyclopedia* (Orion, 1987), some 3,000 alphabetically arranged topics and definitions have been brought together with beautiful photographs (most in color), star maps, and explanatory diagrams.

Biological Hazards: An Oryx Sourcebook. By Joan R. Callahan. 2002. 385p. Greenwood, $64.95 (1-57356-385-4).

Chapters in this readable volume divide hazards into categories: human pathogens in water, food, and air; those transmitted by contact; plant and animal pathogens and pests; venoms, toxins, and allergens; and animals that are a threat for predatory or other behavior. Another chapter provides information on controversial topics such as immunization and biological warfare.

Encyclopedia of Addictive Drugs. By Richard Lawrence Miller. 2003. 491p. Greenwood, $75 (0-313-31807-7).

This volume contains alphabetical listing for drugs "which have been declared a public concern by government officials, medical caregivers, or news media." Highly readable discussions cover uses, drawbacks, abuse factors, some drug interactions, cancer risk, pregnancy effects, and more.

Encyclopedia of Computer Science and Technology. By Harry Henderson. 2003. 450p. Facts On File, $82.50 (0-8160-4373-6).

The strength of this resource is its currency. In more than 400 entries, it focuses on computers and issues related to computers, including information on hardware, software, computer languages, operating systems, applications, the Internet, key individuals, and social issues such as the digital divide.

Encyclopedia of Infectious Diseases. 2d ed. By Carol Turkington and Bonnie Lee Ashby. 2003. 397p. Facts On File, $71 (0-8160-4775-8).

Although SARs is too recent to be included in this second edition (updating a volume that was published in 1998), others that have emerged in the last five years, including West Nile virus, are here. Major diseases that have had an impact on the world's population (tuberculosis, AIDs) are covered in depth and include a history. This feature makes the volume useful to researchers and students.

Firefly Encyclopedia of Insects and Spiders. Ed. by Christopher O'Toole. 2002. 240p. Firefly, $40 (1-55297-612-2).

With lush color photographs and lavishly detailed illustrations, this encyclopedia presents a striking abundance of information at a glance. A major article introduces the main classes: insects and arachnids. Articles pertaining to specific species follow. All articles provide current scientific information and research findings relating to physiology and to behavior.

Firefly Encyclopedia of Reptiles and Amphibians. Ed. by Tim Halliday and Kraig Adler. 2002. 240p. Firefly, $40 (1-55297-613-0).

Similar in design and arrangement to *Firefly Encyclopedia of Insects and Spiders* (above) but covering different parts of the animal kingdom.

Van Nostrand's Concise Encyclopedia of Science. Ed. by Christopher G. DePree and Alan Axelrod. 2003. 821p. Wiley, $40 (0-471-36331-6).

Based on the two-volume, ninth edition of *Van Nostrand's Scientific Encyclopedia* (Wiley, 2002) but written at a level accessible to the general reader, 5,000 entries cover physics, chemistry, earth sciences, space sciences, life sciences, energy, environmental sciences, materials sciences, and information sciences.

Twenty Best Bets for Student Researchers

by Mary Ellen Quinn

As the new school year gets under way, our annual "Best Bets" list features titles we reviewed in the past 12 months that are targeted specifically for students from the elementary- through high-school levels.

The American Heritage Student Science Dictionary. 2002. 376p. Houghton, $18 (0-618-18919-X).

An attractive volume designed to help users in grades seven and up understand the important concepts of science. The 4,500 entries provide pronunciation, part of speech, and definition, with enough detail to explain the scientific meaning and relevance of each term. The overall design will appeal to students who might be intimidated by larger scientific dictionaries. [RBB D 1 02].

Bowling, Beatniks, and Bell-Bottoms: Pop Culture of 20th- Century America. Ed. by Sara Pendergast and Tom Pendergast. 5v. 2002. 1,320p. UXL, $225 (0-7876-5675-5).

Geared for middle-school and high- school users, this ambitious set examines the foremost fads and styles emblematic of the last century's culture. Each volume covers two decades, and for each decade, A–Z entries are sorted into nine categories, including "Fashion," "Food and Drink," and "TV and Radio." [RBB F 15 03].

Britannica Online School Edition. 2002. [Online database]. Britannica, $545 [http://eb.com].

For K–12 settings, Britannica has gathered *Encyclopaedia Britannica* (geared to high- schoolers), *Britannica Student Encyclopedia* (geared to middle-schoolers), *Britannica Elementary Encyclopedia, Britannica Internet Guide,* and video and media (photos and audio clips). Altogether, these five databases offer 118,000 articles, 22,000 images, and 2,000 video clips. [RBB N 1 02].

Drugs, Alcohol, and Tobacco: Learning about Addictive Behavior. 3v. Ed. by Rosalyn Carson- DeWitt. 2002. 839p. Macmillan, $295 (0-02-865756-X).

Articles from the *Encyclopedia of Drugs, Alcohol, and Addictive Behavior* (Macmillan, 2d ed., 2001) have been revised to suit the needs of students in middle school and up. More than 200 alphabetically arranged articles address the nature of, treatments for, and social issues surrounding addictive substances and behaviors. [RBB My 15 03].

Drugs and Controlled Substances for Students. Ed. by Stacey L. Blachford and Kristine Krapp. 2002. 495p. Gale, $115 (0-7876-6264-X).

Another set on drugs, this one written for the teen reader, with many references to teen usage. Each of the 50 entries includes the names of the substance—brand, generic, chemical, and street names—along with overviews, chemical composition, usage reason and method, the effects of usage as well as reaction with other substances, consequences (personal, social, and legal), and treatment and rehabilitation. [RBB Mr 15 03].

Encyclopedia of Careers and Vocational Guidance. 4v. 12th ed. Ed. by Andrew Morkes. 2002. 3,216p. Ferguson, $159.95 (0-89434-418-8).

Now in its twelfth edition, this guide profiles 92 career fields and more than 700 specific careers. It also offers articles on career guidance. An essential tool for high-school libraries. [RBB F 1 03].

Exploring Animal Rights and Animal Welfare. 4v. 2002. 512p. Greenwood, $128 (0-313-32245-7).

In volumes titled *Using Animals for Food, Using Animals in Research, Using Animals for Entertainment,* and *Using Animals for Clothing,* this set for middle-schoolers examines the ways animals are treated or mistreated by humans. All sides of the issues are spelled out. The text is easy to read and delivers information in an unbiased manner. [RBB Mr 1 03].

Favorite Children's Authors and Illustrators. 6v. Ed. by E. Russell Primm III. 2002. Tradition; dist. by Child's World, $357 (1-59187-026-7).

A well-designed and easily accessible resource intended to satisfy the browsing and research needs of middle-grade readers. It offers more than 220 biographical essays on "young readers' favorite authors and illustrators," primarily from the twentieth century. Each essay is brief but informative and contains a wealth of information useful to student researchers. [RBB Mr 1 03].

Great American Writers: Twentieth Century. 13v. Ed. by R. Baird Shuman. 1,887p. Marshall Cavendish, $459.95 (0-7614-7240-1).

Most high-school libraries will want this survey of 90 American and Canadian authors who "most frequently appear in high-school and college anthologies." Each volume profiles seven or eight writers in chapters that are up to 25 pages long. The illustrations that enhance most pages are a blend of photographs and well-chosen examples of American artwork. [RBB O 1 02].

Health Matters! 8v. Ed. by William M. Kane. 2002. 1,280p. Grolier, $409 (0-7172-5575-1).

This set serves two purposes: it is a means of answering teens' questions about their health and also a reference source for school reports pertaining to health topics. Each of the eight volumes focuses on a different health-related topic, such as addiction, mental health, sexuality and pregnancy, weight and eating disorders, and sexually transmitted diseases. [RBB S 15 02].

Historic Events for Students: The Great Depression. 3v. Ed. by Richard C. Hanes and Sharon M. Hanes. 2002. Gale, $250 (0-7876-6701-8).

Designed for high-school students, this set examines in great detail an important period in U.S. history, offering social, cultural, and ideological as well as historical perspective. Some 45 key topics are examined in chapters that are 20 pages or more in length and follow a standard format. [RBB D 15 02].

A History of the Third Reich. 4v. By Jeff T. Hay. 2003. Greenhaven, $299.80 (0-7377-1283-X).

Combines A–Z articles, biographical profiles, and primary source material to help high-school students understand the social and political forces that shaped, or were shaped by, the Third Reich. An accessible, reliable source such as this is a useful tool for countering the misleading information and extreme perspectives that students might find on the Web. [RBB Jl 03].

Lifetimes: The Great War to the Stock Market Crash. Ed. by Neil A. Hamilton. 2002. 328p. Greenwood, $74.95 (0-313-31799-2).

This biographical encyclopedia for high-schoolers presents history in an immediate and engaging style. Representative personalities are used to illustrate various aspects of American politics, society, and culture from approximately 1917 to 1930. Sixty individuals are profiled in original biographies accompanied by primary source material. [RBB S 15 02].

Literary Movements for Students: Presenting Analysis, Context, and Criticism on Literary Movements. 2v. Ed. by David Galens. 2002. Gale, $150 (0-7876-6517-7).

Another valuable title in the Gale high-school level For Students line, this set is meant to "provide readers with a guide to understanding, enjoying, and studying literary movements." Twenty- eight literary movements are described in their historical and cultural contexts. Volume 1 includes literature before the twentieth century (alphabetical chapters from "Bildungsroman" to "Transcendentalism"), and volume 2 covers the twentieth century ("Absurdism" to "Symbolism"). [RBB Ap 1 03]

Opposing Viewpoints Resource Center. [Internet database]. 2002. Gale, pricing from $1,250 [http://www.gale.com/OpposingViewpoints/].

The print Opposing Viewpoints series, which provides pro and con arguments for various current-events-related topics, has long been a staple in secondary school and young adult collections. The digital counterpart includes more than 2,000 articles from more than 170 titles in the Opposing Viewpoints and other series plus topic overviews; statistical tables, charts, and graphs; images; full- text periodicals and newspapers; and links to more than 1,000 Web sites. [RBB N 1 02].

Peoples of Europe. 11v. 2002. 648p. Marshall Cavendish, $471.36 (0-7614-7378-5).

Similar to the publisher's *Peoples of the Americas* (1999), this attractively designed set for grades four to eight "uses geography and national identity to organize information" on 44 countries. Entries deal with the people occupying each nation today and treat religion, housing, clothing, language, health and education, food and drink, family and social life, and art and music. The multiple indexes add value. [RBB Mr 1 03].

Renaissance and Reformation Reference Library. 5v. Ed. by Peggy Saari and Aaron Saari. 2002. UXL, $225 (0-7876-5466-3).

Coverage focuses on major events and individuals in European history between the mid-1300s and the early 1600s. Like numerous other UXL sets, this one is divided into *Almanac* (two volumes), *Biographies* (two volumes), and *Primary Sources* (one volume) and is aimed at middle-schoolers. [RBB D 15 02].

Reptiles and Amphibians. 11v. 2002. 1,568p. Marshall Cavendish, $657.07 (0-7614-7390-4).

This appealing set provides thorough coverage of the field of herpetology for students in grades eight and up. Seventy alphabetically arranged entries treat topics ranging from *African reed frogs* to *Worm lizards*. Students will appreciate the appealing layout and the accessibility of information. [RBB F 15 03].

A Student's Guide to Biotechnology. 4v. 2002. 576p. Greenwood, $160 (0-313-32256-2).

This attractive set is designed to help students in grades 6 through 12 understand the issues that make up the biotechnology debate. It defines terms, profiles people who have made significant contributions to the field, provides a historical overview, and investigates the controversies associated with biotech research. [RBB Mr 1 03].

World of Animals: Mammals. 10v. Ed. by Pat Morris and Amy-Jane Beer. 2003. Grolier, $419 (0-7172-5742-8).

Important mammal groups and species are arranged according to scientific classification in the first 10 volumes of a five-set *World of Animals* collection intended for the middle-school level. Clear, concise text is intermingled with many color photographs and illustrations. Subsequent sets, each also consisting of 10 volumes, will cover birds, insects and other invertebrates, fish, and amphibians and reptiles. [RBB Ag 03].

Focus Reviews

Ancient Europe, 8,000 B.C.–A.D. 1,000: Encyclopedia of the Barbarian World. 2v. Ed. by Peter Bogucki and Pam J. Crabtree. 2003. 658p. bibliogs. glossary. illus. index. maps. Scribner, $240 (0-684-80668-1). 936.

A superbly written work that covers a history all but ignored in conventional historical surveys, *Ancient Europe, 8,000 B.C.–A.D. 1,000* features 212 essays written for a general readership by 131 contributors. The span of years covered by the set is explained in the introduction of the first section: "The beginning is marked by the freeing of Europe from glacial ice . . . and the end is determined by the spread of Christianity across northern and eastern Europe and the establishment of many European states that persist into the present." Many of the contributors are archaeologists, and the set is focused accordingly.

Arranged in seven sections, the set proceeds in chronological order once past the first section, "Discovering Barbarian Europe," which provides overview essays such as "Trade and Exchange." Each section features several essays—most about eight pages in length—many followed by somewhat shorter "feature essays" that deal with more specific topics. The eight-page essay "Bronze Age Britain and Ireland," for example, is followed by the six-page essay "Stonehenge," the three-page "Flag Fen," and the three- page "Irish Bronze Age Goldwork," each separately authored. There are black- and- white photographs and maps throughout. Each volume also has a section of line maps and a chronology at the start as well as eight pages of color plates in the middle. Each essay concludes with an up-to-date bibliography and cross-references to other articles. In a work that is not alphabetically arranged, it would have been helpful to have these cross-references include specific page numbers rather than just volume and part number.

Libraries that purchased the recent *Encyclopedia of Barbarian Europe* [RBB N 15 2003] may be tempted to pass on this more expensive set. In fact, the two works are complementary. The *Encyclopedia of Barbarian Europe* offers accessible A–Z entries on people, places, and events; the present set not only encompasses a much wider time frame but offers a different perspective. Any public and academic library that has a clientele interested in European archeology or the featured historical period covered will find this a valuable purchase.—*Ken Black*

★**The Chicago Manual of Style.** 15th ed. 2003. 956p. appendixes. bibliog. glossary. index. Univ. of Chicago, $55 (0-226-10403-6). 808.

The Chicago Manual of Style maintains its vitality by adapting to its ever-changing environment. None of the changes from one edition to the next are capricious; that which remains vital carries over, and that which must change, changes.

From the 1906 first edition's limited focus as "a compilation of typographical rules" for books, it has evolved to provide guidance to authors and editors working in other forms and media such as journals, newsletters, Web sites, and even, with the fifteenth edition, American Sign Language. The editors now "assume throughout that most writers and editors, whether preparing print or nonprint works, use computer software." That assumption is most visible in the chapter dealing with presentation in type of mathematical expressions and formulas. Software has collapsed the division of labor between author and typesetter, giving the author the power to fulfill both roles simultaneously. Mathematicians have faced that special challenge; all scholars have been vexed by uncertainty about citing electronic resources.

Various specialized manuals from other publishers have attempted to codify practices for citing electronic publications, but none has enjoyed the authority *Chicago* has earned over nearly a century. The fifteenth offers deeper guidance for citing electronic books, articles in e-journals, electronic editions of older works, and online newspapers and magazines. The clear, practical, and easily applied rules for citing these sources recognize the problem an author must solve when a URL is subject to change; they also offer advice on matters such as when to provide the date a cited e-work was accessed. U.S. copyright law, driven by the same technologies the fifteenth edition addresses, has also experienced significant changes. An expanded section on copyright offers clear albeit not exhaustive coverage of the current complexities of copyright. All authors would do well to study this primer.

Chicago's mantra throughout is consistency in support of clarity. Helping authors and editors achieve consistency in practice when creating or editing a manuscript and presenting it to readers is *Chicago*'s raison d'être. The prescriptive tone of some entries serves consistency, but usage is determined by users of the language. *Chicago* acknowledges variants in practice, often noting that an author may use a variant even though its entry first describes preferred practice. Bowing to popular influence, the editors concede that they "no longer urge deletion of the *n* in 2nd or the *r* in 3rd" and they "now recommend the month-day-year form of dates" prevalent in the U.S. The editors also have the wisdom and the experience to uphold rules that, if ignored, can create confusion in readers' minds. All of the rules and recommendations are easily accessible through the thorough index, a hallmark of every recent edition.

New to the fifteenth is a lively chapter on grammar and usage contributed by Bryan A. Garner, author of *Garner's Modern American Usage* (2d ed., Oxford, 2003; formerly *A Dictionary of Modern American Usage*). Its first part reviews basic rules of English grammar, and the second offers succinct explanations of words easily misused *(decimate, precondition)* or confused (e.g., *healthy* and *healthful; purposely* and *purposefully*). Added features discuss bias- free language and prepositional idioms.

Evolution is never a lockstep uniform process. Although the heart of *Chicago* embraces changes wrought by digital publishing, its concluding bibliography lags. Only the print editions of general- purpose encyclopedias and several English-language dictionaries are noted. Even though the entry for the *Oxford English Dictionary* indicates its availability on CD-ROM, it neglects to mention its online incarnation. But one must not miss the forest for these few trees. As it has done again and again, *Chicago* offers sensible, clearly articulated, and defensible advice to authors and editors who want to do their best to present an author's text to readers. Every library that serves authors, especially those producing scholarly works, simply *must* have the current edition of *Chicago*.

—James Rettig

Dictionary of the Middle Ages: Supplement 1. Ed. By William Chester Jordan. 2004. 772p. bibliogs. illus. index. maps. Scribner, $135 (0-684-80642-8). 909.07.

The 13-volume *Dictionary of the Middle Ages* (DMA), begun in the 1970s and published 1982–89, remains the only successful comprehensive encyclopedia of the medieval world. More recent, specialized reference sources complement DMA primarily because they incorporate a global, interdisciplinary approach to medieval studies that transcends traditional geographic limitations equating the Middle Ages with western Europe. Containing 320 articles, this is the first supplement to DMA, and its designation, *Supplement 1,* suggests that future supplements might be forthcoming.

Since DMA was completed, new trends have emerged in both medieval scholarship and popular interest. Paul Freedman, of Yale University, addresses these trends in his *Supplement* article *Medieval Studies.* Among the changes, he notes the development of feminist scholarship and "a growing sophistication in investigating voices not readily transmitted through official sources." The *Supplement* is intended to address the "problems and lacunae of the original *Dictionary,*" including a bias toward northwestern Europe and the omission of topics that are now "required reading," such as gender, race, ecology, and sexuality. Articles on gender and sexuality include *Abortion, Gynecology, Pornography, Sexuality,* and *Widowhood. Medievalism* examines fascination with the Middle Ages from Spenser's *Faerie Queen* to the Society for Creative Anachronism and the *Lord of the Rings* film trilogy. Several articles debunk popular misconceptions (*Chastity belt, Pope Joan*). Readers interested in the Middle East will find articles such as *Hagiography, Islamic; Ottoman art and architecture; Persian language;* and *Hebrew language* supplementing articles in DMA on *Islam; Jews in Europe; Mohammad; Sects, Islamic;* and *Sephardim.* The index indicates coverage of Islam and Judaism within many additional *Supplement* articles. Historical revisionism and its attention to subjects ignored by the traditional academy resulted in articles on *Archaeology; Architecture, Domestic; Ovens; Pilgrim souvenirs; Poverty;* and *Religion, Popular.*

Supplement articles sampled ranged from one or two pages (*Astral magic, Uppsala, Pollution and taboo*) to more than 10 pages in length (*Gothic architecture, Women, Paganism and pagan gods*). Most include bibliographies with ample evidence of up-to-date research, with many citations published in 2000 or later and some as recently as 2003. For example, the article *Women* includes references to 28 primary and secondary sources, with 3 of the primary sources and 20 of the secondary sources published after the DMA was completed. While current research and references are among the *Supplement*'s strengths, the contributors do not neglect important primary and older secondary sources. *Etiquette and manners* includes as a primary work Christine de Pisan's *The Treasure of the City of Ladies; or, the Book of the Three Virtues;* the article on *Gothic Architecture* includes a reference to Erwin Panofsky's 1946 classic, *Abbot Suger on the Abbey Church of St.- Denis and Its Art Treasures.*

The *Supplement* is the work of scholars who are at least as prominent as those who contributed to the DMA. They include John Block Friedman, editor of *Trade, Travel, and Exploration in the Middle Ages: An Encyclopedia* (Garland, 2000); Pam Crabtree, editor of *Medieval Archaeology: An Encyclopedia* (Garland, 2000); and Stephen Murray, author of three university press books on gothic cathedrals and creator of a virtual tour of Amiens Cathedral [http://www.arch.columbia.edu/DDL/projects/amiens/]. The premier medieval studies institutions at the University of Toronto, Princeton, and Yale are represented; editor William Chester Jordan, of Princeton, contributed more than 30 articles.

The 100 black-and-white illustrations and sidebars are thoughtfully selected and carefully reproduced. Intriguing examples include a photo of trinkets and badges sold as souvenirs at the shrine of Thomas Becket at Canterbury (*Pilgrim souvenirs*), a movie still of orc warriors from *The Fellowship of the Ring* (*Medievalism*), and a fifteenth-century German woodcut depicting the birth of the Antichrist by cesarean section (*Childbirth and infancy*). Sidebars include excerpts from primary sources, such as "A Cure for an Intermittent Fever" from an English common place book compiled in the 1470s (in the entry *Religion, popular*). The index is not cumulative; it pertains only to the *Supplement* and does not include articles in DMA. However, individual entries include *see also* references to both DMA and other *Supplement* articles.

While DMA remains after 15 years the ultimate medieval encyclopedia, its *Supplement* brings freshness and liveliness to the period. It is, however, a static resource, designed to endure on the shelf. None of the articles examined included references to Web sites, and only one passing reference to Internet resources was found, in the article *Medieval Studies.* Scholars, students, and nonspecialists interested in medieval studies will want to explore Web resources that provide primary sources, maps, collections of further Web links, and myriad other resources. Two excellent Web sites, both active for approximately 10 years, are the Orb: Online Reference Book for Medieval Studies [http:// www.the-orb.net/index.html], which recently moved to a new home at the College of Staten Island, City University of New York; and the Labyrinth: Resources for Medieval Studies, sponsored by Georgetown University [http://labyrinth.georgetown.edu/]. The Orb is an online encyclopedia with peer-reviewed articles written by medievalists, resources for teachers, and a section of medieval resources for nonspecialists. The Labyrinth is a portal providing access to primary texts, databases, images, articles, and other resources worldwide, including some pedagogical materials.

Scholars and nonspecialists interested in the Middle Ages will enjoy browsing the DMA's first supplement for research trends, suggested readings, and illustrations that have not become overly familiar through repeated publication. The *Supplement* is essential for all collections with the DMA; it may even inspire readers to revisit the original set. And perhaps they will not have to wait 15 years for another supplement.

—Christine A. Whittington

★**Europe, 1450 to 1789:** Encyclopedia of the Early Modern World. 4v. Ed. by Jonathan Dewald. 2003. bibliogs. illus. index. maps. Scribner, $695 (0-684-31200-X). 940.2.

In the distinguished tradition of its *Encyclopedia of the Renaissance* (1999) and *Dictionary of the Middle Ages* (1982–1989), Scribner has published an encyclopedia that is even grander than these award-winning works. *Europe, 1450 to 1789* spans the mid-fifteenth century, a period of relative stability following the chaos of the late Middle Ages, to the French Revolution. The focus is on Europe within the context of world history, including meaningful developments in the arts, religion, politics, exploration, and warfare. Alphabetical entries range from broad and expected topics like the Enlightenment and the Renaissance to the more narrowly defined, such as *Advice and etiquette books, Balloons,* and *Tulips.* Cross-references are numerous, and each signed entry is followed by a bibliography and *see also* references.

The 1,100-plus entries range in length from half a page to eight pages, and the number of bibliographical references from a few to 40. Major topics are represented by extended, in-depth essays, but the more tangential entries—*Concubinage, Sanitation, Virtue*—are also informative. More than a third of the entries are biographical. The first volume contains a helpful 120-page chronology dividing notable subjects into three categories—"Art and Architecture," "Drama and Music," and "Literature and Scholarship." Volume 6 has a "Systematic Outline of Contents," so users can locate all entries under a broad topic like "Law," "Religion," or "Science." Each volume lists the contents of all volumes in the set (though there is only one index at the end of the last volume), and each includes the same six maps representing major political changes during this period. Overall, there are 90 archival maps in the set. Gorgeous illustrations are sprinkled throughout, including an eight-page color section in the middle of each volume. Breathtaking reproductions of paintings provide a good argument for print encyclopedias over their online counterparts. Landmark pieces of art and architecture are also splendidly exhibited. Additionally, there are 750 black-and-white illustrations.

This user-friendly encyclopedia attempts to bridge "the gap between researchers and nonspecialist readers" in covering the early modern era. Another goal, as the introduction explains, was to include subject areas often ignored until recently—women's roles, Judaism, Islam, Eastern Europe, Africa, and "how ordinary Europeans lived and thought." This is a fine set, from its beautiful physical appearance to the scope and depth of its coverage. Recommended for academic and large public libraries.

—Michael Tosko

Gale Virtual Reference Library. [Online database]. Gale, pricing varies [http://www.gale.com/eBooks/]. (Last accessed February 18, 2004).

Oxford Scholarship Online. [Online database]. Oxford, pricing from $1,425 [http://www.oxfordscholarship.com/oso/public/index.html]. (Last accessed February 18, 2004).

Gale Virtual Reference Library is an electronic implementation of 85 (and growing) of Gale's reference publications. The content is stellar; it includes some fine encyclopedias, almanacs, and other reference books. It has clear records, nice up-front print or e-mail options, and a helpful "how to cite" feature. It also has a user-friendly interface and intuitive search features. The dictionary feature is an added benefit. Libraries may select from among the available titles to customize their electronic collections. Gale considers the business model that of a purchase, but there are still annual fees to have access to the materials. All purchases include unlimited access.

Searches can be performed on article/entry title, keyword (the first 50 words of an article as well as index terms), image caption (less useful), source, and print and e-book ISBN. From a document record, the searcher can link not only to the article but also to the table of contents, index, and list of illustrations—all searchable and clickable—in the book where the article appears. Entries are electronic versions of their printed counterparts and can be displayed either as text with graphics or as PDF files. In addition to the *see also* references that appear in the print version, each entry also includes a linked list of relevant terms from the back-of- the-book index. Web sites in the bibliographies are also linked. As part of the "how to cite" feature, the *Gale Virtual Reference Library* includes field identifiers that could be used in EndNote or other bibliographic database management software.

If patrons are going to experience confusion with this product, it will be because there are too many choices. Searching by article entry is usually better than keyword or full text because of the number of hits. Searching by a specific encyclopedia may be the best way to find information. For example, a basic search on the keyword AIDS produces 518 hits, that is, 518 articles in various books that contain the term. These hits can be sorted by article title, source, or relevance (which Gale is still refining). However, choosing Advanced Search, specifying *Encyclopedia of Public Health,* and searching AIDS as an article/entry title produces one very relevant entry. As another example, searching *diversity* as a keyword produces 183 hits. A search on *diversity* as an article/ entry title produces 6 hits on topics like biological diversity, diversity in the workplace, and the Unity and Diversity World Council. A good way to use this product is in conjunction with the online catalog. Patrons may find a catalog record for an e-book and search that specific title for the information that they are seeking.

The *Gale Virtual Reference Library* has good content and a well-designed interface and is easy to use. Recommended for libraries of all sizes that can afford it.

Oxford Scholarship Online builds upon the successes of other Oxford electronic products. It is an e-book publishing service with titles currently available in (for now) four modules: Economics and Finance, Philosophy, Political Science, and Religion. It includes 700 Oxford publications with the promise of more than 200 new titles per year. *Oxford Scholarship Online* has a nice interface that fully utilizes the power of e-books. The content is scholarly and of a high quality. Libraries can purchase one or more modules, and a subscription allows for multiuser, institutionwide access, including remote users. Access to abstracts, tables of contents, and keywords for each book is free.

The user can look for terms or phrases using Quick Search or Advanced Search or browse the available titles by author, title, and subject. In Advanced Search, the user can search by one or more fields, among them title, author, keywords, abstract, ISBN, and publication date. From the Result page, users can link to the full text of titles or chapters. The e- books can be viewed as an entire book, or chapter by chapter, or just one page. Bibliographic citations and footnotes are linked to external resources such as online journals and reference databases, depending on an institution's subscriptions.

Records contain bibliographic information, a small graphic of the cover, and an abstract created by the book's author. After the abstract is a list of searchable keywords that are linked to other titles, and following this the book's clickable table of contents is displayed. Readers can view either the full text or an abstract of a selected chapter. When another chapter is referred to with the text, it is linked. Index entries are also linked, which speeds access to other parts of a book.

There are a few minor navigational difficulties. To retrieve a list of titles within a category, the user must click on *A–Z* links, one at a time. It would be faster to scroll through all 22 titles in the microeconomics category, to take one example, or, for categories with more titles, to choose settings for how many titles are displayed. Within a book's index, there is no "jump to" feature; the user has to scroll through the index to reach the Ws. Finally, getting back to the main page of a book can be confusing.

Despite these small inconveniences, *Oxford Scholarship Online* is a superior e-book implementation. It joins the ranks of other successful Oxford products, such as *Oxford English Dictionary Online,* the *American National Biography Online,* and *Oxford Reference Online.* Highly recommended for academic and larger public libraries.

—Jack O'Gorman

★**A History of Women in the United States:** State-by-State Reference. 4v. Ed. by Doris Weatherford. 2003. 1,680p. appendixes. bibliogs. illus. index. maps. Grolier, $399 (0-7172- 5805-X). 305.4.

In a set designed for "researchers at the high school, college, and university levels" as well as for general readers, U.S. women's history is filtered through the 50 states, plus Puerto Rico and Washington, D.C. Editor

Weatherford is the author of several other resources on women's history, including *History of the American Suffragist Movement* (ABC-CLIO, 1998) and *Milestones: Chronology of American Women's History* (Facts On File, 1997). Joining her here are almost 70 contributors, primarily responsible for sidebar material.

The set begins with nine introductory essays, each between six and nine pages long. The first five essays take a chronological approach, tracing women's experience as Americans from the 1600s through the 1950s. These are followed by essays that explore various themes: feminism, political participation and social activism, race and ethnicity, and "cultural representations." Each essay is signed by its author and includes a bibliography.

Main entries are organized alphabetically by state. Averaging 23 pages in length, each state history is ordered in a way that generally conforms to the eras outlined in *The National Standards for United States History*. Biographical profiles in each entry offer brief accounts of women (anywhere from around 10 to more than 40) chosen primarily on the basis of historic milestones. Examples include Maggie Smith Hathaway, who helped integrate California golf courses, and Deborah Stabenow, Michigan's first female U.S. senator. The fact that Weatherford herself seems to have written all of the state histories and one other author was responsible for biographical material accounts for the remarkable consistency in tone. A list of prominent places provides information on museums, churches, theaters, inns, restaurants, and other locations in each state that played a role in women's history. A fairly extensive list of resources cites historical texts, biographies and autobiographies, Web sites, and selected organizations and institutions. State maps, time lines, quotations from literary works, excerpts from primary sources, a smattering of black-and-white photographs, and sidebars highlighting aspects of women's experience add interest as well as further levels of informative detail.

In the final volume the reader will find several appendixes: a chronology (1530–2003), a few key documents, statistical tables, and a general bibliography. Given the set's arrangement, the index is a crucial tool, and fortunately this one is up to the job of helping readers pull together all the strands of information on the abolition movement, Susan B. Anthony, or aviators, to give just a few examples.

The past few years have seen the publication of several other multivolume women's history resources. The biographical *Women in World History* (Gale, 2002) provides comprehensive global coverage. *Encyclopedia of Women in American History* (Sharpe, 2002) offers biographical and topical entries within a chronological framework. This newest addition's state-by-state perspective makes it unique. Authoritative, highly readable, and very nicely organized, it is recommended for high-school, public, and academic libraries.

—Mary Ellen Quinn

★**Merriam-Webster's Collegiate Dictionary.** 11th ed. 2003. 1,623p. index. Merriam-Webster, $25.95 (0-87779-807-9). 423.

The first *Merriam-Webster's Collegiate Dictionary* (M-W) was published in 1898, and the tenth edition had a copyright date of 1993. The eleventh edition brings many new words, a CD-ROM, and a free one-year subscription to Merriam-Webster Collegiate.com, which includes the text of the dictionary as well as the *Collegiate Thesaurus, Collegiate Encyclopedia,* and *Merriam-Webster's Spanish-English Dictionary*.

Now for the numbers. M-W has a paper file of 15,700,000 citations from which their lexicographers chose 10,000 new words, for a total of 165,000 entries and 225,000 definitions. There are 100,000 "changes" from the tenth edition. Users asked for more usage examples and idioms and phrases, so there are now 40,000 examples and a "significant" increase in idioms. There are 91,000 pronunciations, 33,000 etymologies, 2,700 illustrative quotations, 650 foreign words and phrases, and 700 illustrations.

As the world rushes on, so does the time taken for words to become accepted. It used to be at least ten years before a new word was considered for inclusion; now it may take as few as four years. M-W staff certainly have become the purveyors of the words that we use. Terms added to this edition include *Botox, comb-over, crunch-exercise, dead-cat bounce, dead presidents, dead tree, def, exfoliant, gimme cap, identity theft, phat,* and *tweener*. As would be expected, some entries had to be eliminated because words are invented faster than they go out of favor. Anyone seeking definitions of *record changer* and *pantdress* will need an unabridged or older dictionary.

M-W still includes separate sections for geographical and biographical names, but abbreviations are now interfiled in the main section. Perhaps the next edition will interfile the other two sections.

Criticisms of the eleventh edition are mostly cosmetic. The use of photographs and shaded boxes for usage notes would make it more attractive to users. There are, however, more than 200 new black- and-white line drawings. The *Collegiate Dictionary*'s closest competitor, the *American Heritage College Dictionary* (4th ed.), published last year, makes good use of photographs and illustrations in the margins. It contains a number of words (*gangsta, goth*) that are also new to this edition of M-W.

The online version has a number of search options, including a reverse dictionary (if you can think of the correct words), the etymology of words, and those that are the same part of speech. The most interesting option is the date feature. Paging through the words attributed to a particular year is a definite retrospective of recollections. Words of 1980 include *balsamic vinegar, exit poll, NIMBY,* and *ziplock*. An improvement to the online version would be a search button so the back button doesn't need to be used as much. It would be less cumbersome if the illustrations were included with the definitions rather than requiring another click. Because the one-year free subscription to the online version is only mentioned on the dust jacket, some users will fail to see it. Unfortunately, the free subscription is not available free to libraries or schools. One wonders if the CD-ROM is really necessary because it provides only basic searching.

For serious dictionary collections and fans of dictionaries from this venerable publisher, now in partnership with Britannica, the eleventh edition is a definite buy. With a list price of $25.95, it is a bargain for individuals. Libraries with limited budgets that purchased the *American Heritage College Dictionary* in 2002 may not need another college dictionary this year.

—Christine Bulson

Rx for Consumer Health Reference:
One-Volume Medical Encyclopedias

by Barbara Bibel

Single-volume medical encyclopedias are an important part of public and consumer health library reference collections. They are also used in the home. Since medical information changes rapidly, these sources need to be replaced periodically. Fortunately, several of the most popular medical encyclopedias have released new editions within the past year. All provide basic information that is easy for lay readers to understand. Choosing one or more for a library collection will depend on community needs and preferences. All of these new editions now include information about complementary and alternative therapies, environmental health issues, and domestic violence.

American Medical Association Complete Medical Encyclopedia. 2003. 1,408p. Random House, $45 (0-8129-9100-1).

This encyclopedia has a good series of flowcharts that include questions that lead to suggestions for emergency care, urgent care, or a routine appointment. It also has a fascinating section about the latest advances in medical research. The alphabetical entries for diseases and conditions are brief, but there are sample forms for advance health-care directives and information about the Health Insurance Portability and Accountability Act (HIPAA) and privacy of information.

Complete Home Medical Guide. 2d ed. 2003. 1,104p. DK, $50 (0-7894-9673-9).

As always, the outstanding feature of this DK book is illustration. Published under the auspices of the American College of Physicians, it has more than 2,000 color pictures. It also has a fine series of flowcharts, both general and specific, for men's, women's, and children's symptoms. The book is organized by broad topics: "Taking Control of Your Health," "Assessing Your Symptoms: Looking for Disease," "Your Body and Disease," "Treating Disease." Added features include first-aid information, a drug glossary, and a good list of Web sites.

Mayo Clinic Family Health Book. 3d ed. Ed. by Scott C. Litin. 2003. 1,448p. HarperResource, $49.95 (0-06-000250-6).

The Mayo Clinic's new encyclopedia is also organized by broad topics: "Living Well," "Common Conditions and Concerns through Life's Stages," "Making Sense of Your Symptoms," "First Aid and Emergency Care," "Diseases and Disorders," "Tests and Treatments." The symptoms section is brief and narrative, making it less useful than a flowchart. There is very good coverage of immunization, the aging process, and nutrition, including diet pyramids for Mediterranean, Asian, Latin American, and vegetarian diets as well as the USDA pyramid. The book also has a 40-page section of color plates illustrating anatomy and diseases.

The Merck Manual of Medical Information: Second Home Edition. By Mark Beers. 2003. 1,946p. Merck Research Laboratories, $37.50 (0-911910-35-2).

This new edition of the lay version of a medical reference classic has the most detailed information about diseases and conditions. It is organized by organ systems and includes a great deal of information about anatomy and physiology, genetics, and drugs as well as an explanation of medical terminology. The book also covers travel health and diseases of unknown cause and offers a good selection of Web sites for further information. It is available free online along with the other Merck Manuals at [http://www.merckmanuals.com] in English and Spanish.

With tight budgets, it would be difficult to buy all of these encyclopedias. *The Merck Manual of Medical Information: Second Home Edition* provides the most information for your money. DK's *Complete Home Medical Guide* has the best illustrations as well as explanations of procedures. A good consumer health collection should include both of these titles. The *Mayo Clinic Family Health Book* and the *American Medical Association Complete Medical Encyclopedia* both provide good basic medical information. They would be excellent in circulating and home collections.

Spanish-Language Online Encyclopedias

by Barbara Bibel

Hispanics comprise the largest and fastest-growing ethnic group in the U.S. Libraries serving this group usually have bilingual staff and books and videos in Spanish, but current encyclopedias are difficult to find. Those available in print are often out-of-date. Fortunately, the major publishers of online encyclopedias have added Spanish-language sources to their collections. Britannica and Grolier have adult encyclopedias, while World Book has one for young children. All encyclopedias were last accessed on August 29, 2003.

Enciclopedia universal en español. Britannica, call 1-800-621-3900 for pricing [http://corporate.britannica.com/library/online/eue.html].

Enciclopedia universal en español is the largest of the online encyclopedias in Spanish. It has 47,000 articles, 8,300 photographs and images, 390 maps, 500 tables, and 65,000 dictionary entries. The content is based on *Enciclopedia Hispanica*. The search box has a nice feature, a row of Spanish characters with diacritical marks above the typing area. Users may click on the appropriate letter to insert it so that they can search precisely even though they do not have a Spanish keyboard. They may enter individual terms or use Boolean operators. Users can also browse by letter or historical period. Combining a geographic area or subject with a time period produces a very nice time line with illustrations. The summary results screen offers the choice of looking at the article text, the illustrations, tables, maps, graphs, Datapedia (showing current available economic and population statistics for countries), related articles, or Web links. Users may print or e-mail articles. The editors provide citation information in both the Modern Language Association and American Psychological Association formats.

The article on Afghanistan (*Afganistán*) is current through 2001 and Karzai's election. A search for Osama bin Laden brought up a biography and links to articles on the Taliban (*Talibanes*) and terrorism (*terrorismo*). The Taliban article links to an article on religious fundamentalism (*fundamentalismo religioso*), which discusses only Christianity and Islam. The article on HIV/AIDS (*SIDA*) has a good overview of the disease, noting the existence of HIV I and HIV II as well as the major impact of this disease in Africa.

Looking up the date September 11 leads to biographies of people who fought in battles on that date throughout history as well as to articles about Osama bin Laden, Pervez Musharaf, the Taliban, and Hamid Karzai; biographies of people born on that day; terrorism; and New York. Articles on countries are reasonably current. Clicking on the Datapedia link will bring up the most current available statistics.

Although the search engine needs some refining, *Enciclopedia universal* is a good Spanish-language source for academic and large public libraries serving users who are fairly sophisticated.

Nueva enciclopedia cumbre en línea. [Internet database]. Grolier, pricing from $490 [http://go.grolier.com].

Nueva enciclopedia cumbre en línea is an encyclopedia for middle- and high-school students and the general public. It has more than 17,500 entries, 7,000 illustrations, 315 maps, 150 sounds (all national anthems), and 20,345 Web links. Among the 250 new articles in the 2003 editions are biographies of Henry Cisneros, Oscar Hijuelos, and popular women writers such as Elena Poniatowska. This encyclopedia is primarily for Spanish speakers in the U.S., so the editors have added a great deal of new content on U.S. history and culture. All of the articles on the states and the Canadian provinces and territories have been replaced with translations of the articles from the *Grolier Multimedia Encyclopedia*. Contributors have rewritten more than 300 biographies of ancient, medieval, modern, and contemporary philosophers. Eighty short articles on American and British literary figures have been replaced with articles from the *Grolier Multimedia Encyclopedia*, too. Updated articles include those on Israel, George W. Bush, and Argentina. There are 165 new illustrations in this edition. None of the articles are signed, and there are no bibliographies. Users cannot print or e-mail articles.

The search box allows users to enter terms and employ Boolean operators and truncation. They may search the full text or the article titles or browse subject areas such as history or technology by checking boxes. They also have the option of using the search box for all of *Grolier Online*, which appears in the right-hand corner at the bottom of each screen. This is a useful feature for bilingual users or those studying Spanish or English as a second language. If one wants to compare all of the articles on a given subject in both languages, the search term must be spelled the same way. Finding all of the articles on Mexico is easy, but using Spain as a search term only brings up those in English. To find the article in Spanish, one must enter *Espana*. The article on Afghanistan in *Cumbre* is quite current. Hamid Karzai is listed as the head of the transitional government, and the 2002 earthquake is covered. There are no articles about al-Qaeda, but it is mentioned in the articles about Osama bin Laden and George W. Bush. The entry for Taliban (*Talibanes*) covers events through 2000. The article on Mexico is current through the election of Vicente Fox as president in 2000. The fact box has the estimated population for 2002. The article on AIDS (*SIDA*) explains the virus and the transmission of the disease well. The first hit in a search on September 11 is Osama bin Laden. The others deal with unrelated people or events that occurred on that date throughout history.

Nueva enciclopedia cumbre en línea is an excellent choice for school and public libraries with Spanish-speaking patrons. The ability to search it as part of the *Grolier Online* package is a definite advantage, but the fact that users cannot print or e-mail articles is a disadvantage.

Enciclopedia estudiantil hallazgos. [Internet database]. World Book, pricing from $445 for subscription to World Book Online Reference Center [http://www.worldbookonline.com/].

Enciclopedia estudiantil hallazgos is the Spanish-language version of *World Book Student Discovery Encyclopedia*. Available only to libraries that purchase a subscription to *World Book Online Reference Center*, it is a small resource for elementary-school students. This encyclopedia has more than 2,200 articles, 250 maps, 250 flags, 330 tables and fact boxes, and links to 1,150 Spanish-language Web sites. World Book began adding illustrations in September, 2003, and plans to add 100–200 illustrations a month. An application change has made the site more ADA-compliant.

Searching is completely menu-driven. Users click on a letter of the alphabet, which leads to alphabetical subdivisions with a list of articles. They may choose a short specific article (e.g., *Saturno* for information about the planet Saturn) or a longer general article (e.g., *planeta* for information about planets). The print is large, and the short articles contain very basic information. The articles have citation information and links to related articles and Web sites. Users may print or e-mail articles.

The article about Afghanistan has simple information about that country's history and geography. The only reference to current events is a statement that the U.S. accused the Taliban of the attack on the World Trade Center. There is nothing about the war, al-Qaeda, or Osama bin Laden. The article about AIDS has a good basic explanation of how HIV attacks blood cells. The article about Latin American literature is a single paragraph listing a few of the most famous writers. It does not even include the titles of their works, but it does note that Gabriel García Márquez won the Nobel Prize for literature in 1982.

Enciclopedia estudiantil hallazgos is useful for elementary-school libraries and the children's rooms of public libraries that need a Spanish-language resource. It is also useful for low-literacy users. World Book should consider producing a Spanish-language online version of its regular encyclopedia, which would serve both children and adults well.

Reference on the Web

Baseball Statistics 15
Cut Me Some Slang 16
Fashion, Turn to the Left 16
Harlem Renaissance 17
Hinduism 17
How Stuff Works 18
Naming Pains 18
No, Not *Those* Primaries 19
Today in Literature 19
Too Much TMTT 20

Baseball Statistics

by Keir Graff

Some baseball fans find that their blood stirs at the crack of the bat, the roar of the crowd, or an off-key rendition of "Take Me Out to the Ballgame." Others feel ball games are an excellent chance to drink a beer or six, catch up with friends, and wave their arms while saying, "Can you see me now?" into their cell phones. A more cold-blooded group seems to believe the purpose of athletic contests lies in generating dense columns of numbers, which they scrutinize with the fervent passion of religious scholars.

Although I worry that these last folks need more sun, they number too many to dismiss. (Furthermore, I must acknowledge that a judicious use of statistics does actually enhance enjoyment of the game: if you know that the leadoff man is 4 for 13 in base-stealing attempts, it's a lot more exciting when he takes off for second.) And the Web is the perfect way to feed a stats habit. The print world offers periodicals and annual compendiums, but the Web can be updated daily, can be made searchable, and is the perfect way to look busy while hunting for trivia about Lou "The Mad Russian" Novikoff. (All sites last visited July 18, 2003.)

baseball-reference.com. [http://www.baseball-reference.com/].

This site offers information dating back to 1871 on players, teams, and leagues, along with managerial data, awards, team schedules, and more. There are nearly 25,000 individual pages on this site—yet, to find information, users will most likely have to work their way through the site's navigation. Searching is limited to a box labeled "Players."

Headings on the splash page include Players (alphabetized, includes batting and fielding stats, appearances on leaderboards and awards, similar batters, likelihood of entering the Hall of Fame, and even salary history); Teams (with year-by-year records, league and division, position at end of season, manager, players with highest on-base plus slugging [OPS] and highest ERA); Leagues (with season-by-season statistical totals, even for obsolete leagues like the 1884 Union Association); Leaders (with breakdowns of who was best at what and when); Awards (with voting summaries); Postseason (all series helping to decide the World Series); Managers (including a roster ranked by number of wins); Games (see more below); Travel (also below); and Frivolities (trivia).

Two of my favorite sections were Games and Travel. The first allows for interesting sorting: head-to-head records between any two teams, league standings for any date in any season, top team performance over a specific stretch, and more. The second allows users to enter a zip code and find the closest opportunities to see baseball, whether major league, minor league, or independent team.

CBS SportsLine.com. [http://cbs.sportsline.com/u/baseball/mlb/stats.htm].

League Leaders by Timeframe allows users to find hitting and pitching leaders (in categories from triples hit to shutouts pitched) with the added bonus of sorting by year to date, the last seven days, or yesterday only.

ESPN.com: Statistics. [http://sports.espn.go.com/mlb/statistics].

For a quick look at current statistics, ESPN's site allows users to get the picture with a minimum of clicking. Batting, pitching, and fielding, by individual players or whole team, can be sorted by National League, American League, or all of Major League Baseball. Team stats can similarly be accessed by a simple drop-down menu. Top-five individual leaders in batting, home runs, and RBIs, as well as leaders in pitching wins, ERA, and saves, are posted toward the bottom of the splash page. More esoteric data, such as OPS and grounded into double play (GIDP), are only a link away.

mlb.com. [http://mlb.mlb.com/NASApp/mlb/index.jsp].

For in-depth, individual player statistics, individual team sites can be accessed through the drop-down menu on the splash page of Major League Baseball's official site. Using my heart problem–inducing fave team as an example (go Cubbies!), I click on the Cubs, then on Hee Seop Choi, then on the Stats tab. Here I find career hitting and fielding stats for the second-year Korean first baseman—the first a rather disappointing .225 (although slack must be cut for the injury that disrupted his play this year). But the nitty-gritty lies behind three buttons above: Splits (how Big Choi fares versus left-handed pitching, or on grass versus turf); Game by Game Log (stats for each game of the season); and Hitting Chart (a graphic demonstration that shows exactly where he hits what and in which stadium).

Cut Me Some Slang

by Keir Graff

Print dictionaries have always lagged behind English as it is spoken; judiciously, editors want to make sure a new word or new use of a word will last before they influence its chances. Even dictionaries specializing in slang may be slow: the print cycle for books can last years; linguistics professors may, for all their research, be a mite out of the loop when it comes to the way 17-year-olds talk; even regional differences may affect which words make the cut and which do not.

And yet language seems to be evolving more rapidly than ever. Thanks to the Internet, e-mail, cheap cell-phone minutes, and a generally mobile population, new slang can spread across the country or even the globe within days of its origination.

Fortunately, the Internet also helps us decipher the unfamiliar words it spreads. At this time last year, Mary Ellen Quinn examined Wikipedia, an open-content encyclopedia; in this issue, I'll be looking at open-content slang dictionaries. As with all Internet ventures, there are pros and cons to this approach. Some nominees may have unorthodox or inconsistent spellings. Others might be used only by a small group of friends. Worse, some words may be posted only as jokes.

But, taking all this into account, slang sites can provide instant hip for the hopelessly square. When an acquaintance says, "Ay yo trip! That girl from around the way? I'm a get my beemer bumpin', spend mad bank on some bling, and mack on her tonight," do you reply, "Straight up"? Or "Wack"? (All sites last visited August 4, 2003.)

The Online Slang Dictionary. [http://www.ocf.berkeley.edu/~wrader/slang/].

Maintained by UC–Berkeley student Walter Rader (and apparently founded in 1997), this site "depends entirely on your contributions"—and no, he's not asking for ducats. At present, terms are browseable by A–Z listings, although Rader plans to introduce searchability and a thesaurus (the latter is, by my lights, the most useful way to find slang). Submissions and clarifications are bylined and dated, and the range of words is wide and unpredictable. Most words are rooted in U.S. usage. Rader disparages drug references (thus, you won't find *blunt*).

There is intriguing browsing here: the meanings of some words, such as *nastafied* ("*adj* gross. ['That girl is completely nastafied']") might be deducible from context; others are counterintuitive, such as the delightfully illustrated *no diggity* ("used as an agreement. Note: may or may not be paired with another phrase. ['No diggity, Einstein was smart!' or simply 'No diggity!']").

The Rap Dictionary. [http://www.rapdict.org/].

This site originated way back in September 1992 with a series of postings to the alt.rap newsgroup, and Patrick "Tricky" Altoon has been keeping it real ever since. In a simple A–Z format, from *a* ("[v] Going to. 'I'm a do it like this.'") to *zootie* ("[n] A joint laced with crack."), he lists terms that will help even ABBA fans make sense of Jay-Z's lyrics. Many terms are sourced, and although this is not a true open-content dictionary, Altoon encourages challenges and clarifications. Warning: some hip-hop lingo may curl some readers' ears.

Slangsite.com. [http://www.slangsite.com/].

Owned by Impulse Communications, a prolific creator of Web sites (from DancingBush.com to CouponFrenzy.com), Slangsite.com is currently not accepting new submissions. Listings (A–Z) are quite extensive, however, covering words (*aazing*: "Like amazing, but not quite"); acronyms (*T.O.U.*: "Techy One-Up. Spotting an elementary error of a technical/nerdy nature made by a colleague [sic] who really ought to know about that sort of thing, and the subsequent gloating over one's own cleverness"); and phrases (*watch the scenes*, "to watch the whole movie"). Includes nonsense or made-up words (*inflajeatorant*, "a large and insatiable ducklike mammal"); "Webspeak" (*fark*, "fuxk, used to bypass email [sic] scanners when emailing [sic] from the workplace"); colloquialisms (*parking nazi*, "parking meter enforcement officer"); and manufactured jargon (see *infotoxin*). Nearly all entries include examples.

A sign of the times is *a sims moment*: "Brief moment in which you can relate something in real life to something in the computer simulation game The Sims. Usually occurs after rounds of playing said game. *Example*: 'I'm having a sims moment. This kitchen looks almost like what I did in The Sims last night.'"

Browsing slang on the Web can be addictive. There are sites with jargon for ultimate Frisbee players (Ultilingo.com), mountain bikers (The Dictionary of Mountain Bike Slang), spelunkers (Cavers Slang Dictionary), convicts (A Prisoner's Dictionary), Dubliners (the O'Byrne Files), even residents of Antarctica (English, as She is Spoke at McMurdo).

Fashion, Turn to the Left

by Keir Graff

Ever since humans swapped animal skins for woven fabrics, they have balanced the desire for comfort and functionality with the desire to look good—although even in the hide-and-pelt days, there were undoubtedly some Cro-Magnons who liked to let their furs fall off the shoulder just so. Because we're an industrious lot, the evolutionary cycle for garments has grown shorter and shorter: if the burka has, in some countries, remained de rigueur since 622 C.E., here at home, four-inch cuffs on stovepipe jeans had about a six-month run before the mavens deemed them "so last year."

This might seem irrelevant to those of us with no desire to stride the scissors' edge. Let the purple-haired club kids set the trends, we say, and let them risk the ridicule—we'll happily buy the watered-down, mass-produced version four years later, on markdown, at Marshall's. But there is a certain amount of keeping-up we must all do. Just try interviewing for a job in paisley and bell-bottoms, for example, or speed-dating in acid-wash jeans, pixie boots, and a fringed leather jacket.

"Fashion is made to become unfashionable," said Coco Chanel (of all people), her statement a corrective for the in-the-know who insist on being-of-the-moment. But, if leafing through *Fashion, Costume, and Culture* (see p.46) is a fascinating look at how little our clothes have to do with simply keeping warm, it's also a reminder of how unlikely we are to stop fetishizing couture. The following sites were recommended in the back of the book. (All sites last visited on May 17, 2004.)

The Costumer's Manifesto. [http://www.costumes.org/].

This project is part site, part portal. There are links to information about Halloween costumes, costumes for sale, costuming supplies, and many eclectic byways. For our purposes, the most useful thing is History Sorted by Period, a massive collection of links to sites about clothes, ranging from Barbarian Europe to Corporate Goth. A site so large, maintained by one woman, seems destined to suffer some broken links, as this does. But it's a great jumping-off point.

La Couturière Parisienne. [http://marquise.de/index.html].

Treating "period costume" from the Middle Ages through the early twentieth century, this site offers a database of 4,000 images, hundreds of articles, and even some clothing patterns. *Costume* here means clothes, not fancy dress, and is mostly European, as this amazing site is apparently the work of a single German woman. Everything is well organized, and text and images are both searchable (the English version of the site uses British spelling). Preconfigured searches, such as Ancient Rome or Film: *Sleepy Hollow*, return a wide array of related images. Among the few men's patterns are a series of scans from a men's tailoring book. A great resource for reenactors, would-be costumers, and people who are sick of wearing Tommy Hilfiger.

Fashion-Era. [http://www.fashion-era.com/index.htm].

Ironically, this site devoted to fashion is a little, um, unhandsome (pink scroll bars and gold lettering? please!). But this labor of love, from a husband-and-wife team in Droitwich Spa, England, is actually a fairly successful populist look at the last two centuries of fashion. Searching quality varies, but clearly labeled categories make it easy to look for La Belle Époque or Fashion after 1980. Images include snapshots and magazine cutouts. Writing is pithy and entertaining ("Zip fronted boiler suits were a development from space clothes of 1969 and when made up in fabric like stretch velours were exceptionally sexy 1970's party gear"). There's obviously an English bias, but good taste knows no borders, don't you agree?

Metropolitan Museum of Art: The Costume Institute. [http://www.metmuseum.org/Works_of_Art/department.asp?dep=8].

Unfortunately, the Met's famed Costume Institute displays only a tiny fraction of its 75,000-costume collection online (1/1500th of the collection, to be precise). But these beautiful photographs of mostly twentieth-century clothes will make any fashionista turn chartreuse with envy. Not much use for anthropologists—unless their area of study is the Upper East Side, the Gold Coast, and Beverly Hills—but worth a look all the same.

Harlem Renaissance

by Keir Graff

First known as the "New Negro Movement," the Harlem Renaissance was a time of cultural flowering for black Americans. During the affluent post–World War I period, huge numbers of southern blacks migrated north to industrial cities, New York—and Harlem, a three-square-mile neighborhood—in particular. The concentration of so many black people, and so many talented black people, provided fertile soil for creative growth. The first shoots were literary, as talented writers working in fiction, poetry, drama, and the essay broke the constraints of dominant white culture to incorporate African American traditions and explore themes (alienation, repression, assimilation) that spoke strongly to black audiences. Other arts flourished, too: music (jazz, blues, and spirituals); painting; and politics (from "back to Africa" movements to integration) all saw growth in sophistication and popularity.

The Great Depression hit Harlem hard, and many key figures were forced to move or sustain themselves with mundane work, largely bringing the renaissance to a close. As the *Encyclopedia of the Harlem Renaissance* (see review p.72) suggests, however, study of this influential period is still necessary and popular. Bibliographic information on the subject is easy to find online, but the following sites provide some of the color necessary to understand this dynamic era. (All sites last visited December 30, 2003.)

Harlem: Mecca of the New Negro. [http://etext.virginia.edu/harlem/index.html].

A fascinating chance to feel the intellectual excitement of the times, this is a "hypermedia edition" of the March 1925 issue of *Survey Graphic*. The magazine includes essays, articles, stories, and poems by many prominent thinkers (Alain Locke, W. E. B. DuBois, Arthur Schomburg) and writers (Countee Cullen, Langston Hughes). Pages are reproduced in facsimiles that run side-by-side with (sometimes hyperlinked) transcriptions. Even advertisements are included, making this an extremely appealing time capsule.

Harlem, 1900–1940: An African-American Community. [http://www.si.umich.edu/CHICO/Harlem/index.html].

A Web version of a 1991 publication (a project of the New York Public Library's Schomburg Center for Research in Black Culture), this research tool is intended for students and teachers. Though the years covered are much greater than those of the Harlem Renaissance, the renaissance lies at the core of the 40-year period. Entries can be read page by page, as if strolling through a museum exhibit. A well-written, succinct article about Marcus Garvey and his Universal Negro Improvement Association (with photo) is followed by an article about two NAACP publications, the short-lived *Brownies' Book* and the still-going *Crisis*. The third entry covers the Silent Protest, a landmark march in 1917 addressing violence against African Americans. Entries continue in this vein, covering cultural and political figures, organizations, and landmarks. The site includes a time line, a teachers' section, a bibliography, and links (some of which are broken or out-of-date).

Perspectives in American Literature: Chapter 9: Harlem Renaissance, 1919–1937. [http://www.csustan.edu/english/reuben/pal/chap9/CHAP9.HTML?Submit=9.+The+Harlem+Renaissance].

Paul P. Reuben, English professor at Cal State–Stanislaus, has built upon his print work, *PAL (Perspectives in American Literature): A Research and Reference Guide* (8th ed., California State Univ., 1995), to create a much-lauded project online. He provides an extremely substantial bibliography of books and articles; an outline-style introduction that includes an overview, prominent personalities, a year-by-year chronology, and a discussion of themes; research topics; and 26 author entries, from Gwendolyn Bennett to Walter White. Author entries often include photos and brief biographies; seemingly all contain lists of works and bibliographies of relevant books and articles.

Rhapsodies in Black: Art of the Harlem Renaissance. [http://www.iniva.org/harlem/].

Focusing on the visual arts, this extremely attractive site juxtaposes short essays with paintings (Aaron Douglas, Jacob Lawrence) and sculptures (Sir Jacob Epstein, Ronald C. Moody) to relate themes of the era with the then-emerging art. Really an introduction to an exhibition of the same name, organized by London's Hayward Gallery in collaboration with Washington, D.C.'s Corcoran Gallery and the Institute of International Visual Arts, Rhapsodies in Black provides a brief but compelling portrait of the time.

Hinduism

by Keir Graff

Many Americans' acquaintance with Hinduism may come from *The Simpsons:* Apu, the indefatigable Kwik-E-Mart owner, struggles to educate Springfield's loutish citizens ("Please do not offer my god a peanut"). Even if we do have some non-pop-culture awareness of Hinduism, it's often limited to thoughts that (a) its adherents are Indian and (b) it has fascinating-looking deities, such as the blue-skinned Shiva, the four-armed Vishnu, and, yes, the elephant-headed Ganesha. As this belief system looks nothing like our monotheistic, good-versus-evil Western tradition, few of us can provide a passable definition of it.

Hinduism is the Western name for Sanatana Dharma ("eternal religion") or Vaidika Dharma ("religion of the Vedas"). Some debate whether it is monotheistic, polytheistic, henotheistic (worship of one god without denying others exist), or even Trinitarian, but it's generally agreed that its deities represent different aspects or forms of the same god. Complicating matters further, however, God, or Brahman, exists in every living being, so the divine may be found in each person. Hindus see existence as a cycle of birth, death, and rebirth (transmigration), governed by a balance of good and bad deeds (karma).

Hinduism is the world's third-largest religion, with as many as 900 million adherents (although India and Nepal are the only countries with Hindu majorities). Its venerated texts, the Vedas, date back to 1200–200 B.C.E. (and far earlier orally); it may well be the world's oldest organized religion still practiced today. Interestingly, Hinduism is not considered to have a founder or primary teacher or any prophets.

But no religious tradition can be adequately summed up in three paragraphs; these Web sites offer further reading. (All sites last visited August 18, 2003.)

The Hindu Universe. [http://www.hindunet.org/].

A project of the Boston-based Hindu Students Council, the Hindu Universe has an FAQ, a glossary, and a very extensive amount of educational material. But it also serves as an online community for Hindus, with current news, discussion groups, a calendar, and much, much more. A great way to see what's important to U.S. Hindus today.

Hinduism for Schools. [http://www.btinternet.com/~vivekananda/schools1.htm].

A project of the Vivekananda Centre London, this site provides plain-English answers about many aspects of Hinduism. Though written for UK schools (primary and secondary), there is no reason this would not be helpful in the U.S. as well.

Kashmir: Hindu Deities. [http://www.koausa.org/Gods/].

Some sites give better explanations of the deities, but the combination of concepts, symbolism, and illustrations here provide a great one-stop study aid.

Sacred-texts: Hinduism. [http://www.sacred-texts.com/hin/ index.htm].

Offering straight text of the important works of Hinduism—the Vedas and Upanishads—along with national epics *The Mahabharata* and *The Ramayana* and other important works. Some, such as *The Bhagavad Gita*, come in several translations.

TempleNet. [http://www.templenet.com/].

This fascinating site focuses on Indian temples, which dot the subcontinent in multitudinous variety. In explaining the form and function of these wondrous edifices, quick lessons are offered on Hinduism and history as well. Temples are organized by major deity and region, and subsections offer primers on both architecture of the temples and beliefs and legends related to them. A detailed glossary explains any confusing terms.

Valmiki's Ramayana. [http://www.askasia.org/adult_free_zone/ virtual_gallery/exhibitions/index.htm].

Graphic novel version of the 24,000-couplet epic by the Sanskrit poet Valmiki. Hugely influential in Hindi art and culture, this will interest kids with its colorful stories and exciting battles.

How Stuff Works

by Keir Graff

HowStuffWorks. [http://www.howstuffworks.com/index.htm]. (Last accessed October 15, 2003.)

After my maternal grandfather passed away several years ago, I stumbled across a wonderful book on his bookshelf, called *How Things Work*. By then a yellowing paperback with a brittle spine and a separated cover, it was inscribed by the friend who'd given it to him during an illness. I'd always held my grandfather in quiet awe. A pleasant, unassuming man, he was a successful banker who was also highly skilled with his hands. He seemed to know everything about making and fixing things, whether he was building a beautiful bed and hope chest for my parents or, more controversially, a crossbow for my brother and me.

My own father taught me more about literature and history than carpentry and electricity, but finding the book gave me hope that there were still shortcuts to being the kind of guy for whom a toolbox was more than a prop. Granted, its explanations of toasters and light bulbs seem a little quaint in an era of PDAs and picture phones, but many of the principles are still relevant.

Now, accessible via what is arguably the least-understood technology in common use, there's a Web site that helps us make sense of the technology we live with. HowStuffWorks is the online offering of a company that produces books, a magazine, and a CD, all in the same vein. The idea is simple: devices or concepts are presented—boomerangs, gas prices, patents—and the way they work is explained in terms that anyone should be able to understand.

Users looking for a particular topic can use the search box, while browsers can choose splash-page buttons for particular areas: computers, cars, electronics, science, home, entertainment, health, money, travel, and people (that is, culture, government, and public works). Each area has a home page with different categories and subcategories clearly listed. Computers, for example, are divided into hardware, Internet, peripherals, security, "ShortStuff" (quick answers), software, and a library that seems to list all computer-related articles. The security subcategories include topics like firewalls, facial recognition systems, and surge protectors.

"How Facial Recognition Systems Work" is a four-page, illustrated, hyperlinked article that is refreshingly jargon free. One of the illustrations is actually an animation, and another uses a smidge of humor, which is nice. How *do* they work? The words *nodal points, biometrics,* and *algorithm* may strike fear into the hearts of liberal arts majors like myself, but after reading the article I feel pretty confident that I could explain the basics to anyone (computers scan video images and measure the distance between facial features to create a code, then try to match the code against others already on file). The last page of the article is a bibliography of related articles on the site and of links to articles published elsewhere. (Helpful hint: the Printable Version button also makes the articles easier to read on your screen by arranging them on one scrollable page rather than sequential pages you "turn.")

Because this site is clearly put together by technophiles, it's a welcome surprise to see some mention of the possible negative repercussions of biometric (using biological information to verify identity) technology. Granted, it's not at the same level we find on the American Civil Liberties Union site [http://www.aclu.org/], but in an era when scientists blend the genes of fish and strawberries, a note of restraint seems necessary even when discussing the most wondrous discoveries.

The number and breadth of articles is impressive. From hydraulic cranes to hurricanes, movie screens to MRI (although, incredibly, they do forget to spell out the acronym—Magnetic Resonance Imaging), and seat belts to smart windows, some explanations demystify things you've always found confusing, while others expose seemingly forgettable processes as amazing in their own right.

There are a few exceptions: "How Frequent Flier Programs Work" (under Money, then Business) seems like filler. Reading like a promotional brochure for the concept of using frequent flier miles, the article uses too many exclamation points and offers little information that wouldn't readily be available from any airline. A Krispy Kreme article, too, seems more like a triumph for the doughnut maker's tireless publicity machine than a legitimate educational experience.

HowStuffWorks has a wide appeal, from would-be and actual handymen and compulsive book-stall browsers to students doing reports and parents with young children. Searching *Why is the sky blue?* leads to an article called "Why Is the Sky Blue?" that explains the phenomenon succinctly. Alas, however, there are no corresponding articles for the questions "Why am I here?" or "Are we there yet?"

Naming Pains

by Keir Graff

Naming things satisfies uniquely human needs. It helps us make sense of the world (a terrifying monster becomes *Ursus arctos horibilis*), take ownership of it *(Queensland)*, advertise ourselves *(Bank One Ballpark)*, and gratify our egos *(Trump Tower)*. Although naming children works somewhat similarly, it is fraught with hidden perils. We've all heard of unfortunates whose parents didn't think through all the dangers: too-creative spelling *(Britani Kaytlyn)*, ethnic collisions *(Günter Littlefeather)*, mouthfuls that can't be shortened *(Ebenezer)*, smirk-inducing initials *(Pamela Michelle Smith)*, painful puns *(Sandy Beach)*, unfortunate double entendres *(Peter O'Toole)*, Biblical names that inspire un-Christian mockery *(Nimrod)*, and flamboyant handles that read like early appointments for therapy *(Scarlett O'Hara)*.

Yet the task can't be shirked. We can't trust children to choose names they will still appreciate when they become adults *(Cool Superdude)*, nor would we want them to go through life with a placeholder name *(Kid A, Sanchez #37)* until they're old enough to choose wisely.

My wife, Marya, and I are expecting our first child, and strangely, diapering and burping seem less daunting than giving the little critter a name. After all, we can learn the best way to fasten a diaper or pat a baby's back, but what makes a good name is purely subjective. (All sites last visited November 25, 2003.)

Baby Zone. [http://www.babyzone.com/babynames/babynames.asp].

This site features lists of popular, cool (according to the editors), international, twin, celebrity, and, yes, Shakespearean names *(Polixenes,* perhaps?); detailed articles with advice and humor about naming babies; and tools such as an advanced search allowing users to input name beginnings, endings, letters, origin, gender, and syllable count. Baby Names around the World is especially helpful—I find that Germanic first names sound better with *Graff* than many others, for instance. But the Baby Name Wizard didn't work its magic for me, however; the random generator produced such gems as *Ffesteb* and *Tucl* for a boy, *Quados* and *Wnee* for a girl, and *Grylerena* and *Rillilil* for either-gender names. My guess is, parents who care for the schoolyard safety of their progeny won't leave their choices to chance. All in all, though, this site seems to have strong, useful lists of names.

BabyCenter. [http://www.babycenter.com/pregnancy/babynaming/index].

This site's name finder promises to help sort names by any combination of gender, beginning or ending letter, origin, and syllable count, but my first half-dozen attempts returned zero results. Name meaning is reverse-searchable and more useful (although I would never have guessed *Marcel* meant "warlike"). Another tool allows users to poll their friends (and, if they like, BabyCenter visitors) if they need help narrowing down the choices—although some friends may wonder why you surrendered *their* names (and e-mail addresses) to a commercial Web site when you could have just sent your own e-mail. In addition to articles, bulletin boards, and various polls, useful features include reader response to naming dilemmas ("Should I name my baby after a victim of the 9/11 attacks?"), state-by-state baby-name popularity breakdowns, and historical name popularity (*John* ruled supreme from 1880 through 1920).

BabyNames.com. [http://www.babynames.com/V5/].

With a database of 6,500 names and meanings, this site is only one-fourth the size of some books. Still, it is searchable by meaning and top names of recent years (useful if you want to make sure your kid doesn't need a last initial appended in every classroom) as well as Shakespearean names, soap-opera names, and Tolkien names (*Elbereth Githoniel*, anyone?). Users can offer their opinions on names or even let the staff choose names for their babies (six names cost only $24.95, and major credit cards are accepted)—or even themselves, if they're tired of their monikers (I prefer my given name to *Roosevelt Remedy Graff*, thank you). This site is pleasingly jumbled and multicultural, though the ability to search by ethnic origin might help some users find names consonant with their own surnames.

Looking at names for long periods results in a syndrome known as *name fatigue*. In this state, it's hard to recognize even excellent names, and bad names can seem perfect. So, if you'll excuse me, I'm going to wrap this column up and see how Marya and little Grylerena are doing.

No, Not *Those* Primaries

by Keir Graff

When the vast potential of the Web was first glimpsed, scholars were drunk with excitement about the intellectual possibilities, and rightly so. Here was a wonder worthy of science fiction, where in theory any person in the world could, with a few keystrokes, have access to all humankind's collective learning—science, art, history, philosophy, religious texts, and knock-knock jokes.

Suffering the hangover of reality, their heads throbbing from blinking banner ads, pop-ups, pornographic spam, and viruses, those visionaries may be wondering whether they're looking at a cathedral of learning or a stripmall of sleaze. But still, those who have little interest in using cyberspace to hawk penis-enlargement technology toil on. Internet information may be notoriously unreliable, but the increasing amounts of digitized primary-source documents do much to counterbalance that failing. To complement the starred review of *American Decades Primary Sources* (see p.87), I offer a small selection of related sites. But finding this stuff is easy—just type *American history primary sources* into Google, or the name of the document (quotes are helpful) if you know what it is. Do, however, take a look at who posted the material. As a general rule, www.yale.edu is a better bet than www.billybobsweekendfunzone.com. Although Billy Bob may just have been kind enough to scan his family's authentic, handwritten copy of the Emancipation Proclamation. (All sites last visited February 23, 2004.)

Amdocs: Documents for the Study of American History. [http://www.ukans.edu/carrie/docs/amdocs_index.html].

This portal, from the University of Kansas, is organized as a time line from 1492 (with a document detailing Columbus' mission) to 2003 (George W. Bush announces the end of major combat operations in Iraq). Most documents are transcribed, with a few files in PDF or Real Audio (a sample of the Nixon tapes).

American Memory: Historical Collections for the National Digital Library. [http://memory.loc.gov/ammem/].

This offshoot of the Library of Congress offers more than seven million items from over 100 historical collections. Materials are searchable and browsable by broad topic (Agriculture; Recreation and Sports), original format (written materials, sound recordings), time, region, library division, and digital format. An exhaustive delight: within a minute of browsing, I'd stumbled on a reproduction of an 1884 panoramic map of my hometown.

Smithsonian American Art Museum. [http://nmaa-ryder.si.edu/].

Art both reflects society and draws it in new directions. The extensive online collections and exhibits at the Smithsonian allow users to search or browse by category (the American West, Urban Scenes). Ansel Adams' pristine nature photographs and John Humble's shots of L.A. for the Los Angeles Documentary Project both have much to tell us. Viewing art online reminds us of the Web's shortcomings, but until hologram technology gets a lot better, we'll have to make do.

U.S. National Archives and Records Administration: Exhibit Hall. [http://www.archives.gov/exhibit_hall/index.html].

Online exhibits include Charters of Freedom, with high-resolution images of our founding documents (Declaration of Independence, Constitution) and When Nixon Met Elvis, featuring an evidentiary look at the famous meeting between the King and the Crook.

www.ourdocuments.gov. [http://www.ourdocuments.gov/index.php?flash=true&].

This snazzy-looking government site (a cooperative effort among several agencies) pays tribute to "100 milestone documents of American history." Includes old favorites (Bill of Rights, Marbury v. Madison) as well as some dark horses (Zimmerman Telegram, Transcript of John Glenn's Official Communication with the Command Center). Explanatory passages help users make sense of what they're looking at, and images of the documents themselves are just plain cool. A great stop for students and educators.

Today in Literature

by Keir Graff

Today in Literature. [http://www.todayinliterature.com]. (Last visited September 10, 2003).

This high-tech page-a-day calendar offers an "original biographical story each calendar day about the great writers, books, and events in literary history." Articles are footnoted with a wide variety of links to related articles and texts. Use requires registering as a member, which is free and doesn't require the user to give up any painful personal information. Registered users receive an e-mail newsletter (they can choose weekly or daily), access to all recent stories (up to 21 days old), and limited access to archived articles. Paid users (the cost is $19.95 per year) receive unlimited access to archives, permission to use materials in the library or classroom, and, best of all, the ability to search the archives (although stories are indexed by author even for nonpaying users).

On September 10, the day's offering was titled "Emerson, John Brown, Russell Banks." The interesting article begins with a speech Ralph Waldo Emerson gave in 1856 in support of Kansas abolitionists, such as John Brown, whom Emerson later eulogized. A portion of Brown's trial speech is excerpted in the context of Emerson's high regard for Brown, and then Banks' novel *Cloudsplitter* is discussed—Banks' Brown thinks little of the sophisticated Sage of Concord.

At the bottom, there are buttons for "Ralph Waldo Emerson Stories, Books & Links" and related authors Henry David Thoreau, Henry Wadsworth Longfellow, Iris Murdoch, Louisa May Alcott, Nathaniel Hawthorne, and Walt Whitman. The former links to two previous stories of the day, about Emerson's death and about Mark Twain's poorly received roast of Emerson, Longfellow, Oliver Wendell Holmes, and John Greenleaf Whittier, "a club of the great and triple-named in which Samuel Langhorne Clemons [sic] eyed a chair." The funny Twain story uncovers an overlooked moment of literary history, more important than trivia but light enough for browsing.

Readers curious about Murdoch's connection to Emerson, however, will remain unenlightened, for the Murdoch story (published on July 15, her birthday) doesn't mention it. It's still a well-written biography, with personal information, writing themes, and pop culture neatly bound in a half-dozen paragraphs. Links are more extensive here than after the Emerson story, however. In addition to a selected bibliography of works by and about Murdoch, there are links to elsewhere-published articles, such as Joyce Carol Oates' 1978 essay, "Sacred and Profane Iris Murdoch," reprinted on the Celestial Timepiece Web site.

Unfortunately, nonpaying users are given a limited number of "credits" for use in viewing full articles on the site. After jumping from Murdoch to a piece on Shakespeare—"Essex Loses Head over *Richard II*"—I've used my third and last credit. The tale of the Earl of Essex's unsuccessful attempt to create a groundswell of revolt by remounting *Richard II* at the Globe (on February 7, 1601) is good reading and provides the context high-school students need if they are to realize that iambic pentameter was once used to rouse people instead of putting them to sleep. Again, however, those already unenlightened about Murdoch's relation to Shakespeare will remain in the dark.

Fortunately, I'll be given another credit when I return another day, allowing me another enjoyable browse in the archives (for real research I'd need the paying subscription). Today in Literature does an admirable job of straddling the line between service and commerce (the limited access gives me more than a Web site that shares the lead paragraph only yet still motivates me to purchase a paid subscription) and recreation and scholarship. Teaching literature demands that dry text be watered and brought to bloom; both students and book lovers will enjoy stopping to smell these flowers.

When There's TMTT

by Keir Graff

New technology brings new terminology. There is, of course, the geek-speak that engineers use for the nuts and bolts (or firewire and mother boards) that bring the widget to life, and there are the words advertisers use to make Project 17584-A sound cool (Blackberry, iPod). And then there are the terms actual users adopt to talk about—or, increasingly, *with*—the gadget in question (BTW, LOL).

It started with e-mail, which is a cold medium. If we're kidding, there's no way to wink as we type *You blew that one*—and a sarcastic *Nice job* comes across as genuine approval. Enter the smiley, or emoticon (though the latter term makes me think of a romance writers' convention). Approximating facial expressions, they're easily read by tilting your head to the left and can be simple—the classic :-) signals good humor while :-(signals sadness—or less so, such as :-& for *tongue-tied*. These clues to the writer's intent are, in our culture of irony, apparently more appealing than straightforward honesty (*You have disappointed me, o colleague*).

Of course, e-mail is old hat. True technophiles don't bother much with e-mail, which is still often thought to require complete sentences, or even the amazing conversational capability offered by cell phones. No, the bleeding-edge hip prefer the space-age equivalent of classroom notes or telegrams. Whether they're firing off lightning-fast messages via Instant Messaging (IM) or trying to avoid finger cramps as they use cell phones for Short Text Messaging (SMS), they use all available shortenings—both abbreviation and acronym fall short in defining them—to feed their need for speed. Thus, GMTA—BCNU F2F L8R ;-).

Books have been published on these phenomena, but this shorthand world evolves so quickly there's rarely time to RTM. Not only that, paper works covering the wired world fall quickly out of date. After all, this fab vocab is driven by young users, and why on earth would they want their parents to be able to read over their shoulders?

IMHO, electronic correspondence deserves the same care as anything else we write—grammar and punctuation are still important. But that doesn't mean I'm not resourceful enough to decode foreign terms from time to time, TYVM. (All sites last visited February 2, 2004).

Abbreviations. [http://acro.harvard.edu/GEI/smileys.html].

Includes the handy TMTT (Too Much To Type), the unfortunate IANAL (I Am Not A Lawyer, But . . .), and the ridiculous TANSTAAFL (There Ain't No Such Thing As A Free Lunch). If you find yourself typing nine letters to abbreviate a cliché, remember the saying, "Avoid clichés like the plague" (ACLTP?)—itself a cliché by now.

Acronym Finder. [http://www.acronymfinder.com/].

A terrific shortcut if you don't care to browse but just want to find out what WTF means (warning: it's not at all polite). More than 334,000 abbreviations and acronyms of all sorts.

Cknow.com: Emoticons. [http://www.cknow.com/ckinfo/emoticons.htm].

A stupendously long list of emoticons, many impossibly specific (check out *William Shatner in a high wind*)—making the point that probably only a handful of emoticons actually aid communication.

High-Tech Dictionary: Emoticons. [http://www.computeruser.com/resources/dictionary/ emoticons.html].

From *Computer User* magazine, this list even includes historical figures, such as =):-)= for Abraham Lincoln, and literary creations, such as [:-| for Frankenstein's monster. Truly, as suggested, you may want to print this page for your reference. I can't count the times I've been discussing Mary Shelley over IM and my fingers stumbled over the endless typings of *Frankenstein*.

Taming the Beast: Smileys, Emoticons, Text Messaging Lingo and Abbreviations Dictionary. [http://www.tamingthebeast.net/ ringtones/smileys-emoticons-sms.htm].

This site has some artfully rendered emoticons, such as the @};---, which is the world's cheapest way to offer a rose to someone, or (::()::), band-aid, an offer of help. My personal useless favorite is Homer Simpson, (_8(|). And an abbreviation such as ASL (*age, sex, and location*) reveals how flirty chat rooms can get.

TUCAA: The Ultimate Computer Acronyms Archive. [http://www.acronyms.ch/servlet/welcome].

This archive is so massive—it includes more than just Net lingo—it works better for searching than browsing. (It's an easy way to decode the introduction above, too.) As an added bonus, you can download the whole thing.

Reviews

Generalities

Reference Universe. [Internet database]. Paratext, pricing from $995 [http://www.paratext.com/ru_intro.htm]. (Last accessed September 5, 2003).

Here is a database that librarians will really appreciate. We have spent countless hours selecting, storing, and carefully weeding our reference collections. But patrons would rather search on the Internet, and get any old answer, than use our pride and joy, our reference collections. *Reference Universe* has taken article titles and indexes from more than 2,000 reference works "from both major and minor reference publishers." These entries have been compiled into a user-friendly database that covers topics from a wide variety of disciplines. It is searchable by singular or plural forms, word variants, exact phrase, or exact words. It also includes searches by all of the words and any of the words. Searches can be limited by publication date and by number of hits (the default being 1,000). A Browse Mode allows users to browse for books by publisher, title of work, subject, or Library of Congress classification number or to browse the Reference Universe index of terms.

After searching, the system presents a list of reference titles in relevancy-ranked order. Besides the title, the brief display includes publisher and date and the total number of index entries or article titles containing the term. There are also links to the local catalog, a full-text e-book version if it is available, article titles and index terms, and a fuller bibliographic record. The full record in turn links to other reference books on the subject, other reference books by the author, the record in MARC format, and a review from *ARBA Online*, available to subscribing libraries. A notes field generally contains brief bibliographic information. As of this writing, Paratext plans to add reviews and publisher links and has installed a prototype that will automatically indicate whether a library owns a title that appears in a list of results.

Do you remember *First Stop: The Master Index to Subject Encyclopedias*, published by Oryx Press in 1989? *Reference Universe* has a similar idea but with a modern interface. Titles indexed seem to have good recency, and keeping the electronic version up-to-date will be easier than updating a printed version. General searches will produce many hits. It may take discernment to determine which subject encyclopedia is best for a particular query, but because this is a librarian's tool, finding the best references for a patron shouldn't be a problem.

This metaindex is an exciting product that will get a lot of use at reference desks in both public and academic libraries and also has uses as a collection development tool. Highly recommended.

A to Z of Computer Scientists. By Harry Henderson. 2003. 308p. bibliogs. glossary. illus. index. Facts On File, $45 (0- 8160-4531-3). 004.

Facts On File has issued another in the Notable Scientists series. The purpose of the series is to provide students at the high-school through early college level with relevant information on great scientists in history as well as lesser-known ones, especially in the disciplines not usually covered in the more well known biographical reference sources. Although other aspects of each scientist's life are covered, the emphasis is on the work and contributions to the discipline and to society.

Coverage in the computer science volume ranges from Charles Babbage, who in 1836 conceived of the first computer, to Shawn Fanning, the Napster entrepreneur who created a method for computer users to grow their music libraries by swapping MP3 files over the Internet. The alphabetically arranged entries profile more than 150 computer scientists who blazed the trail for the pervasiveness of computer technology in our lives. Each entry begins with a heading that lists field of occupation, birth and death dates, and nationality and ends with a list of further readings. Essays range in length from 900 to 1,750 words, and many are accompanied by a black-and-white photograph. A very valuable feature is the index, which lists topics, computer languages, research centers, computer companies, and other points of access to the entries. Also useful are a time line, a glossary, and a list of entries organized by field of activity, such as engineering, mathematics, and programming.

Like other titles in the series, this one is recommended for high-school, public, and undergraduate libraries. In high schools, the series would be a useful career as well as biographical reference.

International Encyclopedia of Information and Library Science. 2d ed. Ed. by John Feather and Paul Sturges. 2003. 688p. bibliogs. index. Routledge, $195 (0-415-25901-0). 004.

The world of information and library science is changing, so it makes sense to update the 1997 edition of this reference work. As the title indicates, the volume seeks to include a world perspective and focuses on present practice and research. Although it does include an entry for each continent, it is largely British in nature. Of the approximately 200 contributors, about 80 percent are associated with the UK.

Articles are arranged alphabetically and vary from a paragraph to 19 pages. About half of the articles are signed and include short bibliographies. The editors do not claim to give equal treatment to all subjects but intend to provide longer articles for topics of greater importance. Therefore, it seems surprising that rare book libraries would get more coverage than public libraries or school libraries. Twelve major articles (about eight pages each) form the backbone of the volume: *Communication, Economics of information, Informatics, Information management, Information policy, Information professions, Information society, Information systems, Information theory, Knowledge industries, Knowledge management,* and *Organization of knowledge*. These entries demonstrate a theoretical and managerial approach. In contrast, the entry for *Book* is one-third of a page, and there is no mention of genres or young adult literature. Indeed, youth resources and services are underrepresented. Biographical entries are also disappointingly few in number. Twenty black-and-white diagrams and 17 tables complement the text.

This volume offers an alternative to U.S.-centric librarianship. However, it does not offer a robust picture of the world but rather starts with a British perspective and branches out. Still, the conceptual articles are valuable, and readers interested in librarianship will find succinct definitions for many professional terms. This work will probably find its home in library and information studies collections.

The Basic Business Library: Core Resources. 4th ed. Ed. by Rashelle S. Karp. 2003. 288p. index. Greenwood, $64.95 (1-57356- 512-1). 016.0276.

This revised edition reflects the dramatic changes in the world of business reference and resources over the past seven years. Since the last edition, the Internet and online access to information have become more affordable and more pervasive in libraries of all sizes.

Part 1, "Core List of Printed Business Reference Sources," has been extensively examined, evaluated, updated, and revised. Titles selected for inclusion—a collection of 210 resources with a 2002 total cost of $65,204.98—reflect the changes in the economy and business culture. Whenever possible less costly alternative titles are mentioned, and there are suggestions for items that could be purchased every two, three, or even five years. Each entry is listed alphabetically by title in the core list and includes title, author, place of publication, publisher, date, cost, publisher URL if available, authority and scope, and short evaluation of the resource's strengths and weaknesses. This list is essential as a checklist for business reference tools.

A new, important chapter, "Marketing the Business Library," has been added to part 2, "Business Reference Sources and Services: Essays." The chapter "Continuing Training of the Business Information Professional in the 1990s" was dropped. A bibliographic essay on business libraries replaces the chapter on "Literature of Business Reference and Business Libraries." The other essays were totally revised by expert practitioners. Most have new authors, and the online databases chapter was reviewed by three consultants. Prices for online resources are not included because many factors influence them.

In its fourth edition, this book will once again be used as a guide to best practices for small libraries seeking assistance in business reference. Lorna Daniells' *Business Information Sources* (Univ. of California, 1993), long a standard in business reference, is now very out of date. *The Basic Business*

Library should be used in conjunction with Michael R. Lavin's third edition of *Business Information: How to Find It, How to Use It* (Oryx, 2001) to complete the business resources picture.

Consumer Health Information Source Book. 7th ed. Ed. by Alan M. Rees. 2003. 325p. indexes. Greenwood, paper, $65 (1-57356-509-1). 016.613.

Ever since the first edition of the *Consumer Health Information Source Book* appeared in 1981, librarians have relied on it for collection development and referral information. In its seventh edition, this classic source has kept pace with changes in both the health-care and the information-delivery systems.

Although the format has not changed, the focus is narrower and more selective. This smaller volume is still a guide to the "myriad of popular American health information resources, both print and electronic, available to the general public." But for this edition, editor Rees has selected rather than compiled, including only sources with positive value. The book contains more than 2,000 descriptive evaluations of 385 books, 165 popular health magazines and newsletters, 1,500 English-language pamphlets, 850 Spanish-language pamphlets, 215 toll-free information hotlines, 325 health resource and referral organizations, 31 online and fax-based information services and CD-ROMs, and 40 medical textbooks, monographs, and journals.

An introductory chapter examines recent trends in medical consumerism and the resulting need for accurate information that lay readers can understand. Chapter 2 lists 151 outstanding sources, giving them from one to three stars. These sources are discussed in subsequent chapters. The amount of information provided in these chapters varies. For example, entries for clearinghouses and information centers include the name, address, telephone number, and URL if available as well as a brief annotation about the services and publications that they offer; associations have only a name and address. The best magazines and newsletters, Web sites, and books are indicated by asterisks. The chapter on professional literature is especially useful for collection development because it offers a core list of basic sources and recommended texts and journals in the medical specialties.

A chapter on the library's role as a provider of consumer health information is a new feature in this edition. It includes profiles of 12 outstanding consumer health libraries associated with hospitals, health-care agencies, or public libraries. The *Consumer Health Information Source Book* remains a key resource for all libraries that provide health information to the general public.

Crime Fiction IV: A Comprehensive Bibliography, 1749–2000. By Allen J. Hubin. 5v. 2003. Battered Silicon Dispatch Box, P.O. Box 122, Sauk City, WI 53583, $449 (1-55246-501-2). 016.823.

Hubin's *Crime Fiction, 1749–1980* was published in 1984 in a single volume, followed by a supplement in 1988. *Crime Fiction II*, which appeared in 1994, cumulated the earlier volumes and extended coverage through 1990. *Crime Fiction III*, issued in a CD-ROM version but not in print, continued coverage through 1995. In the fourth edition of what has become a benchmark reference work, Hubin expands and updates his exhaustive record of English-language mystery, detective, suspense, thriller, gothic, police, and spy fiction through 2000.

Hubin lists more than 109,000 book titles, up more than 10,000 from *Crime Fiction III*. Magazines, children's fiction, and anthologies are excluded. The author index now takes up three volumes. Headnotes provide birth and death dates and list series characters, settings, and general reference works in which the author is significantly cited. Titles are listed in alphabetical order following the headnotes. Information includes publisher and date of first U.S. and/or British editions. Other information found in the author entries can include type of material, such as short stories (when this is not obvious from the book title), play, or novelization. In the case of short story collections, individual stories are listed. Theatrical film adaptations are noted as well.

Volume 4 contains the title index. The series, settings, movies, screenwriter, and director index are found in volume 5. The settings index has been expanded to include 480 different settings. The series index now identifies more than 8,600 series/author pairs. The contents of story collections and the listing of film adaptations have been expanded as well.

Crime Fiction IV represents 30 years' labor, and Hubin has said that this edition will probably be the last. No library that is serious about crime fiction can afford to be without it.

Dictionary of Historic Documents. Rev. ed. Ed. by George Childs Kohn. 2003. 646p. bibliogs. indexes. Facts On File, $75 (0-8160-4772-3). 016.90908.

This revised edition of the *Dictionary of Historic Documents* continues in the same vein as the first, with brief descriptions of historical documents such as treaties, charters, laws, and some speeches and decrees as well as some important works of fiction and nonfiction. With some exceptions, the main focus is again on the last 300 years and on Western civilization. Kohn has expanded his work to nearly 2,400 entries (more than 100 of them new), each of which is roughly a paragraph in length. The intended audience is high-school students, undergraduates, and the general public. Well versed in the arena of reference works, Kohn has also given us such titles as the *Encyclopedia of Plague and Pestilence* (Facts On File, 1995) and the *Encyclopedia of American Scandal* (Facts On File, 1989).

Entries are arranged in alphabetical order by document name and include helpful cross-references. Along with an alphabetical index, there is also an index by category, a select bibliography, and a timetable of documents. There are several key differences between this and the previous edition. Most obviously, the entries have been updated and include more recent documents, such as the Maastricht Treaty and "Megan's Law." Also included are documents from previous eras that were not included last time, such as the Japanese Constitution of 1946. Another major difference is that there is a further reading section after each entry, which often suggests where one might find the document's text. This is in addition to the bibliography at the end of the book. The author has also made an effort to provide URLs to documents that are available online.

Since its previous incarnation, this book has improved on several levels, incorporating changes that we suggested in our 1991 review. The value is increased by identifying sources that contain the texts of individual documents. Recommended for high-school, undergraduate, and public libraries.

Film Noir Guide: 745 Films of the Classic Era, 1940–1959. By Michael F. Keaney. appendixes. bibliog. index. 2003. 541p. McFarland, $75 (0-7864-1547-9). 016.79143.

Over a six-week period at the end of World War II, French cinema audiences saw a flood of American films. All were crime movies, mostly involving murder. French critics applied the term *film noir* to these, and it stuck. Examples include *The Maltese Falcon* and *Murder, My Sweet*. Since then, of course, the academic definition of this term has been in much dispute, including, but not limited to, when the first and last film was produced. Keaney, a film noir fan, briefly addresses these controversies, but as a true fan he would rather leave the arguments to professors and collect and enjoy the movies even if they fall outside somebody's definition.

The result is this work, a filmography of more than 700 movies released from 1940 to 1959. Each entry includes a cast and crew list; film noir type (for example, "Blackmail," "Femme Fatale") and themes ("greed, lust, guilt, fatalism"); a one- to five-star rating; and a synopsis and brief examination written in an easy, familiar style that serves to inform and entertain. Keaney is not a blind fan, as he does recognize the faults and problems with the films he includes. The features he appends to most entries add interest. One feature highlights "Memorable Noir Moment(s)." For example, for *The Maltese Falcon* (1941) he notes: "Psychotic gunman [Elisha] Cook, fed up with Bogey's [Humphrey Bogart] lack of respect, warns him, 'Keep on ridin' me, they're gonna be picking lead out of your liver.'" He also identifies "Familiar Faces from Television," cluing viewers into early appearances of *Star Trek*'s Dr. McCoy or *F Troop*'s Sgt. O'Rourke. The work is completed by lists of films by director, type, and year of release; a collector's guide; and a very useful annotated bibliography.

As a popular film reference resource, this is a worthy addition to public libraries, and even specialized or research libraries might be interested in it for the filmography alone.

Korean War Filmography. By Robert J. Lentz. 2003. 486p. appendixes. bibliog. illus. index. McFarland, $45 (0-7864-1046-9). 016.79143.

Author and movie fan Lentz states that "one of the many ways to gauge the social impact of the Korean War is to examine Hollywood's various depictions of the conflict." The 91 English-language films he covers in this volume had to meet at least one of two criteria: at least some of the film's story and action must be set in Korea during the war, and the war must be important enough to the film's story that it affects character action. Lentz admits that most of the movies examined are from Hollywood and therefore are primarily from an American frame of reference. Examples include *The Bridges at Toko-Ri, Love Is a Many-Splendored Thing, The Manchurian Candidate,* and *M*A*S*H.*

The entries first list film credits and cast. Then the author provides ratings for historical accuracy and the level of patriotic propaganda included (Low, Medium, High). Additional "elements" highlighted in the film are also listed with each entry—aircraft carriers, bridge bombings, romance, or politics, for example. Each plot is discussed in great detail, with occasional quotations from movie critics. Black-and-white photographs and movie posters illustrate the text.

The filmography includes seven appendixes: a chronology of films in order of their theatrical release; a listing by production company and distributor; a listing (according to the author's judgment) by levels of accuracy and propaganda; a listing by subject and theme; additional films with only incidental Korean War references; documentary and compilation films; and South Korean films about the Korean War. These appendixes are most useful and add to the book's utility.

Finally, Lentz provides a film-by-film bibliography, including reviews in newspapers and magazines. The *Korean War Filmography* will make a useful addition to academic or special library collections supporting film studies and will appeal to serious movie fans.

Latina and Latino Voices in Literature: Lives and Works. Rev. ed. By Frances Ann Day. 2003. 353p. appendixes. bibliogs. illus. indexes. Greenwood, $55 (0-313-32394-1). 016.8109.

Thirty-five Latina and Latino authors of books for children and young adults are profiled in this work, 12 more than in the first edition. Entrants range from authors and illustrators of bilingual picture books to novelists such as Denise Chávez and Isabel Allende. In addition to updated biographical material, more than 135 additional titles are discussed. An introductory section entitled "Evaluating Books for Bias" has been adapted from criteria published by the Council on Interracial Books for Children. This information is useful for teachers and librarians to have when evaluating children's books dealing with other cultures.

Entries are arranged alphabetically by author and begin with a photograph, essential biographical data, and a contact address. There are also quotations that summarize the person's philosophy of writing. Following this introductory information are lists of works, a biographical profile, and a list of resources for additional information. Selected works are then discussed in entries that range in length from a few lines to two pages. Also provided for each title are grade levels, subject headings, and a list of awards.

Four appendixes contain a list of awards for Latino children's books; a calendar of important holidays and resources for how to celebrate them; a list of cultural organizations and other resources with both Web sites and mailing addresses; and a lengthy section of activities to be used in the classroom to "extend the literary experience" of the various authors' books. There are two indexes, one by title and one by topic.

As communities experience an influx of the Latino population, this resource can be useful in assisting libraries and schools to develop their services and collections. It is an essential reference tool for any library interested in serving this fast-growing population.

United States History: A Multicultural, Interdisciplinary Guide to Information Sources. 2d ed. By Anna H. Perrault and Ron Blazek. 2003. 661p. indexes. Libraries Unlimited, $70 (1-56308-874-6). 016.973.

With the assistance of graduate students in library schools at the University of South Florida and at Florida State University, Perrault and Blazek have updated and expanded their 1994 bibliographic tool.

The 1,250 selected sources (printed reference tools, online databases, Web sites, CD-ROMs, and microforms) include old standards but emphasis is on recent (1980s–2002) publications that focus on the social science aspects of U.S. history. Choices were based on favorable reviews in *Reference Books Bulletin, American Reference Books Annual, Choice, Library Journal,* and *Reference Services Review* and on firsthand knowledge. The Web sites that are listed are current as of November 7, 2002.

The introduction offers users an overview of trends in historical research and reference-source publishing, including electronic sources and networked materials. Part 1 covers general sources (biographical, chronological, statistical, geographical, and demographic). Part 2 is arranged by broad topics and a diverse array of subtopics. For example, chapter 6, "Social, Cultural, and Intellectual History," includes sections on Jewish genealogy, women's suffrage, Korean Americans, higher education, capital punishment, radio and television, and baseball, among others. Each chapter and many of the sections begin with an overview noting relevant organizations and their publications and directions in research. Besides bibliographic information, the annotated entries offer descriptions and often suggest search strategies. Annotations are 85 to 250 words in length. An author-title index and a subject index are provided.

The guide will be helpful for collection development as well as for research and is recommended for academic and large public libraries. The authors recommend retaining the first edition for use in conjunction with the second "to assure comprehensive coverage."

Biology Resources in the Electronic Age. By Judith A. Bazler. 2003. 286p. glossary. index. Greenwood, $49.95 (1-57356-380-3). 025.06.

Chemistry Resources in the Electronic Age. By Judith A. Bazler. 2003. 291p. glossary. index. Greenwood, $49.95 (1-57356-379-X). 025.06.

Here are two useful resources with identical formats and the same purpose: to provide a gateway to authoritative Web sites suitable for use in teaching and learning. The first chapter in each, "The Basics," contains short descriptions of a variety of electronic resources and formats, terms, and some information on searching and on copyright. The bulk of each volume is a bibliography of Web resources grouped by topic within the discipline. Each record includes title, URL, grade level (ranging from elementary to postgraduate), a suggested search engine for hunting similar information, suggested keyword(s), and a detailed annotation. Among the 37 topic categories in the biology volume are "Animal Behavior," "Diffusion," "Heredity," and "Viruses." The chemistry volume has 45 categories, including "Chemical Reactions," "Equilibrium," "Lab Techniques," and "Periodic Table."

These are very useful references for building discipline-, course-, or assignment-specific Web pages. Had the author left out the rather unnecessary suggested search-engine lines from entries, there would have been room for a number of additional sites. The chapters about biology and chemistry suppliers' Web addresses and catalogs are handy directories. Each volume has a brief chapter with a collection of career-related links to associations, universities, and similar resources; the biology volume also offers 14 entries for museums and science centers. The detailed indexes are the best entry point for finding sites for topics that may be in several categories.

These books will be useful for the public, but librarians can also use them to build excellent reference Web pages. They should be especially helpful in libraries serving students from the junior- high-school through lower-division undergraduate levels.

★**The Medical Library Association Encyclopedic Guide to Searching and Finding Health Information on the Web.** 3v. Ed. by P. F. Anderson and Nancy J. Allee. 2004. bibliogs. index. Neal-Schuman, paper, $395 (1-55570-494-8). 025.06.

The amount of information available on the Web is overwhelming. Finding what one needs and making sure that it is accurate and reliable can be a daunting task; searching for health and medical information may literally be a matter of life or death. This guide, written and edited by a group of experienced medical librarians, provides a framework for obtaining the best results from an online search. It will be useful for both consumers and librarians, and it is an outstanding resource for training.

The three volumes cover search techniques as well as information about research on specific subject areas. Volume 1 covers basic elements in a search, among them understanding the question that is being asked, choosing concepts and search terms, and selecting a search engine. The reader will also find a complete step-by-step search procedure, information about the limitation of search engines, a list of more than 2,000 commonly used health and medical terms, forms that can be used for organizing searches, and criteria for evaluating Web sites. Volume 2 deals with specific illnesses, diseases, and conditions, both physical and mental. In addition to an overview and a list of relevant Web sites, each section includes recommended search terms, questions to ask, starting points, additional strategies, and a "Topic Profile"—the who, what, where, and when of each disease and disorder. Volume 3 covers broader topics dealing with health and wellness, life stages, and reproduction, among them diet and nutrition; safety issues, such as bioterrorism and traffic accidents; alternative and complementary therapies; multicultural health; lesbian/gay/bisexual/transgender health issues; chronic illness; disability; and pain.

The Medical Library Association Encyclopedic Guide to Searching and Finding Health Information on the Web lives up to its title. Covering a wide range of health and medical topics, it will help both librarians and consumers search with confidence. The price may be a problem in this era of shrinking budgets, but medical, consumer health, and large public libraries should give it serious consideration. It is essential for libraries involved in teaching information literacy. A CD-ROM that may be purchased separately for $395 or with the print volumes for $495 has an HTML version of the text along with live links to almost 11,000 Web sites.

Grolier Student Encyclopedia. 17v. 2004. 1,088p. illus. index. maps. Grolier, $249 (0-7172-5865-3). 031.

This set, a general encyclopedia with more than 700 entries arranged alphabetically, is intended to introduce children to reference skills as well as to help them develop proficiencies in research and writing. The volumes are 64 pages in length and were designed with young students in mind. For example, the U.S. entry includes volume and page numbers for all of the entries on individual states. The layout is simple and straightforward and includes large print that would be appealing to upper-elementary students. Most of the entries range in length from one to two pages. The writing is clear and should be accessible to students in grades three and above. The intended audience is grades three through six.

Each begins with a brief introduction and concludes with a list of *see also* references to other related topics in the set. Two additional cross-referencing devices are used: *see* references (*Scorpion see Arachnid*) and "Look in the Index for" references that point the student to information contained within entries. For example, there is no entry for Charles Darwin, but a "Look in the Index for" reference in the spot where a Darwin entry would be instructs the user to look up Darwin in the index. Some of these references are awkwardly placed, so they may not be clear to the encyclopedia's intended audience. Each volume concludes with a comprehensive index.

Entries are enhanced with color photographs, illustrations, diagrams, time lines, and maps. The picture captions supplement the text nicely. Special boxes cover specific subjects in extra detail. The types of boxed information include "Key Facts," "Did you know?" "Amazing Facts," and "Biography," the last of which introduces certain important personalities. The "Key Facts" boxes provide facts and figures about U.S. states, U.S. presidents, Canadian provinces, countries, and planets. "Did you know?" boxes offer detailed information about a broad variety of topics, and "Amazing Facts" boxes highlight fun or interesting facts about the natural world and modern technology. The text also includes a special set of articles intended to help students with their reports. These include *Book report, Debating, Grammar, Note taking, Punctuation, Research,* and *Revision*.

This set provides a solid introduction to general topics for students in the primary grades, though it will not provide enough information to meet the research needs of older students. Nevertheless, it would be a useful addition to public and school libraries.

The Oxford Dictionary of Modern Quotations. 2d ed. Ed. by Elizabeth Knowles. 2003. 483p. index. Oxford, $35 (0-19-866275-0). 082.
The Oxford Dictionary of Phrase, Saying, and Quotation. 2d ed. Ed. by Susan Ratcliffe. 2003. 696p. index. Oxford, $45 (0-19-866269-6). 082.

New editions of reliable reference books inevitably invite comparisons with earlier versions, and that is certainly the case here. Although both titles have kept their original format, they have also added new material, deleted less popular passages, and expanded their indexing. In the second edition of *The Oxford Dictionary of Modern Quotations, modern* now refers to the twentieth and twenty-first centuries and "authors who were alive in or after 1914," while the first edition concentrates on the twentieth century and quotations from those "still alive after 1900." While retaining most of the quotations found in the earlier edition, this one adds a number of new selections, such as quotations referring to the terrorist attacks of 9/11. Once again, the quotations are listed chronologically under each of the alphabetically arranged authors' names. Several special features are included: 14 "special categories," including "Advertising Slogans" (found under "Anonymous" in the first edition), "Misquotations," "Opening Lines" and "Taglines for Films," which present these quotations alphabetically by the first word of each passage; an expanded keyword index; and a "Selective Thematic Index," which points the way to quotations on such motifs as "America," "Britain," "Computing," and "Royalty."

The second edition of *The Oxford Dictionary of Phrase, Saying, and Quotation* has been similarly updated. Themes such as "Computers and the Internet," "Management," and "Photography" have been added to the list of topics that opens the book. As in the earlier edition, the material is arranged by subject and then further categorized as "Proverbs and Sayings," "Phrases," and "Quotations." Although this edition retains the format of its predecessor, there has been an effort to strengthen "the links between individual remarks and fixed phrases and sayings," which are the hallmark of this particular work. Modern sayings related to the topic at hand as well as earlier (sometimes the *earliest*) forms of an adage have been added to many sections. The keyword index has been expanded and now forms almost one-fourth of the entire book.

Although there is some overlap between editions and even between these two titles, large or comprehensive collections will want to add both new editions as well as keep the earlier ones. A collection can never have too many quotation sources.

Philosophy, Psychology, Religion

The Gale Encyclopedia of the Unusual and Unexplained. 3v. By Brad Steiger and Sherry Hansen Steiger. 2003. bibliogs. glossaries. illus. index. Gale, $175 (0-7876-5382-9). 130.

In 14 chapters, these volumes cover broad concepts from "Afterlife Mysteries" to "Invaders from Outer Space." Each chapter begins with an overview and an outline of the topics and subtopics that are covered. Within the chapters, entries are generally arranged in alphabetical order. Each ends with a further reading list called "Delving Deeper." Glossaries are appended to each chapter and cumulated in volume 3. Occasional cross-references appear in bold type within the text to refer the reader to other entries, but since the set does not have a strict *A–Z* arrangement, one must use the index to determine where those entries are located. Because of the set's topical arrangement, the index is essential.

The Steigers, prolific writers on the paranormal, have written an encyclopedia for believers. The volumes are meant to "explore and describe the research of those who take such phenomena seriously." Almost everything from mediumship to crop circles is taken at face value. Even Houdini's attacks on phony mediums are interpreted to suggest he was taking on frauds and not real mediums. *Fraud* does not appear in the index, nor are alternate suggestions of how phenomena could have occurred presented. Only in a few instances is some skepticism applied.

The work covers material of interest to a large segment of the public in a way that is clear and readable. Many works in the "Delving Deeper" sections will provide the beginning student of the paranormal with good starting points. Recommended for medium- size to large public libraries and for academic libraries with comparative religion, folklore, and popular culture collections.

The New Encyclopedia of the Occult. By John Michael Greer. 2003. 555p. bibliog. illus. Llewellyn, paper, $29.95 (1-56718-336-0). 133.

In his introduction, Greer states that his book is the first written by an "occult practitioner" who has consulted the scholarly texts that have recently been written about the history of occult traditions. This combination has produced a reference work that is sympathetic to the arcane lore but avoids many of the common errors found in occult literature. The volume arranges its 1,500 entries in alphabetical order. Topics include magic, Tarot, astrology, and other forms of divination; magical orders such as the Golden Dawn; biographies of significant individuals; and spiritual movements such as Wicca, Theosophy, and the modern Pagans. Where appropriate, entries contain *see* references to other entries and to books found in the extensive bibliography. Illustrations include charts, diagrams, and photographs.

The essays are clearly written and are very informative. The book is useful for the practitioner as well as for the curious because the contents are factual and concise. The author promises that as new information becomes available on topics, he will publish a revised edition to maintain the integrity and accuracy of the volume. This is an important source for libraries to have in their collections to assist anyone seeking information about the many aspects of occult traditions.

★Encyclopedia of Bioethics. 5v. 3d ed. Ed. by Stephen G. Post. 2003. 3,062p. appendixes. bibliogs. index. Macmillan, $595 (0-02- 865774-8). 174.

When the first edition of the *Encyclopedia of Bioethics* appeared in 1978, the discipline was new and relatively undefined. The second edition, in 1995, kept pace with the rapid changes in the field. Continuing advances in biological and medical research have created the need for yet another edition. Bioethics has become a recognized field, "the interdisciplinary examination of the moral and ethical dimensions of human conduct in the areas of life sciences and health care." With such a broad, rapidly changing subject area to cover, editor Post (Department of Bioethics, School of Medicine, Case Western Reserve University) has assembled an international group of more than 500 scholars from 18 major disciplines— behavioral sciences, medicine, economics, ecology, philosophy, religion, and so on— to write 448 articles.

The third edition has 120 new articles, among them *Artificial nutrition and hydration, Bioterrorism, Cloning, Cybernetics, Dementia, Managed care,* and *Nanotechnology*. Some 200 articles have been extensively revised, and 100 additional articles have new bibliographies. The alphabetical entries address a wide range of topics that raise difficult and important questions. Abortion, genetic screening, female genital mutilation, the right to die, health issues of immigration, and corporate responsibility are but a few. The contributors discuss the issues from many points of view. The abortion article includes sections covering medical perspectives, contemporary ethical and legal aspects, and Jewish, Catholic, Protestant, and Islamic religious perspectives. There are also articles about bioethics in Buddhism, eugenics, health policy, women as healthcare professionals, whistle-blowing in health care, and veterinary ethics. All of the articles are signed, and all have bibliographies. Ample cross-references help readers find related useful material. A list of all the articles and a topical outline appear in volume 1. A series of appendixes offers codes, oaths, and directives related to bioethics; additional resources; key legal cases; and an annotated bibliography of literary works that have a medical component. A detailed index helps users find material that may be scattered over numerous entries, such as information about surrogate motherhood.

This new edition of a classic work, which addresses timely issues such as same-sex marriages and direct advertising of prescription drugs, belongs in all academic libraries and all but the smallest public libraries. It is an outstanding resource for students, professionals, and the interested public.

RoutledgeCurzon Encyclopedia of Confucianism. 2v. Ed. by Xinzhong Yao. 2003. 932p. bibliogs. indexes. Routledge, $150 (0-700-71199-6). 181.

Confucianism is a difficult concept to define. The *RoutledgeCurzon Encyclopedia of Confucianism* offers welcome assistance in making this tradition accessible to a Western audience.

The set begins with an introductory essay by the editor describing Confucianism as a tradition as well as a subject of study. A team of international scholars is responsible for the more than 950 alphabetically arranged entries, which have been signed, are nicely cross-referenced, and often conclude with bibliographic references. They include important individuals, ranging from Confucius himself to Liang Shuming, a twentieth-century Chinese intellectual who combined Confucian and Chinese Buddhist ideas into a unique philosophy of culture. Biographical information is also provided for some Christian missionaries (e.g., Matteo Ricci) and Western scholars (e.g., William Theodore de Bary) important to the introduction of Confucianism to the West and its understanding there. Other entries include important texts, doctrines, schools, sacred places, and rituals. Although many of these can be quite specific or narrow, there are some more general surveys on Confucianism and the arts, education, government, literature, music, and religion; Confucianism and the religious traditions of Buddhism, Christianity, Islam, and Shinto; and Confucianism during particular periods in Chinese history as well as Confucianism in Japan, Korea, Vietnam, Southeast Asia, and the West. The set concludes with separate indexes for names, subjects, and texts. Use of the indexes will be necessary for many readers as texts and subjects are listed under their transliterated form (e.g., *Lunyu* instead of Analects of Confucius; *Tian* instead of heaven).

Sources such as the *Encyclopedia of Religion* (Macmillan, 1987) and the *Encyclopedia of Asian Philosophy* (Routledge, 2001) treat Confucianism more generally. But the *RoutledgeCurzon Encyclopedia of Confucianism* is a first step toward filling the void of specialized English-language reference tools for many such traditions. Those interested in varied aspects of Asian studies will find it useful. Recommended for academic and large public libraries.

African-American Religious Leaders. By Nathan Aaseng. 2003. 264p. bibliogs. illus. index. Facts On File, $44 (0-8160-4878-9). 200.

Facts On File books are generally well researched, well written, and useful for libraries. This new volume in the A to Z of African Americans series is in the same tradition. More than 150 religious leaders are profiled here. Entries are alphabetical (*Abernathy, Ralph* to *Youngblood, Johnny Ray*) and describe each person's early life, family, and involvement in religious and social issues. Most are about one page long and include recent reference books (often Gale titles), periodical articles, and Web sites for further reading. Attractive black-and-white photos illustrate about one-third of the articles.

Included are the names you'd expect—Jesse Jackson, Martin Luther King Jr., Elijah Muhammad, Adam Clayton Powell Jr. and Sr.—along with important but lesser-known individuals such as Calvin Butts, Barbara Harris, Ben Chavis, and Lucy Smith. Others not usually thought of as religious leaders, among them George Foreman, Mahalia Jackson, Hiram Revels, and Sojourner Truth, are also profiled.

Several indexes make it possible to locate individuals by religious affiliation (including nondenominational *Cornel West*) and year of birth (1737 to 1962) as well as subject *(Civil War, Million Man March, Morehouse College)*. Articles objectively describe even unpleasant events and situations. Some inevitable repetition between articles exists (for example, the 1787 remodeling of St. George's Episcopal Church in Philadelphia to provide separate seating for blacks is described in the entries on both Richard Allen and Absalom Jones), and of course many of the individuals may be found in other similar titles.

Since religious leaders are not commonly studied, this is probably not an essential purchase. It will be useful for high-school collections where brief biographies are well used as well as for public and undergraduate libraries.

Religion and American Cultures: An Encyclopedia of Traditions, Diversity, and Popular Expressions. 3v. Ed. by Gary Laderman and Luis Leon. 2003. 1,046p. bibliogs. illus. index. ABC-CLIO, $285 (1-57607-238-X). 200.

According to the foreword of this set, there is a movement in scholarship, begun in the 1970s with the works of Clifford Geertz, that advocates viewing religion as a cultural concept. Overall, the foreword continues, it has proven easier to view religions in distant places from this perspective, rather than the local American varieties. The intent of this encyclopedia seems to be to support this anthropological view of religions and to provide reference material on American religions as "forms of cultural expression."

Each of the three volumes has very different content, though all relate to the central focus. Volume 1 contains 13 long chapters on major divisions within American religion, whether defined by ethnic tradition ("African American Religions," "Asian American Religious Communities") or by belief system ("Catholicism in America," "Islam in America), with several distinct sections within each chapter. Each section, the work of an individual contributor, ends with *see also* references and a bibliography. While what has been chosen for inclusion seems appropriate and instructional, it is necessary to consider what has been left out. For example, "Protestantism in America" is merely 20 pages long and does little to define the differences, cultural or otherwise, separating the denominations. There is not even a word in this chapter on either the Amish or the Mennonites, each surely worthy of mention in any discussion of religion and culture.

The second volume covers concepts, again grouped into 13 chapters with several sections in each. Among chapter headings are "Death," "Popular Culture," "Ritual and Performance," and "Sexuality." While all are interesting, again one must wonder about what has been left out. The chapter "Sacred Space" has sections on cyberspace, Las Vegas, nature, shopping malls, shrines (including Niagara Falls and Graceland), and the suburban home, but a sociological and anthropological definition of *sacred* opens up many other possibilities.

Volume 3 contains primary documents. Many of these are essential to such a collection, like the Maryland Toleration Act and Thoreau's "A Plea for Captain John Brown." With others, such as Eisenhower's "Military-Industrial Complex Speech," the rationale is unclear.

While this reference set has little competition from what currently exists, and though there is certainly a need and interest in the topic, this particular work does not provide the overall, balanced, cross-cultural information on American religion and culture that one would hope for. If academic and large public library budgets are sufficient, this could do until something better comes along.

The Encyclopedia of Angels. 2d ed. By Rosemary Ellen Guiley. 2004. 398p. bibliogs. illus. index. Facts On File, $75 (0-8160-5023-6); Checkmark, paper, $24.95 (0-8160-5024-4). 202.

Like its first edition (1996), this encyclopedia is devoted to angels and "angelology"—drawn from the Judeo-Christian tradition as well as other religions and belief systems. More than 600 new entries expand the coverage of individual angels and also add details from apocryphal, mystical, and esoteric texts. Numerous entries have been revised. Each of the entries, arranged alphabetically from *Abaddon* to *Zuriel*, concludes with a short list of suggested readings. A bibliography concludes the volume. Illustrations, photographs, and numerous cross-references support the text.

The encyclopedia traces the development of the concept of angels in Western thought and also explores the roles of angels in modern life. Content is not limited to named angels but also includes things *(Amulets, Alphabets)*; special terms or categories; and historic figures. The inclusion of entries on figures such as Charles Lindbergh and Pope Pius XI to try to describe the role of angels in various individuals' lives is interesting but not necessarily convincing. Some errors from the first edition (for example, "Church of Christ of Latter-day Saints" instead of Church of Jesus Christ of Latter-day Saints) persist.

Although this volume will enable ready-reference questions on different angel names or angel orders or ministering angels, it also is a very readable book that could be part of the circulating as well as the reference collections of public libraries.

Men and Women of the Bible: A Reader's Guide. By Nancy M. Tischler. 2003. 267p. bibliogs. illus. index. Greenwood, $59.95 (0-313-31714-3). 220.9.

Here is a helpful resource for students and general readers seeking information on 100 biblical characters and their cultural significance in Western civilization. The guide covers the entire span of biblical history, from the creation of Adam to the apocalyptic visions of the end times. Entries are arranged alphabetically from *Aaron* to *Zephaniah*, concisely written, and adhere to a uniform pattern. Subjects are listed by name with the addition of etymological information. A synopsis of the relevant biblical story follows, utilizing the King James version of the Bible. The author indicates that she chose this translation because of its impact on English and American literature.

Considerable text is given to explicating the historical context and archaeological evidence surrounding each biblical personage. The author also includes information on each person as a character in later works, including Western literature, legend, and painting. The entry *Stephen* mentions a medieval tale of a corpse moving aside to provide space for the body of Stephen as it was being reburied in Rome. Completing each entry is a thorough list of journals, commentaries, and resource books used in crafting the text. Tischler, professor emerita at Pennsylvania State University, wonderfully combines her love of literature and the biblical story into an accessible and authoritative resource that is recommended for public and academic libraries.

Jesus in History, Thought, and Culture: An Encyclopedia. 2v. Ed. by Leslie Houlden. 2003. 984p. bibliogs. glossary. illus. index. ABC-CLIO, $185 (1-57607-856-6). 232.

Jesus in History, Thought, and Culture aims to collect and organize a myriad of scholarly commentaries on the life and influence of Jesus of Nazareth. Houlden, professor emeritus at Kings College London, utilizes the expertise of some 100 leading authorities across the globe to clearly articulate the unique position of Jesus Christ in world civilization. These scholars each add their singular interpretations based on academic background, religious affiliation, gender, and nationality to create this encyclopedic mosaic of Jesus. Although heavily influenced by British academics, the text has an international flavor.

The alphabetical arrangement of this set is easily browsed thanks to numerous *see also* references to parallel or derivative themes. Each of the 200 precisely written and signed articles range in length from two pages *(Crossan, J. D.; Didache; Manichaeism; Masculinity; Paranormal)* to forty pages *(Art,* on Jesus' depiction in art through the ages). A sampling of other articles includes *Adoptianism; Baptism; Chinese Christianity; Gnosticism; Hinduism; Jesus, parables of; Second Coming of Jesus;* and *Wealth.* A bibliography is provided for each entry suggesting additional reading for study or reflection. In its entirety, almost every aspect of the historical Jesus, subsequent theologizing, and cultural interpretation is given a fair and balanced treatment. Reference aids include both a convenient alphabetical and topical list of entries and a concluding glossary of technical terms and comprehensive 80-page general index. Black-and-white illustrations make this encyclopedia aesthetically pleasing. Recommended for academic libraries and large public libraries as well as for appropriate smaller collections.

Biographical Dictionary of Evangelicals. Ed. by Timothy Larsen and others. 2003. 789p. bibliogs. indexes. InterVarsity, $45 (0-8308-2925-3). 270.8.

Here is a welcomed and essential title for understanding the impact that particular evangelical Christians have had. This alphabetically arranged reference work selects 400 men and women who have significantly influenced the theology, pastoral practice, and piety of evangelicals in the English-speaking world. Although 1730 is accepted as the beginning of the evangelical movement by most scholars, the dictionary includes some earlier luminaries such as John Calvin, Jan Hus, Martin Luther, and John Wyclif. It must be noted that editor Larsen, associate professor of theology at Wheaton College, also selected 1935 as the cutoff date for inclusion in the dictionary. Contemporary evangelicals born after this date are not chronicled. The impressive list of contributors numbers about 200, hailing from countries across the globe and consisting of prominent scholars, preachers, and authors.

Each succinctly written article gives sufficient detail, making this much more than a simple who's who. Such evangelists as Oliver Cromwell, Frances Crosby, Billy Graham, Dwight Moody, and William Tyndale are subjects of well-developed essays that are both factual and critical. Most are several pages in length. Entries are signed and conclude with bibliographies encouraging the reader to pursue additional biographical or autobiographical sources. The dictionary has three indexes—names, subjects, and articles.

Comprehensive, balanced, and fairly priced, this title is recommended for academic and public libraries with strong theology collections.

The Encyclopedia of Protestantism. 4v. Ed. by Hans J. Hillerbrand. 2003. 2,195p. appendix. bibliogs. index. Routledge, $595 (0-415-92472-3). 280.

Scholars from all over the world have contributed to these volumes filled with more than 1,000 lengthy signed articles, each with a bibliography. Editor Hillerbrand, from Duke University's Religion Department, proposes a definition of *Protestantism* as "whatever is not Catholic (or Orthodox)." This broad scope fairly well encompasses all manifestations of Christianity not otherwise categorized.

The encyclopedia offers a large number of biographical articles. Also here are entries on cultural and social issues, countries, institutions, movements, and theology as well as the expected coverage of denominations and "isms." According to the editor, there is something of a historical bias in the selection of topics and the way they are treated. This allows readers to see how the development of the various denominations and movements is tied closely to the social and political events surrounding their inception. Articles such as *Abortion, Capital punishment,* and *Homosexuality,* which present a balanced view of controversial areas, also have a historical dimension. These topics and others such as *Civil rights movement* and *Homeschooling* are enhanced by history's eye on what we might consider more exclusively "modern" concerns.

The first volume has a list of all the alphabetical entries as well as a thematic list of entries that broadly groups the topics. The fourth volume has an index, which includes the article titles as well as subsidiary topics. A list of contributors with their affiliations and the articles they wrote precedes the index, and an extremely useful and informative appendix containing statistical tables (which supplement a very nice article on statistics within the body) completes this work.

Overall, this is a very handsome set, well conceived and substantial looking. Its high price may make it a difficult choice, but it should have a place in any academic or large public collection. There are other encyclopedias that cover the subject of religion, but until now there has been nothing in English that can be said to concern itself exclusively with Protestantism.

Encyclopedia of Religion and War. Ed. by Gabriel Palmer-Fernandez. 2003. 530p. bibliogs. illus. index. Routledge, $125 (0-415-94246-2). 291.1.

Another in the series of Routledge Encyclopedias of Religion and Society, this work has a "narrow focus" because "it looks to one part of religion, not to the whole." Its intended audience is students at the undergraduate and high-school levels, professionals, and general readers. Content is meticulously organized so that the researcher may find the entries easily and may also find further information if desired. The more than 130 entries are arranged alphabetically and contain *see also* references and lists of further reading suggestions. Many of the entries have sidebars containing primary source material, either excerpted or whole. For example, the entry *World Council of Churches* includes the WCC's statement on the 2003 Iraq War.

According to the introduction, the volume does not examine religious teachings on love, compassion, or benevolent service to others. Instead, it provides "authoritative historical and cross-cultural information that will help readers understand war and other forms of political violence in the major religions of the world." The encyclopedia includes many of the world's religions but is not exhaustive. Among the Western religions covered are Judaism, Christianity, and Islam. Eastern religions covered include Buddhism, Hinduism, Confucianism, and Daoism. Lesser-known systems such as *Manichaeism* and *Zoroastrianism* are defined, and their connection to war is examined. Other entries discuss regional religious conflict (*Afghanistan, Hindu-Muslim violence in India, Northern Ireland*); religious movements (*Millennialism, Wahhabism*); and religious wars (*Crusades, Thirty Years' War*). Related topics such as *Jihad, Ku Klux Klan, Liberation theology*, and *Martyrdom* are also explored.

Scholars and researchers interested in the connection between religion and war will find this encyclopedia useful. The complexity of the information recommends this resource for academic and large public libraries.

Encyclopedia of Science and Religion. 2v. Ed. by J. Wentzel Vrede van Huyssteen. 2003. 1,050p. bibliogs. index. Macmillan, $265 (0-02-865704-7). 291.1.

This encyclopedia, intended for "a wide readership from high-school students to independent researchers and academics," deals with all aspects of the conflict and dialogue between science and religion. The list of scholars who have contributed is impressive, and the project had as a consultant and contributor Ian Barbour, physicist, theologian, and well-known author on the interplay of science and religion. The editorial point of view is that the formal consideration of the relationship between science and religion has become a new academic field of study. The troublesome potential of new technologies has brought questions into the public arena as well.

The 400-plus alphabetically arranged entries range from broad essays on topics such as *Biotechnology, Causation,* and *Sociobiology* to shorter pieces on terms such as *Cybernetics, Eco-feminism,* and *Entropy*. There are also 20 biographies of important figures in the dialogue between science and religion, from Aristotle to Stephen Jay Gould. The fore matter includes an alphabetical list of all articles as well as a synoptic outline, which enables one to see all of the articles related to, for example, physical sciences or Chinese religions. The historical and contemporary relationships between the realm of science and the major religious groups—Judaism, Islam, Christian traditions, Chinese religions, Buddhism, and Hinduism—are treated individually. Major scientific and academic fields are examined in the context of the encyclopedia's focus. Close to 70 articles on the physical sciences, for example, include entries on all the major arenas of the field: chemistry, particle physics, quantum physics, etc., each providing an overview of early research, contemporary developments and lessons, or applications to religious thought. All of the articles are signed and have bibliographies, some extensive. In addition, a nine-page annotated bibliography serves as a guide for further reading (and collection development) in various topics such as the human sciences and religion. A detailed index makes the wealth of material even more accessible.

The History of Science and Religion in the Western Tradition: An Encyclopedia (Garland, 2000) covers much of the same ground. Both are reference works of very high quality with scholarly contributors, several of them in common. But the approach of the earlier work is to treat fewer topics in broader essays. Some of the treatments are more substantial in the Garland work: medicine is covered in seven pages as opposed to two and a half. The Macmillan work does have a more global scope, including non-Western religions or belief systems. The references and bibliography of the set under review are much more up-to-date.

The comprehensive, global treatment of the historical and contemporary tensions and interplay between our sacred and secular knowledge make this an excellent addition to academic and large public libraries.

The Facts On File Encyclopedia of World Mythology and Legend. 2v. 2d ed. By Anthony S. Mercatante and James R. Dow. 2004. 1,096p. bibliog. illus. indexes. Facts On File, $104.50 (0-8160-4708-1). 291.1.

Dow, a German professor and linguistics chair at Iowa State, has done a substantial revision of the first, 1988 edition, compiled by Mercatante, now deceased. Entries have been added, as have cross-references at the ends of most entries. Entries are in alphabetical order and numbered, and the general index and cultural and ethnic indexes refer to the entry numbers. There is an annotated, updated bibliography.

Most of the entries are related to Europe, but there is a substantial number of entries from Asia, Australasia, South and Southeast Asia, Africa, and the Americas. Each entry has a headword, variant spellings of the word, translation, definition, and cross-references. The writing is formal but clear. A pronunciation guide would have been useful. Illustrations are small black and white line drawings and reproductions of woodcuts.

Some omissions are curious—there is no article on Mordred, one of the central characters of the Arthurian mythos, although many other Arthurian characters, even Lancelot's sword, have entries. The entry on the Great Stone Face mentions that it is part of American folklore but not where the face was located in the Americas. There are also some errors. The entry on Aaron mentions his "flowing wand," which should probably be "flowering wand." The *Appomattox Apple Tree* entry mentions the "tree under which General Lee surrounded to General Grant."

Academic and larger public libraries with the first edition should consider replacing it with this edition. It is an optional purchase for most other folklore collections.

Greek and Roman Mythology A to Z. Rev. ed. By Kathleen N. Daly and Marian Rengel. 2003. 146p. bibliog. illus. index. Facts On File, $35 (0-8160-5155-0). 292.1.

Norse Mythology A to Z. Rev. ed. By Kathleen N. Daly and Marian Rengel. 2003. 126p. bibliog. illus. index. Facts On File, $35 (0-8160-5156-9). 293.

These well-received and accessible books for young adults have been updated. They are part of an expanded Mythology A to Z series that also includes volumes on Egyptian mythology (2000) and Japanese mythology (2003). Other volumes will cover African, Celtic, Chinese, Native American, and South and Meso-American mythologies.

The Greek and Roman volume has more than 500 alphabetically arranged entries, ranging in length from a paragraph to several pages. Of these, more than 60 are new, and many others have been expanded. The Norse volume is somewhat shorter, with closer to 400 entries, but includes almost 70 new topics. Each title features occasional black-and-white illustrations—some full page—a detailed index, and extensive cross-referencing. Each volume also offers a bibliography of mainly adult-level books published the past several decades.

Not as visually enticing as the DK *Illustrated Dictionary of Mythology: Heroes, Heroines, Gods, and Goddesses from around the World* (DK, 1998), and featuring dictionary-type articles as opposed to retellings of legends or sagas, these nevertheless serve as solid, reliable starting points for student research. Mythology remains a curriculum mainstay and a topic of perennial student interest. Collections that purchased the earlier versions have probably noticed considerable wear and tear and will want to update. Other libraries that serve students in grades 4 through 10 should seriously consider this basic reference set.

The Oxford Dictionary of Classical Myth and Religion. Ed. by Simon Price and Emily Kearns. 2004. 599p. bibliog. maps. Oxford, $39.95 (0-19-280288-7). 292.1303.

The content of this encyclopedia is a selection of entries from the third edition of *The Oxford Classical Dictionary* (3d ed., 1996). The entries are broad in range, covering not just mythology but also "religious places and religious officials, divination, astrology, and magic." In addition, there are many entries on Judaism and Christianity, providing broader context to religious life in the Greco-Roman world.

Although entries have been taken from *The Oxford Classical Dictionary*, changes have been made. Some entries have been shortened. Untransliterated Greek, references to ancient texts within the body of an entry, and what the editors term obscure language have been deleted. Supplemental bibliographies have also been eliminated, although entries for individuals (e.g., *Hecuba, Poseidon*) often conclude with some references to their appearance in ancient texts by such authors as Homer, Hesiod, and Livy. The work also includes a short annotated bibliography to serve as a guide for further reading. An introductory essay describes local, Panhellenic, and Roman myths and their reception throughout history. A thematic index groups entries by broad subject area (e.g., "Gods and Heroes," "Places"), and there are *see* references throughout the work. A few maps serve as the only illustrations.

Libraries owning *The Oxford Classical Dictionary* will not gain much by purchasing *The Oxford Dictionary of Classical Myth and Religion*. The elimination of much of the scholarly content may diminish its usefulness to academic collections. On the other hand, some public and high-school libraries may find the work more accessible and thus of greater benefit. In this case, consideration ought to be given first to the *Cassell Dictionary of Classical Mythology* (1998). Although its scope is somewhat narrower, the entries are thorough, scholarly, and accessibly written; there are many illustrations; and the scholarly apparatus of references to ancient texts and other supplemental material is unobtrusively included for those wishing to pursue their research further.

Dictionary of Buddhism. By Damien Keown. 2003. 357p. appendix. illus. Oxford, $35 (0-19-860560-9). 294.3.

The Buddhist tradition is a venerable one, widely practiced and studied. Yet, until recently, substantial reference works have lagged behind the interest in the subject. Most available in English are single-volume works that address terms, concepts, or deities. Oxford's new dictionary, although also a single volume, treats doctrines, practices, biography, scriptures, schools and sects, art, architecture, and more.

More than 2,000 entries are alphabetically arranged from *abhabbatthana*, the five things of which an arhat, or enlightened one, is said to be incapable, to *Zimmè Paññasa*, the Burmese term for a collection of birth stories of the Buddha. Most entries are transliterations from Sanskrit, Chinese, Japanese, Pali, and so on, giving the work a very academic flavor and seeming to require some prior knowledge of the subject. In fairness, the author does state in his preface that this work is more of a companion to the growing literature on Buddhism rather than an introduction to it. The treatment of particular countries (e.g., *China, India*) as well as those for collections of sacred texts can serve as introductory essays of a sort. There are entries for terms in English (e.g., *Diet, Reincarnation*), including some on contemporary issues, such as *Cloning* and *Stem cell research*.

Despite the work's academic bent, entries provide no supplemental bibliographies. This is an especially disappointing omission in the appendix, which outlines the divisions of the three main collections of canonical scriptures (i.e., Pali Canon, Chinese Canon, and Tibetan Canon), as finding translations of particular sacred texts can be difficult.

The *Concise Encyclopedia of Buddhism* (Oneworld, 2000) also lacks a true index and supplemental bibliographies for entries but has some features the Oxford title doesn't, namely, a nice introductory essay on Buddhist history, doctrines, and literature as well as a thematic bibliography. Its coverage, however, is not as comprehensive, with just over 900 entries. Although Oxford's *Dictionary of Buddhism* may not be all it could be, it does provide authoritative and convenient treatment of a wide range of subjects. Academic and public libraries would do well to acquire it.

Encyclopedia of Buddhism. 2v. Ed. by Robert E. Buswell Jr. 2003. 981p. appendix. bibliogs. illus. index. maps. Macmillan, $265 (0-02-865718-7). 294.3.

Buddhism, according to the editor in chief of this encyclopedia, "is one of the three major world religions, along with Christianity and Islam." Unlike the other two, however, Buddhism lacks substantial reference works in Western languages. The majority are single-volume works, defining terms, concepts, deities, etc. The *Encyclopedia of Buddhism*, on the other hand, "seeks to document the range and depth of the Buddhist tradition in its many manifestations."

The nearly 500 entries are alphabetically arranged, signed by their authors, and conclude with *see* references and supplemental bibliographies. Article length ranges from 50 to 4,000 words. There are illustrations throughout, including three maps on the diffusion of Buddhism in Asia as well as an eight-page insert of color plates in each volume. The set ends with several time lines of Buddhist history and a good index. Given the long history Buddhism has enjoyed and the many different cultural regions and national traditions in which it has developed, two volumes are not enough to do the subject justice. Consequently, the entries tend to be thematic and inclusive in nature, with specific mention of, say, an individual or place being made within a broader survey article. While the cosmological, doctrinal, and ritual aspects of Buddhism are covered extensively, entries also treat the cultural, social, and political contexts that have shaped and been shaped by Buddhist thought (e.g., *Economics, Education, Law*). Entries for geographic locations provide nice historical surveys of the development of Buddhism to the present day and include the U.S. and Europe. Buddhism's interaction with other world religions and philosophies (e.g., *Christianity and Buddhism, Communism and Buddhism, Jainism and Buddhism*) is treated. Finally, recognizing that Buddhism is a force in the world today, the editor has included entries that provide Buddhist perspectives on issues of contemporary concern (e.g., *Abortion, Gender, Modernity and Buddhism*).

The editor is correct to point out that covering Buddhism in its entirety is impossible in so short a work. Nevertheless, the *Encyclopedia of Buddhism* is a welcome addition to the reference literature for the tradition itself and, more broadly, Buddhist and Asian studies. Public and academic libraries serving readers with interest in these areas would do well to acquire it.

Handbook of Hindu Mythology. By George M. Williams. 2003. 372p. appendix. bibliogs. glossary. illus. index. ABC-CLIO, $75 (1-57607-106-5). 294.5.

Williams has compiled a learned text based on sound knowledge of the Hindu religion. His methodical coverage of variant spellings, pronunciation, and capitalization in the preface is a valuable guide to writers and researchers. The division of the subject into periods and themes in the introduction simplifies the task of comprehending beliefs and rituals that evolved over five millennia. The text is meticulously compiled, with ample cross-referencing. Attractive illustrations contribute to the understanding of Indian lore in art.

A–Z entries on "Characters, Themes, and Concepts," among them *Brahmâ, Mahâbhârata, Pârvatî, Vishnu,* and *Yoga,* make up the bulk of the text. An appendix charts Vedic gods by periods as a handy guide to development of the Hindu pantheon. A summary of resources suggests readings at various levels, including children's books. The annotated bibliography lists works as old as James Hastings' revered *Encyclopaedia of Religion and Ethics* (1908–1929) and as recent as online Sanskrit dictionaries. A seven-page glossary offers uncomplicated definitions of 246 pivotal terms. The work concludes with a detailed index containing numerous cross-references for maximum accuracy.

Overall, the handbook is a prize catch for public, church, temple, school, and college libraries. In the style of a patient, respectful teacher, Williams has introduced one of the world's long-lived belief systems.

The Oxford Dictionary of Islam. Ed. by John L. Esposito. 2003. 359p. Oxford, $45 (0-19-512558-4). 297.03

In this volume "designed for general readers with little or no knowledge of Islam," more than 2,000 alphabetically arranged entries treat "the religion of Islam and its impact on history, politics, and society." Editor Esposito also edited the four-volume *Oxford Encyclopedia of the Modern Islamic World* (1995), from which the new work extracts and updates material. Recent developments are reflected in the entries *Bin Laden, Osama; HAMAS; Palestine Liberation Organization (PLO); Qaeda, al-;* and *Taliban*. There are also entries that describe Islam in various countries and regions, while the religious foundation of Islam is treated in the entries *Pillars of Islam* and *Quran*. The Islamic perspective on topics such as abortion and homosexuality is also provided. Although the focus is on the nineteenth and twentieth centuries, the inclusion of important persons and places in the history of Islam broadens the scope of the work.

The goal of creating a compact resource for the general reader may account for the lack of features such as supplemental bibliographies and an index. Cross-referencing isi nsufficient. The entry for *Pillars of Islam* has no *see* reference from "Five Pillars," a name by which they are also commonly known. Further, this entry fails to point the reader to the entries for each of the individual pillars, something an index and *see also* references could easily accomplish.

The standard reference tool for Islam is the ongoing *Encyclopaedia of Islam* (Brill, 1954–). Densely academic, it is beyond the scope of many libraries and contains little in the way of contemporary issues. Another option is the single-volume *The New Encyclopedia of Islam* (AltaMira, 2001), which includes suggestions for further reading, illustrations, and better cross-references, though it, too, lacks an index and bibliographies for entries.

World events have sparked a keen interest in Islam. Despite its drawbacks, *The Oxford Dictionary of Islam* would be a useful addition to public and academic libraries.

The Encyclopedia of Celtic Mythology and Folklore. By Patricia Monaghan. 2004. 512p. bibliogs. index. Facts On File, $65 (0-8160-4524-0). 299.

Celtic mythology is a mystery even to the experts. Trying to sort out what is purely Celtic and what has been altered by the Greeks, Romans, and Christians is an impossible task. Trying to reconcile written records with archeological evidence is difficult if not impossible. The reader is then left with a jumble of names, stories, traditions, and places under the rubric "Celtic mythology."

This latest attempt to bring order out of chaos is an encyclopedia of approximately 1,000 entries covering individuals both mythological and quasi-historical, epics, themes, religious concepts, places, and artifacts. Irish mythology predominates, but continental Celtic figures, even those who are only a name in a local region, such as Britovius, are included.

Organized alphabetically, the entries range in size from several sentences to more than a page. Many end with a short list of sources. The work concludes with a seven-page bibliography and an index with major entries in boldface. An introduction explains Celtic history and culture and describes how the author has handled the entries, especially in regard to spelling.

Other dictionaries and encyclopedias have tackled this topic. *An Encyclopedia of Celtic Mythology* (Contemporary, 2000) uses a thematic approach, with chapters on druids, fairies, etc. *Dictionary of Celtic Mythology* (ABC-CLIO, 1992) uses alphabetical entries and has a bibliography but does not include sources with each entry. Another volume, *Dictionary of Celtic Myth and Legend* (Thames and Hudson, 1992), has 400 entries. *The Encyclopedia of Celtic Mythology and Folklore* has more entries and provides sources for many of them. In libraries with a high demand for or interest in Celtic mythology, this would be a worthwhile purchase. For libraries with moderate interest that already own one of the earlier encyclopedias or dictionaries, this would be an optional purchase.

Sociology, Anthropology, Political Science

Encyclopedia of International Media and Communications. 4v. Ed. by Donald H. Johnston. 2003. 2,733p. bibliogs. glossaries. illus. index. Academic, $750 (0-12-387670-2). 302.2.

This encyclopedia comes when a good synthesizing reference source is needed to provide a history and a recent snapshot of the world's media. Among the 219 articles are discussions of historic topics, such as the role of the media in the cold war, and of freedom of the press, the development of the computer, and the role of television. The future of books, newspapers, radio, and television also receives treatment. Other entries cover media types, formats, outlets, genres, interrelationships, issues, and concepts as well the status of the media in 61 geopolitical locations (individual or groups of countries).

Each of the signed articles begins with a small table of contents and a glossary and concludes with *see also* references and bibliographies of books, journal articles, and Web sites. Length averages a generous 11 pages. Each volume has a complete table of contents, contents by subject area, and a directory of contributors. The index is quite detailed, sometimes even referring users to information in illustration captions.

One can learn about the history and current status of comic strips and comic books; the basics of intellectual property law; the place of photojournalism, poetry, drama, and fiction; and many more topics in this comprehensive resource. The scholars and journalists who wrote the essays represent colleges, universities, and other institutions throughout the world (though most are from the U.S.), making this an international product. Knowing a bit about the media of a country or region of the world is an important step in understanding the culture and politics of the area. This set provides students and the interested public with important facts and insights into the changing roles and functions of old and new media. Expensive but a good value, it is recommended for academic and large public libraries.

Encyclopedia of Terrorism. By Harvey W. Kushner. 2003. 523p. appendixes. bibliogs. illus. index. maps. Sage, $125 (0-7619-2408-6). 303.6.

Although there is coverage of groups such as the Irish Republican Army and events such as the Munich Olympics massacre, the emphasis of this book is on terrorism in, or against, the U.S. In 300 A–Z entries Kushner, a well-respected researcher in this area, covers terrorist-related events, groups, individuals, methods, activities, and responses. Although he began work on the book a year prior to the events of September 11, 2001, he writes in his introduction that those events made the need for an authoritative reference source on terrorism more urgent, and many of the entries are connected to 9/11.

Entries generally range in length from half a page to three pages and include further readings. There is good basic coverage of internal American terror activities, including those by ecoterrorists, anticommunist Cubans, antiabortionists, and white supremacist groups. Cross-references help to direct reading within the text. Following the encyclopedia portion of the volume are several appendixes, including maps showing the locations of various terrorist events and a chronology of attacks on U.S. interests at home and abroad. The chronology lists as terrorism the assassinations of President William McKinley, Martin Luther King Jr., and Robert Kennedy, but not that of President John Kennedy. An excellent bibliography lists a great deal of extended reading. A reasonable collection of Web sites gives a variety of news, research, and government sites; a nice addition to this list would be Web sites that offer dissenting and terrorist group views on their actions. A "Reader's Guide" at the front of the volume sorts entry headings into 32 categories, from "Abu Nidal Organization" to "World Trade Center Bombing, February 1993."

Encyclopedia of World Terrorism: 1996–2002 [RBB Ag 03] is more international in scope. Although its global coverage is not comprehensive, *Encyclopedia of Terrorism* is a solid piece of work with thorough coverage of U.S. terror groups of all varieties. It is worthwhile for its coverage of the topic and is recommended for academic and public libraries.

Propaganda and Mass Persuasion: A Historical Encyclopedia, 1500 to the Present. By Nicholas J. Cull. 2003. 479p. bibliogs. illus. index. ABC-CLIO, $85 (1-57607-820-5). 303.3.

This work has been designed as an easily readable survey of propaganda and its history from 1500 to the present. An extensive introduction defines propaganda and traces its origins, concluding with a discussion of the importance of propaganda in the twentieth century and the increasing prominence given to it. The introduction also notes that, although propaganda often serves to "dictate what one should think," it is not necessarily evil.

The encyclopedia contains more than 250 entries, from *Abolitionism/antislavery movement* to *Zionism*. Many of the entries concern individuals who had any connection with propaganda, such as Hitler, Osama bin Laden, and several U.S. presidents. Various countries of the world and their connection to propaganda are also discussed. Other entries cover events (*Gulf War, Reformation and Counter-Reformation*), institutions (*CNN, KGB*), documents and artifacts (*Triumph of the Will, Uncle Tom's Cabin*), movements (*Civil Rights Movement, Environmentalism*), and techniques (*Advertising, Censorship, Television*). Each entry contains a definition of the topic and its connection to propaganda and is enhanced by cross-references and references to source material. The index is quite extensive.

This specialized encyclopedia does a good job of exploring the different uses of propaganda. It would be worthwhile purchase for academic and large public libraries and would also be accessible and interesting to high-school students.

Talking Terrorism: A Dictionary of the Loaded Language of Political Violence. By Philip Herbst. 2003. 220p. bibliog. index. Greenwood, $49.95 (0-313-32486-7). 303.6.

As opposed to the recent spate of reference materials covering terrorism, this text does not define the numerous individuals, groups, and causes that have been involved in terrorist activities over the years. Instead, it discusses the definitions given 150 key terms used by politicians and propagandists who seek to distort or alter the view of an issue for different purposes. The author also wrote *Wimmin, Wimps, and Wallflowers: An Encyclopaedic Dictionary of Gender and Sexual Orientation Bias in the United States* (Intercultural, 2001) and *The Color of Words: An Encyclopaedic Dictionary of Ethnic Bias in the United States* (Intercultural, 1997).

Many more terms are discussed in the articles than are used as the 150 entry headings, and *see also* references and a general index guide the reader through the definitions. In addition to the excellent general bibliography, citations are included within the definitions so that it is easy for a researcher to identify respective sources.

An excellent introduction to the topic of terrorism and use of language by politicians frames the discussion of the terms. Of particular interest is a discussion of how some may fault this text for challenging freedom of speech. The author prefers to see the book as a means of raising awareness of biased language. The entry for *Freedom fighter* demonstrates some of the points he is trying to make. During the most recent conflict in the Balkans, the U.S. government refers to the Kosovo Liberation Army as freedom fighters or terrorists, depending on whether the group was invading Serbia (considered a good war by the U.S. government) or Macedonia (considered a bad war). Similar discussions on the various issues of vocabulary are what make the book a fascinating and necessary addition to available material on language as well as on terrorism. Recommended for academic and public libraries.

Ancestry in America: A Comparative City-by-City Guide to over 200 Ethnic Backgrounds—with Rankings. 2003. 3,045p. index. Grey House, paper, $225 (1-592-37029-2). 304.6.

Using raw data from the 2000 census, this reference work pulls together comparative statistics on the ethnic makeup of 4,206 municipalities in the U.S. with populations of over 10,000. Statistics were drawn from three different sections of the census: "Race," "Hispanic Origin," and "Ancestry." Content is divided into two sections: statistics by place and comparative rankings. "Section One: City-by-City Listings" lists the places by state and then alphabetically, with their population and percent of the total population for each ethnic background. In "Section Two: Comparative Ranking Tables," the top 150 places for each racial and ethnic category are listed by name, by population number, and by population percentage. Using this easy-to-navigate section, users can immediately find out which place has the highest and lowest percentage of each ancestry—of the top 150 places with people reporting Swedish ancestry, Jamestown, New York, has the highest percentage, and Columbine, Colorado, has the lowest. The index provides an alphabetical listing of every place that is included.

This compilation will serve a wide range of research requests for population characteristics. Because it reports data on more than 200 different ethnic and racial categories, it offers much more detail than other sources, such as the publisher's *Profiles of America* (2d ed, 2003). A companion CD-ROM, which has data for 33,150 places regardless of total population size, is available on request for purchasers of the volume.

The Atlas of U.S. and Canadian Environmental History. Ed. by Char Miller. 2003. 248p. bibliogs. illus. index. maps. Routledge, $150 (0-415-93781-7). 304.2.

This chronological account in the form of a series of signed essays about the events, people, issues, movements, politics, philosophy, and science related to environmental history since 1492 is an attractive and accessible presentation. The book is divided into seven chapters, each representing an era. Within each chapter are from 12 to 17 essays, each about two pages long and accompanied by maps, tables, charts, illustrations, photographs, sidebars, and short lists of books for further reading. The essays discuss different aspects of the same themes: agriculture; wildlife and forestry; land use management; technology, industry, and pollution; human habitats; and ideology and politics. The final essay deals with the conflict between environmental and economic globalization, coming full circle back to the issues discussed in the first essay on the economic and cultural forces that fueled the early exploration of North America. In between, one is introduced to cattle ranching, the fur and lumber trades, utopianism, urbanization, water issues, the conservation movements of Canada and the U.S., social Darwinism, nuclear power, public and private lands, eco-radicalism, and more.

U.S. history and issues form the majority of the book, but Canadian history and issues are included. The extensive bibliography suggests general environmental and cultural resources, resources specific to the U.S. or Canada, resources for each of the eras, and resources for the major themes. The detailed index is very thorough.

The 44 contributors are mostly academic historians but also include a few geographers, political scientists, and freelance writers. They have certainly done a fine job in writing for the general audience and students. This atlas is recommended for high- school, public, and academic libraries.

Encyclopedia of Population. 2v. Ed. by Pat Demeny and Geoffrey McNicoll. 2003. 1,040p. appendix. bibliogs. charts. index. tables. Macmillan, $265 (0-02-865677-6). 304.6.

Population means more than people, births, and deaths. Population studies measure how people live, the environment they live in, and the resources to support life. The 336 articles in the *Encyclopedia of Population* discuss topics as varied as *Divorce, Immigration, Land use,* and *Prehistoric populations*. A topical outline provides a thematic view of the encyclopedia's content, which ranges from population theory to the cultural and political aspects of population.

Each entry is 500 to 1,000 words in length, contains a bibliography, and is signed by one of 278 authors—all published scholars from around the world. Among the longer entries are *Climate change and population; Diseases, infectious;* and *Sexuality in humans*. As is expected within the field of population, many charts, tables, and graphs accompany the text, including several in an appendix. Biographical entries on 60 individuals whose work was important in the development of population studies—for example, Thomas Malthus, Karl Marx, and Margaret Sanger—are included. Finding aids include an alphabetical list of articles, *see* and *see also* references, and an extensive index.

The *Encyclopedia of Population* is a successor to the *International Encyclopedia of Population* (Free Press, 1982). This earlier work focused on entries by country, whereas the later title focuses on themes and topics in population. Although the number of entry headings has doubled, the page numbers haven't, so expect concision and some dropped content. Appropriate for academic libraries, particularly those with programs in population studies, world economics, political science, and world development.

Encyclopedia of World Environmental History. 3v. Ed. by Shepard Krech III and others. 2003. 1,429p. bibliogs. illus. index. maps. Routledge, $395 (0-415-93732-9). 304.2.

Aimed at a broad audience of students, scholars, professionals, and general readers, this reference work contains 520 signed articles providing current, comprehensive coverage of environmental history from ancient times to the present. The well-written, alphabetically arranged articles range in length from one column to multiple pages.

Interdisciplinary and cross-cultural in approach, the encyclopedia covers a broad range of general topics, including arts, literature, biomes, climate, natural events, economic systems, energy, ancient civilizations, exploitation, philosophies, law, people, plants, animals, nonliving resources, places, religion, technology, and science. Examples of specific articles are *Animal rights, Aristotle, Buddhism, Coffee, Danube River, Ecofeminism, Eden, Environmental ethics, Free trade, Germany, Global warming, Pleistocene overkill, Snail darter, Trans-Alaska pipeline,* and *Wilderness*.

The text is augmented by 20 maps and more than 100 photographs. Some 115 sidebars provide engaging supplemental material, including extracts from historical documents, firsthand accounts, ethnographic accounts, environmental literature, poetry, and religious traditions. Suggestions for further reading accompany each article. Although the index to this otherwise excellent encyclopedia is adequate, it could use some improvement. For example, the index heading *doves, house* should be *dove, rock*. Two pages are listed in the index for Arne Naess, but references to him in the article on deep ecology, of which he is a prominent philosopher, are missed. Further, the index does not indicate main entries.

Environmental history should be of great interest to anyone concerned with our present global environmental dilemmas. The *Encyclopedia of World Environmental History* is a worthwhile investment for those in need of a scholarly reference source on this timely topic as there are no other single works that provide comparable breadth and authoritative coverage. It is recommended for academic, public, and special libraries.

Indigenous Peoples and Environmental Issues: An Encyclopedia. By Bruce E. Johansen. 2003. 506p. bibliogs. illus. index. Greenwood, $85 (0-313-32398-4). 304.2.

Australia, Burma, Peru, Russia (Siberia), Turkey, Tibet, the U.S., and Zambia are among the more than 50 countries discussed in this encyclopedia. Indigenous peoples, in the definition presented here, are "groups of human beings who have occupied an area before other groups intruded." Author Johansen has written widely on environmental issues of Native Americans, and the purpose of this work is to describe foreign intrusions (usually destructive) and their effects on indigenous peoples and their environment. Aimed at a level accessible to high-school students and the general reader, the geographically arranged chapters range in length from 1 to 84 pages.

Country chapters are divided into stand-alone essays that present various facets of environmental issues confronting specific peoples. Examples of essays within country chapters include "The Mapuche: Oil Contamination" (in "Argentina"); "The Inuit: Dioxin and Other Persistent Organic Pollutants" (in "Canada"); "Deaths of Bauxite Mining Protestors" (in "India"); "The Ogoni: Oil, Blood, and the Death of a Homeland" (in "Nigeria"); "The Saramaka Maroons: Gold Mining and Logging" (in "Suriname"); and "The Zuni: Sacred Waters and Coal Strip Mining" (in "United States"). A guide to related topics alerts the user to various environmental issues found within the country chapters. Additional chapters address broader topics, such as "Climate Change and Indigenous Environmentalism," "The Haudenosaunee (Iroquois) Environmental Worldview," and "Native American Conceptions of Ecology."

A few black-and-white photographs supplement the text. References are included with each essay, and a 31-page bibliography provides information on related books, articles, and Web sites. Since the book deals with issues current at the time of publication, some articles may become outdated rather quickly.

There are no other current reference books specifically devoted to the global environmental issues of indigenous peoples. This volume is particularly recommended for public and academic libraries.

The Newest Americans. 5v. 2003. bibliogs. glossaries. illus. indexes. maps. Greenwood, $200 (0-313-32553-7). 304.8.

This set looks at 34 national groups that, according to the U.S. Bureau of Immigration, represent the largest number of immigrants to the U.S. since 1965. An introduction (reprinted in each volume) provides historical background; a time line of pertinent legislation; definitions of refugees, asylees, illegal immigrants, and naturalized citizens; and a discussion of American attitudes toward immigration. Following this introductory material are individual chapters arranged alphabetically according to parent nation. Chapters average 18 pages and follow a common format. Roughly half the material is devoted to each country's political, historical, and cultural foundations; remaining portions deal with immigrants' new lives in America and coping with changing social, family, work, school, religious, and dietary norms. Several special features, such as biographical "spotlights," boxed inserts, and full- page treatments on religions—Islam, Buddhism, etc.—appear throughout, as do occasional black-and-white photos, charts, and graphs. Volume-specific bibliographies (including print and electronic sources), glossaries, and indexes are also included.

Eleven of the 34 groups originate in the Western hemisphere, 10 in Asia, 7 in Africa, and 3 apiece in Europe and the Middle East. There are no surprises—anyone who follows world events could identify many of these populations. Nor is there anything particularly compelling about the background information, which reiterates standard material found in basic social studies references. What is unique are the individualized studies of assimilation attempts into mainstream American culture and the particular difficulties each group faces. Cultural differences regarding basic social functions such as body language, invitations, eating habits, eye contact, and giving and receiving compliments are explained, as are resulting sources of friction or perceived rudeness.

This is more accessible than recent adult offerings (*American Immigrant Cultures: Builders of a Nation* [Macmillan, 1997]; *Encyclopedia of American Immigration* [Sharpe, 2001]) and narrower in scope but much more detailed than *American Immigration: A Student Companion* (Oxford, 2001). *The Newest Americans* will be helpful as schools expand their curricula to reflect a global perspective and add units on character development and citizenship. Recommended for school and public libraries serving students in grades 6 through 12.

American Masculinities: A Historical Encyclopedia. Ed. by Bret E. Carroll. 2003. 562p. bibliogs. illus. index. Sage, $150 (0-7619-2540-6). 305.31.

Men and Masculinities: A Social, Cultural, and Historical Encyclopedia. 2v. Ed. by Michael Kimmel and Amy Aronson. 2003. 892p. bibliogs. illus. index. ABC-CLIO, $255 (1-57607-774-8). 305.31.

It seems so simple, American masculinity—that social archetype that can never be attained but must be proved again and again. Yet the nearly simultaneous publication of two sweeping encyclopedias devoted to the subject testifies to its complexity, as do their differences in content. Their shared subject yields duplication of articles such as *Bogart, Humphrey; Dean, James; Death of a Salesman; Eugenics; Fathers' rights; Marlboro Man; Prostitution; Shaft; Slave narratives;* and *Violence.* The subject's complexity ensures many more entries unique to each—*Chivalry, Father's Day, Gambling, Manifest Destiny, Outdoorsmen,* and *Suburbia* in *American Masculinities* and *Domestic violence, Hazing, Male strippers, Shell shock,* and *Suicide* in *Men and Masculinities.*

Both encyclopedia offer substantial articles on a wide range of relevant topics, individuals, creative works and characters, theories, and events that over centuries have shaped the notion of American masculinity and its implications for men and women. That is not, however, a monolithic notion. Together the encyclopedias explore masculinities other than that those assumed and accepted by most and reinforced by countless cultural signals. These include female masculinity, androgyny, homosexuality, post-Vietnam masculinity, middle-class manhood, the men's movement, and transvestism.

American Masculinities will be accessible to a broader audience than will *Men and Masculinities.* The latter hints at the difference by the frequency in which articles explicitly cite scholarship and by its lengthier bibliographies. Furthermore, *Men and Masculinities* is not immune to the bloodless prose of the social sciences, as in the following from the article on premature ejaculation: "Enacted masculinity is displayed sexually by effectual accomplishment." But it ranges more widely, especially in its treatment of twentieth-century popular culture (*Lolita, Rap, Tootsie*) and the ways in which it both mirrors and modifies popular perceptions about masculinity.

Long—perhaps too long—in coming, these informative encyclopedias demonstrate the maturity of the men's movement and the interdisciplinary breadth of men's studies since these began to emerge three decades ago. They will provide information, help clarify the issues in play, and raise the consciousness of many not yet aware of the vitality of this small movement and its related academic discipline. Despite their many similarities, their differences, not unlike the similarities and the differences between American women and men, advise that reference collections in academic and large public libraries make both available to their users.

Encyclopedia of Children and Childhood in History and Society. 3v. Ed. by Paula S. Fass. 2003. 1,055p. bibliogs. illus. index. Macmillan, $325 (0-02-865714-4). 305.23.

Intended to provide "the interested reader with a necessary introduction to the wide range of issues that define the field" of children's history, the volumes of this encyclopedia draw on the expertise of more than 300 scholars from around the world for 445 articles arranged in alphabetical order. Among the contributors are authors of several important books written about the history of children over the past two decades, including Paula Petrick, who wrote *Small Worlds: Children and Adolescents in America, 1850–1950* (Univ. of Kansas, 1992), and Joseph E. Illick, author of *American Childhoods* (Univ. of Pennsylvania, 2002).

Articles vary in length from 500 to 5,000 words and cover topics in such broad areas as history, social sciences, literature, medicine, and law as they relate to the history of childhood and children. *Bicycles and tricycles; Cassatt, Mary; Charter schools; Child pornography; Halloween; Infant rulers; Islam; Lindbergh kidnapping; Montessori, Maria; Multiple births; Orphanages; Shyness; Teen drinking; Temple, Shirley;* and *Theories of play* are examples of entries that demonstrate the set's range. The encyclopedia has discussions of literature that has been an important ingredient in the lives of Western children, such as the Bible, ABC books, fairy tales, Nancy Drew, Harry Potter, and comic books. Each entry ends with *see also* references and a bibliography. A wide variety of black-and-white illustrations, many of them significant representations of children in art, illustrate the text. Volume 3 contains an annotated collection of 50 primary sources identified as essential documents in the field, reproduced in whole or in part. A topical outline appears in volume 1, and volume 3 has an excellent comprehensive index.

Volumes in ABC-CLIO's the American Family series (*Adolescence in America, Boyhood in America, Girlhood in America, Infancy in America* [all 2001]) cover some of the same topics but are narrower in geographic scope. They are also more centered on the experience of children and youth rather than on childhood as an idea. The *Gale Encyclopedia of Childhood and Adolescence* (1997) is more concerned with child development. For its worldwide historical scope, *Encyclopedia of Children and Childhood in History and Society* is a recommended purchase for history collections as well as collections that focus on the study of children and children in families. It is also recommended in the broader sense as a great background tool for any public and academic library with patrons concerned with the study of topics relating to children.

Encyclopedia of Modern Ethnic Conflicts. Ed. by Joseph R. Rudolph Jr. 2003. 375p. appendix. bibliogs. illus. index. Greenwood, $74.95 (0-313-31381-4). 305.8.

The *Encyclopedia of Modern Ethnic Conflicts* consists of 38 articles focusing on specific ethnic conflicts around the world. The articles are substantial, covering the historical background of the conflict's characteristics, management, and significance and including a chronology, cross-references, and a bibliography. Examples include "Central Europe: The Romany, a Stateless Minority in a World of States"; "United Kingdom: Scotland and Scottish Nationalism"; and "Western Sahara: Ethnic Conflict and the Twentieth Century's Last Colonial War." Arrangement is alphabetical based on country or geographic area. An appendix lists the volume's contents by region, and an extensive index gives good access.

Averaging about 10 pages in length, the articles provide excellent, in-depth treatment of each conflict. The limited number of articles means that the coverage is highly selective, but the editor did a good job of choosing conflicts that are prominent in the news and likely to be of interest to library patrons. Selective detailed coverage combined with a global reach set this source apart from related reference tools. Other sources with a global scope, such as *Ethnic Relations: A Cross-Cultural Encyclopedia* (2d ed., ABC-CLIO, 1998), have shorter entries on a wider variety of topics. Sources such as *Racial and Ethnic Relations in America* (Salem, 2000) focus on particular geographic areas. Even for collections with other sources on ethnic conflicts, *Encyclopedia of Modern Ethnic Conflicts* will be a useful addition and is recommended for academic and public libraries.

Encyclopedia of Retirement and Finance. 2v. Ed. by Lois A. Vitt. 2004. 869p. appendixes. bibliogs. charts. graphs. index. Greenwood, $149.95 (0-313-32495-6). 305.26.

This multidisciplinary work is a "comprehensive inventory of policies, institutions, practices, and problems" associated with retirement and finance and is a revised and enlarged edition of the *Encyclopedia of Financial Gerontology* (Greenwood, 1996).

More than 185 A–Z entries fall within nine core topics—"Advisors, Advice and Support"; "Economic and Income Security"; "Employment, Work and Retirement"; "Family and Intergenerational Issues"; "Financial Investments and Insurance"; "Health Care and Health Coverage"; "Housing and Housing Finance"; "Legal Issues"; and "Quality of Life and Well-Being." Sample entries are *Accelerated death benefits*, *Baby Boomers and retirement*, *Guardianship*, *Identify theft*, *Medicare*, *Retirement planning*, and *Widowhood*. The signed entries contain *see also* references, related organizations, suggested readings, and references. *See* references are used to point the reader from an unused entry to the correct term. Figures and tables are included where appropriate.

Especially helpful are the four appendixes. The first, "Chronological Summary of Post-ERISA Benefit Legislation," starts with the Employment Retirement Income Security Act of 1974 and covers related legislation through 2002. The second appendix is "Major Post-ERISA Benefit Legislation," a list by year of the legislation. The third appendix lists organizations and resources and gives addresses, telephone numbers, and Web addresses. The fourth appendix is "Types of Benefits by Tax Treatment and by Function." A name and subject index completes the encyclopedia.

The entries are very readable and provide excellent insight into the area of retirement and finance. Although this work could be used as a textbook, its major contribution will be as a reference tool, and it will undoubtedly be an extremely useful addition to academic and public libraries.

Encyclopedia of Women in the American West. Ed. by Gordon Morris Bakken and Brenda Farrington. 2003. 381p. appendix. bibliogs. illus. index. Sage, $125 (0-7619-2356-X). 305.42.

A companion to Sage's *Handbook of American Women's History* (2000), this alphabetically arranged encyclopedia focuses on ways in which women had an impact on the history of the West from the mid-1800s to the present. Signed articles written by approximately 60 subject experts, most college or university affiliated, run from a partial column to better than 10 pages. Most of the entries are biographical, covering 150 women as varied as Barbara Boxer, Saint Frances Xavier Cabrini, Willa Cather, Molly Ivins, Maxine Hong Kingston, and Sarah Winnemucca. The weighting is appropriate, with shorter entries for biographical profiles and longer ones for general areas of study, such as *Conservation movement, 1870–1940; Education;* and *Prostitution.* Coverage is selective rather than comprehensive; for example, the only state that has an entry is Kansas, to give an idea of "how to structure a work on women in a place." Each article concludes with a bibliography. The number of sources cited depends on the depth of treatment of the topic. Frequent well-reproduced black-and-white photographs illustrate and extend the accessible articles. Despite the many contributors, the style is remarkably uniform and easy to read.

In addition to an alphabetical list of entries, the "Reader's Guide," which precedes much of the front matter, lists articles in nine different categories, among them agriculture and ranching, arts and letters, education, law, and women's organizations. Cross-referencing is provided in the form of *see also* references in the accurate index, but otherwise cross-references are absent. The volume concludes with a chronology (1804–2003), a list of women's organizations, a helpful essay on researching women's history, a comprehensive bibliography, and the aforementioned index.

Despite the price, this is a sound purchase for college and university libraries with women's studies or American West programs as well as for large public libraries.

★The Greenwood Encyclopedia of Women's Issues Worldwide. 6v. Ed. by Lynn Walter and others. 2003. bibliogs. illus. indexes. maps. Greenwood, $550 (0-313-32787-4). 305.4.

In a global survey of the conditions under which contemporary women live, this resource divides the world into six regions: Asia and Oceania, Central and South America, Europe, the Middle East and North Africa, North America and the Caribbean, and sub-Saharan Africa. Each volume is organized alphabetically by country or in some cases by region (for example, the chapter "Central Asia" covers Tajikistan, Kazakhstan, Turkmenistan, and Kyrgyzstan). A general introduction provides an overview of contemporary women's issues worldwide, written by the editor in chief, a professor of women's studies at the University of Wisconsin. Volume editors and contributors are likewise university affiliated. The volume editors provide introductory essays treating the situation of women in the particular region or regions addressed.

Across the volumes, chapters are organized almost identically. A profile of the nation or region is followed by an overview of women's issues. Subsequent sections on education, employment and economics, family and sexuality, health, politics and law, religion and spirituality, violence, and the outlook for the twenty-first century offer a clear and comprehensive picture of women's everyday lives. Subsections under each heading allow for in-depth treatment. For example, "Politics and Law" is divided into smaller sections on "Suffrage," "Political Participation," "Women's Rights" (in turn subdivided into "Feminist Movements" and "Lesbian Rights"), and "Military Service." Chapter length averages 24 pages, with that for French Guiana, at 8 pages, being the shortest and that for Jordan, at 50 pages, being the longest. Both the volume introductions and the chapters conclude with notes; a resource guide listing suggested readings, videos and films, Web sites, and organizations; and a selected bibliography.

Clear black-and-white line maps begin each of the country or region chapters, and black-and-white photos, though infrequent, do extend the text. Each volume contains an index of subject and person entries, with a comprehensive set index at the end of the volume on sub-Saharan Africa. Despite the number of contributors, the text is remarkably uniform in its objective tone and clear sentence structure. The full page, noncolumnar layout is inviting, and the organizational structure facilitates ready access to information.

Though the excellent *Routledge International Encyclopedia of Women: Global Women's Issues and Knowledge* (2000) is a bit stronger on statistical and demographic information, *The Greenwood Encyclopedia of Women's Issues Worldwide* provides stiff competition with its wealth of information clearly and accessibly presented. There is room in most collections for both. Recommended for libraries serving patrons from high-school age and up and especially for colleges and universities with strong women's programs.

Peoples of North America. 10v. 2003. bibliog. glossary. illus. index. maps. Grolier, $359 (0-7172-5777-0). 305.8.

A multitude of native peoples and immigrant groups have populated North America throughout the centuries. This encyclopedia, geared to upper-elementary through senior-high students, is a survey of the North American population at the start of the twenty-first century and profiles well-established ethnic groups, relatively recent immigrants, and indigenous peoples who "survive in significant numbers."

Approximately 200 distinct groups appear alphabetically (*Afghans* to *West Africans*). Entries range in length from two or three paragraphs (*Afghans, Ecuadoreans, Greenlanders, Hispanic Americans*) to eight pages (*African Americans*). Additional entries examine topics such as *Agriculture, Music, Racial prejudice and racial theories,* and *Religion* from a cross-cultural perspective. Each entry contains a "Fact File" of special boxes that provide facts about key people, immigration history (first immigrants and dates of major arrivals.) common names, typical jobs held in North America, dominant religions, festivals, languages, national or traditional foods, and population statistics. (The 2000 U.S. Census or the 1996 Canadian Census is utilized for this data, unless otherwise specified). A distribution map shows states and cities where major communities live today and often the region of origin. Boxes listing Web sites and community organizations provide links to additional resources. A listing of *see also* references at the end of each article helps students locate related articles throughout the set. Color and black-and- white photographs, all featuring captions, appear throughout.

Each volume concludes with a one-page set glossary, resources for further reading, a brief immigration time line from 1492 ("Christopher Columbus sails to North America") through 2003 ("U.S. forces attack Iraq"), and a set index. A useful look at Native North Americans by region is included in volumes 7 and 8.

The brevity of the fact boxes means that some, especially those dealing with jobs and food, have data that seem overly generalized and even stereotypical. Although this is often balanced by more detailed information in the text, students will be likely to turn to the fact boxes first as convenient sources of information.

Though different in arrangement (by country rather than ethnic group), the excellent 11-volume *Peoples of the Americas* (Marshall Cavendish, 1999) is similar in scope and more comprehensive, including both Central and South America as well as offering several highly useful indexes. *Peoples of North America* is accessible and provides information that students will find useful when completing school assignments. School and public libraries that need a reference source focused solely on North America will find this purchase serviceable.

★**Encyclopedia of Lesbian, Gay, Bisexual, and Transgender History in America.** 3v. Ed. by Marc Stein. 2003. 1,423p. appendix. bibliogs. illus. index. Scribner, $380 (0-684-31261-1). 306.76.

At a time when marriage equality is being championed and challenged, the publication of this resource on lesbian, gay, bisexual, and transgender (LGBT) identities, communities, cultures, and movements in the U.S. could not be more timely. A carefully constructed entry list includes more than 500 entry subjects. A wide spectrum of subject areas is covered: people; politics; culture and the arts; academic disciplines and fields; identities, communities, and cultures; geographical locations; law and public policy; economics and labor; sex, sexuality, intimacy, and relationships; religion and spirituality; language, symbols, signs, and concepts; social life, issues, and institutions; and social, cultural, and political processes. More than 400 years of historical developments are chronicled.

A–Z entries range from slightly less than a page to eight pages in length and include cross-references and sometimes substantial bibliographies. A directory of LGBT libraries and archives throughout the U.S. and Canada, a directory of contributors with their primary institutional affiliations and the entries they prepared, and a comprehensive index conclude the set. *Arab Americans, Class and class oppression, Gentrification, Native Americans, Republican Party, Sexual revolutions,* and *Visual art* are some of the subjects covered. Also here are biographical entries for more than 250 individuals, among them Josephine Baker, Hart Crane, David Hockney, Billie Jean King, Jerome Robbins, Billy Tipton, and Carl Van Vechten. Contributors have maintained a high level of scholarship throughout the set, and entries are characterized by evenhandedness.

The encyclopedia succeeds in opening up for contemporary readers the complex history of LGBT life in the U.S. Garland's two-volume *Gay Histories and Cultures: An Encyclopedia* (2000) might appear to be closely comparable. Readers are reminded, however, that significant differences exist between these two works—Garland includes separate volumes on lesbian histories and cultures and gay histories and cultures, its focus is on history and culture, and its scope is international. Libraries that own the Garland set will want, therefore, to make room for *Encyclopedia of Lesbian, Gay, Bisexual, and Transgender History in America* in their reference collections. It an exceptional work that should be useful for academic and public libraries. General readers, students, researchers, and members of the LGBT communities alike will find this to be a most welcome resource.

Handbook of Death and Dying. 2v. Ed. by Clifford D. Bryant. 2003. 1,088p. bibliogs. charts. index. tables. Sage, $350 (0-7619-2514-7). 306.9.

Although the U.S. is considered a death-denying society, a focus on understanding the social and cultural issues around death has been gathering momentum since the 1960s and 1970s, a result of demographic changes, medical advancements and resulting ethical issues, and other factors.

Topics in the *Handbook of Death and Dying* are presented as a collection of 103 comprehensive essays clustered in 10 general areas. The field of death studies is multidisciplinary; the more than 100 contributors are academics in sociology, psychology, social work, theology, history, medicine, law, and other areas of inquiry as well as practitioners in medicine, law, public policy, and mortuary sciences. Essays are gathered under general rubrics: in the first volume the section "Death in the Cultural Context" treats issues in confronting death, with essays on fear of death, death in popular culture, spiritualism, and more. The 12 essays that make up "Death in the Social Context" consider topics such as trends in mortality, accidental death, and terrorism. Suicide, capital punishment, euthanasia, and the hospice movement are among other topics in the first volume. The second volume deals with the response to death—the social ceremonies, the different ways of disposing of bodies, and the experiences of bereavement and survivorship. Ten essays on various aspects of the legalities of death are followed by a section on the response to death in literature, music, and art. The substantive essays are generally between 9 to 15 pages, with extensive bibliographies. A very deep and detailed index, close to 50 pages, easily leads the reader to more specific information.

The single-volume *Encyclopedia of Death and Dying* (Routledge, 2000) is much less comprehensive. *Death and the Afterlife: A Cultural Encyclopedia* (ABC-CLIO, 2000) deals with the funeral and afterlife beliefs of various cultures. In breadth and heft, the *Macmillan Encyclopedia of Death and Dying* (2003) is most similar to the *Handbook of Death and Dying*. It is in a more traditional encyclopedic format with a mix of brief and longer entries. One can find similar information in both, and the two works share many of the same contributors, but the *Handbook* is perhaps more scholarly overall in tone. Both works are excellent and highly recommended. Although each has it strengths and slight differences in coverage (including the quirky—Elvis sightings in *Macmillan,* taxidermy as art in the *Handbook*), smaller libraries may be satisfied with the Macmillan work if it is already in the reference collection.

How People Live. 2003. 304p. illus. index. maps. DK, $29.99 (0-7894-9867-7). 306.

The advances in technology over the past 25 years have created the global village in ways that Marshall McLuhan could never have imagined. DK has published a book that brings together a collection of photographs and facts from around the globe to inform readers about the diversity of cultures that make up our world and to celebrate the common bonds that bind us together. The title page shows Australian Aborigine children wearing traditional body decorations while playing with a laptop computer.

The book begins with general information explaining the international borders of the world map, and the people who inhabit it. Subsequent sections are divided into geographic regions beginning with North and Central America and continuing by continent. Each section is introduced with a map and boxes with statistics and facts about the region. Within each section, two- page spreads treat different population groups (*Amish, Bengalis, New Zealanders, Persians*) or, in the case of the U.S., different regions (*East coast, Southern states*). As in other DK publications, the text is brief, with photographs dominating the pages.

Although the book features more than 80 different peoples, it is impossible to profile every group in a single volume. The spectacular photographs make this an appealing browsing item for children and adults. The brief text is both a strength and a weakness, supplying essential information for the casual reader but limiting the volume's use as a reference source for reports or school assignments. Affordable for even the smallest library with limited funds, the volume is recommended as a supplemental resource in school and public libraries.

Encyclopedia of Community: From the Village to the Virtual World. 4v. Ed. by Karen Christensen and David Levinson. 2003. 1,839p. appendixes. bibliogs. illus. index. Sage, $595 (0-7619-2598-8). 307.

Subject encyclopedias generally cover a well-defined academic area, historical period, or topic. The *Encyclopedia of Community* focuses on the hard-to-define concept of community and works to explore and position that concept within many disciplines and contexts. Entries such as *Apartheid, Blogs, County fairs, Eugenics, Gangs, Shtetls, Social Darwinism,* and *Third places* display the wide scope that the editors and contributors give to the notion of community.

Experienced reference book editors Christensen and Levinson (*Encyclopedia of Modern Asia* [Scribner, 2002] and *Encyclopedia of World Sport* [Oxford, 1999], among others) have assembled an international group of scholars to produce a set containing 500 signed entries, arranged in alphabetical order, with bibliographies and cross-references where appropriate. Some 266 of the entries are supplemented with sidebars that contain additional information, much of which comes from primary sources. An example is Emma Goldman's address to the jury during her trial as a sidebar to the entry *Anarchism*. The encyclopedia opens with lists of entries, sidebars, and contributors. A "Reader's Guide" groups the entries into 20 general categories, offering a thematic alternative to the alphabetical arrangement.

There are four potentially useful appendixes. "Resource Guides" offers 21 broad subject areas (not the same as those in the "Reader's Guide" mentioned above), each with a definition, list of applicable entries, books and Web sites for further research, journals, and organizations. "Libraries Build Community" is designed to assist librarians by describing different kinds of outreach activities. "Community in Popular Culture" lists books, movies, television programs, and other resources on the theme of community, and the "Master Bibliography of Community" compiles most of the works cited in the articles. The entries themselves are clearly written and intended for a general researcher.

In spite of all the positive aspects of this work, it is necessary to question how essential it might be to a general academic or public collection. As most of the topics can be found in other subject encyclopedias, unless the focus on "community" matches a specific need, this may not be worth the price. For collections supporting community studies programs, as well as for comprehensive collections in sociology, urban planning, and the like, it is a good choice.

Profiles of America: Facts, Figures & Statistics for Every Populated Place in the United States. 4v. 2d ed. Ed. by David Garoogian. 2003. 10,058p. indexes. maps. Grey House, paper, $595 (1-891482-80-7). 307.

This new edition of a work published in 1995 by Toucan Press is an expansive compilation of statistical information on more than 42,000 places in the U.S. There are four regional volumes: *Southern Region, Western Region, Central Region,* and *Eastern Region*. Individual volumes are organized alphabetically by state, county, and place and include maps from the Bureau of the Census. According to the publisher, more than 20 information sources were used to compile the data. These include the Bureau of the Census, Bureau of Labor Statistics, *Columbia Gazetteer of North America* (2002), FBI, and U. S. Department of Health and Human Services.

State entries in the individual volumes begin with a black-and-white census map and an alphabetical place index. Counties (parishes in Louisiana) are given a brief geographical description and yearly weather chart followed by summary statistical profiles of population, religion, economy, income, taxes, education, housing, health, and presidential election returns in 2000. Contact information is provided for government offices and local chambers of commerce, and any national or state parks in the area are noted. Following the county summaries are community profiles (39,141 in all). These communities may be cities, towns, villages, boroughs, postal areas, unincorporated postal areas, or CDPs (census designated places). The profiles begin with a brief geographical description and include historical background. Statistical profiles are similar to those for the county or parish as a whole with the addition of information on hospitals, safety, newspapers, airports, and transportation.

A "Master Alphabetical Place Index" at the conclusion of volume 4 supplements the individual state indexes interspersed throughout the set. This is useful for those who wish to locate each Arlington, Burlington, or Franklin (there are 62 in all, with 16 in Pennsylvania alone!) or verify that there is in fact a Toast, North Carolina. The statistical data are compiled in a manner useful to the general user, and the volumes are easy to browse. Though much of the information can be located elsewhere (on the Web directly from the Census Bureau or FBI, for example), public and academic libraries will appreciate having so much data available in a single source.

Dictionary of the Modern Politics of Japan. By J. A. A. Stockwin. 2003. 291p. bibliog. index. maps. Routledge, $95 (0-415-15170-8). 320.952.

"There is no country with which Japan's relationship has been more important than the United States since 1945," states Stockwin, Nissan Professor of Modern Japanese Studies at Oxford University, at the beginning of his entry on U.S.-Japan relations. That alone should warrant a closer look at a book whose title suggests analysis of a relatively narrow sector of a world power over a relatively short period of its existence. This book began, notes Stockwin, as an answer to the demands of his students for a factual database of the "increasingly confused, and confusing" subject of Japanese politics since the end of World War II.

Stockwin has written all of the clear, alphabetically arranged entries as well as a general introductory essay and another on theories of Japanese politics. Some 250 entries cover prime ministers, party leaders, and other politicians; political parties and other political entities; political crises and scandals; interest groups; the constitution and related issues; and areas of government policy. Each is followed by a list for further reading, gathered in fuller form in separate bibliographies of English-language and Japanese-language sources. A comprehensive index with extensive cross-referencing fails to cite Emperor Hirohito, for whom there is also no main entry; one will have to know to look at the entry for *Emperor (Tenno) and politics*. Nor is Herbert P. Bix's award-winning *Hirohito and the Making of Modern Japan* (HarperCollins, 2000) listed in the bibliography, although it is cited (not by title) within the entry *Emperor (Tenno) and politics*. The Constitution of 1946, although ably summarized in the appropriate entry, is perhaps short enough to have been included in its entirety as an appendix. These quibbles aside, *Dictionary of the Modern Politics of Japan* is highly recommended for academic and larger public libraries, especially where there is keen interest in Japan or world politics. *Encyclopedia of Contemporary Japanese Culture* (Routledge, 2002) is highly recommended for a comprehensive view of Japan covering the same time period.

Encyclopedia of Public Administration and Public Policy. By David Schultz. 2003. 526p. bibliogs. illus. index. Facts On File, $75 (0-8160-4799-5). 320.973.

In an effort "to clarify what government agencies and their public administrators do and why," A–Z entries on American bureaucracy focus on events, topics, and personalities in public administration. More than 350 signed entries describe the functions, background, and importance of federal programs and agencies (e.g., *Aid to Families with Dependent Children, Department of Agriculture*); important laws (e.g., *Clean Air Act*); and public administration concepts and issues (e.g., *Faith-based initiatives, Earned income tax credit, Eminent domain, Lobbying, Police power*).

Information differs depending on the type of entry. For instance, the entry on a governmental concept such as *Progressive property tax* includes several paragraphs explaining the concept and its use in local government as well as implications for the future use of this tax as a revenue source. Biographical entries provide both birth and, if relevant, death dates (years only) and a short profile that emphasizes the subject's impact on public administration. Biographical subjects include some presidents; social reformers and activists (Jane Addams, Mary Parker Follett); public administration authors (Frank Goodnow, Dwight Waldo); and behavioral scientists (Abraham Maslow, Max Weber).

The encyclopedia has an index as well as some standard federal documents such as "How a Bill Becomes a Law," the U.S. Constitution, the Bill of Rights, and a helpful chapter, "Looking for Government Information."

This volume is suitable for readers at the high-school level and up. Its value for the general public is in helping the average person get a better understanding of government and the public policy process. For public administrators the volume should be used as a desk reference, kept near the phone book, annual report, personnel manual, and budget documents. Recommended for public and academic libraries.

Encyclopedia of American Religion and Politics. By Paul Djupe and Laura Olson. 2003. 512p. bibliogs. illus. index. Facts On File, $85 (0-8160-4582-8). 322.

This encyclopedia brings together "in one place 'the facts' about the people, groups, jurisprudence, forces, and phenomena that together tell the story of the interaction between religion and politics in America." A team of 135 scholars wrote the more than 600 entries, which focus on several themes, among them the roles played by religious organizations and beliefs in shaping American politics; religion and the Constitution; and the intersections between religion, political theory, and public policy.

The A–Z entries include discussions of the *Abolitionist movement, Anti-Defamation League, Christian social ethics, Focus on the Family, Gay and lesbian marriage,* and *Raid on Waco,* among other topics. Numerous men and women who had influence on the world of religion and politics, such as Ralph Abernathy, Mary Baker Eddy, Cotton Mather, and several U.S. presidents, are included. There are also entries for court cases that left their mark on the religious and political landscape of the U.S. Other entries cover different religious traditions, including Christian Science, Hinduism, Islam, and Judaism. Length ranges from approximately half of a page to two pages. Many entries conclude with a list of further readings.

This work offers general information for the beginning researcher and could be used as a springboard to further research. It joins two similar-sounding but older titles. *Encyclopedia of Religion in American Politics* (Oryx, 1998) covers many of the same topics in its 700 short entries and also provides some supporting material, such as a collection of speeches and documents and a time line. *Encyclopedia of Politics and Religion* (Congressional Quarterly, 1999) offers a global perspective. Academic and larger public libraries that don't already have a resource on the relationship between politics and religion in the U.S., or that need to expand or update their holdings, might do well to include this newer volume in their collection.

Encyclopedia of Religious Freedom. Ed. by Catharine Cookson. 2003. 555p. bibliogs. illus. index. Routledge, $125 (0-415-94181-4). 323.44.

The fourth volume in Routledge's Religion and Society series, this encyclopedia covers key concepts and issues related to religious freedom, topics in U.S. and world history, world religions, the rights of religious minorities, and the philosophical and legal framework of religious freedom, among many other topics. The 140 essays vary in length from one to several pages and are mostly written by college professors. The quality and usefulness of individual entries vary: two entries on Jehovah's Witnesses (international and U.S.), for example, provide an excellent overview; other entries, such as *Middle East,* attempt to survey very broad topics in too few words.

The chronological scope and geographical range of coverage are impressive: the entries include *Augustine on religious coercion* (fourth century C.E.), *Imperial China,* and the *Universal Declaration of Human Rights* (1948). Especially noteworthy are the generally excellent bibliographies at the end of each entry. The prominent sidebars scattered throughout the volume—helpfully citing the source—provide useful and, occasionally, very hard-to-locate documentary material (e.g., a list of Coptic Christians tortured in Egypt in 1998). The topical list of entries in the introduction and a well-organized index facilitate access.

This volume fills a void in reference sources on this increasingly important topic and is recommended for academic and large public libraries.

The Greenwood Encyclopedia of African American Civil Rights: From Emancipation to the Twenty-First Century. 2v. Ed. by Charles D. Lowery and John F. Marszalek. 2003. 920p. bibliogs. illus. index. Greenwood, $175 (0-313-32171-X). 323.1.

This set is a revision of *Encyclopedia of African American Civil Rights* (1992), providing updates; an enlarged chronology; and, perhaps most impressive, 120 primary documents. Entries are alphabetically arranged and cross-referenced, and each is followed by a selected bibliography. Many of the entries focus on seminal political issues of the 1950s and 1960s—*Black Power, March on Washington, Voter Education Project*—but also cover important developments both before and after this time. Other entries are biographical, ranging from politicians to writers, artists, actors, musicians, and athletes. Important literary documents are covered, including not only novels, plays, and political treatises but also journals, such as the long-gone *Negro World* and the still-published *Journal of Negro Education.* Some entries are more cultural than political (*"Black Is Beautiful,"* for example), but all are well written and concise.

The entries are followed by a detailed time line beginning in 1859, with the opening of a few schools for blacks, and ending in 2003, with the Supreme Court decisions on affirmative action at the University of Michigan. An eight-page selected bibliography follows.

More than half of the second volume of this encyclopedia is devoted to primary documents. These are most often only excerpts, though in some instances entire documents are included. For example, Justice John Marshall Harlan's dissenting opinion on *Plessy* v. *Ferguson* is included in full, as is Lincoln's Emancipation Proclamation. Other materials include poems (like Claude McKay's "If We Must Die"), speeches (Martin Luther King's "I Have a Dream"), interviews with and essays by famous writers and politicians ("Maya Angelou on the 'Plague of Racism'"), and constitutional amendments and acts of Congress (the Civil Rights Act). The plethora of materials here is striking in its range and variety, and citations are listed after each. The preface to the primary documents notes that materials representing "setbacks in the struggle" have been intentionally left out. No further explanation is given, but the decision seems questionable when considering that in a movement for cultural and national change much can be learned from failures, as well as successes.

The editors have attempted to bring all of the information up-to-date to September 2003. Like the previous version, this set is recommended for high-school, public, and academic libraries.

The Wilson Chronology of Human Rights. Ed. by David Levinson. 2003. 573p. bibliog. index. Wilson, $100 (0-8242-0972-9). 323.

This chronological history of human rights documents thousands of human rights struggles and violations from as early as 3,000 B.C.E. to 2002. The chronology is arranged in nine chapters covering topics such as "Civil Rights," "Children's Rights," "Gay Rights," and "Refugee Rights." Editor Levinson, a cultural anthropologist, is author or editor of more than 30 books, including the *Encyclopedia of Cultural Anthropology* (Holt, 1996), the award-winning *Encyclopedia of World Cultures* (G. K. Hall, 1996), and *The Encyclopedia of Human Emotions* (Macmillan, 1999).

Within each chapter, events are arranged year-by-year and described in entries that average around six lines in length. When warranted, events are recorded in multiple sections; for example, the papal bull of 1484 and related events in 1486, condemning the spread of witchcraft in Germany, are under both "Women's Rights" and "Religious Rights." As with any chronology, content is not exhaustive. The "Indigenous Rights" section begins in 1492 with Columbus' voyage to the New World although human rights violations against the indigenous peoples began long before 1492. For example, the Japanese began a campaign against the indigenous Ainu almost 600 years before Columbus landed on the island of San Salvador (Guanahani). There is no mention of the Ainu until 1984, in an entry that references their conquest in the ninth century.

Despite any missing content, the chronology is copious, well arranged, and extensively indexed. The 82-page subject index lists general topics, personal names, organization names, and places. A 65-item bibliography includes books, journals, Web sites, and organizations.

Magill's Great Events from History II: Human Rights Series (Salem, 1992) is similar in concept but has a scope of 1900 to 1991. *The Wilson Chronology of Human Rights* is recommended for academic and public libraries.

★**American Presidential Campaigns and Elections.** 3v. Ed. by William G. Shade and Ballard C. Campbell. 2003. 1,137p. appendixes. bibliogs. glossary. illus. indexes. maps. Sharpe, $325 (0-7656-8042-4). 324.973.

Professors Shade and Campbell are respectively affiliated with Lehigh University and Northeastern University. With the assistance of 44 contributors, they have compiled this set intended for general readers and scholars. It contains 62 signed essays, six appendixes, and two indexes. The first eight essays cover an assortment of topics, among them the electoral college, the role of the media, and campaign finances. Following this there is an analysis of every presidential election from 1788–89 to 2000.

Each election chapter offers a description of the issues, conventions, campaigns, and election results; a chronology; a "highlight" sidebar focusing on an interesting aspect of the election; a vote analysis in chart and map form; a bibliography; and a collection of between five and seven documents. Examples of the highlight essays include a discussion of the Missouri Compromise of 1820 and an analysis of the "Willie" Horton story and its role in the election of 1988. Among the documents are Thomas Jefferson's first message to Congress in 1801; excerpts from the Lincoln-Douglas debate on October 15, 1858; and "Who Will Then Speak for the Common Good?"—Barbara

Jordan's keynote address at the Democratic National Convention in 1976. Other documents include letters, slogans, campaign songs, speeches, editorials, and cartoons. Also provided are more than 170 fact boxes presenting brief biographical summaries for each candidate, including place and date of birth, political party, parents' names, schooling, marriage, family, military service, career, and death information. The vote analysis shows both the popular and electoral vote returns, and the 54 maps show the electoral vote. Numerous black-and-white illustrations are appropriately placed throughout the text. Each volume comes with a table of contents and a list of features—fact boxes, highlights, election returns, maps, and documents—for the set. The separate list of features is a useful aid.

Several appendixes round out the work. The first contains excerpts on the electoral college and the presidency from the U.S. Constitution. This is followed by a glossary with definitions of 77 terms. Next are two chronologies, one of political parties and one of events; a bibliography with more than 500 citations; and an extensive list of the sources used for election statistics. The general index is arranged by subject, and a biographical index directs users to all references to people throughout the text. Both indexes are repeated in each volume.

Although there are other reference sources that cover various aspects of U.S. presidential elections, none provide this kind of detailed election-by-election history. The text is both readable and informative, enhanced by good organization, well-chosen features, and attractive design. This reference will prove valuable to high- school, academic, and public library reference collections.

Encyclopedia of Presidential Campaigns, Slogans, Issues, and Platforms. By Robert North Roberts and Scott John Hammond. 2004. 395p. appendix. bibliogs. illus. index. Greenwood, $75 (0-313-31973-1). 324.973.

The authors' intention in this volume meant for college undergraduates and high-school students is to "support the initial stages of a student's inquiry and ensure the continued legacy of a particularly fascinating aspect of the American political past—presidential politics." Part 1 explores each presidential campaign from 1789 through 2000. Each entry examines issues and slogans and briefly describes the course of the campaign. Important issues, programs, slogans, and platforms make up the alphabetically arranged entries in part 2 and include both broad, general entries (e.g., *Affirmative action, Iran hostage crisis, School prayer issue*) as well as shorter entries focused on specific events, individuals, slogans, or phrases (e.g., *"Daisy" campaign ad, Fireside chat, "Happy Days Are Here Again," "Read My Lips, No New Taxes"*). Entries for presidential candidates are cross-referenced to the appropriate campaigns in part 1. Cross-references are heavily used as boldface terms or as *see also* references at the end of each entry. Suggested readings are also included with each entry.

A "Guide to Related Topics," which groups topics under general headings such as "Campaign Management and the Tools of Political Persuasion," "Elections Decided by Electoral College Contrary to Popular Vote," and "Presidential Candidates," offers a quick summary of themes found throughout the book. Historical context is provided by a "Timeline of Presidential Campaigns." The appendix includes a table of selected major party platforms from 1840 to 2000. The planks are grouped under economic policies, social and political principles, civil rights and liberties, foreign affairs, and others. A selected bibliography and an index complete the book.

The goal of stimulating the student toward further exploration and research into presidential politics and its rich history is well served by this clearly written and easy-to-use tool. It will be an excellent addition to high-school and undergraduate libraries as well as public libraries.

United States Gubernatorial Elections, 1776–1860: The Official Results by State and County. By Michael J. Dubin. 2003. 300p. bibliog. index. tables. McFarland, $75 (0-7864-1439-1). 324.973.

This reference source claims to be unique in its coverage of providing complete returns for all gubernatorial elections of the period. Three groups of data sources were used to assemble the returns: journals of the various legislatures, original manuscript data, and returns as published in newspapers.

Organization is in two parts. The annual summary consists of statewide votes for each year beginning in 1776, providing state, date of election, total votes, and percentage of votes. The second section contains returns by county for each state, arranged alphabetically by state and then chronologically within each state. In this section, besides the county returns, other data are given, including the date when the state entered the union, the date of the first gubernatorial election, the term of the governor, election day, and any limits on the office. Population figures for each of the decades are also provided. A candidate index, arranged by state, gives the name of the candidate and the date he was elected. Another special feature is two pages of statistical tables that provide the length of term of each of the governors, the methods of election, term limits, and party affiliation.

This type of reference work requires a great deal of research using materials that vary from state to state and election to election. It's too bad that all libraries really cannot justify this reference volume's purchase. Although *United States Gubernatorial Elections, 1776– 1860* is a unique source, it would probably only be valuable in a larger public library, state library, or university reference collection.

Colonialism: An International Social, Cultural, and Political Encyclopedia. 3v. Ed. by Melvin E. Page. 2003. 1,208p. bibliogs. illus. index. maps. ABC-CLIO, $285 (1-57607-335- 1). 325.

Page, professor of history at East Tennessee State University, has edited a work that deals with "modern" colonialism, from about 1400 C.E. to the present. Its intended audience is high-school students, undergraduates, and the general public. There are more than 600 entries varying in length from half a page to four and a half pages. Entries cover geographical concepts and entities (*Angola, Johannesburg, Spanish empire, U.S. empire*); ideas (*Absolutism, Pacifism*); events (*Boxer Rebellion, Crimean War, Lewis and Clark expedition*); peoples (*Incas, Kurds, Puritans*); and individuals (Dean Acheson, Christopher Columbus, Rudyard Kipling, V. S. Naipaul), among a slew of other topics. The documents section that comprises volume 3 includes material like the Monroe Doctrine, Ho Chi Minh's Independence Speech, and the U.S. Declaration of Independence. Page is no stranger to the subject of colonialism, having also written *Africa and the First World War* (St. Martin's, 1987) and *The Chiwaya War: Malawians and the First World War* (Westview, 2000).

The first two volumes of the set contain the alphabetical entries as well as a section of empires' chronologies, which helps put the entries into context. Each entry includes a list of further readings, but there is no general bibliography. Entries are signed by their authors, and they include cross-references to other pertinent entries. The work also includes photographs and maps.

Balanced and wide ranging, this encyclopedia is a very helpful tool for those interested in or doing basic research on modern colonialism. Primary documents can be difficult to find, so their inclusion in volume 3 will be especially useful for the novice researcher. One minor flaw is the exclusion of a holistic bibliography. The set is recommended for public, high-school, and undergraduate libraries.

Encyclopedia of American Foreign Policy. By Glenn Hastedt. 2004. 562p. bibliogs. illus. index. maps. Facts On File, $85 (0-8160- 4642-5). 327.73.

Written by a professor of political science, this reference work provides an accessible introduction to U.S. foreign policy from the American Revolution to present-day events such as the war in Iraq. The volume contains about 500 entries, which are arranged alphabetically and range from a few paragraphs to several pages in length. Access to articles is aided by cross-references and a precise index. Many articles include suggestions for further readings. The encyclopedia also contains a detailed bibliography. Black-and- white pictures and maps complement the text.

Hastedt states that his choice of entries reflects both the "standard coverage" of American foreign policy and his own approach to teaching and research. The articles discuss important figures (*Kissinger, Henry*), key events (*Vietnam War*), relevant organizations (*North Atlantic Treaty Organization*), major legislation (*National Security Act, 1947*), countries (*Cuba*), and key concepts (*Brinkmanship*). There is coverage of both traditional foreign-policy topics (*Cold war, Détente, Diplomacy*) and contemporary matters (*Environment, Globalization, Women and American foreign policy*). However, there are some gaps. For example, in contrast to other recent reference works on American foreign policy, there is no discussion devoted to African Americans or race. Furthermore, the encyclopedia includes entries on some of the nations of the former Soviet Union, including *Baltic states* and *Central Asian republics,* but there are no entries on Belarus or Ukraine. Although it is impossible to cover every aspect of American foreign policy, these omissions seem to be a significant oversight.

The work provides a beginning point for the study of American foreign policy. It is less comprehensive than the *Encyclopedia of American Foreign Policy* (2d ed., Scribner, 2001) and the *Encyclopedia of U.S. Foreign Relations* (Oxford, 1997), although it is more current, covering topics such as the Patriot Act and the terrorist attacks of September 11. Suitable for high-school, academic, and large public libraries.

Encyclopedia of the Central Intelligence Agency. By W. Thomas Smith Jr. 2003. 282p. bibliog. illus. index. Facts On File, $60 (0-8160-4666-2). 327.1273.

A freelance writer with military experience has brought together more than 500 historical, biographical, and general entries about the intelligence-gathering, covert-action agency established in 1947. Drawing from nearly 300 resources (books, articles, Web sites), the author describes events, lives, operations, and terms. Cross-references, black-and-white photos, acronyms and abbreviations, an organization chart, frequently asked questions sent to the CIA Web site, a list of directors and deputy directors, a current bibliography, and an accurate index add to the reference value.

Current through March 2003, the encyclopedia also covers predecessor organizations such as the World War II–era Office of Strategic Services (OSS). Entry length varies from a few lines for *Chief of outpost* and *Safe house* to more than two pages, with the longer entries generally treating individuals such Aldrich Ames and Fidel Castro. Information is duplicated in some entries, such as in *Walker, John Anthony, Jr.* and *Walker family spy ring*, and in individual entries on the Watergate figures. The work covers terrorism extensively, not only in the entry *September 11, 2001, terrorist attacks on the United States*, which is one of the longest in the volume, but also in entries for Osama bin Laden and the Department of Homeland Security, among others.

Although much of the information is available in other resources, the book brings together a large array of pertinent detail and will be useful in high-school, public, and academic libraries.

Work in America: An Encyclopedia of History, Policy, and Society. 2v. Ed. by Carl E. Van Horn and Herbert A. Schaffner. 2003. 741p. appendixes. bibliogs. illus. index. ABC-CLIO, $185 (1-57607-676-8); e-book, $200 (1-57607-677-6). 331.

It is always a pleasure to handle a well-produced, accessible reference source, and this is an outstanding example. In 256 *A–Z* signed, well-written entries, it conveys the impact of the workplace throughout the nation's history. The editors are with the John J. Heldrich Center for Workforce Development at Rutgers University, and the 73 other contributors are from a variety of universities, with several from Rutgers.

Focusing on developments since the Industrial Revolution, entries cover specific businesses, industries, and types of work; labor relations; compensation and benefits; notable individuals, groups, and organizations; theories and trends; legislation and public policy; training; immigration issues; and more. In addition to the table of contents, there is a listing of entries by category. The articles, including the ones on the work life of Native Americans, mid-twentieth-century mine union leader John L. Lewis, and environmental concerns in NAFTA, are balanced in presentation. Further readings at the end of each entry document the article and lead the user further, as do *see also* references. The length is sufficient to fully explain the topic; for example, *American slavery* is seven and one-half pages long. Material is current into 2003.

An accurate index, appendixes, black-and-white photos, and extensive references enhance articles on historical and contemporary issues and individuals. This appears to be the first comprehensive reference work on labor in America. *Encyclopedia of American Social History* (Scribner, 1993) is broader in scope, and the *St. James Encyclopedia of Labor History Worldwide: Major Events in Labor History and Their Impact* (St. James, 2004) covers 300 key events. Although many entries are covered in other sources, this work will fill an information need in large public and academic libraries.

Business, Economics, Resources

Ferguson's Career Guidance Center. [Internet database]. Ferguson, pricing on request [http://www.fergpubco.com]. (Last accessed September 5, 2003).

Expanding on Ferguson's *Encyclopedia of Careers and Vocational Guidance*, the gold standard of multivolume print career reference sources, and Facts On File's Career Opportunities series, this is an update of the online *Career Guidance Center*. The newly named *Ferguson's Career Guidance Center* contains a total of 2,050 articles on careers and lists some 23,000 industry resources.

Navigation of the uncluttered screens is straightforward, the writing is uniformly clear, and the breadth of coverage is unsurpassed. Depth of coverage for a career or vocational choice, when combined with the additional sources of information provided and the easy links to related careers, is just about everything one could ask of a comprehensive career source. The 94 industry categories of *Encyclopedia of Careers and Vocational Guidance* are used to classify all career articles; each industry category, from *Accounting* to *Wood*, has a helpful profile (which is, in many cases, the Background section of the *Encyclopedia*). The industry profile for *Accounting* links to 7 career descriptions and 37 additional related careers. The seven printed pages for the first of these career descriptions, *Accountants and Auditors*, gives summary information, job history, duties, work environment, salary range, employment prospects, advancement prospects, education and training needed, experience/skills/personality traits, best geographical location, licensure/certification requirements, job exploration, tips for getting the job, and resources for further information (including addresses, phone numbers, Web links, and e-mail addresses).

It appears that the majority of career articles and all of the industry profiles are taken directly from the *Encyclopedia*. Among the new features are a more accessible interface, ability to search by U.S. and Canadian government career indexes, and a link to Ferguson's bimonthly *Career Opportunities News*, whose latest brief articles include "Résumés Should Not Be Works of Fiction" and "New Test Seeks to Validate MBA Degrees." Finally, one may search for academic or athletic scholarship information, data on and links to colleges and universities with cooperative education programs, careers that do not require four-year degrees, and a checklist of basic employability skills. A search for athletic scholarships resulted in 1,519 hits, while a search for music scholarships produced only 6 hits; libraries should not rely on this as their only source of scholarship information.

This database is highly recommended for high-school, academic, and public libraries. Libraries already owning the superb *Encyclopedia of Careers and Vocational Guidance* will have to weigh the added value of *Ferguson's Career Guidance Center*.

HQ Online. 2004. [Online database]. Omnigraphics, pricing from $185 [http:// www.headquartersonline.com]. (Last accessed April 22, 2004).

The print directory *Headquarters USA* is now available as a searchable electronic database called *HQ Online*. Like the print edition, it includes individually selected associations, consulates and embassies, convention centers, military bases, sports teams, and UN missions, as well as nationally significant businesses in construction, retail, manufacturing, communications, mining, service, and wholesale industries. Also included are government agencies, cultural and educational institutions, and prominent leaders and other people of national interest. Public companies are selected on a variety of criteria including size; companies in certain technological fields that may be of special interest, such as the 334 biotechnology companies listed, are included regardless of size.

Listings can be searched by name or by subject. In Name Search, listings are searchable by ticker symbol and by name; limits by city, state, zip code, and telephone area code are available. Users can also limit to organizations that have toll- free or fax numbers or Web sites. In Subject Search, users can enter keywords, select from a list of general subjects like Arts and Humanities or Clothing and Textiles, or browse an alphabetical list of all subject headings from *Abilene, TX—Radio Stations* to *Zoos and Wildlife Parks*. A further search option is provided by the Quick Links. Users can drill down from very general categories like Attractions or Magazines and Newspapers to specific listings for sports museums or trade magazines and then limit by state. Under the People category users can browse lists of business leaders, print journalists, motivational speakers, TV news personalities, and more and find contact information. Though parts of the database include Canada in searches, the Government section concentrates on the U.S. Most listings include links to relevant Web sites.

Downloading is simple and fast. Check boxes next to each listing allow the selection of specific records, and selections can be downloaded in text format. A maximum of 25 records can be downloaded at one time. One glitch occurs in searching for individuals. Entering a person's name in Name Search works only if the user figures out that the last name of the individual must be entered first. If users enter *George Bush*, they get the

George Bush Library and Museum but neither President Bush. An example showing users how to enter personal names would be a help. Another drawback is the limited search engine. None of the options that many users would be accustomed to, such as AND operators and phrase searching, are available, and Advanced Search only allows users to limit searches by city, state, zip code, or area code.

Making all their lists and data more searchable in a "Google-esque" fashion would be a big improvement for *HQ Online*. Still, the database is definitely more versatile and user-friendly than a print directory, and libraries where the print version is heavily used will want to consider it.

The American Economy: A Historical Encyclopedia. 2v. Ed. by Cynthia Clark Northrup. 2003. 709p. bibliogs. index. ABC-CLIO, $185 (1-57607-866-3); e-book, $200 (1-57607-867-1). 330.973.

This is a work designed as "a reference tool for anyone who wishes to learn more about the role of economic policy in American history" from colonial times to the present. Volume 1 provides more than 500 brief, alphabetically arranged entries with information on, among other topics, concepts such as *Ecosocialism, Globalization,* and *Industrial heartland;* prominent individuals such as Henry Ford, John Maynard Keynes, and Ralph Nader; and events such as *French and Indian War, Industrial Revolution,* and the *Yazoo land companies* scandal. Most of the contributors are faculty connected with higher education. The writing style is geared to upper-level secondary-school students.

Volume 2 presents 31 essays and 20 primary source documents. The signed essays are intended to be read as a whole, often running from three to five pages. Unlike the short entries in the first volume, they offer relatively comprehensive treatment of a subject and its history, connection with other events, and contemporary impact on American society. Essay topics range from "Energy Policy" to "Intellectual Property" to "Urbanization," and all contain a brief bibliography of serial and monographic sources. As with any collection of essays, writing style varies by contributor. The primary source document section gives readers the full text of, for example, the Treaty of Guadalupe Hidalgo, the Emancipation Proclamation, and Lyndon Johnson's Great Society speech. Volume 2 concludes with a lengthy bibliography and very detailed subject index.

This is the type of reference source that will hold its value even as more and more reference materials migrate from print to electronic format (although it is also offered in an e-book version). Rather than attempting to offer up-to-date facts and figures, it focuses on definitions, identifications, and carefully considered overviews. It will be a welcome addition to reference collections serving primarily secondary-school and undergraduate students.

Distinguished Women Economists. Ed. by James Cicarelli and Julianne Cicarelli. 2003. 244p. appendix. bibliogs. index. Greenwood, $65 (0-313-30331-2). 330.

The 51 entries in this biographical dictionary represent women who have advanced the field of economics through breakthroughs in theory, dissemination of knowledge, and application of economic reasoning. Although not every one of the women presented here is a trailblazer, each one "has made a difference in the scope, depth, or use of economics." The women who are covered range from Jane Haldimand Marcet (1769–1858), who wrote popular books on economics for young people, to Caroline M. Hoxby (1966–), an expert on the economics of education.

Each entry provides a short introduction, a biographical sketch, a summary of contributions, and a selected bibliography. The introductions are designed to tag the subject and distinguish her from the other entries. For example, the introduction to Harriet Hardy Taylor Mill (1807–1858) indicates that she was a "free thinker and a creative intellectual" who was unable to "escape the prejudices of her era." Although her husband, economist John Stuart Mill, acknowledged their intellectual partnership, history largely forgot the considerable contributions she made to his famous nineteenth-century works. *Principles of Political Economy* and *On Liberty,* both traditionally attributed solely to J. S. Mill, were written to a significant degree by Harriet Mill, and this is clearly stated in J. S. Mill's *Autobiography.* Quoting directly from *Autobiography, Distinguished Women Economists* nicely integrates primary source material within the information it presents.

Bibliographies generally contain a dozen or so book and journal citations, some as recent as 2002. Following the entries is a list of individuals arranged by date of birth.

With any one-volume biographical encyclopedia, one has to consider whether the cost may be justified in light of how easy it is to simply enter a name on a standard Internet search engine. On the other hand, *Distinguished Women Economists* pulls information on 51 women into one easily accessible book, and the reader can be sure of academic credibility. It is probably worth its price for any large public or academic library supporting programs in either women's studies or economics.

Industrial Revolution: Almanac. By James L. Outman and Elisabeth M. Outman. 2003. 242p. bibliogs. glossary. illus. index. UXL, $55 (0-7876-6513-4). 330.9.

Industrial Revolution: Biographies. By James L. Outman and Elisabeth M. Outman. 2003. 218p. bibliogs. illus. index. UXL, $55 (0-7876-6514-2). 330.9.

Industrial Revolution: Primary Sources. By James L. Outman and Elisabeth M. Outman. 2003. 212p. bibliogs. illus. index. UXL, $55 (0-7876-6515-0). 330.9.

Like other sets in the UXL history series for middle school through high school, each volume in this new offering—*Almanac, Biographies,* and *Primary Sources*—may be purchased separately. A set index is also available.

The *Almanac* consists of 8 chapters, approximately 60 black-and-white photographs, sources for further study, a time line, a glossary, and an index. The first four chapters focus on England, where the first phase of the Industrial Revolution (1750–1850) was dominated by the coal-driven steam engine and textile machines. The last four chapters focus on the second phase, which occurred mainly in the U.S. and continental Europe, from 1850 to 1940, and was driven by the internal combustion engine and electricity.

The 25 essays in *Biographies* provide biographical information with an emphasis on each person's contribution or impact on the Industrial Revolution. Personages include economic philosophers (such as Karl Marx and Adam Smith); innovators (Henry Ford, Robert Fulton, Eli Whitney); financial giants and robber barons (Andrew Carnegie, John D. Rockefeller); crusading journalists (Upton Sinclair and Ida Tarbell); and unionizer Mother Jones. More than 50 black-and-white photographs complement the text together with further reading, a time line, and index.

Primary Sources offers 27 full or excerpted documents, speeches, or testimony from the period. The documents are arranged in four thematic chapters with each entry including an introduction, "Things to Remember" while reading the document, definitions of difficult terms, and a follow-up of what happened after the document was published. Among the documents are excerpts from Adam Smith's *Wealth of Nations* and Upton Sinclair's *The Jungle,* letters from Luddites, newspaper accounts regarding the telegraph, and an excerpt from the U.S. Supreme Court decision *Northern Securities Co. v. United States,* 1904. Forty black-and-white photographs, sources for further reading, a time line, and an index round out the *Primary Sources* volume.

This is an excellent adjunct to American and world history units and classes on economics and labor movements. The primary documents meet the needs of student researchers. Recommended for school and public libraries.

The Oxford Encyclopedia of Economic History. 5v. Ed. by Joel Mokyr. 2003. 2,800p. bibliogs. illus. index. Oxford, $695 (0-19-510507-9). 330.

Economist John Hicks wrote that "a major function of economic history . . . is to be a forum where economists and political scientists, lawyers, sociologists, and historians . . . can meet and talk to one another." Similarly, scholars and students in these disciplines, as well as business and public administration, will find *The Oxford Encyclopedia of Economic History* a valuable interdisciplinary reference tool. More than 875 signed articles cover all aspects of economic history, including concepts and definitions, institutions, historical events, and people. Major entries address macroeconomic topics such as consumption, national income accounts, and economic growth. Money, banking, and finance are well covered with essays ranging from the history of banking to the futures market. In addition, the set includes entries on the economic histories of more than 100 countries and regions and 36 cities as well as surveys of more than 80 industries. These surveys provide a historical overview of the industry and a discussion of technological change, organization, markets, and trade. Biographical essays of 36 economists and economic historians will be welcomed by students researching the individuals covered, who range from Adam Smith (1773–1790) to Robert Fogel (1926–). Also here are essays on inventors, entrepreneurs, bankers, and labor leaders.

The interdisciplinary nature of the encyclopedia is illustrated by entries encompassing *Child care, Pollution, Public health,* and *Religion.* Volume 5 includes a topical outline of articles, which librarians should consult upon receipt of the set to familiarize themselves with the many areas of study to which the essays will be relevant. This volume also offers a list of relevant Internet sites and an extremely comprehensive index. Each essay has a bibliography with an average of about 10 sources, although some are much longer.

Although there are numerous encyclopedias of economics and two widely held encyclopedias of U.S. economic history (*Encyclopedia of American Economic History* [Scribner, 1980] and *Gale Encyclopedia of U.S. Economic History* [1999]), there is no source comparable to this. Highly recommended for all academic libraries as well as larger public libraries.

Career Discovery Encyclopedia. 8v. 5th ed. 2003. glossary. illus. index. Ferguson, $175 (0-89434-275-4). 331.7.

In its latest edition, this career resource continues to provide very basic information for upper-elementary and middle-school students. More than 650 entries cover careers from *Accountants* and *Actors* to *Zookeepers* and *Zoologists.* Among the more than 70 new entries are *Animal handlers, Campaign workers, Epidemiologists,* and *Science and medical writers.*

Entries are arranged alphabetically. Each two-page spread is divided into sections that briefly explain what people in the career typically do, what education and training are required, what the prospects for growth are, and how to obtain more information. This last section provides contact information for relevant organizations and associations, most of which appear to be well chosen. Additional entry features include a black-and-white photograph and a box summarizing relevant school subjects and personal interests, minimum education level, salary range, and outlook. Another box refers the reader to entries for jobs that are related. Each volume concludes with the same two-page glossary and set index. Volume 8 also contains a "Guide for Occupational Exploration Index" and "National Occupational Classification System Index" as well as the standard "Dictionary of Occupational Titles Index" and the new "Occupational Information Network–Standard Occupational Classification Index."

Do libraries that own the fourth edition, published in 2000, need to update? Unlike other career reference sources, *Career Discovery Encyclopedia* is not heavy with statistical information that quickly becomes obsolete. On the other hand, many entries have been revised to reflect the conditions of the last two or three years. For example, *Cruise ship workers, Hotel and motel managers and workers,* and *Pilots* all refer to the downturn in travel and tourism after September 11, 2001. It is important to supply students with fresh materials in this popular subject area, and the new edition of *Career Discovery Encyclopedia* is definitely recommended for school and public libraries.

Historical Encyclopedia of American Labor. 2v. Ed. by Robert E. Weir and James P. Hanlan. 2004. 733p. appendix. bibliogs. illus. index. Greenwood, $175 (0-313-31840-9). 331.88.

Like the recent *Work in America* [RBB My 1 04], this wonderful resource redresses the absence of the organized labor movement in American social history reference material. The struggles and achievements of women and minority groups continue to be documented in information resources, but until now organized labor's story has been lacking. The authors, history professors in Massachusetts who have written about the working class, have enlisted 79 other contributors, primarily from universities in the Northeast.

The 400 alphabetically arranged and signed entries on unions, leaders, statutes, court cases, and terms range from one paragraph to several pages, as the subject requires. Cross-references, highlighted related entries, exact birth and death dates, and suggested readings with each entry are very helpful.

Important leaders, such as Dolores Huerta, who worked with Cesar Chavez in organizing farm workers, and significant but less known organizations (for example, 9 to 5, the National Association of Working Women) have prominent entries. Both are mentioned in *Work in America* but only in a larger context. The earlier resource does have a four-page article on the North American Free Trade Agreement, as compared with one paragraph in the current work. It also has solid entries on ergonomics, workplace safety, and Native Americans, which are not included here. *Historical Encyclopedia of American Labor* is very good on social and leadership changes in unionism; women and minority issues; political radicalism throughout labor history; and economic changes, such as automation and globalization. It is balanced and accurate.

The 55 alphabetically arranged documents in the appendix, many of them little known, encompass nineteenth- and twentieth-century statutes, worker interviews, congressional testimony, passages from literature, and articles. An extensive 12-page bibliography of books and Web sites, an accurate index, and 100 illustrations enhance the work.

Outstanding in concept, coverage, layout, and documentation, this work is highly recommended for public, academic and high-school libraries even if they have the earlier work. It will be useful for student reports, research projects, and learning about less known people, ideas, events, and organizations that have been crucial in American history.

A World History of Tax Rebellions: An Encyclopedia of Tax Rebels, Revolts, and Riots from Antiquity to the Present. By David F. Burg. 2003. 502p. appendix. bibliogs. illus. index. Routledge, $95 (0-415-92498-7). 336.2.

The author of this resource has written other reference works, mainly on U.S. history. In the current book, we learn about the long, historical struggle against taxes over many civilizations and across centuries, from measures taken to relieve oppressive taxes in Babylonia around 2350 B.C.E. to a protest on Ascension Island in 2002. Tax revolt has been part of larger economic, political, social, and religious issues in every nation.

After a 10-page chronological list of rebellions over the centuries (nearly every year in the past few centuries), the author provides an 8-page cross-cultural summary of terms and strategies, such as *underground economy.* Subsequent chapters cover the "Ancient World"; "Early Middle Ages, A.D. 365–1199"; "Late Middle Ages, 1200–1500"; "Renaissance to Enlightenment, 1500–1700"; "Eighteenth Century"; "Nineteenth Century"; and "Twentieth and Twenty-First Centuries." The format for each chapter is the same: chronological entries on revolts ranging from a paragraph to a few pages, with running dates in the margins, and a bibliographic reference for each entry. The work concludes with brief biographies, a list of tax-revolt events arranged by empire or nation, a bibliography, and an accurate 34-page double-column index.

This work appears to be unique with its wide span of nations and times. It will be valuable in academic libraries, especially where there is a business school, as well as larger public libraries.

Business and Industry. 11v. Ed. by William R. Childs and others. 2004. 1,584p. bibliogs. glossaries. illus. indexes. Marshall Cavendish, $459.95 (0-7614-7430-7). 338.

Targeted for high-school students, this encyclopedia introduces them to the effect business and industry have on people's daily lives. Focusing on the U.S., the articles present an overview of how capitalism works and how it is different from competing economic systems like mercantilism, socialism, and communism. Individuals who have been important to the evolution of capitalism, like Henry Ford, Alan Greenspan, and Adam Smith, have biographies, as do more than 50 other entrepreneurs, labor leaders, economists, and venture capitalists. Mold- or glass-ceiling-breaking women like Mary Kay Ash, Martha Stewart, and eBay CEO Margaret Whitman and individual companies like small-scale Ben and Jerry's Homemade, giant General Motors, new economy Amazon.com, and old economy General Electric all have individual entries.

Other entries explore economic concepts (*Competition, Division of labor, Recession*); industrial and economic sectors (*Internet, Retail and wholesale, Utilities industry*); and aspects of finance, labor, and legislation and public policy. The editors also hope to inspire readers to participate in the world of business and industry, and to this end there are entries discussing various topics in operations and management. The global economy is not ignored, with articles on foreign firms like British Airways and the Royal Bank of Canada as well as international agreements and organizations like the WTO and NAFTA. Numerous color pictures, sidebars, diagrams, flow charts, and graphs add interest.

Each volume is arranged alphabetically, and cross-references are provided to lead readers to related entries and information. The "Thematic Outline of Contents" at the beginning of volume 1 organizes the articles into nine broad categories to help readers access specific material in areas of interest. Each volume is indexed, and volume 11 has a very detailed index of the entire set. Each entry has a further reading list that is amplified in volume 11 with a thematically organized bibliography, followed by a listing of resources available on the Web. Statistics and excerpts from important laws are also featured in volume 11.

Presenting basic business information in a clear, readable style accessible to the intended audience, this set is recommended for high-school and public libraries.

Distinguished Asian American Business Leaders. By Naomi Hirahara. 2003. 242p. appendix. bibliogs. illus. index. Greenwood, $69.95 (1-57356-344-7). 338.0973.

This is the second book in Greenwood's Distinguished Asian Americans series, joining *Distinguished Asian American Political and Governmental Leaders* [RBB S 1 03]. Although *The Asian American Almanac* (Gale, 1995) includes biographical sketches of 19 Asian Americans who gained prominence in the business field, this work is the first reference source to focus entirely on business leaders from the Asian American community. *Business leader*, according to the author, is defined broadly to include those who showed determination and perseverance while overcoming prejudices, learning the English language, and succeeding in the world of commerce. Other factors in her selection of the subjects include philanthropic activities, differing personal philosophies, and ethnic and regional diversity. Nautica Apparel cofounder David Chu, Toys "R" Us CEO Robert Naksone, and PepsiCo president Indra Nooyi are among the individuals included.

The 96 profiles are arranged alphabetically by surname and include information compiled from secondary sources between 1999 and 2001. Many include photographs, and all point the reader to other sources for additional reading. The sketches are simply written and organized to provide full name at birth, education, positions held, honors and awards, and career highlights.

The appendix lists subjects by field, such as "Cosmetics," "Financial Services/Insurance," and "Tourism." An index helps the reader find articles by a key term (*Charley's Steakery*, *daisy-wheel printer*, and *Japan Society*, for example). A finding aid to locate subjects by country of origin would be useful.

Although readers will need to do additional research to analyze why these individuals have been so successful, this will be a useful source for identifying American entrepreneurs with Asian backgrounds. Recommmended for high-school, public, and academic libraries.

Encyclopedia of American Business. Ed. by W. Davis Folsom. 2004. 516p. bibliogs. index. Facts On File, $95 (0-8160-4643-3). 338.0973.

Designed as a nuts-and-bolts guide to business jargon for students and nonspecialists, this work will help users understand the complex world of U.S. business, the largest economy in the world. Five general areas of business are covered: accounting, economics, finance, management, and marketing. Terms, concepts, laws, and institutions defined were drawn from two sources, the *Wall Street Journal* and "principles" texts used in introductory courses. Sample entries include *Deming's 14 points, Interlocking directorate, National Industrial Recovery Act, Underground economy,* and *World Bank*. Entries are short, generally a page or less. Many entries have one or two further reading suggestions, which are often very current and frequently refer readers to URLs. Entries often are followed by *see also* references, and *see* references from not-used topics to related or similar topics are frequent. The 80-plus contributors are librarians and academics involved in teaching business courses at colleges and universities.

A lengthy bibliography of current resources is provided after the alphabetical entries. A thorough, detailed index provides many additional access points and acts as a good acronym dictionary. Readers seeking to learn more about associations and federal acts will really benefit from the outstanding index and its cross-references. This encyclopedia presents up-to-date, solid, easy-to-understand information. High-school and college students, as well as interested laypersons, will find this title useful to expand their knowledge of the business world and business lexicon. Public libraries and academic general collections will want to add it to their collections.

Law, Public Administration, Social Problems and Services

CQ Researcher en español. 2004. [Online database]. CQ, pricing varies [http://www.cqpress.com]. (Last accessed February 16, 2004).

CQ Researcher is a mainstay of library reference service for students and interested patrons who need current, objective information about contemporary issues. Founded in 1926 as *Editorial Research Reports, CQ Researcher* appears 44 times per year in print and online, offering original, in-depth information and analysis prepared by experienced investigative reporters. The Spanish-language version, also available both in print and online, provides reports that appeared in English from 1999 to 2003 on education, health, youth, and social issues as well as all 2004 reports. Four of the 36 reports that will appear in 2004 will be original Spanish-language documents on subjects of interest to Latinos.

The report format includes a general overview of the topic, historical aspects, the present situation, perspectives on the future, opposing viewpoints, special information on other aspects of the issue, and a chronology. The writers cite a variety of sources to provide a balanced view. They provide bibliographies and contact information, but they do not update the reports. Among the topics recently available on *CQ Researcher en español* are hazing (*Novotadas*), the future of Latinos (*El futuro de los latinos*), the shortage of nurses (*Escasez de enfermadoras*), and film rating (*Clasificación de películas*).

There are several search options on the home page (*Inicio*). Users may select *Informe actual* (current reports) or *Noticias recientes* (recent news) or enter keywords in the search box (*Búsqueda rápida*). There is also an option to search by year (*Busque por fecha*) as well as an advanced search (*Búsqueda avanzada*). In advanced search, searches can be limited by date, title word, text word, subject heading, and section (e.g., Cronología, Pros y Contras), and results can be sorted by relevance, year, or article title. A subject search (*Búsqueda temática*) takes users to an alphabetical menu of subject headings.

After selecting a report, users may look at the entire text; choose a section of it to read, print, or e-mail; mark documents; and create a citation in several formats. They can also print the document in PDF format in color or black and white. Users may create and save a search profile and save up to 25 searches or 50 documents for later use. A PDF subject index will be available after March 23. The publishers plan to introduce a bilingual interface in spring 2004 also. This will allow librarians who do not know Spanish to help Spanish speakers use the database. If the library subscribes to the English-language database, users will be able to link from the Spanish to the English version of each report section or view the two versions in a parallel display.

CQ Researcher en español is an excellent resource for libraries serving Spanish speakers. It provides objective information about current events and offers students high-quality research for reports.

Encyclopedia of Constitutional Amendments, Proposed Amendments, and Amending Issues, 1789–2002. 2d ed. By John R. Vile. 2003. 635p. appendixes. bibliogs. index. ABC-CLIO, $85 (1-85109-428-8). 342.73.

Updating a 1996 title, this *A–Z* source now contains 100 new entries, increasing the total number of articles from 400 to more than 500. Like the previous edition, the new one covers 27 amendments as well as notable proposed amendments, along with related issues, individuals, organizations, and Supreme Court decisions, among other topics. A new "A to Z List of Entries" makes a handy addition. The author is professor and chair of the Department of Political Science at Middle Tennessee State University and has authored several other books, including the 1996 edition.

Articles range from a single paragraph (e.g., *Office of the Federal Register*) to six pages (e.g., *History of constitutional amendments in the United States*). Almost every article includes a list of suggested further readings. Examples of new entry titles include *Flag salute, National Initiative for Democracy, Reverence for the Constitution,* and *Terrorism.* Many of the entries that appeared in the earlier edition have been updated. For example, *Patents and copyrights* now includes the 2003 Supreme Court decision on the Copyright Term Extension Act. For ease of use, subheadings have been added to some articles as well as additional *see* references.

Five appendixes provide the Constitution, amendment proposal and ratification dates, number of amendments by decade (e.g., 2,598 for the 1960s), a listing of popular amending proposals and key related events by year, plus two new appendixes: "Chronological List of Proposals by Individuals outside Congress Significantly to Revise or to Rewrite the U.S. Constitution" and "Major Proposals by Institutions outside Congress Seeking Major Constitutional Changes."

The bibliography lists mostly books and articles with publications up to 2002. The index includes cases as well as personal names and topics. Bold type makes identifying main entries a snap. This update is a useful and unique item for academic, public, and high-school libraries, even those owning the earlier edition.

Women and the Law. By Ashlyn K. Kuersten. 2003. 256p. bibliogs. illus. index. ABC-CLIO, $85 (0-87436-878-2). 342.7308.

Describing the evolution of women's legal rights in the U.S. from the Revolutionary War to the present, this volume uses biographical sketches of key individuals, summaries of significant court cases and legislative victories, definitions of major concepts, and selected important documents.

A 19-page introduction and a chronology provide an overview of gender equality in the U.S. from colonial times forward. Around 200 entries are arranged alphabetically within broad categories ("Key Historical Concepts and Pioneers," "Constitutional Equality," "Education," "Family Law," "Reproductive Rights," "Violence against Women," and "Workplace Rights"). A comprehensive index, references and further reading lists at the end of each section, and *see also* tags at the end of most entries allow researchers to learn more about each topic. The "Table of Cases" directs readers to the published court texts, and a collection of 21 documents provides relevant declarations, speeches, constitutional amendments, and legislative acts verbatim.

A caveat: editing is sometimes weak. For example, Hillary Rodham Clinton is credited with making history in November 2000 "when she became the first lady ever to be elected as a U.S. senator." "First First Lady" would have been correct. The occasional errors, however, do not detract from the volume's usefulness.

Although other reference sources contain much of this information (*Handbook of American Women's History* [Sage, 2000], *The Reader's Companion to U.S. Women's History* [Houghton, 1998], *Encyclopedia of Women's History in America* [Facts On File, 1996], *Women's Rights in the United States: A Documentary History* [Greenwood, 1994]), Kuersten's volume is more current and focuses on women in the legal and political arenas. It should prove useful in academic and large public libraries.

Great American Judges: An Encyclopedia. 2v. Ed. by John R. Vile. 2003. 981p. appendixes. bibliogs. illus. index. ABC-CLIO, $185 (1-57607-989-9). 347.73.

Great American Judges fills a gap in the judicial reference category by providing biographical information on the great federal and state judges, both living and dead, in one collection. It covers a diverse array of 100 judges who were selected on the basis of frequent mention in various sources and results of a survey sent to legal scholars.

The set begins with a rather lengthy forward on the role of judges in American history. Next come profiles arranged in an *A–Z* format. Each entry includes a portrait (when available) and introduction summarizing the salient points in the subject's judicial career. Following the introduction, the profile covers the subject's personal and professional career and court experiences. Rounding out each entry is a list of references and further reading. Sidebars treat an additional 60 or so "outstanding and/or newsworthy individuals," among them Clarence Thomas and Judge Judy.

There are several appendixes, one of which is a table of the 100 great judges listed by date of birth and showing years of life, nation or state of birth, colleges attended, and courts over which they presided. From this table it is possible to identify the oldest living great judge (Luther Lee Bohanon, Senior Judge, U.S., Oklahoma, 103 years), and the shift from obtaining a legal education by reading law under a judge or lawyer to an emphasis on training in a university setting. Another supplemental feature is a trivia quiz, "How well do you know your Great American Judges?"

Great American Judges is a valuable tool for providing current and retrospective biographical information on the nation's "best" judges. Academic and larger public libraries would find the source a welcome addition.

Landmark Legislation, 1774–2002: Major U.S. Acts and Treaties. By Stephen W. Stathis. 2003. 429p. bibliog. index. CQ, $130 (1-56802-781-8). 348.73.

Stephen W. Stathis is a senior researcher with the Congressional Research Service of the U.S. Congress with over 30 years experience. He is the author or co-author of at least 21 major studies for Congress and has contributed to numerous scholarly publications and conferences.

This reference surveys the early Continental Congress and the 107 Congresses from 1774 through 2003. The author has perused thousands of laws and treaties that were enacted and selected about 1,181 that have had significant influence on the U.S. A preface and introduction discuss the legislative process and describe how legislation evolves. Assisting users is a 22-page "Finders Guide" in which the laws and treaties are arranged under 41 subject headings. The text is arranged chronologically by congress.

Headings provide the dates of each congress and session and identify the president in office at the time. This is followed by a one- to two-and-a-half page description of the historical background of legislation in each congress, and an annotated list of major acts. Each annotation tells the purpose of the act and the date passed, and provides a citation to a copy of the full text. Following the main text, an extensive "Sources for Further Study" is arranged by approximately 74 subject headings. Rounding out the volume is a 34-page index in which entries in boldface type refer to major acts in the text.

This well-organized volume will allow users to quickly find a description of important legislation and determine where they can locate the full text. It will also allow researchers to determine what legislation was produced during various congresses and administrations. Users can also easily see how legislative subjects have evolved over several generations. This will be a useful source for academic and public libraries.

★**Major Acts of Congress.** 3v. Ed. by Brian K. Landsberg. 2003. 1,175p. appendixes. bibliogs. glossary. illus. indexes. Macmillan, $290 (0-02-865750-0). 348.73.

Written in a clear and accessible style, with sidebars, illustrations, and definitions of terms, *Major Acts of Congress* will be a top-tier reference work for students and laypersons researching federal legislation. It contains signed articles summarizing and analyzing 262 statutes selected on the basis of their historical significance, contemporary impact, and contribution to an understanding of American government. The articles, which vary in length from 300 to 2,500 words, span legislation enacted between 1787 (Northwest Ordinance) and 2002 (Department of Homeland Security Act). Important pieces of legislation affecting civil rights, crime, copyright, education, the environment, civil service, immigration, labor, national security, social programs, taxation, telecommunications, trade, and transportation are covered. Many statutes that are the subject of ongoing interest (and often selected as term-paper topics by students) have been included, such as the Americans with Disabilities Act, the Brady Handgun Violence Prevention Act, the Endangered Species Act, the Family and Medical Leave Act, the Flag Protection Act of 1989, No Child Left Behind, the Sherman Antitrust Act, and the USA Patriot Act.

Entries are arranged alphabetically; a topic outline helps integrate related acts, as does the liberal use of *see also* references. Public Law and Statutes at Large citations are included in the body of each article; a separate table of acts and citations would have been useful. Bibliographies conclude each entry. Most bibliographic references are to books, although some government documents, law reviews, and journals are included. Internet resources are generally listed separately; government sites predominate and thus should be accurate for longer than is typical for Web addresses. In addition to summarizing and often excerpting the acts, most articles discuss the underlying need for congressional action, prior attempts at legislation, lobbying efforts for and against the legislation, court challenges, amendments, and effects of the act. Liberal use of white space, shading, and different typefaces for excerpts, blurbs, and sidebars help readers focus on important elements. Photographs, editorial cartoons, and scanned documents also enrich the work. Each volume includes the same five appendixes. Two are useful to repeat: a cumulative index and a glossary. However, the decision to include the U.S. Constitution, a time line, and an index of court cases in each volume unnecessarily increases the size of the set. Highly recommended for high-school, college, and public libraries.

U.S. Laws, Acts, and Treaties. 3v. Ed. by Timothy L. Hall and Christina J. Moose. 2003. 1,666p. bibliogs. indexes. Salem, $188 (1-58765-098-3). 348.73.

Part of the Magill's Choice series, *U.S. Laws, Acts, and Treaties* is a collection of 433 major U.S. acts of Congress and U.S. treaties covering the time period from 1776 through 2002, beginning with the Declaration of Independence and ending with the Homeland Security Act. Those laws and treaties most likely to be a part of classroom discussions were chosen for inclusion. All of the essays except for 50 new ones were compiled and updated from 16 Salem Press reference works published from 1992 through 2002.

Coverage includes a wide variety of topics, such as African Americans, civil rights and liberties, education, immigration, the military and national security, religious liberty, and voting and elections. The essays, chronically arranged and varying in length from 500 to 2,000 words, cover the historical origins and main provisions of each law or treaty. Each entry provides alternative popular names (if applicable); the date of enactment or signing; U.S. Code, U.S. Statute, or Public Law number; subject categories; and a brief summary of the act or treaty. Selected sources for further study and *see also* references conclude each essay. An alphabetical listing of contents by popular name is included in each volume.

Volume 3 includes the Declaration of Independence, the Constitution of the United States, and the Amendments to the Constitution. Another important and helpful feature of the volume is a section on legal resources explaining primary sources of the law and how to find them. Web addresses are given for online resources. Mailing addresses, telephone numbers, Web addresses, and e-mail addresses are given for both government organizations and offices and for legal organizations.

Many reference works in this area are highly technical or are limited in scope and geared to narrow coverage of a topic, such as education or civil rights. U.S. government online databases are available but require targeted searches. This set presents a good coverage of landmark laws and treaties in a concise, easy-to-read, and easy-to-use work. It is geared toward high-school and undergraduate students but would also make a useful and functional reference tool for public libraries.

Presidents, Vice Presidents, Cabinet Members, Supreme Court Justices, 1789–2003: Vital and Official Data. Ed. by Keith L. Justice. 2003. 297p. appendixes. index. McFarland, $45 (0-7864- 1044-2). 351.73.

A complete revision of the 1985 book *Public Office Index: Vol. 1, U.S. Presidents, Vice Presidents, Cabinet Members, Supreme Court Justices*, this volume lists vital and official data for the categories of individuals named in the title. The first section, "Administration and Cabinet Summaries," lists vice presidents and Cabinet officers for each president. The following sections contain chronological listings of and biographical summaries for presidents, vice presidents, Cabinet members, and Supreme Court justices. Arranged in alphabetical order by person's name, the biographical data vary somewhat in each section but generally include date and state of birth and state of residence; date of and age at inauguration or appointment; dates of assuming and exiting official position; and date of and age at death. Other information might include reason for leaving office, president served, other offices held, and length of service.

One change to this edition is that Cabinet officers are listed more than once if they served more than one president. John Forsyth (1780–1841) served as Andrew Jackson's Secretary of State from 1834–1837, but since he was appointed again by Martin Van Buren, he is listed a second time. Another new feature is the numerical indicators used to show the number of days a person held office; Forsyth's was 2,435 days. The appendixes contain time lines, facts about each office, and listings of total length of service, longest and shortest time in office, and ages at time of inauguration or confirmation. A separate appendix on women in the cabinet is also included.

This volume is recommended for academic and public libraries, especially where the 1985 edition has been useful.

The United States Executive Branch: A Biographical Directory of Heads of State and Cabinet Officials. 2v. Rev. ed. Ed. by Robert Sobel and David B. Sicilia. 2003. 698p. appendixes. bibliogs. illus. Greenwood, $150 (0-313-31134-X). 351.73.

A number of researchers have contributed to this work on the men and women who have served in the cabinets of American presidents. Since the 1989 edition 50 new entries have been added, including those for George W. Bush's initial cabinet officers. Only individuals confirmed in office by the U.S. Senate are covered.

A chronological listing of the members of each presidential administration is repeated in each volume, followed by a list arranged by department. These features make information readily available for the researcher looking for a few quick names and dates, such as the name of the first attorney general under President Dwight Eisenhower. Each of the more than 600 A–Z entries offers a detailed chronological summary of significant events in a subject's career as well as personal information such as education, family, religious affiliation, and awards and honors. If any of the men and women have significant publications, these are also noted. The date and place of death are included where appropriate. Bibliographic references to important primary and secondary works are provided and may be consulted for additional information. The set concludes with additional lists that organize entrants according to other government offices they held,

military service, and place of birth. Other lists provide educational and marital information.

This work is a valuable addition for any library, especially an academic institution. Having convenient listings as well as more in- depth information make it a handy resource. Highly recommended for academic and large public library collections.

African Americans at War: An Encyclopedia. 2v. By Jonathan D. Sutherland. 2004. 819p. bibliogs. illus. indexes. ABC- CLIO, $185 (1-57607-746-2). 355.

This encyclopedia is devoted exclusively to the war experiences of African Americans, beginning with King William's War in the late seventeenth century and extending to events just before the outbreak of the second Gulf War. The alphabetically ordered entries conclude with *see also* and further reading references. There are more than 250 entries conveying biographical, thematic, and conceptual information. Well-known leaders (Colin Powell), groups (Buffalo Soldiers), specific units (Fifty-fourth Massachusetts Infantry Regiment, made famous in the movie *Glory*), and battles (Bunker Hill) have their own entries. So do landmark legislation (G.I. Bill), long-forgotten governmental agencies (Bureau of Colored Troops), and notable speeches (Call to Rebellion, delivered at the 1843 National Negro Convention).

Most entries range from half a page to three pages, and the references range from one to six sources, including Web sites. Entries covering major conflicts, from the American Revolution to Vietnam, are among the longest, with World War II receiving almost 50 pages. These longer entries are made more user-friendly with subheadings like "The Impact of the Draft" and "Experience in Combat." There are pleasant surprises among entries focusing on lesser-known subjects, for example, an article on Phoebe Jeter, "the only African American woman to direct the launch of a Patriot missile during the first Gulf War," and Z-Gram 66, a policy directive issued in 1970 by Admiral Zumwalt in response to declining African American participation in Vietnam.

Volume 2 contains an excellent and detailed 40-plus-page chronology, as well as the formation, service records, battles, and postings of colored troops through the years and Medal of Honor recipients. More than 100 photos are interspersed throughout the set, and numerous charts and statistics are included (number of blacks in the armed services, African Americans in certain military ranks, etc.).

The inclusiveness and comprehensiveness of this encyclopedia make it impressive, though it will no doubt need to be updated eventually to include the second Gulf War. This is a superb resource for any high-school, public, or undergraduate library looking to enrich its history, military, or African American studies collections.

African Americans in the Military. By Catherine Reef. 2004. 256p. bibliogs. illus. indexes. Facts On File, $44 (0-8160-4901-7). 355.
African-American Political Leaders. By Charles W. Carey Jr. 2004. 322p. bibliogs. illus. indexes. Facts On File, $44 (0-8160-5138-0). 973.

Two more titles in the attractive Facts On File series A to Z of African Americans. Like other volumes in the series (e.g., *African Americans in the Performing Arts* [RBB Ag 03], *African-American Religious Leaders* [RBB F 15 04]), they are well written, well researched, and useful (but not essential) purchases for school and public libraries.

Each alphabetically arranged entry provides a one- to two-page biography with cross-references, photo, and suggestions for further reading (many with Web sites). A bibliography and indexes by office or branch of service, year of birth, and keyword follow the text. *African Americans in the Military* includes more than 125 individuals from Clara Leach Adams-Ender (Army Nurse Corps) to Matthew Zimmerman (army chief of chaplains) and from the Revolutionary War to the present. *African-American Political Leaders* includes 185 individuals from Ethel Allen (Pennsylvania secretary of state) to Coleman Young (mayor of Detroit) who have been elected to federal, state, or local office or have served in cabinet- level posts. Chronological coverage begins with John Langston (1829–97), the first African American elected to public office. However, Education Secretary Roderick Paige and the current Wilmington, Delaware, mayor—James Baker—are not included.

There is some overlap with other works, such as *Distinguished African-American Political and Governmental Leazders* (Oryx, 1999), and even with other volumes in the series. Buy where reports and interest make these needed.

★**Amazons to Fighter Pilots:** A Biographical Dictionary of Military Women. 2v. Ed. by Reina Pennington. 2003. 760p. appendixes. bibliogs. illus. index. Greenwood, $175 (0-313-29197-7). 355.

The role of women in the military has traditionally been a topic of contention, particularly when the focus is the assignment of women to combat roles. With the advent of the war in Iraq and the visible role of women as POWs, the publication of this title could hardly be more opportune. It covers the history of women in the military, focusing on women who fought, from ancient times to the present. The body of the work, written by more than 100 university and college-affiliated subject experts, consists of alphabetically arranged profiles of more than 300 women or groups (e.g., *Spanish Civil War, women in; WASP [Women's Airforce Service Pilots]*), followed by a section that treats World War II Soviet military units, such as the Forty-Sixth Taman'sky Guards Bomber Aviation Regiment, listed by number.

As indicated, treatment is international as well as historical in scope. Presented in brisk, readable prose, entries run between a third of a page to six pages for more prominent figures or groups, such as Elizabeth I of England or the women involved in the Israeli War of Independence. Following a brief fact summary, entries treat the history of the person or group from birth or inception to death or disbanding. Some group entries include brief profiles of "representative participants." The focus is on the specific military operations in which the subject was involved. Cross-references are noted in bold within the body of the entry, and each entry ends with a brief bibliography. Additional information such as quotations, statistics, and related facts appear in sidebars throughout the text. Some entries are accompanied by clear black-and-white photographs or reproductions.

The first volume opens with an engagingly written introductory essay, and the second includes both a 125-page time line and bibliographic surveys of materials on "Women as Prisoners of War" and "Women, Medicine, and the Military." Each volume contains lists of entries by geographic region, time period and conflict, role or branch of service, prisoner or POW status, and groups and organizations. The second volume closes with a comprehensive bibliography, good index, and notes on the contributors.

With its international scope and its emphasis on women in combat, this title complements Victoria Sherrow's *Women and the Military: An Encyclopedia* (ABC-CLIO, 1996), which focuses on the U.S. and includes coverage of events, wars, laws, and military branches as well as women who served in noncombat roles. *Amazons to Fighter Pilots* is a necessary addition to college and university libraries and a sound selection for high-school and public libraries.

Dictionary of Military Terms: A Guide to the Language of Warfare and Military Institutions. 2d ed. Ed. by Trevor N. Dupuy and others. 2003. 271p. illus. Wilson, $85 (0-8242-1025-5). 355.

When it was published in 1986, the first edition of *Dictionary of Military Terms* was greeted enthusiastically by reviewers as there had been no standard reference work on this subject that was satisfactory to both the military profession and to laypersons. One of the compilers, Colonel Trevor N. Dupuy, was a noted military theorist, historian, teacher, and decorated World War II veteran. Building on the work of Dupuy and his associates, this second edition is equally welcome. Many things have changed in these last 17 years, and entries needed to be updated, added, and, in some cases, even deleted.

There are now approximately 3,500 terms as compared to 2,500 in the first edition. Examples of new entries are *Abrams (M-1); Abu Nidal organization; Fedayeen Saddam; Gulf War; Hawk (MIM-23); Moro Liberation Front (MLF); Oslo Accords; Scud;* and *World Trade Center and Pentagon attacks, 2001.* As in the first edition, all aspects of military affairs are covered: strategy, tactics, fortifications, weapons, ranks, organization, and administration. The concise entries are arranged alphabetically, and *see* and *see also* references are included. The definitions emphasize military meanings and cover military affairs and military history from ancient times to the present; this is not an etymological dictionary. Photographs and line drawings illustrate some terms.

This is a very readable book for the general reader and will make a great addition to public, academic, and some high-school libraries as well as being useful for military professionals.

Encyclopedia of American Military History. 3v. Ed. by Spencer C. Tucker. 2003. 988p. bibliogs. glossary. illus. index. maps. Facts On File, $225 (0-8160-4355-8). 355.

Approximately 200 individuals from both academic and military backgrounds contributed to this encyclopedia on American military history. The time period covered is from the colonial wars through the events of September 11, 2001, which, the editor says, "like December 1941, will probably stand as a major turning point in our history."

Even though the book has more than 600,000 words, the editor acknowledges the impossible task of including all information about U.S. military history. The focus is on key individuals, including women and minorities; overviews, causes, and effects of America's wars; overviews of weapons systems; and key technological developments. The selective bibliography includes general works, monographs listed by historical periods, miscellaneous works, and encyclopedias and atlases. Basic military terms are described in the glossary. An index to the complete work is included in each volume.

Arranged alphabetically, each signed entry opens with dates, if appropriate, and in most cases a short description of the subject (e.g., *Crazy Horse [Tashunca-uitco] [ca. 1842–1877] Oglala Sioux chief and one of the most effective Native American war leaders*) followed by a longer discussion. *See also* references are found at the end of each entry along with a short list of works for further reading. The majority of entries average one half page, but some, such as *Aircraft, fixed-wing* and *World War II, course of U.S. involvement: Europe,* run several pages because of their significance and complexity.

According to the editor, "Understanding the history of America's wars and its military establishment helps us understand ourselves and our world a bit better." This set does an excellent job of furthering that understanding in a nicely condensed manner. The entries are easy to read, and the entire set presents a pleasing appearance. Black-and-white photos and maps are scattered throughout. This work would make an excellent addition to high- school, public, and academic libraries.

Directory of Drug & Alcohol Residential Rehabilitation Facilities. 2003. 320p. indexes. Grey House, paper, $135 (1- 59237-031-4). 362.29.

A 2001 survey by the U.S. Department of Health and Human Services determined approximately 4.6 million Americans to be in need of some degree of substance abuse treatment. The *Directory of Drug & Alcohol Residential Rehabilitation Facilities* contains comprehensive information on 1,300 treatment centers. In addition to the standard contact information, each profile contains the center's general description, treatment philosophy, treatment programs, acceptable age groups, total number of residents and counselors, average length of stay, fees, acceptable insurances, license and certification, key personnel, and, when given, clinical staff.

Generally, treatment philosophy falls into two categories—harm reduction and faith-based therapies—both of which are clearly explained in the *Directory's* introduction. Available treatment types are both inpatient and outpatient, long and short term, and may include specialized programs (behavior modification, continuing education, sober housing, etc.).

Since arrangement of the 1,300 profiles is alphabetical first by state, then by facility name, the three indexes are essential. Profiles are identified by entry number. There is the obvious name index; an age-range index, which divides the facilities into six age brackets (all ages, under 13, 13–17, 18–25, 18 and up, 30 and up); and a treatment program index. The programs are as varied as the facilities. Among those included are 12- step recovery, Alzheimer's, detox, dual diagnosis, group therapy, employee assistance, relapse prevention, and eating disorders. Some programs are available in Spanish. An extensive listing of support groups, research centers, resource organizations, periodicals, pamphlets, conferences, trade shows, and Web sites immediately precedes the indexes. This excellent, much needed directory fills an important gap created by the cessation of *Drug, Alcohol, and Other Addictions: A Directory of Treatment Centers and Prevention Programs Nationwide* (2d ed., Oryx, 1993).

Encyclopedia of Health Care Management. Ed. by Michael J. Stahl. 2003. 621p. bibliogs. index. Sage, $150 (0-7619-2674-7). 362.1.

Make no mistake—medicine is big business and promises to become even more so. Within the health-care industry, health-care management is a burgeoning field in its own right, encompassing a broad variety of business and management issues including accounting and activity-based costing, economics, health policy, human resources, information technology, legal and regulatory issues, managed care, marketing and customer value, operations and decision making, pharmaceuticals and clinical trials, quality, statistics, and data mining.

Containing about 600 entries contributed by more than 160 expert contributors, this reference covers the aforementioned facets of health-care management and more, such as institutions and organizations and international health-care issues. Readers will find entries on *Balanced scorecard and health care, Episodes of care, Facilities management, Health insurance, Inpatient services, Outsourcing, Physician extenders, Structured settlement, Utilization review, Vicarious liability,* and *Zero defects,* among others. The focus is primarily on the U.S. Although there are eight entries specifically on international health-care issues, readers looking for a more international perspective will be disappointed—something that Sage might want to ponder when contemplating further development of its health services and public health administration reference lists. Signed articles are accompanied by short lists for further reading; some contributors have elected to include URLs in these lists. Access is facilitated three ways—by a list of entries, a reader's guide that classifies entries into 16 general categories, and an index.

The most comprehensive one-volume reference work on health-care management published in the last 10 years, this work brings together much useful information and will appeal to a broad audience. Health science libraries, college libraries, and large public libraries will want to invest in this title. Although the treatment is probably not deep and critical enough for major research libraries, they should consider purchase in the absence of recently published comparable works.

The Encyclopedia of Suicide. 2d ed. By Glen Evans and others. 2003. 329p. appendixes. bibliog. illus. Facts On File, $65 (0-8160- 4525-9). 362.28.

In the decade from 1990 to 1999 more than 300,000 people in the U.S. and 8 million people worldwide died by their own hands. The second edition of *The Encyclopedia of Suicide* is a comprehensive A–Z introduction to suicide from ancient times to the present. It is a heavily expanded, updated, and revised edition of the 1988 encyclopedia, reflecting the most current data available. Among the compilers are a former member of the American Association of Suicidology and the director of the L.A. Suicide Prevention Center.

The entries deal with a wide range of issues, such as causes, history, and psychology of suicide. Length varies from a short paragraph to as much as a page. Entries cover such individuals as Herbert Hendin, the medical director of the American Suicide Foundation, and Herodotus, the Greek historian who describes the custom of institutional suicide in which a man's widows vie for the honor of being the deceased's most loved. Also included are organizations such as the Voluntary Euthanasia Society and Survivors of Loved Ones Suicide, plus topics like survivor guilt and biblical suicides. New entries cover topics such as gender differences, suicide bombers, school violence and suicide, and ethnicity and suicide. Appendixes provide a listing of associations, government agencies, suicide prevention agencies, and crisis hotlines in the U.S. plus a table showing international suicide rates. The short bibliography mostly references materials that are new since the previous edition. The index is detailed. This revision is recommended for academic, high-school, and public libraries.

Encyclopedia of Forensic Science. By Suzanne Bell. 2003. 350p. appendixes. bibliogs. illus. index. Facts On File, $75 (0-8160-4811-8). 363.25.

The popularity of books by Patricia Cornwell and television crime-solving shows like *C.S.I.* has brought forensic science to the forefront of popular culture. The *Encyclopedia of Forensic Science* seeks to narrow the gap between forensic fiction and the actual capabilities of forensic science by providing an overview to a very complex discipline.

With an emphasis on science, this volume covers such experiment and laboratory concepts as *Control samples, Density,* and *Null hypothesis,* along with laboratory equipment and various lab tests like chromatography and immunoassay. In addition to explaining the science of forensics, Bell, a research professor in forensic chemistry, reviews various disciplines related to forensic science, among them entomology, odontology, and psychology. Other entries cover professional organizations, government agencies, famous names in the field of forensics, evidence, and legal issues. There are also entries for cases such as the O. J. Simpson trial and the Lindbergh kidnapping. More than 600 topics related to forensic science are treated.

Descriptions vary in length from a sentence to four pages. Longer entries often have suggestions for further reading, usually one to three citations. There are illustrations and photographs throughout, as well as an eight-page color photograph insert. Numerous cross-references within entries provide a better understanding of the relationships among terms. In addition to the encyclopedia entries, Bell has also included 14 feature essays on such topics as "Myths of Forensic Science," "Careers in Forensic Science: A Reality Check," and "The 'Top Ten' Cases in Forensic Science."

This volume has substantially more entries than *Encyclopedia of Forensic Science: A Compendium of Fact and Fiction* (Oryx, 2002), though readers hoping for more case examples may prefer the latter. *Encyclopedia of Forensic Sciences* (Academic, 2000) is a much more scientific treatment. With its clear language and brief entries, the current volume will provide readers with a nuts-and-bolts understanding of the real world of forensic science and is recommended for public and undergraduate libraries.

The FBI Encyclopedia. By Michael Newton. 2003. 440p. appendixes. bibliog. index. McFarland, $95 (0-7864-1718-8). 363.25.

Newton, author of two other books on the FBI, asserts that "nearly everything you know about the FBI is wrong" and the organization is "deliberately shrouded in mystery." Newton's purpose is to eliminate some of the secrecy that surrounds the FBI while acknowledging that it is impossible to disclose a complete picture of an organization whose records are in large part unavailable to the public.

Coverage begins in 1908, the year of the bureau's creation, and ends in early 2003. Entries are arranged alphabetically and range from a single paragraph to several pages. Access to articles is aided by cross-references directly in the text and a detailed index. Entries fall under broad categories: biographical sketches *(Hoover, John Edgar)*; organizational practices *(Wiretapping)*; programs *("COINTELPRO")*; notable cases *(Watergate scandal)*; federal legislation authorizing investigations *(Mann Act)*; histories of other relevant organizations *(KGB)*; and miscellaneous entries *(Prohibition)*. The text is supplemented by appendixes, including a chronology that is current as of November 2002 but omits some significant events, such as the Oklahoma City bombing. Finally, the book contains an extensive bibliography of both scholarly and popular sources.

The work successfully reveals the sinister side of the FBI, such as its surveillance of individuals and groups, questionable information-gathering practices, and J. Edgar Hoover's inaction with respect to civil rights investigations. Articles are generally well written in a journalistic style; however, information is not always presented in a neutral tone. Furthermore, the text contains typographical errors, which detracts from the quality of the writing.

The FBI Encyclopedia covers material similar to *The FBI: A Comprehensive Reference Guide* (Oryx, 1999), though Newton's offering is neither as scholarly nor as objective. It is useful as an overview that is accessible to a general audience. Moreover, it contains articles on topics of current interest, such as the USA Patriot Act, the anthrax cases of 2001, and spy Robert Hanssen. This work is suitable for public libraries.

The Grey House Homeland Security Directory. 2003. 669p. indexes. Grey House, paper, $195 (1-59237-035-7). 363.3.

Here is an easy-to-use guide to the newly formed Department of Homeland Security and the various governmental, private, and nonprofit organizations that support it. Nearly 700 pages of directory information divided into five sections include federal agencies, state agencies, private company profiles, industry resources, and indexes to key personnel and products and services.

The federal agency section contains 40 pages outlining the Department of Homeland Security. Entries include a description of each office, top officials, and standard directory information of address, phone, fax, and occasional URLs and e-mail addresses. An additional 110 pages contain directory information on the Office of the President, Senate, House, and 12 of the 15 cabinet-level departments—excluding Labor, Housing and Urban Development, and Veterans Affairs. Top department officials are listed along with selective offices that support Homeland Security. House and Senate committees related to Homeland Security are included.

Likewise, the state agency profiles arranged by state include the State Homeland Security Office, governor and lead state officials, and related homeland security offices such as public safety, National Guard, public health, emergency management, air traffic control, and port authority.

Company and industry sections contain 1,175 private company profiles and a multitude of associations, periodicals, directories and databases, trade shows, and seminars. Entries are alphabetical within each category and include a general business description, directory information, and, when available, URL, number of employees, and budget data.

Comparable information can be found online or in print publications such as the *State Yellow Book, Federal Yellow Book, U.S. Government Manual,* and Grey House's *Directory of Business Information Resources*. However, *The Grey House Homeland Security Directory* compiles this information in one place and is discerning in content. A useful purchase for public and academic libraries.

Pollution A to Z. 2v. Ed. by Richard M. Stapleton. 2003. 756p. bibliogs. glossary. illus. index. maps. Macmillan, $195 (0-02- 865700-4). 363.73.

Intended for use in high-school, public, and academic libraries, these volumes include articles on various causes of pollution and their effects on human and environmental health, on people and organizations that have been active in cleanup, and on agencies and legislation related to these issues. Contributors are connected with government agencies, universities, or scientific organizations.

There are 264 alphabetically arranged articles, from *Abatement* to *Zero population growth*. Some articles, such as the excellent *Global warming* and *Space pollution*, deal with specific issues related to pollution. Others, such as *Popular culture, Risk,* and *Writers,* might seem like odd choices but add a more conceptual dimension. The articles conclude with lists of Internet sites as well as bibliographies that list many publications that are dated before 2000. The set is attractive and inviting, illustrated with charts, photos, maps, and drawings. Each volume commences with a table of contents and topical outline for the set and lists of acronyms and abbreviations and ends with a glossary and set index. The index entry for *Tankers, oil* incorrectly cites pages 104–405, instead of 104–105.

There are several older reference sources, among them *Encyclopedia of Environmental Issues* (Salem, 2000) and *Encyclopedia of Environmental Science* (Oryx, 2000), that treat many topics related to pollution but have a broader overall scope. Others, such as *Environmental Disasters: A Chronicle of Individual, Industrial, and Governmental Carelessness* (Facts On File, 1998) and *Toxic Waste Sites: An Encyclopedia of Endangered America* (ABC-CLIO, 1997), are more narrow. *Pollution A to Z* is an attractive, informative, current work that could be useful in high-school and public library collections.

The Dictionary of Crime Terms. By Carl Sifakis. 2003. 272p. bibliog. index. Facts On File, $60 (0-8160-4548-8). 364.
The Encyclopedia of High-Tech Crime and Crime-Fighting. By Michael Newton. 2003. 377p. bibliog. glossary. illus. index. Facts On File, $75 (0-8160-4978-5). 364.16.

Here are two reference volumes that tackle topics related to crime.

In *The Dictionary of Crime Terms,* Sifakis, who also wrote *The Mafia Encyclopedia* (Facts On File, 2d ed., 1999), has brought together the language of Mobspeak—what wise guys and other American criminals say among themselves, not what is fabricated by writers or the media. The focus is mainly on Mafia-related terms, such as *ace of spades* (the widow of a departed criminal big shot), *buckwheats* (vicious spite killings), *midnight flips* (the law enforcement tactic of arresting mobsters between two and four o'clock in the morning), and *sparkplugs* (the most feared Mob killers), rather than street crime. Arrangement of the 900 clearly written entries is alphabetical, and there are some cross-references. The bibliography is current and comprehensive. The index is accurate and very helpful. In addition to book sources, the author has drawn on newspaper files and two attorneys with "special knowledge."

In 420 entries, the alphabetically arranged *Encyclopedia of High-Tech Crime and Crime-Fighting,* by prolific crime writer Newton, examines how technology combats crime and also makes crime possible, such as through the many Internet hoaxes (the *Miller Beer giveaway,* the *Tweety Bird chain letter*) and viruses *(Rainsong, Rhapsody, Xalnaga, Xanax)*. There are entries for individuals who have been convicted based on DNA evidence as well as for hackers, computer saboteurs, and software and satellite TV pirates. The book also describes how technology is being used to free the innocent, particularly the huge number of persons who have been exonerated by DNA test results. Scope is international. Following the entries are a glossary, a bibliography, and an index.

Both *The Dictionary of Crime Terms* and *The Encyclopedia of High-Tech Crime and Crime-Fighting* are recommended for criminal justice collections in academic and public libraries.

Encyclopedia of Murder and Violent Crime. Ed. by Eric Hickey. 2003. 603p. appendixes. bibliogs. glossary. illus. index. Sage, $125 (0-7619-2437-X). 364.15.

Edited by a specialist in criminal psychology, this volume contains more than 200 signed entries from more than 116 contributors on a variety of topics related to violent crime and murder. The majority of the alphabetically arranged entries can be divided into two categories: biographies of murderers or violent groups and overviews of theories of violence, legal processes, or types of violence. There are also several short articles on issues that do not address violence directly but are related somehow (e.g., *The Brady Bill*). The biographical entries range from less than one page for Al Capone and Jack the Ripper to four or five pages for Charles Manson and Osama bin Laden. While the focus is on American criminals and crime, there are several entries for international figures (for example, Andrei Chikatilo, the "Russian Ripper"). The articles on types of violence average three to four pages and cover the expected topics (*Rape, School shootings, Serial murder,* and *Stalking* are but a few). Articles on court or legal procedure also average three to four pages and are written in clear language. The most interesting component is the inclusion of articles related to theories of violence, such as *Aggression: Psychological theories* and *Violent behavior: Personality theories*. This gives the book a psychological and sociological slant that sets it apart from similar publications, such as *Encyclopedia of American Crime* (2d ed., Facts On File, 2000).

Encyclopedia of Murder and Violent Crime is a good single-volume introductory source. It is written in a very readable style and presents controversial topics without bias. It is well indexed and includes listings of murderers and organized crime figures in the appendixes. For libraries that own the three-volume *Violence in America* (Scribner, 1999), this would be a useful companion purchase as it contains information from recent headlines (for example, the Beltway Snipers and Andrea Yates) and provides better coverage of the psychological aspects of violence and crime. A superior purchase for academic and public libraries.

Education, Commerce, Custom

Directory of Distance Learning Opportunities: K–12. 2003. 302p. indexes. Greenwood, $69.95 (1-57356-515-6). 371.3.

Designed for librarians, parents, and school counselors looking for information on specific K–12 distance learning courses of study, this work contains an overview of the current status of distance education in the U.S. and in-depth information on more than 6,000 courses offered by 154 U.S. institutions and consortia. Information was obtained from respondents to a request from the publisher. Both print-based (correspondence study) and electronic (via the Internet, satellite broadcast, or interactive television) programs are included.

Main entries are arranged alphabetically by name of institution and contain full contact information, description of the institution, grade level, admission requirements, fees, equipment requirements, grading, and accreditation (this is important if the student wishes to transfer the credit or intends to use it for graduation). Course descriptions, emphasis, and approach, as well as general requirements are also included. A subject index provides access to courses by grade level, and a geographic index is helpful because some course offerings are limited to residents of particular states. An index that separated courses by delivery system—print, online, satellite broadcast, or interactive TV—might have been useful.

The demand for distance education is growing thanks to schedule conflicts in traditional schools, a desire for AP classes and enrichment opportunities, and interest in homeschool options. This directory is sure to be a welcome addition in public and school libraries. Nothing else pulls so much information together in one print source. Users can contact specific institutions by e-mail or visit their Web sites for additional information.

Education and Technology: An Encyclopedia. 2v. Ed. by Ann Kovalchick and Kara Dawson. 2003. 713p. bibliogs. charts. glossary. index. ABC-CLIO, $185 (1-57607-351-3). 371.33.

"It has never been easy to define educational technology or the scope of the profession." The editors of this encyclopedia use the introduction to try and define the phrase as well as discuss the broad aspects of it. The aim is "to provide an opportunity for those who have had little or no formal introduction to the field of educational technology to learn about its numerous applications and to recognize the relevance of educational technology to many endeavors."

More than 200 alphabetically arranged entries are the work of more than 120 contributors and fall into seven broad categories, as outlined in the topical contents list: "Foundations" (*Cognitive psychology, Human-computer interaction*); "Implementation" (*Knowledge management, Rapid prototyping, Webcast*); "Issues" (*Assistive technology, Copyright, Digital divide*); "Leaders"; "Professional Associations"; "Projects" (*Apple Classroom of Tomorrow Project, JSTOR*); and "Research and Theory" (*Computer-Supported Collaborative Learning [CSCL], Visual literacy*). Average entry length is five pages. Each selection includes a *see also* note and references. A glossary, an index, and a list of contributors are all included in volume 2.

Despite its stated aim, this work seems best suited to students majoring in education and professionals in the education field. Those who have no background in either education or technology might find these volumes difficult to use. The encyclopedia is recommended for academic libraries.

Encyclopedia of Distributed Learning. Ed. by Anna DiStefano and others. 2004. 549p. appendixes. bibliogs. index. Sage, $125 (0-7619-2451-5). 374.

Despite the fact that education is an area that has no lack of reference resources, there is surprisingly little available on the "hot" topic of distance learning. Even Macmillan's *Encyclopedia of Education* (2002) has only a four-page article and assorted short references to cover something that is touted to be in all our futures. *Encyclopedia of Distributed Learning* should therefore be a very welcome addition to nearly every reference collection, and for the most part, it performs the function that collection development librarians would want from it. The title phrase *distributed learning* usually refers only to electronic distance learning, but this volume seems to cover all aspects, electronic or not.

This is a volume that adheres to high production standards. The editors have respectable academic credentials and are affiliated with the Fielding Graduate Institute, an academic entity whose presence is largely "distant." The list of contributors includes faculty from both virtual and "brick and mortar" institutions. All entries are listed at the beginning of the book, a reader's guide section groups headings thematically to assist the researcher, and an appendix provides an annotated list of programs that offer distance degrees.

The body of the volume has an *A–Z* arrangement, with most of the 174 entries being several pages long. They are signed and include cross-references and a bibliography. The topics covered include *Assessment of prior learning, Cultural diversity, Ethics, Library services,* and *Team teaching*. Much of the content covers the technology of distributed learning and therefore is likely to become dated quickly. However, since topics such as *Learning platforms* and *Meta-communication* are not easily found elsewhere, what this encyclopedia adds to the literature, along with its relatively modest price, will make it worth the risk of becoming outdated. Recommended for large public and academic libraries.

★Museum of Broadcast Communications Encyclopedia of Radio. 3v. Ed. by Christopher H. Sterling. 2003. 1,650p. bibliogs. illus. index. Fitzroy Dearborn, $375 (1-57958-249-4). 384.54.

This new set is a companion to the *Museum of Broadcast Communications Encyclopedia of Television* (Fitzroy Dearborn, 1997) and echoes its predecessor's format while featuring a broader topical scope to reflect the medium of radio's advanced development. The 670 alphabetically arranged entries, written by scholars and experts, range from 1 to 10 pages and explore various aspects of radio broadcasting within radio's historical context. Types of entries include programs (*The Green Hornet*), people (*Keillor, Garrison*), networks and organizations (*National Broadcasting Company*), regulations and policies (*Equal Time Rule*), audience research (*RADAR*), evolving technology (*Internet radio*), radio stations (*KYW*), and radio's interaction with other societal forces (*Violence and radio*). Some entries are accompanied by one of 200 black-and-white photographs. The encyclopedia's scope is international, but treatment of non-U.S. radio is often done in broad surveylike entries such as *Africa, Asia,* and *New Zealand*. The majority of entries emphasize U.S. radio practices, with a secondary emphasis on key English-speaking nations like Britain and Canada.

A substantial general annotated bibliography precedes the entries, and within each entry is a bibliography for further reading. The index is fairly comprehensive but could be expanded even more to accommodate geographical interests. For example, it would help to list entries for individual radio stations under the cities in which they are located.

Several competent encyclopedias already exist with information on American radio programs and their performers, such as Luther Sies' *Encyclopedia of American Radio, 1920–1960* (McFarland, 2000) and *On the Air: The Encyclopedia of Old-Time Radio* (Oxford, 1998), also covering the "golden age" of radio. These are more inclusive of the less well known but lack the biographical details in *Museum of Broadcast Communications* and the scholarly yet accessible narrative bent that places each entry in its broader context. *The Encyclopedia of American Radio: An A–Z Guide to Radio from Jack Benny to Howard Stern* (Facts On File, 2000) covers recent years but has shorter entries and lacks the international scope of the current encyclopedia. The new encyclopedia is a major addition to radio reference works. It makes a fantastic complement to a detailed radio program chronicler, but it can also stand alone. If libraries can only afford one major reference work on radio, this is the best choice. Enthusiastically recommended for academic and public libraries.

Fashion, Costume, and Culture: Clothing, Headwear, Body Decoration, and Footwear through the Ages. 5v. By Sara Pendergast and Tom Pendergast. 2004. 1,040p. bibliogs. illus. index. UXL, $275 (0-7876-5417-5). 391.

From the furry hides probably worn by Neanderthals to designer jeans, this set intended for middle-schoolers surveys how people have covered and adorned themselves through the ages and around the world. The volumes cover *The Ancient World; Early Cultures across the Globe; European Culture from the Renaissance to the Modern Era; Modern World Part I, 1900–1945; and Modern World Part II, 1946–2003*.

Within each volume, organization is by culture ("Ancient Rome," "African Cultures") or by period ("The Sixteenth Century," "1946–1960"). Following a brief introduction that provides background and context, each chapter is divided into sections covering "Clothing," "Headwear," "Body Decoration," and "Footwear," and within each of these categories are an overview and between one and 20 alphabetically ordered entries on specific items or styles. For example, the chapter on Europe in the seventeenth century has entries for breeches, bustles, stomachers, and waistcoats, among other articles of clothing. The chapter on Africa describes beadwork, body painting, and lip plugs, among other types of decoration. There are 430 entries in all, ranging from a paragraph or two to a page, and each concludes with citations to a few references, including Web sites, for additional information. Sidebars highlight related topics, such as hygiene and sumptuary laws.

Each volume contains the same glossary, time line, and general bibliography. Also repeated in each volume are several access aids, including a set table of contents, an alphabetical list of entries, a list of entries by category (clothing, headwear, etc.), and an index.

Although profusely and colorfully illustrated with photographs and reproductions of paintings, the set could use some drawings as well. It's hard to picture what a farthingale, a *fontange*, or a *haori* actually look like based on descriptions in the text. This aside, the work is notable for its organization, breadth of coverage, and attractive design. Strongly recommended for school and public libraries, it will likely appeal to an audience beyond its targeted readers.

Encyclopedia of Christmas and New Year's Celebrations. 2d ed. By Tanya Gulevich. 2003. 977p. bibliogs. illus. index. Omnigraphics, $68 (0-7808-0625-5). 394.261.

Featuring 240 *A–Z* entries on Christmas and New Year's ritual and lore, Gulevich's volume is a worthy addition to the cultural reference shelf. Well researched and appealingly illustrated with black-and-white sketches, the text outlines holiday customs in easy-to-read language. There are entries for the ancient Roman festival of Saturnalia, the Salvation Army kettles, and Charles Dickens' Christmas writings, to cite a few examples. The entry on Christmas carols offers a succinct overview from the time of the gospels to the present day. Coverage has been expanded from the first edition, *Encyclopedia of Christmas* (2000), to encompass New Year celebrations in entries such as *Resolutions* and *Times Square, New Year's Eve in*. There is also more coverage of Christmas around the world. Around 30 national traditions are described in entries such as *Iran, Christmas in* and *Mexico, Christmas in*. The text contains reference helps: a sprinkling of cross-references, 70 pages of meticulous indexing, and 5 pages of illuminated lettering with Christmas motifs.

Weaknesses fall mainly in the category of omissions or lack of upgrade from the first edition. An entry on the U.S. national Christmas tree presents a serious examination of the politicizing of an annual tradition. However, the author offers data from 1993 as examples of the number of people attending the ceremony and the number of lights strung on the White House tree. Following entries are resources and Web sites for further study, many of which are seriously out of date. Gulevich fails to include some standard elements of holiday celebration, e.g., the Alfred Burt carols, the popular story "The Fourth Wise Man," and Benjamin Britten's "Ceremony of Carols." Overall, commentary is limited in depth. Nevertheless, the topic is a popular one, especially around holiday time, and school and public libraries will want to add this to their collections. Those already owning the first edition may not consider it essential to update.

The Halloween Encyclopedia. By Lisa Morton. 2003. 232p. appendixes. bibliog. illus. index. McFarland, $39.95 (0-7864-1524-X). 394.2646.

Several hundred A–Z entries cover the history, folklore, symbols, rituals, artifacts, and activities of Halloween. Morton's research extends to Wiccan lore, Celtic observances, and Christian mythology, including the Mexican celebration of the Day of the Dead. She writes enthusiastically about folk customs and is sensitive to the controversies surrounding horror literature, witchcraft, and demonism. Without undue pedantry, she explains the house-to-house souling pilgrimage, the incorporation of cabbages in Scottish holidays, the source of the boogeyman in bogs, and the lengthy training of Druid priests in predicting the future. Contributing to data are detailed photos and line drawings—players enjoying a fireside game of snap-apple, an illustration from the *Luttrell Psalter*, a cook preparing holiday eggs, children around a bonfire. A lengthy entry on Guy Fawkes Day, which absorbed many Halloween traditions, includes a detailed history, an engraving of the gunpowder conspirators, descriptions of regional variations, and the texts of several popular rhymes.

Assisting teachers, researchers, and the media is a two-page chronology of Halloween, beginning with ancient Egyptian writings and a post-9/11 urban legend about going to malls on Halloween. A second appendix lists and summarizes literature and films from 1714 to 2001. The bibliography is thorough, covering early sources as well as recent works. The author could have improved on the list of books by separating primary and secondary sources.

This generously illustrated and indexed overview is a worthy addition to public and school libraries as well as the reference shelves of journalists and leaders of community events. Information on Halloween can be found in resources such as *Folklore of American Holidays* (3d ed., Gale, 1998) and *Holidays, Festivals, and Celebrations of the World Dictionary* (3d ed., Omnigraphics, 2003), but *The Halloween Encyclopedia* offers much more detail.

Holiday Symbols and Customs. 3d ed. Ed. by Sue Ellen Thompson. 2003. 895p. index. Omnigraphics, $68 (0-7808-0501-1). 394.26.

This edition of *Holiday Symbols and Customs* is the newest in a series of books Thompson has written in this subject area. The new edition, which explores the origins of more than 1,000 well-known symbols and customs, has been expanded to include some major annual sporting events, such as the Super Bowl and the Kentucky Derby, as well as more nonreligious events and Native American celebrations. The book is written to appeal to a wide audience, including students, teachers, and librarians seeking information related to a variety of holidays and celebrations.

Entries are arranged alphabetically by the name of the holiday or event. Each identifies the type of holiday; when and where it is celebrated or observed; a list of traditions, symbols, and customs; colors associated with the holiday, if any; closely related holidays; and contact information and Web sites. In addition, each entry includes a brief essay discussing the historic and folkloric origins of the holiday, followed by a section on the meanings of the symbols or customs. Each entry has a list of further reading for additional research.

This book contains more detailed information about holidays than *Anniversaries and Holidays* (ALA, 2000) or *The Folklore of World Holidays* (Gale, 1992). It would have benefited by having a bibliography for the whole volume that includes those works cited repeatedly throughout. The information is easy to read and use, but the choice of entries seems a little unusual (for example, why include the Kentucky Derby but not the Belmont Stakes and why the Arctic Winter Games but not the more well-known Iditarod dogsled races?).

Recommended for those school and public libraries whose budgets will handle another holiday reference book, but for those with previous editions or other holiday reference tools, this may be an optional purchase.

United States Holidays and Observances: By Date, Jurisdiction, and Subject, Fully Indexed. By Steve Rajtar. 2003. 165p. indexes. McFarland, $45 (0-7864-1446-4). 394.26973.

Many libraries are familiar with *Chase's Calendar of Events*, which focuses on proclamations, sponsored events, historic anniversaries, and religious observances. Some may turn to a work such as *Holidays, Festivals and Celebrations of the World Dictionary* (2d ed., Omnigraphics, 1997) to find other international observations. *United States Holidays and Observances* concentrates on observances and holidays established by statute in the U.S. and American Samoa, District of Columbia, Guam, the Northern Mariana Islands, Puerto Rico, and the U.S. Virgin Islands. In addition, UN-designated holidays are included to reflect the membership of the U.S. in the UN.

The text is arranged by month, and chapters for each month are divided into "Observances with Variable Dates" and "Observances with Fixed Dates." Each entry identifies the observance as federal or specific to a state and offers a description that ranges in length from three or four lines to a quarter page. Following the main chapters is a list of unscheduled observations (for example, in Oklahoma each Native American tribe can choose its own official day) and a section on "Holidays and Observances Listed by Jurisdiction." This shows chronologically arranged federal observances first, then lists states and territories in alphabetical order. A subject index and a name index complete the volume. It would be useful to have an observance index as well. Readers who want to know where Juneteenth Day (a fixed holiday in Florida but a variable holiday in Delaware, Oklahoma, and Arkansas) is observed have to guess which heading to look under in the subject index.

With its concentration on U.S. holidays and observations, this reference volume would complement the international scope of Chase's or similar titles. It would be a good addition to ready-reference desks in public libraries and information centers in schools.

World Book's Celebrations and Rituals around the World. 11v. 2003. bibliog. glossaries. illus. indexes. World Book, $249 (0-7166-5019-3). 394.2.

Designed to meet the needs of students in grades four and up researching multicultural holidays and customs, this set features double-paged spreads jammed with color illustrations and photographs. The short (less than 50 pages each) volumes each cover a different theme, such as *Marriage Celebrations* and *New Year's Celebrations*. Within each volume, a simple introduction is followed by a brief presentation on ancient celebrations that fit within the volume theme and then by surveys of celebrations and rituals in six geographic areas. Color coding is used to identify the geographic areas consistently throughout the set. Although each region is described in a small information box, there are no maps to help orient users.

Segments on individual observances often include either craft projects or recipes; for example, the recipe for *buuz*, a meat-filled dumpling that is served as part of the celebration of Tsagaan Sar (the White Month) in Mongolia, is provided in the *Winter Celebrations* volume. Each volume has its own glossary and index. The last volume contains a cumulative glossary and index as well as a list of additional resources.

These volumes are clearly designed for an upper-elementary to middle-school audience. The volume *Birth and Growing Up Celebrations* mentions male circumcision in a matter-of-fact, nonsensational way, but it does not discuss piercing or female mutilation. There is more information here on a wider array of topics than in *Kids around the World Celebrate! The Best Feasts and Festivals from Many Lands* (Wiley, 2000). The less colorful *Junior Worldmark Encyclopedia of World Holidays* (UXL, 2000) deals only with specific holidays like Christmas and does not incorporate information about rituals surrounding life events. The idea of gathering all the traditions from different cultures together by topic—birth, death, marriage, religious celebrations, etc.—rather than having a single alphabetical arrangement of holidays or the more traditional calendar arrangement is unique for this age level and makes it easier for students to compare and contrast rituals from different cultures.

This will be a useful addition to school and public libraries where students are seeking accessible information on rituals and celebrations from many cultures.

African Folklore: An Encyclopedia. Ed. by Philip M. Peek and Kwesi Yankah. 2004. 593p. appendixes. bibliogs. illus. index. maps. Routledge, $175 (0-415-93933-X). 398.

More than 300 entries in *African Folklore* recognize "significant historical and cultural experiences" shared among the wide variety of African cultures, including the diaspora. This encyclopedia offers substantive (averaging about three pages) signed articles, each with references. Sample topics include *Dreams, Films on African folklore, Metallurgy and folklore,* and articles on oral communication types like jokes, riddles, tongue twisters, call-and-response, songs, theater, and more. There are also brief surveys of African countries. Entries reflect the editors' broad concept of folklore as artistic communication inclusive of a variety of expressive behaviors and communicating media and of folklore's existing "primarily to provide group identity and homogeneity." An extensive index and cross-references are helpful navigation aids in addition to the list of entries that begins the encyclopedia. Appendixes—"African Studies Centers and Libraries in the USA and Africa," a bibliography of the Field and Broadcast Sound Recording Collections at the Indiana University Archives of Traditional Music, a filmography, and a partial listing of dissertations and theses on African folklore at four U.S. universities—also add value. The list of contributors includes academic or other institutional affiliation for most of the 161 authors, who come from a variety of subject areas and countries.

The editors also have the backgrounds necessary for this publication. Peek has authored various ethnographic studies of African cultures, including divination, arts, and ceremonies, and has also compiled several bibliographies of African and African American recordings of music and oral data. Yankah has written about political life, language, and folklore in Ghana. Their current project matches Routledge's other folklore encyclopedias in format and depth: *South Asian Folklore: An Encyclopedia* [RBB Jl 03], Jan Harold Brunvand's *American Folklore: An Encyclopedia* (1996), and the forthcoming *Jewish Folklore* and the *Encyclopedia of American Folk Art. African Folklore* fits nicely in the gap between encyclopedias of Africa and encyclopedias of folklore, narrowing and sharpening the focus of each. There is no resource quite like this one. Highly recommended for academic and large public libraries.

Language

The Facts On File Encyclopedia of Word and Phrase Origins. 3d ed. By Robert Hendrickson. 2003. 822p. index. Facts On File, $82.50 (0-8160-4813-4). 422.

This, the third edition of the *Encyclopedia of Word and Phrase Origins,* continues to couple etymology with humor, as did the previous editions, in 1987 and 1997. It contains 30 percent more new material and has more than 12,500 entries (3,500 of which are new). Not only has the author added more entries but he has also lengthened and expanded older ones. Hendrickson has much experience with linguistic reference works and has written *Whistlin' Dixie: A Dictionary of Southern Expressions* (Facts On File, 1993) and *American Talk: The Words and Ways of American Dialects* (Viking, 1986).

The entries in the encyclopedia range in length from one line for *Man* to almost an entire page for *Dutch* (including expressions such as *Dutch courage, Dutch door,* and *Dutch treat*). The work contains an alphabetical index, consisting mostly of individuals' names, and entries have *see* and *see also* references. As noted in our review for the previous edition, though the author claims to record the "living language of the day," he is still often behind the times. For instance, although *Axis of evil* has been added, other new entries in this edition include the already widely used term *make love* and the line *Make him an offer he can't refuse* from *The Godfather*. When it comes to technology, Hendrickson is also behind the times, as evidenced by the fact that he has no entry for something as pervasive in today's world as e-mail.

RBB's previous recommendation stands—this title is recommended for those with an avid, though not scholarly, interest in etymology. High-school, undergraduate, and public libraries that have the previous editions may want to update them. Libraries that own other standard titles such as *Brewer's Dictionary of Phrase and Fable* (HarperCollins, 16th ed., 1999), *Chambers Dictionary of Etymology* (1999), and *The Concise Oxford Dictionary of English Etymology* (1993) and have limited funds may forgo this one.

Garner's Modern American Usage. 2d ed. By Bryan A. Garner. 2003. 879p. bibliog. glossary. Oxford, $37.50 (0-19-516191-2). 423.

Garner's Modern American Usage is the latest by the author and editor of several legal dictionaries (including *Black's Law Dictionary*), among other works on language and style. The second edition maintains the same basic format as the first (called *Dictionary of Modern American Usage*), published in 1998: each entry discusses the usage of the word, provides quotations for illustration, and gives citations. There are two types of entries. Word entries, which are generally short, discuss individual words or groups of words. Essay entries discuss topics related to usage and style, including contractions, danglers, punctuation, and subject-verb agreement, among others. Compared to the first edition's entry for *complexioned; complected,* the second edition makes only minor editorial changes; the real difference is the easier-to-read spacing in the updated volume. The second edition shows more substantive changes in the essay entry for *Passive voice* without changing the basic meaning or adding unnecessarily to the length of the essay. New entries include *DVD, Internet, World Wide Web,* and, as Garner insists, *webpage.*

The *Columbia Guide to Standard American English* (Columbia Univ., 1993) takes a more prescriptive tone than *Garner's* and maintains more succinct entries on usage topics (comparing entries on passive voice, for instance). *The New Fowler's Modern English Usage* (3d ed., Oxford, 2000) is more descriptive, on the other hand, and includes examples from published fiction, where most of *Garner's* quotations come from newspapers and journals. Because of its somewhat conversational style and extensive essays on usage topics like *sexism, Garner's* might be best used, as the author suggests, for "browsing a little at a time or for serious reading" and later consultation. Appended material includes a glossary, "A Timeline of Books on Usage," and a selected bibliography. Recommended for public and academic libraries, especially if the institution does not own the first edition.

Science

The American Heritage Children's Science Dictionary. 2003. 280p. illus. Houghton, $17.95 (0-618-35401-8). 503.

Although there are several fine science dictionaries on the market for students in grades four through six, this one has some attractive features. The 2,600 entries were selected to represent different areas of science such as astronomy, biology, and physics as well as areas like weather and computer technology. Each blue-highlighted entry word has one or more definitions. Entries generally contain a pronunciation guide and a succinct two- or three-sentence definition. Unusual plurals or irregular forms are included, as are notations that alert users to locations of pictures or illustrations and places to look for cross-references or comparisons.

One nice feature is the "Did You Know?" boxes that are interspersed throughout the book and contain extra information about topics like anesthesia or cactus; there are also 150 short biographies on famous scientists, like Barbara McClintock. Larger entries, called "A Closer Look," use captioned pictures to illustrate topics like machines, plate tectonics, and stars. There are also full- and double-page treatments of measurement, the periodic table, geologic time, and other concepts. All of these added features present information in an appealing, user-friendly way. The illustrations that dot the text are small but in full color and generally clarify the entries.

School and public libraries that serve upper-elementary and middle-school patrons will find this a useful addition to their reference collections. It is well bound, attractive, and accessible and has the types of definitions a young patron needs.

The New Encyclopedia of Science. 9v. 2d ed. By John O. E. Clark and others. 2003. bibliogs. glossaries. illus. indexes. Oxford, $299 (0-19-521918-X). 503.

This set is an update to the original *New Encyclopedia of Science,* which was published in 1995. It consists of nine volumes, eight of them devoted to a particular field of modern science: "Matter and Energy," "Animals and Plants," "Chemistry in Action," "Stars and Atoms," "Earth and Other Planets," "Ecology and Environment," "Computing," and "Evolution and Genetics." The set is intended for both general readers with quick questions and students interested in specific scientific topics. The majority of each volume, about 100 pages, is a narrative consisting of approximately

50 topical sections (for example, "Hydrocarbon Chains," "Patterns of Animal Growth," "The Human Genome Project"), each two to four pages in length. Highlighted terms refer the reader to the other major component of the volume, "Keywords," an alphabetic mini-encyclopedia containing more than 400 brief entries. This "Keywords" section cross-references back to the thematic topics. The cross-referencing is only within each volume.

Each volume begins with a "Knowledge Map" that shows how the pertinent areas of science are interrelated as well as defining the major fields. Next, there is an extensive "Time Chart" that traces the development of the science through the key discoveries that shaped it. Each volume concludes with its own "Factfile" offering a wealth of quick information for the casual browser, including data, tables, and statistics chosen for their relevance to the subject. In addition, each volume has its own index and subject-specific recommended further reading list. New to this edition is the ninth volume, which has a full set index and a more general reading list. It also contains a listing of scientific institutions worldwide, recommended Web sites, and places to visit. Other changes include the addition of plant life to the volume on animal life, advances in computer technology, and updates to the "Keywords" and time lines.

The text is written for the less well informed reader and should be accessible to most. The layout is bright and appealing. Color photographs and illustrations appear on almost every page. All of the illustrations include thorough annotations that nicely supplement the text.

Each of these new volumes is excellent as a stand-alone. The addition of a cumulative index enhances their value as a reference set that would be a useful addition to the science collection in public and high-school libraries.

African Americans in Science, Math, and Invention. By Ray Spangenburg and Kit Moser. 2003. 254p. bibliogs. illus. index. Facts On File, $44 (0-8160-4806-1). 509.2.

What do Angella Dorothea Ferguson, Mae Carol Jemison, Garrett Augustus Morgan, and Lloyd Albert Quarterman have in common? They are among the 160 scientists profiled in this addition to the A to Z of African Americans series from Facts On File. Ferguson, a medical researcher and pediatrician, researched the cause and treatment of sickle-cell anemia in children. Jemison, a physician, was the first African American woman in space. Morgan, an inventor, created many useful items, including a gas mask for firemen and an improved traffic signal, and later founded the *Cleveland Call* newspaper. And Quarterman, a chemist, worked on the Manhattan Project.

This volume outlines the lives, challenges, and accomplishments of African American scientists since 1731. One-fourth of the 160 entries are about women. Each entry begins with birth and death dates and the subject's particular area of science. Fifty-six of the entries are accompanied by a black-and-white photograph of the scientist. The entries range in length from 4 to 18 paragraphs, and each entry concludes with suggestions for further reading.

In addition to the entries themselves, the volume contains a list of the entries in alphabetical order and a bibliography, which includes Web sites. Entries are also listed by 62 areas of activity and by the year of birth of the scientist. The volume concludes with a useful general index that enables the researcher to identify biographees who were slaves, attended the University of Chicago, or were awarded patents, to name a few topics.

High-school and undergraduate students and general readers will find this well-written book useful, particularly for less well-known scientists. It will be a good addition to any school or public library that does not already have a concise overview of African American scientists in its collection.

The Oxford Companion to the History of Modern Science. Ed. by J. L. Heilbron. 2003. 941p. bibliogs. illus. index. Oxford, $110 (0-19-511229-6). 509.

This is not a science encyclopedia but, as the title states, a companion guide to the history of science. The time covered is from the Renaissance (about 1550) to the beginning of the twenty-first century. It is similar to other Oxford Companions, such as *The Oxford Illustrated Companion to Medicine* (2001). The editor is widely published in the history of science, and he worked with a distinguished editorial board, along with 217 international contributors. The intended audience is scientifically curious adult readers. The volume is appropriate for undergraduate science majors.

The 609 entries cover scientific disciplines, historical developments in science, people, institutions, and other topics. Examples include *Astrolabe, Astrophysics, Botanical garden, Hypothesis, Nazi science, Navigation, Oxygen,* and *Scientific Revolution*. About 100 of the entries are biographical. Entries are signed and accompanied by solid bibliographies. Most of the recommended readings are books, but Web sites and journals are also included. There are four pages of color plates, and black-and-white photos and illustrations are interspersed in the text. Cross-references, a list of entries by broad topic, and an index (not always found in Oxford Companion titles) facilitate access.

This volume makes a good supplement to an encyclopedia of scientific history, such as Scribner's *History of Modern Science and Mathematics* [RBB D 1 02]. For example, biology is treated in 3 pages in *The Oxford Companion* and 32 pages in *History of Modern Science and Mathematics*. *The Oxford Companion to the History of Modern Science* is recommended for science reference collections in large public and academic libraries.

Science in the Enlightenment: An Encyclopedia. By William E. Burns. 2003. 355p. bibliogs. illus. index. ABC-CLIO, $85 (1-57607-886-8). 509.

This book is the second in the History of Science series and is a follow-up to *The Scientific Revolution: An Encyclopedia* (ABC-CLIO, 2001). It provides coverage of the great minds behind the developments of the Enlightenment as well as lesser-known ideas and scientists of the times. More specifically, it covers the period from the reorganization of the French Royal Academy of Sciences in 1699 until the 1820s. The preface provides a brief overview of science in the Enlightenment, primarily in Europe and the U.S. Attention is also paid to the controversies and challenges that many of the scientific discoveries posed to the major religions of the time.

The book begins with a topic finder that offers a listing of the entries by subject, for example, "Instruments and Devices," "Scientific Disciplines," and "Theories and Ideologies." The more than 200 entries appear in alphabetical order, from *Academies and scientific societies* to *Zoology*. Also included are entries for *Berlin Academy* and *Newtonianism* as well as individuals such as Antoine-Laurent Lavoisier, Carolus Linnaeus, and Voltaire. Each of the entries is one or two pages in length and includes bibliographic citations to works for further research as well as numerous *see also* references. The text is complemented by a variety of black-and-white illustrations.

The entries, although brief, are dense in content and would best serve those with some subject specialization. The text concludes with an annotated chronology; a substantial bibliography that will be extremely valuable for researchers; a brief, annotated list of useful Web sites listing only 11 sites; and a thorough index.

The book is intended for people in high school, college, and beyond. The text includes many scientific terms, and novice readers would have benefited from a glossary. Still, this volume fills a need, as there is little published that is devoted to this particular era of scientific discovery. This would be a useful resource for high-school, college, and large public libraries.

The Facts On File Geometry Handbook. By Catherine Gorini. 2003. 280p. appendix. bibliog. glossary. illus. index. Facts On File, $35 (0-8160-4875-4). 516.

The Facts On File Marine Science Handbook. By Scott McCutcheon and Bobbi McCutcheon. 2003. 266p. appendixes. bibliog. glossary. illus. index. Facts On File, $35 (0-8160-4812-6). 551.46.

With these titles, Facts On File continues its Science and Math Handbooks series designed to give both beginning and advanced students "quick, direct answers to basic science and math questions." Each consists of four major sections: glossary; biographies; chronology; and charts and tables. There are also appendixes in each, as well as good black-and-white illustrations and photographs. *Geometry* covers Euclidian and non-Euclidian geometries including projective geometry, affine geometry, vector spaces, knot theory, and topology. *Marine Science* covers everything having to do with the sea, including navigation, exploration, weather, geology, and creatures.

The glossaries are extensive although not exhaustive. The definitions are clear and easy to understand. The brief biographies are balanced in terms of gender, ethnicity, and specialization. Some have portraits. Charts and tables are well chosen, offering a wide variety of information. Especially helpful are the prefix and suffix charts in *Marine Science* and the constants, abbreviations, and symbols in *Geometry*. The recommended reading list in *Geometry* is more extensive than that in *Marine Science* and includes Internet sites, multimedia, and teaching resources as well as books at both the introductory and advanced level. The indexes are just adequate and in extremely small print, but the cross-references in the body help make up for that. In every section there are guide words at the top and bottom of each page that include first and last terms on that page.

Some definitions in *Geometry Handbook* are either too simplistic, too difficult, or confusing. The term *amplitude* is not defined. The reader is referred to two other terms, but neither definition uses the word *amplitude* or explains the referral to the term. There are some errors, including phrase duplications at page breaks. Pronunciation guides would have been a good addition.

Both of these handbooks will be useful to teachers. Students will find the *Marine Science* handbook more accessible than *Geometry*. Recommended for academic, public, and some high-school libraries.

Firefly Atlas of the Universe. By Patrick Moore. 2003. 288p. glossary. illus. index. Firefly, $45 (1-55297-819-2). 520.

Updating Moore's *Atlas of the Universe,* first published in 1970 and last revised in 1994, this edition utilizes color maps, charts, drawings, and photos to communicate information about the universe obtained on recent space probes. The book is organized into a series of two-page spreads tracing the history of astronomy, space exploration, and telescopes; exploring the solar system in detail; investigating outer-space objects (e.g., meteors, asteroids, and comets); and discussing the sun and other stars. A final section, entitled "The Practical Astronomer," advises amateur astronomers on how to select a telescope and set it up in a home environment.

Each of the two-page overviews packs a great deal of textual and graphic information into its compact format. The narratives are clearly written; however, they discuss complex scientific theories and technological concepts, and they sometimes contain mathematical calculations that require prior familiarity with the subject in order to be understood (e.g., the chapters dealing with star maps and solar system planets). Readers with little scientific background should refer to the nine-page glossary at the end of the book to understand some of the subjects discussed in the main body of atlas.

Almost every two-page spread appears to be revised somewhat from the last edition. The text has been updated and rewritten, and many of the photos were taken within the past five years using advanced telescopic and photographic technology.

The *Firefly Atlas of the Universe* provides current, accurate, and detailed information on the universe. It is more comprehensive and current than the *National Geographic Picture Atlas of Our Universe* (rev. ed., 1994), and it is especially helpful when used with Moore's excellent award-winning *Astronomy Encyclopedia* (Oxford, 2002), which defines and explains many of the concepts of astrophysics integrated into the atlas. Highly recommended for most public and academic libraries, whether or not these libraries have an earlier edition in their collection.

The Cambridge Guide to the Solar System. By Kenneth R. Lang. 2003. 452p. appendixes. bibliog. index. illus. maps. Cambridge, $60 (0-521-81306-9). 523.2.

Libraries will find a use for this book both in the reference and in the circulating collections. The photographs are stunning, the numerous charts and graphs are exemplary, and the narrative is bulging with all the important information about the solar system that is available to date. The author has done a wonderful job of making many of the complicated scientific concepts accessible to the layperson. The language is challenging for students younger than high school, but many of the charts, graphs, maps, captions, sidebars, and introductions should be understandable to middle- school readers.

The beginning chapters are an overview of the field of space science, with emphasis on discoveries, discoverers, and tools. The major planets and the moon have their own chapters. Uranus and Neptune are treated in the same chapter, because they are so similar. Pluto has no chapter at all, because it is no longer considered a major planet. Chapters on comets, asteroids and meteorites, and colliding worlds end the narrative. The lengthy chapters follow the same layout, beginning with lists of important fundamental facts, histories of explorations and discoveries, and descriptions of the atmosphere, landforms, and moons. Each planet chapter ends with a summary diagram of the essential makeup of the planet. The numerous photographs are a balanced mixture of large black and white and color, most from NASA files. There are rich appendixes of books and Web sites and a good index.

Anyone with a need for information on the solar system should find fulfillment in the pages of this handsome work, and it is a beautiful browsing book. More current and less technical than *Encyclopedia of the Solar System* (Academic, 1998), it is recommended for high-school, public, and academic libraries.

Religious Holidays and Calendars: An Encyclopedic Handbook. 3d ed. Ed. by Karen Bellenir. 2004. 406p. appendixes. bibliog. illus. indexes. Omnigraphics, $84 (0-7808-0665-4). 529.

Following the scope of the first two editions (1993 and 1998), the third covers "holidays with a sacred component that celebrate, commemorate, or honor people, places, events, and concepts important to a specific religious community." Included are the world's major faiths and other smaller faith communities that were chosen for their historical and current cultural impact in the U.S. Religious authorities and members of various religious communities contributed to this handbook in the writing and editing of chapters.

The book is divided into three parts. Part 1, "The History of Calendars," is broken into four chapters that provide information on the development of calendars as well as other methods of timekeeping, such as water clocks and pendulums. "Calendars and Holidays for Religious Groups" comprises part 2 and is the major section of the handbook. The addition of over 100 new entries means that more than 550 religious holidays are listed, beginning with those that originated in the Middle East (Judaism, Zoroastrianism, Christianity, Islam, and Baha'i) and moving eastward around the globe.

Each chapter on a religion or religious group begins with an overview of the religion. A second essay covers specific issues that relate to the religion and its sacred calendar. The last section of each chapter is a chronological listing of holidays and a brief description of each. Each chapter also contains a table that lists each holiday alphabetically.

Part 3 contains appendixes and indexes. The appendixes include Internet and organizational sources for more information, a bibliography, and a five-year chronological list of holidays for 2004 to 2008 based on the Gregorian calendar. There are three indexes: a "Holiday Index," a "Calendar Index," and a master index of personal names, concepts, key terms, holidays, organizations, events, and other significant terms.

All types of libraries would find this a good source of basic information about religions and their holidays.

A to Z of Physicists. By Darryl J. Leiter and Sharon L. Leiter. 2003. 388p. bibliogs. index. Facts On File, $45 (0-8160-4798- 7). 530.

Entries are in alphabetical order in this biographical dictionary of 150 of the most important people in physics, from Archimedes to Stephen Hawking. There is summary material at the beginning of the entry: birth and death dates, nationality, and field of expertise. Entries average around 1,200 words in length, and each ends with a short bibliography for further reading. Many include portraits. The volume's end matter lists physicists by field of study, by country of birth, by country where most of the person's work was done, and by year of birth. There is a wonderful chronology that helps the user visualize which scientists were contemporary to each other. The bibliography at the end of the book includes Internet sites.

What makes this dictionary special is the readability of the text. Physics theories are not the easiest concepts to understand, yet the Leiters take care to convey the importance of each person's work and to explain the nature of the discoveries in terms that make it accessible to a wide audience, including high-school science students. The Leiters also try to convey the personalities and beliefs of these physicists and how these influenced their theories and discoveries. Emphasis is on professional rather than personal life. Quotations in the text are from the person's own writings, including letters, journals, and publications. Cross-references help the reader see the connections between the work of different scientists. Understandably, there are few women profiled, but their entries tend to be longer and point out the discrimination the women faced in their professional lives.

Public libraries will find this a great text to have on hand, and high-school libraries should consider it a valuable addition to their collections.

Building Blocks of Matter: A Supplement to the Macmillan Encyclopedia of Physics. Ed. by John S. Rigden. 2003. 530p. bibliogs. glossary. illus. index. Macmillan, $130 (0-02-865703- 9). 539.7.

Twentieth-century and twenty-first-century elementary particle physics is full of quarks, leptons, antimatter, and dark energy. How is a reader supposed to understand physics when much of what he or she may, or may not, remember from high- school physics is no longer current? This alphabetically arranged guide is intended for a broad audience, including advanced high-school and college students as well as general readers. An international team of physicists contributed 153 entries, each with a bibliography of recommended books, journals, and Web sites. *See also* references appear at the end of each article. Also included are a reader's guide presenting a topical arrangement of entries, a time line, a glossary, and a list of common abbreviations and acronyms. Case studies of experiments such as the measurement of the muon, profiles of important laboratories such as Fermilab, and biographies of physicists such as Paul Dirac are among the entries, which are illustrated with tables, photograph, and schematics.

Building Blocks of Matter is a supplement to the *Macmillan Encyclopedia of Physics* (1996). As such, it will help students understand the physics of elementary particles, that is, particles that cannot be broken down. Because of its focus, it is more specialized than a physics dictionary. Recommended for science reference collections in academic and public libraries, especially those that own the *Macmillan Encyclopedia of Physics*.

A to Z of Marine Scientists. By Barbara Charton. 2003. 230p. bibliog. illus. index. Facts On File, $45 (0-8160-4767-7). 551.46.
A to Z of Scientists in Weather and Climate. By Don Rittner. 2003. 256p. bibliog. glossary. illus. index. Facts On File, $45 (0-8160-4797-9). 551.5.

Two inviting volumes "designed for high school students, researchers, teachers, and general readers." As is typical for the Notable Scientists series, these titles are clearly written and well organized and aim to include male and female contributors in their fields. The authors have included 115 (*Weather and Climate*) and 145 (*Marine Scientists*) scientists from varied educational and economic backgrounds, many countries, and different time periods.

Arrangement is alphabetical by last name, with most entries one or two pages long. Introducing each essay is basic biographical information (birth and death dates, nationality, field, education, and positions held). Emphasis is on how the person's work contributed to scientific understanding. Interestingly, although both titles encompass fields like mathematics, meteorology, and oceanography, there are only a few entries repeated in both books—Vilhelm Friman Koren Bjerknes (his name is spelled differently in each), Benjamin Franklin, Harald Ulrik Sverdrup, and Alfred Lothar Wegener. Librarians will be intrigued to read about Kurt Vonnegut's brother Bernard, who held 28 patents and developed cloud seeding.

Both volumes are well indexed. In addition to general indexes, there are lists of scientists by scientific field, country of birth, country of major scientific activity, and year of birth. Both titles define unfamiliar terms in context, but *Weather and Climate* also includes a glossary of lengthy, very well explained definitions. The bibliography in *Marine Scientists* has two pages of fairly current books and a few Web sites. The *Weather and Climate* bibliography offers eight pages of print and online sources, including much older journal articles. A list of climate-related Web sites is also included.

These volumes are definitely worth the price for high- school and public libraries. They may be useful for reports in middle-school collections too.

Encyclopedia of Air. By David E. Newton. 2003. 252p. bibliogs. illus. index. Greenwood, $79.95 (1-57356-564-4). 551.5.

A worthy complement to its two companions—*Encyclopedia of Water* [RBB S 15 03] and *Encyclopedia of Fire* (Oryx, 2002)—this work continues to blend factual and whimsical information about its subject. With his usual offbeat touch, Newton includes a list of musical references to air and a selection of aphorisms and sayings involving air along with the fundamental information about air.

More than 160 alphabetically arranged entries cover the science of air as well as related chemical and biological science and scientific concepts; devices such as air bags, wind tunnels, and zeppelins; mythology; recreation; and transportation. Biographical entries cover such individuals as Archimedes, Robert Boyle, and Amelia Earhart. Most entries have short bibliographies that include Web sites, and there is a general bibliography before the index. The index facilitates specific searching, but this is also a wonderful browsing book. There is a smattering of black-and-white images.

The thematic "Guide to Selected Topics," which precedes the entries, offers a snapshot of the diversity of content, which is also demonstrated by adjoining entries: *Airbrush* followed by *Air cavalry*; *Clear the Air* (a national education program) and *Coriolis, Gaspard Gustave* (a mathematician whose theory explaining curved paths is applied to air and ocean currents); and *National Wind Technology Center* and *Nitrogen*. One criticism is that the book is much shorter than its companion titles but also more costly. Nevertheless, high- school, public, and academic libraries will find it a useful addition, especially if they have acquired the volumes on water and fire.

Encyclopedia of Water. By David E. Newton. 2003. 401p. bibliogs. illus. index. Greenwood, $75 (1-57356-304-8). 553.7.

Just as he did in the *Encyclopedia of Fire* [RBB S 15 02], Newton includes entries on the physical and chemical aspects of his subject and also the "philosophical, mystical, metaphorical and symbolic" nature of water in human society. From *Acid rain* to *Zooplankton*, there are entries as diverse as *Holy water* and *Hydrogen bonding*, *Water rights* and *Watercolor*, and *Deluge* and *Drought*. It is a wonderful browsing book where one can learn about the ancient art of dowsing and also find a discussion of limnology, "the study of all types of inland waters." Also here are profiles of individuals such as Rachel Carson, Jacques Cousteau, and Dixy Lee Ray, who was a marine biologist as well as Washington State governor.

Entries vary from a paragraph to several pages in length. Many have several references for further reading and addresses for further information. All the further reading references are gathered into an eight-page bibliography. Entry headings are sorted into broad topic areas at the front of the volume, and the detailed index directs readers to more specific information. The book is an attractive resource for public and academic libraries and might also be considered for high-school libraries, where it could be useful for reports.

Water: Science and Issues. 4v. Ed. by E. Julius Dasch. 2003. 1,474p. bibliogs. glossary. illus. index. Macmillan, $395 (0-02-865611-3). 553.7.

Ben Franklin observed in *Poor Richard's Almanac* that "When the well's dry, we know the worth of water." This encyclopedia is an effort to educate users about water's worth before the well runs dry. With more than 300 topical entries, it is a good starting place for anyone desiring to learn about a wide array of topics surrounding the nature, sources, use, desecration, and protection of this most valuable resource. *Acid rain, Bottled water, Careers in oceanography, Hoover Dam, Leonardo da Vinci, Plankton, Salmon decline and recovery,* and *Wetlands* are examples of entries and help illustrate the set's range.

The topical outline at the beginning of all volumes groups entries into 28 categories such as "Agriculture," "Aquatic Animals," "Biographies," "Using Water," and "Weather and Climate." The outline also lists the 17 "Selected Sidebars Topics," although, without page numbers, these are hard to locate in the text. Also at the beginning of each volume are several tables: metric conversions; symbols, abbreviations, and acronyms; and geologic eras, periods and epochs. Entries range in length from 500 to 2,500 words and include short bibliographies of print and electronic sources. Pages have wide margins, which contain picture captions, definitions of key terms, and boxes of important facts and explanations (e.g., "Tsunamis Are Not Tidal Waves"). Photographs, illustrations, and tables are attractive and add meaning to the text. Each volume concludes with the 36-page, detailed cumulative index and the 60- page glossary. The glossary is, in itself, a useful reference tool with clear "plain English" definitions of terms like *100-year flood,* one that has a 1 percent chance of happening in a given year, and *senior appropriator,* the holder of the highest or oldest water right.

The scientific and social aspects of water are well introduced in this set, which is recommended for high-school, public, and undergraduate libraries. It is more comprehensive and more useful for student reports than Greenwood's *Encyclopedia of Water* [RBB S 15 03], although that volume has entries for water's philosophical, mystical, metaphorical, and symbolic roles, which *Water: Science and Issues* does not treat.

The Dinosaur Atlas. By Don Lessem. Illus. by John Bindon. 2003. 64p. glossary. illus. index. maps. Firefly, $18.95 (1-55297-830-3). 567.9.
Dinosaurus: The Complete Guide to Dinosaurs. By Steve Parker. 2003. 448p. glossary. illus. index. maps. Firefly, $49.95 (1-55297- 772-2). 567.9.

Here are two more dinosaur books to add to your collection. The first, *The Dinosaur Atlas,* is different from the usual dinosaur book and should be in most school and public library collections. It is written by Lessem, an acknowledged expert on dinosaurs and famous to kids for his work on the *Jurassic Park* movies. The atlas is divided into the three major eras of the dinosaurs. At the beginning of each section is a world map with locations of the different dinosaur finds from that period. The text explains the types of dinosaurs found and the environment of the period. Specific dinosaurs are profiled. The pages that follow focus on the finds on different continents. On each two-page spread is a small globe showing the positions of the continents during that period, a time line of the period, and a sidebar labeled "Dino Don Says," with tidbits of explanation about dinosaurs or paleontology. Back matter includes addresses for active dinosaur digs that students can go to as well as Internet sites for virtual experiences. The illustrations are excellent, although they often cover parts of the maps, which might be confusing to younger readers. Kids will love the details in the Dino Don sidebars. The text is good but brief; the value of the book is in the graphic material.

Parker's *Dinosaurus* is magnificent in its breadth and illustration. Arrangement is by group, and 500 dinosaurs are described. Each entry includes an illustration and brief information about the dinosaur's discovery and characteristics. Each entry also includes a "Dino Factfile" containing data on scientific name with pronunciation and meaning, location, size, diet, and time period. The luscious illustrations include photographs of fossils and of living animals related to the dinosaur or artistic renderings. The volume concludes with chapters on nondinosaur creatures of the dinosaur age and evolution since then. The end matter contains maps of main fossil sites, a list of museums, and a glossary. The text is better suited to older readers; younger children will be fascinated by the pictures.

Both of these books compare favorably to *Scholastic Dinosaurs A to Z* [RBB D 15 03]. All three books describe the work of paleontologists and the excitement of discovery. Depending on the popularity of the subject in a particular community, all three should be purchased.

Scholastic Dinosaurs A to Z: The Ultimate Dinosaur Encyclopedia. By Don Lessem. Illus. by Jan Sovak. 2003. 224p. bibliog. glossary. illus. Scholastic, $22.95 (0-439-16591-1). 567.9.

Doing what so many of us wanted as children when we looked for dinosaur books, this one lists dinosaurs in alphabetical order and gives their pronunciation. Other information includes what each dinosaur's name means, its complete taxonomic classification, length, time period, place, diet, and other details. Icons beside each name tell the reader to which class of dinosaur it belongs. Running along the bottom of each two-page spread is a chart identifying these icons. Many dinosaur names are no longer used, and the author explains why the names are not valid.

Almost half of the pages are color illustrations of the dinosaurs mentioned on the facing page's text. Smaller illustrations are liberally placed throughout, including pictures of bones and teeth as they are found at digging sites. Information boxes profile paleontologists or give interesting sidelights about dinosaurs and dinosaur research.

The text is thorough and interesting and not too difficult for elementary-school readers, who will be excited to have this book. The facts and explanations are very interesting and address most of the questions kids have about dinosaurs, how they lived, how they are discovered, and how scientists figure out what they are. The bibliography lists books, videos, reputable Web sites, museums, and expeditions. The author even tells readers how to participate in a dig. This is an excellent purchase for every school and public library, and many children will want their own copies.

Encyclopedia of Life Sciences. 13v. 2d ed. 2003. 1,872p. bibliogs. glossary. illus. indexes. Marshall Cavendish, $459.95 (0-7614-7442-0). 570.

Building on the successful and widely held first edition (1996), this expanded and improved second edition of a set intended for grade 7 and up does not disappoint. The first 12 144-page volumes are a continuously paginated collection of one- to five-page entries on a wide variety of topics. Some 78 new entries bring the total to 481, and the number of volumes has grown from 11 to 13, with volume 13 containing multiple indexes.

Each signed entry is supplemented by useful sidebars addressing relationships and concepts beyond the main essay. Categories of sidebars are color coded—for example, pink indicates evolutionary history, and purple means "Science and Society" (aspects of the topic that affect public life). All entries include cross-references to other entries and a short list of further reading. Each volume ends with its own brief index, a new feature. As in the first edition, entries range from the very general (e.g., *Atmosphere* and *Ecology and ecosystems*) to the very specific (e.g., *Cats* and *Ears*), but given the intended audience, nothing seems particularly out of place. In fact, by encompassing public health topics with entries on abortion and the common cold, animals and plants, and large questions of environment and technology, this encyclopedia has something for everyone in the targeted audience. Welcome additions are the 23 new entries about the lives and work of individuals, among them Rachel Carson, Dian Fossey, Carolus Linnaeus, and James Watson and Francis Crick. The repeated entries from the first edition are largely unchanged.

Although academic libraries will be better served by higher-level academic treatments such as those found in Nature's *Encyclopedia of Life Sciences* (2002), this set is highly recommended for public and school libraries.

Encyclopedia of the Aquatic World. 11v. 2003. 1,582p. appendixes. bibliog. glossary. illus. indexes. maps. Marshall Cavendish, $459.95 (0-7614-7418-8). 578.76.

More than 70 percent of Earth's surface is covered with water. Though these bodies of water vary in temperature, depth, and salinity, life-forms abound in most aquatic environments. This set covers the mammals, fish, birds, amphibians, reptiles, crustaceans, plants, algae, and microorganisms that inhabit the aquatic world as well as its symbiotic relationship with humans.

Seventy-two articles are arranged alphabetically by the commonly used English name for the group or subject. Articles range from 8 to more than 25 pages in length and are color coded into categories: fish and other vertebrates, invertebrates, plants and microorganisms, or habitat and human interest *(Aquarium, Lake and pond, Oceanography)*.

Each article describing a group of plants or animals begins with an introductory profile and a classification panel. A "Family Tree" maps relationships between members of the group. Other sections discuss anatomy, habitat, food, and reproduction or life cycle. Many articles also include sections on related topics such as camouflage and migration. All articles contain "Key Facts," "Focus On," and "Insight" boxes that highlight important or interesting information about the group: for example, how to tell the difference between crocodiles, caimans, and alligators. More than 1,500 full-color photographs, maps, drawings, anatomical charts, and other illustrations are included to enhance learning and encourage browsing.

Volume 1 includes a useful reader's guide, a set table of contents, and a thematic outline of contents. Volume 11 contains an essay on the variety of aquatic life, a set glossary, resources for further study (including Internet resources), resources for younger readers, places to visit, an evolutionary tree, and indexes of scientific names, biological classification, habitat, and behavior as well as a comprehensive set index. Individual volumes conclude with a volume-specific index only.

The absence of *see also* references and pronunciation guides only minimally detracts from this highly browsable and informative set. Designed for students in junior high through high school, this set will serve general browsers as well. The publisher's *Aquatic Life of the World* (2000) is similar in concept and treatment but intended for grades five and up.

Botanica North America: The Illustrated Guide to Our Native Plants, Their Botany, History, and the Way They Have Shaped Our World. By Marjorie Harris. 2003. 665p. bibliog. glossary. illus. index. HarperResource, $59.95 (0-06-270231-9). 581.97.

Harris is currently editor of *Gardening Life*. *Botanica North America*, which took five years to write, is certainly her major work.

In separate chapters North America is divided into 10 plant communities: "The Eastern Forests," "Swamps and Wetlands," "Florida," "The Boreal Forest," "The Prairie," "The Desert," "California," "Montane," "The Tall Trees," and "The Tundra." A map illustrates the areas crossing state and provincial boundaries. The Florida plant community is the southern half of the state, and "Tall Trees" includes part of northern California. Prairie runs from Texas to the southern part of Alberta.

Throughout the text Harris stresses plant ecology and the importance of preserving the natural world. The 420 plants included are native—documented to have been in North America before exploration by Europeans (1450) and still in existence. Plants that are considered the most important historically, ecologically, or economically are first in each chapter, followed by other plants arranged in botanical families. Each entry includes botanical, ethnobotanical, geographical, and historical information. We learn that sphagnum moss was used by Native Americans to line diapers, and in World War I it was encased in muslin and used for surgical dressings. Dogwood berries are high in fat, and robins depend on them for energy in migrating from the south. Quotations, poems, and excerpts from books and articles are scattered through the text and well documented. The photographs are all in full color, and many are full-page or double-page spreads. Unfortunately, the index includes only plant names.

The two-volume *Botanical Garden* (Firefly, 2002) might be considered similar, but it is more of an identification source. *Botanica North America* concentrates less on identification and more on how North American trees, shrubs, perennials, and annuals have survived and flourished. It is a necessary acquisition for public and academic libraries with a strong botanical collection. Gardeners will love to have their own copies to read in the dead of winter or on a warm summer evening.

Grzimek's Animal Life Encyclopedia: v.1: Lower Metazoans and Lesser Deuterostomes. 2d ed. Ed. by Michael Hutchins. 2003. 530p. bibliogs. glossary. illus. index. maps. Gale, $105 (0-7876-5777-8). 590.

Grzimek's Animal Life Encyclopedia: v.2: Protostomes. 2d ed. Ed. by Michael Hutchins. 2003. 569p. bibliogs. glossary. illus. index. maps. Gale, $105 (0-7876-5778-6). 590.

Grzimek's Animal Life Encyclopedia: v.3: Insects. 2d ed. Ed. by Michael Hutchins. 2003. 472p. bibliogs. glossary. illus. index. maps. Gale, $105 (0-7876-5779-4). 590.

Grzimek's Animal Life Encyclopedia: v.12–16: Mammals. 5v. 2d ed. Ed. by Michael Hutchins. 2003. bibliogs. glossary. illus. index. maps. Gale, $475 (0-7876-6573-8). 590.

The final volumes of the massive revised *Grzimek's Animal Life Encyclopedia* have finally rolled off the press. We reviewed volumes 8 to 11 (*Birds*) in the January 1 & 15, 2003, issue, and volumes 4 and 5 (*Fishes*), volume 6 (*Amphibians*), and volume 7 (*Reptiles*) in the December 1, 2003, issue. Volume 17 is a comprehensive index.

H. C. Bernhard Grzimek hoped his original encyclopedia would "disseminate knowledge of the animals and love for them." This is also a goal of the revised edition; it does not disappoint. All volumes follow a similar organization. Introductory chapters, written in a narrative style, are usually followed by taxonomic chapters and species accounts, which follow a prescribed format. There are no page references from the main account of the species to the illustrations; the index at the end of each volume must be consulted. Color photographs, illustrations, and distribution maps supplement the text. Additional resources include references to books, periodical articles, organizations, and Web sites.

Volume 1, *Lower Metazoans and Lesser Deuterostomes* (e.g., sea anemones, sponges, jellyfish, flukes, tapeworms, nematodes), and volume 2, *Protostomes* (e.g., mollusks, gastropods, annelids), represent animals often not well known to nonspecialists. The authors do an excellent job of presenting current research and scientific facts in combination with interesting sidelights. Volume 3, *Insects*, is written in an engaging style and provides a good overview of more than 1.5 million known species. Volumes 12–16, *Mammals*, are a rich source of information on this popular group, from platypuses to moles to bats to wildebeests to whales to humans. The illustrations are of mixed appeal; some look like strained imitations of reality, while others seem as if the animals could walk off the page. A less current revision is McGraw-Hill's 1990 *Grzimek's Encyclopedia of Mammals*, distinguished by exceptional large-format action photographs.

Authoritative writing in a style accessible to the general reader, comprehensive coverage, a taxonomic arrangement to facilitate comparison between species, consistent organization, ample color illustrations and photographs, incorporation of current research, and the inclusion of conservation status and the significance of the animal to humans make *Grzimek's* an excellent choice for academic, large public, and special libraries.

★**Grzimek's Animal Life Encyclopedia:** v.4–5: Fishes. 2d ed. Ed. by Dennis A. Thoney and others. 2003. bibliogs. glossary. illus. index. maps. Gale, $195 (0-7876-6572-X). 590.

★**Grzimek's Animal Life Encyclopedia:** v.6: Amphibians. 2d ed. Ed. by William E. Duellman and Neil Schlager. 2003. 507p. bibliogs. glossary. illus. index. maps. Gale, $105 (0-7876-5782-4). 590.

★**Grzimek's Animal Life Encyclopedia:** v.7: Reptiles. 2d ed. Ed. by James B. Murphy and Neil Schlager. 2003. 593p. bibliogs. glossary. illus. index. maps. Gale, $105 (0-7876-5783-2). 590.

"Enjoyable reading" is not usually a phrase used in descriptions of encyclopedias, yet these four volumes of the second edition of *Grzimek's Animal Life Encyclopedia* provide just that. Part of a 17-volume rewrite of the original 13-volume edition published beginning in 1967, these volumes exhibit excellence in writing, organization, illustration, and editing.

Following an extensive six- to nine-chapter overview, organization is taxonomical. Each family or order is discussed in terms of general description, evolution, structure and function, distribution, habitat, behavior, feeding, reproduction, conservation status, and relationship to humans. These descriptions are generally followed by anywhere from 2 to 20 representative species accounts that include rich illustrations and range maps. Formatting and layout are similar in all of the volumes, making the set consistent and easy to use. Illustrations, photos, and maps are in full color, serving the needs and expectations of today's readers. Editing of the volumes is tight, yielding uniform entries written by numerous expert contributors.

Volume 4 and volume 5—*Fishes 1* and *Fishes 2*—open with an elegant explanation of the diversity of the superclass *Pisces* and the difficulty of giving a general definition for all fish. Treatment is thorough despite the complexity of the topic caused by the sheer numbers of families, species, and habitats. Volume 6, *Amphibians*, includes introductory chapters on larvae and an expanded section on the early evolution and fossil history of amphibians. Volume 7, *Reptiles*, is the strongest of these excellent volumes. The contributors' expert knowledge and love of reptiles is evident. The "Order: Crocodilians" section is particularly well written.

Indexing is good in all volumes, giving access to both taxonomic and common names. Bibliographic references and further readings are well chosen and current. Recommended Web sites are authoritative and well cited. Criticism of these volumes is minor but must include the observation that the glossaries are on the scanty side. Examples of significant terms that should have been included in the glossary for *Reptiles* include *envenomated, hibernaculum, vomeronasal, vomerofaction, TSD* (temperature dependent sex determination), and *GSD* (genetic sex determination). The scientific illustrations are extremely well done, and the illustrations and photos are present in just the right amount—there when needed yet not intruding on the text. The addition of some minor cross-referencing of page numbers between the species/family accounts and the in-text illustrations and maps would be helpful.

These volumes are recommended for academic and larger public libraries.

Firefly Encyclopedia of Birds. Ed. by Christopher Perrins. 2003. 656p. bibliog. illus. index. maps. Firefly, $59.95 (1-55297-777-3). 598.

This encyclopedia provides a good overview of the birds of the world. About 9,800 bird species are included. The signed articles, arranged by family, average two to six pages in length. They are written by subject experts at a level accessible to high-school students and the general reader. The discussion of each family is augmented by a "Factfile," which usually includes a distribution map, habitat, size, plumage, voice, nest, eggs, diet, and conservation status. "Special Feature" articles highlight topics such as peacock display and the effects of pesticides, and the "Photo Story" features use photos and detailed captions to illustrate various types of bird behavior.

Species represented include those common to North America, such as snowy owls, blue jays, golden-crowned kinglets, and indigo buntings, as well as birds native to other parts of the world with intriguing common names like purple-crowned fairy wren, skylark, cuckoo roller, mountain firetail, and pin-tailed whydah. The casual reader could glean many interesting facts from this encyclopedia. For example, we learn that the New Caledonian crow is able to create tools to flush out insects; whooping cranes have been "taught" to migrate by imprinting aircraft as their parents; pigeons produce a crop milk that is similar to mammal milk. Outstanding large-format color photographs and illustrations on every page should appeal to both students and the general reader. A 16-page index provides subject access to the contents.

For high-school, public, and academic libraries, this encyclopedia is a good value for the money. *Grzimek's Animal Life Encyclopedia: v.8–11: Birds* [RBB Ja 1 &15 02] is a more comprehensive and proportionately more expensive set and belongs in larger collections. For smaller collections, the Firefly volume is an excellent alternative.

National Geographic Reference Atlas to the Birds of North America. Ed. by Mel Baughman. 2003. 480p. bibliog. glossary. illus. index. maps. National Geographic, $35 (0-7922-3373-5). 598.

Go to your shelf and take a look at your *National Geographic Field Guide to the Birds of North America* (2002). What you'll find is a detailed listing for each of the more than 800 species of birds that one can expect to see visiting or living in North America. But what about birds more generally? What of the particular characteristics of grebes or finches or crows? How are we to understand the general ranges, overlaps, and connection between closely related species within such groups? Baughman, of the National Wildlife Federation, has brought together an impressive array of experts to create this useful and fun volume, which will be a welcome companion to the *Field Guide*.

The volume begins with an informative essay on bird physiology, evolution, behavior, and classification. Each of the ensuing chapters treats one of the 42 major groups of North American birds, comprising 78 individual families. Following a general essay about the group, chapters provide details on each family, including classification, physical structure, plumage, behavior, ranges, observation tips, and conservation status. Major species are represented with outstanding illustrations, and sidebars treat special topics. A basic glossary of bird terminology, a brief bibliography, and an index that will be familiar to users of the *Field Guide* round out the volume.

The volume is populated with hundreds of very useful maps. Each chapter contains maps that chart the ranges and migration patterns of major species or families. In the "specialty maps" section, there is a wonderful map of "important bird areas in the contiguous United States" (great for vacation planning), and nearly 600 of the small range maps from the *Field Guide* are reproduced.

This is an outstanding companion to the *Field Guide*, but it also stands on its own as an excellent introductory text to the world of birds. It will be at home in public and school libraries and also belongs in all serious recreational and academic collections that serve those interested in birds and birding. More advanced readers may also want to consider the Audubon Society's *Sibley Guide* set (Knopf, 2000).

World of Animals: Birds. 10v. By Ron Hume. 2003. bibliog. glossary. illus. index. maps. Grolier, $419 (0-7172-5731-2).

Birds is the second cluster of the five-set World of Animals collection to be released. It joins *Mammals* [RBB Ag 03], while insects and other invertebrates, fish, and amphibians and reptiles are scheduled to follow. The *Birds* cluster continues set numbering where *Mammals* left off and is numbered volumes 11–20. Libraries that shelve by Dewey decimal number will find that this new set is therefore shelved prior to *Mammals* even though the volume numbers indicate a continuing set.

Geared to upper-elementary- through high-school students, the set groups species that share similar characteristics or have similar lifestyles, such as ground birds, seabirds, insect eaters, and tropical forest birds. More than 250 characteristic species are covered. Each 128-page volume is organized by family and presents information in two types of articles. The first introduces individual or closely related bird families (for example, the ratites) and reviews the variety of birds as well as their relationship with other bird families and orders. The second type, which constitutes the majority of the text, concentrates on birds typical of the family or families (for example, the ostrich, emu, or brown kiwi of the ratite families).

Well-written entries range in length from two to six pages and include numerous full-color photographs and illustrations. These detailed, vivid, and captioned pictures enhance the highly appealing and browsable layout. Cross-referencing in the bottom margin includes bird, volume, and page number for easy additional searching. Each volume concludes with a list of bird orders and families, a set glossary, further reading and useful Web sites, and a set index.

An additional noteworthy feature is the "data panel" found on the introductory page of each individual bird entry. Information provided includes common name, scientific name, family, order, size (imperial and metric), a visual comparison of an adult bird to a six- foot-tall human, key features, habits, nesting, voice, diet, habitat, distribution, International Union for the Conservation of Nature status, and a locator map showing normal range. School and public libraries alike will find that this set contains sufficient information to serve the needs of a variety of student users and will appeal to the casual browser as well.

Medicine, Health, Technology, Management

Salud para todos. [Internet database]. EBSCO, pricing on request [http://www.epnet.com/ifact/Saludmed.pdf]. (Last accessed September 5).

Salud para todos is a Spanish-language database with health information for consumers. It contains more than 300 publications created by 50 research associations and institutes, including nonprofits, federal and state agencies, and pharmaceutical companies. At this time, access is via an English-language interface allowing users to enter search terms in either English or Spanish and receive results in Spanish. Currently a simplified Spanish-language interface is available. EBSCO will soon launch a multilngual interface with all the functionality of the English- language version. Subscribers have unlimited on-site and remote access.

The Basic search mode offers keyword searching that supports Boolean and proximity operators, wildcards, and truncation. Users can refine a search by expanding it to search article text (as opposed to citations) and related words (plurals, synonyms) and also by limiting searches by categories such as Artritis (Arthritis) and Cirugía (Surgery). Advanced search can also be limited by field codes (Au, Ti, Su, etc.). The results are available as PDF or HTML files, which the user can save in a folder, print, or e-mail. Users may also set up an account for current awareness alerts. This feature will run a saved search at specified intervals and send the results to an e-mail box.

Searching is easy, but the results can be mixed. The topic of heart disease in women (*mujeres y enfemidades de corazón*) produced no results using either language in both Basic and Advanced modes. By adding a search for the terms within the text and related words in the Advanced search, one pamphlet from the National Heart, Lung, and Blood Institute (National Institutes of Health) on hypertension appeared. Looking for information about heart attack (*ataque al corazón*) produced one article on returning to normal life after the attack. There is nothing on the basic anatomy of the heart or symptoms of heart disease, but there are several articles on diet and nutrition for cardiac patients. There was more information on pregnancy (*embarazo*), with 60 hits on topics ranging from planning a pregnancy to breast feeding and breast care for mothers who bottle-feed. There are 79 articles about cancer, most on breast cancer, with several duplications. One can also find some material on ovarian, cervical, small-cell lung, and colorectal cancer.

La salud para todos is useful for libraries serving Spanish speakers who need basic health information. The ability to search in both languages makes it easier for librarians who do not know Spanish to locate material, although they may not be able to evaluate what they find. Most of the articles in the database at this time come from *Recursos de la salud en español*, created by the University of Utah Health Sciences Center and from the National Institutes of Health. Both are reliable sources. As the database grows and the multilingual interface becomes available, it will have even more to offer.

Exploring Technology. 11v. 2003. 880p. glossaries. illus. indexes. Marshall Cavendish, $329.95 (0-7614-7406-4).

This latest entry in a series that also includes *Exploring Life Science* (2000) and *Exploring Earth and Space Science* (2001) serves students in grades five through eight. The set offers 280 articles pertaining to all facets of technology from *Abrasive* to *Wood and wood carving*. The history of invention and innovation are also included in the coverage. Volumes 1 through 10 consist of alphabetically arranged articles, and each volume includes its own glossary and index. Unfortunately, terms that appear in the glossary are not indicated within the text of the articles, detracting from its usefulness for students. Volume 1 also includes a comprehensive table of contents and a useful listing of contents that organizes the articles by six main areas of interest. The final volume consists of a comprehensive glossary and index as well as an assortment of lists and concepts including weights and measures, "The Atomic World," the periodic table, time lines of science and inventions, famous inventors, "Places to Go," and "Things to Do."

Each of the articles begins with a brief description of the topic and contains numerous photographs and illustrations along with captions. Generally, the articles range in length from one to four pages and offer a brief overview of their topics. The coverage encompasses agriculture and food, engineering and construction, information technologies, medicine, and transportation. The text is clear and easy-to-read and offers pronunciation guides for hard- to-pronounce words. The layout includes many different feature boxes, among them "Look Closer," offering an in-depth discussion about a topic covered in the main text, and "Highlights," summarizing key information from the article. All of the articles conclude with a set of cross-references referred to as "Check These Out."

The colorful and eye-catching presentation, featuring many color photographs and diagrams as well as the boxed features, will especially appeal to casual browsers. In addition, the articles contain enough information to meet the needs of most upper-elementary and middle-school students. This set fills a need, as there is little on the topic for middle readers, and would be a useful addition to school and public libraries.

How It Works: Science and Technology. 20v. 3d ed. 2003. 2,879p. bibliog. glossary. illus. indexes. Marshall Cavendish, $499.95 (0-7614-7314-9). 603.

This updated edition offers extensive coverage of science and technology. It is intended as a reference for students and others who want to learn more about the technologies that affect modern life but who may not have a scientific background. Volumes 1 to 19, which are each 144 pages in length, include more than 800 articles that are alphabetically arranged. Some of the entries, which vary in length from one to eight pages, include fact boxes that provide supplemental information. The topics covered range from *Abrasive* to *Zoology*. There is a comprehensive index at the beginning of volume 1, and each of the subsequent volumes includes its own table of contents. Entries conclude with an alphabetical listing of their cross-references. This is especially useful, as the first 19 volumes lack individual indexes.

The coverage provided is thorough, the writing style is clear, and explanations are easy to understand. The areas of science covered include astronomy, biology, chemistry, geography, geology, medicine, and physics. Some of the topics in this new edition pertain to recent developments in microelectronics, biotechnology, and computers. The text is complemented by more than 2,800 illustrations, of which 600 are new to this edition. Students will especially appreciate the numerous cutaway drawings showing the inner workings of a variety of objects, including an airplane and an Aqua-Lung.

Volume 20 contains more than 13 different subject indexes in addition to a general index. A sampling of the subject indexes includes "Instrumentation and Analytical Technology" and "Transportation and Leisure." The final volume also includes a section of further reading that suggests titles as well as Web sites, a glossary, a weights and measures conversion chart, a science time line, a geological timescale, and a periodic table of the elements.

The articles are highly informative and would serve students in junior high school and up as well as the browsing lay reader. This would be a useful addition for public and school libraries. For a younger audience, UXL offers the less comprehensive *Technology in Action: Science Applied to Everyday Life* (1998).

The Encyclopedia of Human Ecology. 2v. Ed. by Julia R. Miller and others. 2003. 760p. bibliogs. illus. index. ABC-CLIO, $255 (1-57607-852-3). 604.2.

The complex nature of human ecology is examined in this encyclopedia. Entries are drawn from the studies of individuals and groups (as in psychology and sociology, for example); from the professions "intended to enhance individual and family life" (education, public health, etc.); and from the various disciplines and professions that study environments, both natural and designed. A sampling from the more than 250 entries includes *Aging and technology, Air quality, Child and family poverty, Cognitive and language skills, Contemporary men's movement, Evolution, Family diversity, Functional clothing design, Gender and environment, Juvenile justice system, Osteoporosis, Sustainable development,* and *Youth sports*. Profiles of individuals who have contributed significantly to the field of human ecology are given entries, among them Erik Erikson, Arnold Gesell, and Margaret Mead. Each of these entries provides a brief biographical sketch in addition to a discussion of the individual's work and contributions.

The encyclopedia is arranged in alphabetical order. Following each entry is a *see also* note listing related topics and a "References and Further Reading" section. Complete bibliographic citations range in number from 5 or 6 for some entries to 30 for others. The cited works generally refer to the literature of recent years and should be readily available for more detailed study. Some entries are accompanied by black-and-white photographs.

Other resources addressing human ecology, such as *The A to Z of World Development* (New Internationalist, 1998) and *Human Environments: A Cross-Cultural Encyclopedia* (ABC-CLIO, 1995), are not as comprehensive. The editors have succeeded in their ambitious goal of creating a single authoritative source for the study of human ecology. This unique encyclopedia is recommended for academic and large public libraries.

It Came from Outer Space: Everyday Products and Ideas from the Space Program. By Marjolijn Bijlefeld and Robert Burke. 2003. 242p. appendixes. bibliogs. glossary. illus. index. Greenwood, $55 (0-313-32222-8). 609.

Daily life has significantly changed over the past 45 years thanks to innovations by NASA, among them cordless tools, ergonomic chairs, computer joysticks, heart-rate monitors, and scratch-resistant eyeglass lenses. As stated in the introduction, "This volume contains 67 entries on products and technologies that have been either developed or improved upon because of space-related research and technology development."

Aimed at high-school students, *It Came from Outer Space* is useful for educators as well. One-half of the book has A–Z entries that give historical, scientific, and present-day applications for each item as well as additional readings from technological periodicals and authoritative Web sites. The entries blend information about how the technology was originally developed by the space agency with information on later commercial developments and applications. Technical terminology might make the text difficult reading for some students, but the authors generally succeed in presenting the material in an accessible and interesting way.

The second half of the book contains several appendixes: a history of NASA; guides to NASA's regional technology transfer centers, field centers and facilities, and commercial development centers; lesson plans for grades 9 to 12; an annotated listing of Web sites; and a glossary. The lesson plans are selected from the NASAexplores Web site, and each references the appropriate National Education Standards for science, math, technology, and geography, which are printed following the plans.

This book is recommended for the school and public libraries as well as a professional teacher's library. It will provide ideas for science projects for students and educators and fascinating reading for all patrons interested in learning about products and ideas generated by the space program.

The Merck Manual of Medical Information: Home Edition. 2d ed. Ed. by Mark H. Beers and others. 2003. 1,907p. appendixes. illus. index. Merck, $37.50 (0-911910-35-2). 610.

The Merck Manual, now in its seventeenth edition, has been a standard medical reference source for over 100 years. The first home edition, published in 1997 and translated into 12 languages, was a welcome addition to consumer health reference collections. Just as librarians begin to worry about its age, Merck has released a second home edition. The editors have completely revised and rewritten the manual, adding a great deal of new material in the process. All of the editors, contributors, and editorial board members are physicians or academics with doctorates.

The format of the book has not changed. A detailed table of contents lists 25 sections divided into chapters. The first, "Fundamentals," explains basic anatomy and physiology, the aging process, fitness, communicating with health professionals, and legal and ethical issues. The others cover specific organs, systems, diseases and disorders, drugs, and first aid. The sections dealing with organs and systems begin with the biology of the system and then explain the symptoms, diagnosis, prognosis, and treatment of diseases that may affect it. There are color diagrams of relevant anatomy as well as an eight-page insert of anatomical charts. This new edition has added material on violence against women, sexual dysfunction, chromosomal and genetic abnormalities in children, and travel health. The drug section now includes information about medicinal herbs and nutraceuticals and their interactions with other drugs. A new section called "Special Subjects" covers medical decision making, surgery, complementary and alternative medicine, amyloidosis, familial Mediterranean fever, and diseases of unknown origin. A series of appendixes contains information on weights and measures, common tests, generic and trade names of drugs, and resources for referrals.

Although it has fewer, less colorful illustrations than the *American College of Physicians Complete Home Medical Guide* (DK, 1999) and lacks the flow charts of *The Harvard Medical School Family Health Guide* (Simon & Schuster, 1999), *The Merck Manual of Medical Information* continues to provide the most current, detailed medical information in a format and language that lay readers will understand at a reasonable price. Libraries owning the 1997 edition will want to update and the others will want to add this excellent resource to their consumer health reference collections.

The Encyclopedia of Nutrition and Good Health. 2d ed. By Robert Ronzio. 2003. 726p. glossary. index. Facts On File, $71.50 (0-8160-4966-1). 613.2.

The media constantly bombards us with sound bites and snippets of information about nutrition and health. We hear about the latest diets and research findings that tell us what to eat in order to live longer and healthier lives. The interested and perhaps confused health-information consumer can turn with confidence to this encyclopedia. For the new edition (the first was published in 1997), the number of entries has been expanded to more than 1,800 (including increased coverage of botanicals), and approximately 30 percent of the content has been revised.

The alphabetical entries cover a broad range of topics. Foods, their ingredients, and nutritional values are described. Specific diets (Atkins, Mediterranean) are discussed objectively, with the basic premise of the diet explained along with its pros and cons. Entries on foods and the components implicated in diseases and disorders explain how and why the problem occurs and offer dietary recommendations.

Some articles reflect new health concerns. For example, the *Trans- fatty acids* entry gives a clear explanation of the health risks and offers alternative food options. There is useful information on the food pyramid and food labels. Medical terms, tests, and current research are also covered.

The author intended the encyclopedia as a one-stop introduction to nutrition, and he has covered all the bases. The book will be useful in all types of libraries serving sophisticated information consumers. It complements similar resources such as *The Nutrition Bible* (Morrow, 1995) and the *Wellness Encyclopedia of Food and Nutrition: How to Buy, Store, and Prepare Every Variety of Fresh Food* (Rebus, 1992), whose vocabulary and presentation are more accessible to the lay reader.

Statistical Handbook on Infectious Diseases. By Sarah B. Watstein and John Jovanovic. 2003. 321p. appendix. bibliog. glossary. illus. index. Greenwood, $64.95 (1-57356-375-7). 614.

Here is a volume that successfully pulls together information from print and Web-based sources. The information was gathered from federal and international government agencies as well as nongovernment experts, with complete referencing to the original source. Many of the diseases featured are current topics of news and discussion.

Eleven chapters cover topics such as "Nationally Notifiable Diseases" (the 58 infectious diseases designated as nationally notifiable in 1999), "Waterborne Diseases," and "Bioterrorism." Most of each chapter consists of tables, ranging in number from 8 for "Malaria" to 47 for "Sexually Transmitted Disease." These are accompanied by background discussion of the topic, followed by an overview of the tables themselves. Symptoms, pathologies, diagnosis, and treatment are discussed when appropriate. Types of data expressed in the tables includes U.S. tuberculosis cases by occupation in 1999, numbers of pediatric AIDS cases in the U.S. through 2000, and total numbers of cholera cases and deaths in Europe 1990–1998. Most information is current as of 2000 or later, and URLs are listed for Web identification of data.

A chapter-by-chapter list of tables, a list of World Health Organization regions, a glossary, and a bibliography divided by subject enhance an already effective volume. Recommended for the academic and public library, this handbook will complement any collection on diseases and current medical concerns.

World Epidemics: A Cultural Chronology of Disease from Prehistory to the Era of SARS. By Mary Ellen Snodgrass. 2003. 479p. appendixes. bibliog. index. McFarland, $75 (0-7864-1662-9). 614.4.

Epidemic illness and related topics from antiquity to the present day are described in this work. The chronologically arranged entries range in length from a paragraph to several pages. The information is objectively presented, with no editorial comment. It is left to the reader to deduce the cultural impact of population-devastating disease throughout history and also the impact of history on the spread of disease.

Cross-references help tie some information together. The index can be used to locate all the entries on a disease, but the references are to dates rather than pages, which can make it time-consuming to locate a mention of a particular topic. There are other problems with the index. The entry for *Black Death* gives only three twentieth-century dates in addition to a *see* reference to *plague*. The term *bubonic plague* is not indexed at all, although there are textual entries using the term. To find all the information the user must search through the hundreds of dates indexed under *plague*. More useful are the data charts and tables and the appendixes. One appendix lists epidemic diseases by date and source. Two others, general and disease-specific bibliographies, will be useful to scholars and researchers, who are clearly the target audience for the work.

The general reader will learn more in a less-labor-intensive manner from a work such as *Encyclopedia of Plague and Pestilence: From Ancient Times to the Present* (rev. ed., Facts On File, 2001), which provides a broader approach to the multifaceted impact of epidemics. Serious students of epidemiological history are likely to find the strict chronological arrangement of *World Epidemics* a workable research aid, and it is appropriate for academic and large public library collections.

The Encyclopedia of Complementary and Alternative Medicine. By Tova Navarra. 2004. 276p. appendixes. bibliog. index. Facts On File, $65 (0-8160-4997-1). 615.5.

There are many books on alternative medicine, but not many can be considered quick reference guides. This encyclopedia has 400 entries covering terms, organizations, and personalities related to the field.

Entries vary in length from one-sentence definitions to multipage essays. The shorter entries can be frustrating, and some of the longer ones, less than complete. One example is the entry *Bates Method for improving eyesight*. There is a brief explanation of the relaxation system and of Bates' credentials but no description of the exercises. Some entries on individuals give little or no information about their relevance to the field of alternative or complementary medicine.

On the other hand, the *Yoga* article provides in-depth coverage of the discipline, giving a brief history, the basic principles involved, and descriptions of the 26 branches of yoga. Another article that would have benefited from the same treatment is *Ayurveda*. A description is given, but there are no cross-references to related entries *(Chakra, Doshas)* that provide additional details. The lack of illustrations is limiting; even line drawings of things like acupuncture pressure points would have added value to the book. The appendixes include a list of professional and lay organizations, a list of herbs used in herbal treatments, and a time line of alternative and complementary medical history.

That research projects involving nontraditional medicine are being conducted at prestigious medical schools illustrates the growing awareness and acceptance of holistic treatment methods. As a result libraries will be handling more questions related to the area of alternative medicine. Despite its cursory coverage of some topics, the encyclopedia provides a starting point for further exploration. Public libraries may find this useful, but libraries serving a professional audience will find it lacking.

Encyclopedia of Folk Medicine: Old World and New World Traditions. By Gabrielle Hatfield. 2003. 392p. bibliogs. illus. index. ABC-CLIO, $85 (1-57607-874-4). 615.8.

More than 240 entries representing folk medical practices used in North America, Britain, Ireland, and Scotland were gleaned from extensive research. Articles are followed by no less than a dozen scholarly references related to the study of superstition and folklore. Ranging from a concise paragraph to several pages in length, entries include the treating of ailments and conditions such as *Insect bites and stings* (applying spit, urine, soda, vinegar, or well-chewed tobacco); *Palsy* (ingesting cowslip, applying leeches, or holding a dying chicken); and *Wrinkles* (drinking elderflower water, goat's milk, or an infusion of butterwort) and the supporting of *Contraception* (using birch bark diaphragms, impotence-inducing *Rhus trilobata*, or eating heart ventricles). Other entries discuss the various uses of remedies such as *Dandelion* and *Holly*. *See also* references follow each article, and an index completes the volume.

In concept, this volume is an ambitious effort, an attempt to record for future consideration and study a host of old-world and new-world folk traditions. Such traditions are often passed down by word of mouth from generation to generation, but the current resurgence in using alternative treatment and natural remedies to treat ailments makes examination of this volume worthwhile. This is not a health reference book, however; it would be as much at home in folk culture collections as in a library's medical section. Public libraries with patron interest or academic libraries with collections in traditional medicine would profit from the author's historical approach.

Encyclopedia of Alzheimer's Disease. By Elaine A. Moore and Lisa Moore. 2003. 401p. illus. index. McFarland, $55 (0-7864-1438-3). 616.8.

Amazon lists almost 100 titles on Alzheimer's disease published in 2002 alone. They range from medical texts to children's books as well as personal narratives and caregiver information. A reference title is hard to find, but this one fills the gap. The first of the book's four sections contains entries on disease pathology, brain anatomy, research, current treatment, caregiving, and government programs. Topics such as disease stages, drug action and effectiveness, and clinical trials are covered in definitions ranging from a sentence to several paragraphs.

Section 2 is a national list (by state and city) of long-term care and day-care treatment centers. Information for each facility includes the type of care provided, the number of beds, and the types of insurance accepted. The third section lists institutions involved in government-funded research projects, some of which conduct clinical trials.

"Resources," the last section, contains a list of organizations that either conduct trials or serve as a clearinghouse for this important activity. Also found here are a short bibliography and referral information on a variety of resources for caregivers.

The encyclopedia will be a useful tool for public, academic, and medical libraries and also for health information consumers. The latter group will find not only the names of the most recent drug treatments but also a checklist to assess nursing homes and an entry outlining the progression of Alzheimer's.

For both the professional and the consumer, this title fills a need and provides a starting point for further exploration.

The Encyclopedia of Arthritis. By Michael Stein and Guy Taylor. 2003. 388p. appendixes. bibliog. glossary. index. Facts On File, $71.50 (0-8160-4810-X). 616.7.

Arthritis is the number-one cause of disability in the U.S., and this encyclopedia, written for the lay reader as well as the professional, covers all aspects of the subject. Included are definitions of specific types of arthritis along with their symptoms, causes, diagnoses, and treatments, whether nonpharmacological, proven pharmacological, or surgical.

Written by two experienced medical doctors, this addition to the Facts On File Library of Health and Living provides reliable, comprehensive coverage of the topic in an accessible *A–Z* format. Most articles give the history of the term, symptom, or disease, some of which have been identified from ancient times, while others have been diagnosed only within the last 10 years. Clear explanations of the various clinical types of arthritis, among them osteoarthritis, crystal-induced arthritis, rheumatoid arthritis, and connective tissue disorders, aid the reader.

An appendix gives information on drugs that are used in the treatment of arthritis and includes trade name, side effects, and excellent *see* references. Lists of laboratory and diagnostic tests, general and specific Web sites, a glossary of abbreviations and medical terms, and a bibliography are also provided. The index cites information in the appendixes as well as the encyclopedia portion of the book.

This volume is a one-stop source for a broad subject and is highly recommended for libraries with medical and consumer health collections.

The Encyclopedia of Autoimmune Diseases. By Dana K. Cassell and Noel Rose. 2003. 364p. appendixes. bibliogs. index. Facts On File, $71.50 (0-8160-4340-X). 616.97.

The newest addition to the Facts On File Library of Health and Living series is *The Encyclopedia of Autoimmune Diseases*. Like others in the series, it is a stand-alone reference. With "nearly 100 autoimmune diseases . . . affect[ing] up to 22 million Americans—8 percent of the population," this book is appropriate for both general readers and professionals. More than 300 *A–Z* entries, voluminous appendixes, and bibliography will guide readers in their search for information.

Entries cover terminology, key physicians and researchers, and specific diseases. Specific disease articles contain a historical and general introduction with subsections on causes, clinical features, diagnosis, complications, treatment (drug and nondrug), and other readings. A separate entry on research on the disease follows, where appropriate. Articles on ethnic, age-related, and other specific factors are included (for example, *African Americans with autoimmune diseases, Environment and autoimmune disease*). Familiar conditions such as allergies, AIDS, diabetes, and hepatitis are found along with less well-known diseases such as Evans' syndrome or ocular cicatricial pemphigoid (OCP).

Appendixes list autoimmune diseases, diseases listed by target organs, organizations and help groups, patient research registries, and the National Institutes of Health (NIH) investment in research on autoimmune diseases, among others topics. An extensive bibliography and index round out the encyclopedia.

Highly recommended for the academic and public library collection, this book gives unbiased medical information for the general public as well as the family and friends of a disease sufferer.

The Encyclopedia of HIV and AIDS. 2d ed. By Sarah Barbara Watstein and Stephen E. Stratton. 2003. 660p. appendixes. bibliog. index. Facts On File, $71.50 (0-8160-4808-8). 616.97.

This is the second edition of a 1998 work titled *The AIDS Dictionary*. As with the earlier edition, there are several thousand *A–Z* entries, and the territory covered is enormous. Included is a wide array of topics—medical, cultural, social, personal, and pharmacological.

Changes include both new entries and revisions to existing entries. *Abacavir* is an example of an entry that has been updated. This is a powerful pharmaceutical agent that was headed for FDA approval for use with HIV patients in 1998, the year the first edition was published. In the 1998 entry, concern was expressed about the efficacy of the drug in patients who had already been prescribed other courses of treatment for HIV. Fears of its potential side effects, including anaphylactic reactions in a small percentage of patients, were also described. In the new entry those concerns and fears are both confirmed; however, abacavir's very positive uses are also discussed, as its benefits have emerged over time. Another revised entry, *Pregnancy*, is some six paragraphs long in *The AIDS Dictionary*. In *The Encyclopedia,* it has grown to multiple pages with subheadings such as "Pregnancy and HIV Disease," "HIV-Infected Babies," "Prevention and Treatment," "Knowledge of HIV Transmission," and "Reproductive Rights and Testing."

Aside from the entries, *The Encyclopedia* contains appendixes of value to both librarian and library user alike. The first offers more than 100 "Frequently Used Abbreviations." The second provides many pages of statistics on HIV/AIDS in the U.S. The third appendix provides worldwide HIV/AIDS statistics by country, and the fourth includes selected resources: telephone listings, education sources for physicians, clinical trial information, publications, databases, and Web sites from around the world. An extensive bibliography and index round out this excellent resource. *The Encyclopedia of HIV and AIDS* is recommended for health collections in academic, public, and medical libraries.

The Encyclopedia of Infectious Diseases. 2d ed. By Carol Turkington and Bonnie Lee Ashby. 2003. 397p. appendixes. bibliog. glossary. index. Facts On File, $71.50 (0-8160-4775-8). 616.9.

The recent advent of the SARs virus proves the validity of a statement in the introduction to this title, which says "new viruses may still appear." Although SARs is too recent to be included among the infectious diseases in this second edition (updating a volume that was published in 1998), others that have emerged in the last five years, including West Nile virus, are here. The alphabetically arranged volume covers diseases, treatment options, and relevant organizations. Comprehensive information is provided for each disease and includes its cause, symptoms, treatment, and prevention. Major diseases that have had an impact on the world's population (tuberculosis, AIDs) are covered in depth and include a history. This feature makes the volume useful to researchers and students.

New to this edition are articles on bioterrorism risks and the West Nile virus. Other entries have been updated to include new information. Charts and information boxes, including several on food safety, appear throughout the book. Appendixes include a list of drugs used to treat infectious diseases and a guide to home disinfection. There is also a bibliography and a topical list of organizations.

The readable text and the clear organization of information make this a useful title for secondary-school and public libraries. It will also be useful in consumer health and patient education collections.

The Encyclopedia of Parkinson's Disease. By Anthony D. Mosley and Deborah S. Romaine. 2004. 406p. appendixes. bibliog. index. Facts On File, $65 (0-8160-5032-5). 616.8.

This encyclopedia by a neurologist specializing in Parkinson's disease and a medical writer provides an overview of the illness. More than 600 alphabetical entries with cross-references describe all aspects of the disease. Entries range in length from one paragraph to several pages and include drugs used in treatment (*AADC inhibitor medications, Levodopa*), surgical procedures (*Brain tissue transplant*), anatomy and physiology (*Brain, Lewy body*), related conditions (*Dementia*), practical considerations (*Coping with diagnosis of Parkinson's, Home safety*), biographies (*John Paul II; Parkinson, James*), and organizations (*National Institute of Neurological Disorders and Stroke [NINDS], Parkinson Study Group*). Two appendixes list organizations and resources and state Medicaid offices. A bibliography of books and articles and an index complete the work.

Although general medical encyclopedias have articles on Parkinson's disease, this encyclopedia goes into greater detail. The articles on the practical aspects of life such as clothing, shopping, and home safety are valuable for caregivers. It would have been helpful to include a definition of the disease in the introductory material, as well as in the entry *Parkinson's disease*.

The wide range of information about the disease; current research, support, and useful therapeutic techniques; and a bibliography with clinical information, as well as sources for patients and caregivers, make this a valuable addition to all public, health sciences, and consumer health libraries.

The Encyclopedia of Sexually Transmitted Diseases. By Jennifer Shoquist and Diane Stafford. 2003. 326p. appendixes. bibliog. index. Facts On File, $65 (0-8160-4881-9). 616.95.

Directed to general readers and professionals, this work represents an effort to increase awareness and education about the serious problem of sexually transmitted diseases in the U.S. and worldwide. The introduction gives an overview of the problem, which affects the 65 million Americans who were living with STDs in 2002, according to the CDC, and includes statistics and demographics, the "why" behind the problem and its scope, major STDs, the global HIV/AIDS picture, and recent developments.

In *A–Z* format, entries present material in clear, succinct language. They cover causes, cures, key research, medical terms, symptoms, treatments, trends, organizations, and agencies. Entries such as *Kaposi's sarcoma, Psychiatric disorders, Shingles,* and *Tuberculosis* deal with conditions peripherally associated with some STDs. Other articles giving helpful practical information are *Condom, Insurance, Reporting and confidentiality,* and *Talking with a sex partner*. Although articles on various aspects of HIV are the most prominent, other STDs are well covered.

The bibliography is extensive, and the appendixes are good. They include, among other items, resources for information (Web sites and hotlines), an HIV/AIDS time line beginning in 1980, U.S. Centers for Disease Control and Prevention guidelines for home care for HIV/ AIDS patients, and a convenient "Sexually Transmitted Diseases at a Glance."

Broader in scope than the *Encyclopedia of HIV and AIDS* [RBB D 1 03], this work is appropriate for public and academic libraries. Currency of information and clarity of presentation make it an excellent choice.

The Encyclopedia of Work-Related Illnesses, Injuries, and Health Issues. By Ada P. Kahn. 2003. 434p. appendixes. bibliogs. index. Facts On File, $65 (0-8160-4844-4). 616.9.

With the World Health Organization reporting that nearly 1.1 million people are killed each year by work-related injuries and illnesses, this encyclopedia will provide employers and employees with needed information and resources to help reduce these statistics. It explores the relationship between individual health and the workplace with a focus on the health and safety rights of employees. An introduction explains contemporary workplace issues like safety, ergonomic and biological hazards, economic losses, demographics (such as aging workers), U.S. laws surrounding gender issues, and more.

Approximately 350 *A–Z* entries cover topics such as *Carpal tunnel syndrome; Child labor laws; Endocrine toxicity; Environmental Protection Agency; Karoshi; Slips, trips and falls;* and *Violence in the workplace*. Entries often conclude with contact information for relevant organizations and associations, a list of one or two references, and *see also* references. In some cases, *see also* references refer to nonexistent entries. Sixteen appendixes provide information on absenteeism, mortality rates, work-related homicide statistics, and other topics as well as a lengthy list of resources. Each resource entry includes name, address, toll-free phone, phone, fax, and URL. Following this is a nine-page bibliography divided into numerous subject areas including "Anxiety and Anxiety Disorders," "Environment," "Feminist Viewpoints on Working," and "Unions." Some of the references are rather dated; under "Eating Disorders," the most current book was published in 1994. The index is very detailed, providing a plethora of access points for research and quick reference.

Kahn has written several Facts On File books that have won awards from the American Medical Writers Association. Although not comprehensive, this resource will be used by employers, human resource personnel, employees, students, and faculty to learn about and thereby reduce the number of work-associated diseases, injuries, and distresses. Recommended for public, college, and special libraries.

Human Diseases and Conditions, Supplement 2: Infectious Diseases. 2003. 472p. illus. index. bibliog. Scribner, $90 (0-684- 31260-3). 616.9

This latest supplement to *Human Diseases and Conditions* (Gale, 2000), designed to be accessible to both adults and students at the middle school level and up, will help users understand the process of infection as well as specific diseases caused by bacteria, viruses, fungi, and parasites. The editors are physicians affiliated with the Center for Children's Health Media and the Nemours Foundation of the Alfred I. Dupont Hospital for Children.

The volume begins with a series of essays that examines the impact of infectious diseases in history and explains germ theory, diagnosis, treatment, laboratory tests, drugs, public health, and immunization/vaccination. These essays are extremely useful because the explanations are so clear. Readers will learn about Koch's Postulates (used to identify germs as the causes of particular illnesses) and gain a basic understanding of the complex process of immunity. Approximately 100 alphabetical entries follow, covering specific diseases (AIDS, measles, pinworm infestation), general types of infection (sepsis, zoonoses, skin and soft tissue infections), and related topics (bioterrorism, immune deficiencies). The disease entries define the illness and then explain how it is transmitted, signs and symptoms, diagnosis, treatment, duration, possible complications, and prevention. The page layout, featuring wide, colored margins that contain glossary terms, *see* references, and keywords for Internet searches, helps readers find information quickly. Sidebars with related information and historical tidbits enliven the text. Color illustrations and maps showing disease prevalence help users understand the concepts. All of the entries have brief resource lists of organizations and Web sites. A bibliography of recent books and articles and a cumulative index for the full set appear at the end of the book.

Although readers seeking detailed information about a specific disease will need to consult other sources, this volume provides an excellent introduction to the concept of infection. Libraries that own *Human Diseases and Conditions* will want to add the supplement. Those that do not have the whole set will find it useful as a stand- alone resource. It is highly recommended for school, public, and consumer-health libraries.

The Encyclopedia of Deafness and Hearing Disorders. 2d ed. By Carol Turkington and Allen E. Sussman. 2003. 294p. appendixes. bibliog. index. Facts On File, $65 (0-8160-5615-3). 617.8.

We all know that the sounds assailing us from amplifiers at rock concerts and air hammers alongside our roads can wreak havoc with sensitive human hearing structures. But what about automobile air bags? According to British researchers, the impact of an air bag hitting a passenger's face, coupled with the 150–170 decibel sound as the bag inflates, may, indeed, cause hearing loss. In addition to the entry on *Air bags and hearing loss,* this update to the second edition covers issues ranging from *ABLEDATA,* a database of assistive technology products, to *Xylitol,* a common food sweetener that helps prevent ear infections by inhibiting bacterial growth. The more than 600 entries provide information covering both adults and children.

The *Encyclopedia* is a wonderful reference guide for ear parts, the mechanics of hearing, disease comprehension, demystification of clinical jargon, and legal definitions and public laws. It also ably fleshes out the sociology of deafness through entries such as *Social adequacy index* and *World Games for the Deaf*. The very interesting *Miss Deaf America* entry describes a pageant created as part of the National Cultural Program within the National Association for the Deaf. It was begun by the late Douglas Burke, who was looking for a way to discover deaf actresses at an early age.

Fourteen appendixes and a well-constructed index round out the text. Among the appendixes are "Statewide Services," "Periodicals of Interest to Deaf People," "Religious Ministries and Organizations for Deaf People," "Residential Programs for Deaf/Emotionally Disturbed Children," and "Training Centers for Hearing Ear Dogs."

The *Encyclopedia* provides solid, easily digested, dependable information. Suitable for students, patients, concerned family members, and, certainly, librarians, it is recommended for academic and public libraries with medical and consumer health collections.

Illustrated Dictionary of Automobile Body Styles. By Lennart W. Haajanen. 2003. 165p. appendix. bibliog. illus. McFarland, $35 (0-7864-1276-3). 629.2.

As the preface states, "Few things have been subject to so many confusing type names and designations as automobile models and body styles." Where did the terms *station wagon, sedan,* or *spider* originate, and how have they come to be used? This dictionary is intended for students of automotive history and other car buffs to help them sort out this confusion. Both modern terms *(All wheel drive, Flattop, Hatchback)* and those inherited from the horse-and-buggy era *(Brougham, Cabriolet, Landau)* are included. More coverage is given to innovations and developments in auto body styles in the early twentieth century.

Entries include one- or two-paragraph descriptions of the term, including the period of usage, origins and history, variations, and language varieties. American, British, French, German, and Italian varieties are given, but there is no mention of Japanese, Korean, or other designs. Trucks are excluded, but SUVs and minivans are included. Cross-references include backward and forward pointing arrows for earlier and later usages. Terms in all capital letters have their own entries. Some entries illustrate body styles with generic-looking line drawings.

There are many car books, but no other source provides definitions of body styles. Recommended for libraries with specialized automobile collections.

Pioneer Aviators of the World: A Biographical Dictionary of the First Pilots of 100 Countries. By Hart Matthews. 2003. 208p. bibliog. glossary. illus. index. McFarland, $39.95 (0-7864-1522-3). 629.13.

December 17, 2003, marked the 100th anniversary of the first sustained, manned flight in a heavier-than-air machine. That 12-second flight fueled the dreams and ambitions of people around the world. This dictionary covering the first pilots from 100 countries honors the achievement of the Wright brothers and the accomplishments of aviators worldwide. Although the fliers were from diverse backgrounds, they shared some common ground. Many, like the Wright brothers, were inventors or engineers intrigued with solving the challenge of flight. Others, like Hungary's Ehrich Weiss (aka Harry Houdini), were daredevils in love with the idea of flying.

The entries are arranged by country and vary greatly in length. The U.S. entry on the Wright brothers runs for 11 pages. Documentation and information about pilots from some other countries, among them Albania, Finland, and Uganda, proved more elusive. As a result some entries are little more than a few sentences. Criteria for inclusion required that the pilot flew solo and took off from level ground in a heavier-than-air machine over which he exercised some level of control. Many of the noted flights did not take place in the pilot's country of origin. Some entries favor ancestry over country of birth. For example, the Armenian pilot was actually born in France of Armenian parents. He is Armenia's first because no Armenian-born pilot was found.

A short glossary, a chronology, and bibliography are included. Wonderful photographs, some never before published, accompany most entries. Except for the very brief entries this compilation makes for compelling reading. It explores the scientific challenges involved in building a plane, the sometimes bitter conflicts over who flew first, and the lasting impact flight has had on the world. The dictionary provides an interesting international approach to the fascinating history of flight that public, secondary-school, and college libraries will find useful.

The American Horticultural Society Encyclopedia of Gardening. Rev. ed. Ed. by Christopher Brickell. 2003. 752p. glossary. illus. index. DK, $60 (0-7894-9653-4). 635.

In 1993, when the first edition of *The American Horticultural Society Encyclopedia of Gardening*, the Americanized edition of *The Royal Horticultural Society Encyclopedia of Gardening* (1992), appeared, reviewers used the terms *definitive* and *comprehensive* when describing it. Very often, something of that caliber is difficult to improve. However, a decade later, the American Horticultural Society has done just that in its revised and expanded edition of the 1993 work.

The book remains unchanged in size, appearance, and format. Even most of the photos and actual text are identical. Subtle revisions are scattered throughout the entire work, with the majority and most obvious appearing in the first half, "Creating the Garden." It is here that the latest botanic technology and principles are found. State-of-the-art planning and design concepts now incorporate our various living conditions into today's garden lifestyles. The beauty and elegance of yesteryear's formal estates and traditional gardens have been preserved and at the same time transformed into the more casual landscapes and container gardens. An entire chapter on container gardening has been added. Techniques are discussed and illustrated for achieving the graceful and utilitarian window box, deck, patio, and rooftop gardens so prevalent today. Planning diagrams now take into consideration container sizes, shapes, and styles as well as all types of flowers and plants.

The American Horticultural Society plant codes (also new) guide the selection of the most appropriate plants for the gardening space. These are based on the 2002 USDA Plant Hardiness Zone and 1997 AHS Plant Heat Zone maps found on the end papers in the front and back of the book. A detailed "Hardiness and Heat Zone Index" lies at the end of the text, just ahead of the extensive regular index. As previously, the second half of the encyclopedia pertains to garden maintenance, including pruning, diseases, structures, and surfaces. This outstanding encyclopedia supersedes its first edition and brings gardening into the twenty-first century. Recommended for gardening collections.

The American Rose Society Encyclopedia of Roses. By Charles Quest-Ritson and Brigid Quest-Ritson. 2003. 448p. appendix. glossary. illus. index. DK, $40 (0-7894-9675-5). 635.9.

This encyclopedia, a beautiful tribute to America's favorite flower, contains information on nearly 2,000 roses from the earliest species to the most modern cultivars. Each A–Z entry, accompanied by a short description and a true-to-color photograph, lists both cultivar name and registered or trademark name, synonym and code names, the classification group to which the rose belongs, its origin and parentage, size and scent, flowering information, mature height and spread, hardiness zone, and awards. Since entries are listed by the name the rose was given when introduced, there are numerous cross-references to point users to the correct entry. For example, the *Peace* rose is found under its breeder name of *Mme. A. Meilland*.

Eighty-nine roses are highlighted in special entry boxes where the parent plant and its sports (mutations) are shown together. More than 40 feature panels profile nurseries, rose growers, and famous rose gardens from around the world. There are sections on cultivating roses, a glossary, a species index, a directory of rose societies throughout the world, a list of Web sites, and a very short general index.

The book is lacking in only a few types of information that would have assisted users. Since most gardeners choose roses by color, a color index would be helpful. Similarly, multiple indexes would aid patrons looking for a particular type of rose, such as a climbing rose or a rose with certain properties, such as fragrance or resistance to disease. Some additional cross-references would help with American names of foreign roses such as New Zealand's *Land of the Long White Cloud* (known as *Full Sail* in the U.S.).

These lapses aside, this is an excellent resource about roses. It will delight gardeners whether they wish to find information or merely browse and is highly recommended for both public and academic libraries.

★**Flora:** A Gardener's Encyclopedia. 2v. Ed. by Sean Hogan. 2003. 1,584p. bibliog. glossary. illus. index. Timber, $99.95 (0-88192-538-1). 635.9.

Major garden and plant reference sources are appearing like bulbs sprouting in the spring. A significant contribution to the bouquet is this work from the independent publisher Timber Press, which is celebrating its twenty-fifth year in the industry. The encyclopedia was produced in Australia by Global Book Publishing, and the chief consultant, Hogan, for many years managed the Australia/New Zealand areas at USC–Berkeley Botanic Garden. Most of the 15 contributors are from the U.S. and have credentials or experience in horticulture.

Following some introductory material on hardiness zones and plant nomenclature, the pages are filled with descriptions of 20,000 plants accompanied by 10,000 color photographs. There are entries from all plant groups—trees, shrubs, bulbs, herbs, fruits, vegetables, grasses, etc. They are arranged alphabetically by botanic name and include distinguishing features, commercial use, propagation, and cultivation. Individual species follow with common name, growth habit, flower color, hardiness zone, and width and height. The majority of the plants are cultivated (not wild) and grow in temperate climates. Starred species are those recommended by the consultants.

Many of the pages are more than half-filled with color pictures of various sizes from all over the world—Chile, Namibia, Nepal, Puerto Rico. The great number of species that are in existence is illustrated by 17 pages of irises, 24 pages of camellias, 59 pages of rhododendrons, and 68 pages of roses. Since the plants are listed by genus, it is necessary to use the index to find the common name. However, varieties are in the index only as a subheading of the genus; the "Peace" rose, for example, is listed as *Rosa* "Peace." A small glossary and full-page spreads illustrating leaf, fruit, and flower types complete the work. An accompanying CD-ROM enables a gardener to choose plants by group, hardiness zone, flower, color, and flowering season. For 50 plants, a moving illustration shows the change of seasons on the plant.

Several American Horticulture Society publications are comparable. The *American Horticultural Society A to Z Encyclopedia of Garden Plants* (DK, 1997), with 15,000 entries and 6,000 small colored photos, is not as complete. A 2003 revision of the *American Horticultural Society Encyclopedia of Plants and Flowers* [RBB My 1 03] contains a "Plant Catalog" and also provides step-by-step suggestions for creating different garden designs. Librarians and gardeners will need to look at their budgets before deciding how many plant reference sources are needed, but *Flora* certainly is a beautiful and comprehensive encyclopedia for the serious gardener.

The Kennel Club's Illustrated Breed Standards: The Official Guide to Registered Breeds. Rev. ed. 2003. 416p. glossary. illus. index. Erbury; dist. by Trafalgar, $60 (0-09-189028-4). 636.71.

The Kennel Club was founded in London in 1873. Since then, it has set the specifications for dog breeds around the world. The primary purpose of this volume is to describe Kennel Club Breed Standards for 192 pedigree dogs.

The book is organized by groups of dogs—hound, gundog, terrier, utility, working, pastoral, and toy. Each entry contains a history of the breed, a color photo or illustration, and specifications for eyes, mouth, feet, coat, tail, size, color, faults, temperament, and more. The specifications are used as the basis for judging dogs and provide the latest standards for each breed. An index of breeds, a canine glossary, and a guide to Kennel Club services are also included.

New to this edition are the updated standards for each breed, a general explanation of the breed standards, and the new pastoral group of dogs. The pastoral group was derived from the working group in 1999. Seven new breeds have full entries, and six additional breeds are represented with a photograph.

Libraries that own *The New Encyclopedia of the Dog* (DK, 2000), *The Complete Encyclopedia of Pedigree Dogs* (Southwater, 2000), or *Encyclopedia of Dog Breeds* (Barron's, 1998) may want to add this book for a more technical look at canines. The specifications are also available on the Kennel Club's Web site [http://www.the-kennel- club.org.uk], so for libraries short on budget, the Web site will suffice. However, the reasonable price of this compact, beautifully illustrated guide may justify purchase for some public libraries. Dog lovers will appreciate circulating copies.

The American History Cookbook. By Mark H. Zanger. 2003. 459p. bibliog. illus. indexes. Greenwood, paper, $29.95 (1-57356-376-5). 641.5973.

Zanger's zealous pursuit of populist cookery covers a wide swathe of American history. Concentrating on resources in local food history, he avoids the usual homage to the divas of the American cookery and home economics movements, such as Fanny Farmer and Rose Knox. Instead, he covers Indian bean bread, Pilgrim succotash, New England back-burner standing dishes, slave and ship's galley cookery, school lunch standards, trestle-table specialties from the Amana and Oneida communities, and the favorite recipes of Henry Ward Beecher, Emily Dickinson, and Susan B. Anthony.

The more than 350 recipes for muffins, syllabub, leatherbritches beans, jelly cake, flapjacks, S-O-S, and stewed gizzards were selected from historical cookbooks and other sources because they "tell people's stories" and help illustrate something about U.S. history. Recipes and commentary are arranged in 50 chapters focusing on particular time periods and themes, such as "Temperance and Prohibition Recipes (1837–1930)." Zanger's presentation preserves both history and practicality with the original wording of each recipe followed by an approximation of current cooking styles and measures and substitutions for rare items with available ingredients. The work concludes with a generously annotated bibliography, and chronological, geographical, and subject and recipe indexes.

Enhancing the text are photos and line drawings that resurrect containers and implements long relegated to antique shops. This book is a must-have for food history collections.

Fine Arts, Decorative Arts, Music

Classical Music Library. [Online database]. Classical International, pricing from $995 [http://www.classical.com/]. (Last accessed February 13, 2004).

Classical Music Library (CML), initially called *Classical.com,* is the first streaming classical music service for subscribing libraries and their patrons that is available 24/7 in the library or through remote access.

CML presently contains 20,000 recordings (tracks) from 17 labels, including Arabesque, Hyperion, and Vox. There are companies with specific missions; for example, Cantolopera specializes in operatic arias; CORO specializes in Handel oratorios; Hanssler Classic specializes in recordings of J. S. Bach. Missing from the collection are major labels such as DGG, Angel, and CBS. Consequently, Leonard Bernstein will be found as a composer but not as a conductor. U.S. orchestras are in the minority, but the Cincinnati Pops, Dallas Symphony, and Minnesota Orchestra are represented. There are multiple recordings of some selections so comparisons may be made between performers' interpretations.

The home page has a Composer of the Week feature, News, and "teasers," including selections from recently acquired labels. The page offers a simple search box, with a click for advanced search. There are a variety of other search options, beginning with the broad areas of Orchestra, Chamber, Instrumental, Stage and Screen, Vocal and Choral, and Opera and Operetta. Searches may be refined by genre, composer, artist, period, label, instrument, conductor, and ensemble.

There is a link on the home page to My Playlist, which is a collection of works that the user chooses (a simple registration is necessary) and saves for future listening. There is no limit to the number of tracks on My Playlist, so a user could add all the tracks available. While one is listening to music, links will appear to the Reference Section, which offers biographies of composers, illustrations, and notes on the specific piece. This information is brief and currently written by the CML staff. A suggestion of a newly created advisory board (six librarians, five of whom are U.S. academic, music, or public librarians) was that liner notes of recordings would be useful, and this is what will be provided in the future. Additional features of CML include Discovery Concerts and Playlists. Both of these features are topic-related tracks developed by CML.

Negatives with CML include the limitations of the labels (and music) that are available. There may be problems with streaming on the Internet just as with online radio. A few glitches were noted—music "skipped" and then stopped. There is a pause button but no way to start in the middle of a movement. There is no indication if a selection with a number of movements is complete. Browsing through the list of ensembles, one finds that some are listed under *The,* which is always jarring for librarians.

CML is an interesting concept, and some library consortiums are offering the service to their members. Libraries will have to decide if they need to replace CDs with a ready-made collection. The technology that accompanies the in-library use of the service (high- speed network, sound cards, headphones) is also a consideration. A reserve component is planned for the future. An increasing number of labels and additional enhancements may make CML a useful teaching tool for schools and colleges and a popular listening source for classical music.

Encyclopedia of the Romantic Era, 1760–1850. 2v. Ed. by Christopher John Murray. 2003. 1,277p. bibliogs. illus. index. Fitzroy Dearborn, $250 (1-57958-361-X). 700.

A superb set on one of the most important topics in Western thought and art offers 770 contributed articles on individuals; specific works of literature, art, and music; national developments in cultural areas; and themes, concepts, and events that are significant to the Romantic era. The editor's aim was to look at the time period as broadly as possible to see the changes in thought, philosophy, art, literature, and politics. The encyclopedia does not try to define what Romanticism was but instead to show how the movement manifested itself throughout all aspects of society, culture, and politics. This will be a drawback to a reader looking for a neat definition, but it allows the encyclopedia to cover diverse topics and people, such as Napoleon, Lord Byron, the French Revolution, landscape design, and the symphony.

The bulk of the entries are about individuals, including major writers, poets, artists, and musicians from Western Europe, Great Britain, and America. Focusing on what the person did during this period that contributed to or was influenced by the Romantic movement, biographical articles run one to two pages in length and conclude with a one-paragraph biography, a short list of major works, and a selected bibliography of secondary articles and books. A small number of articles are on individual works of literature, music, or art, chosen because they are representative of the period or because they are historically important. Probably the most valuable articles are the broad surveys that cover such topics as American Romanticism, drama, fiction, German idealism, literary criticism, and science. All entries have numerous cross-references that help the reader find related topics. The set opens with an alphabetical list of entries and then a list of entries by subject and by national developments. There is also a comprehensive index at the end of volume 2.

Through an interdisciplinary approach to the Romantic era, the encyclopedia gives students or general readers an excellent introduction to the movement while allowing them to see its full scope. Highly recommended for all academic and large public libraries.

Latin American and Caribbean Artists of the Modern Era: A Biographical Dictionary of More Than 12,700 Persons. By Steve Shipp. 2003. 864p. appendixes. bibliog. illus. McFarland, $115 (0-7864-1057-4). 704.03.

International interest in the artists of Latin America and the Caribbean has been growing steadily since the late 1950s. Despite this, most of the artists named in this directory are little known outside their home countries, despite representation in major exhibitions and art competitions in both the U.S. and Europe. Organized alphabetically by last name, this work presents entries for approximately 12,700 artists from 39 countries. Using information provided by art galleries and art museums and augmented where possible by personal letters from the artists, most entries include a brief one- to ten-sentence biographical note, citations to print works listed in the bibliography, collections containing works by the artist, date and location of significant exhibitions, and titles of important or defining works. The length of each entry varies from a few lines to more than a page for Fernando Botero and Diego Rivera, to name two examples. Argentina is by far the most heavily represented country, followed by Colombia, Brazil, and Mexico.

The work concludes with several appendixes: a list of artists by country, a chronology of exhibitions from 1819 to 2002, a list of art museums and one of galleries, and the aforementioned bibliography. Listed in alphabetical order by author's last name, the 500- plus titles (many in Spanish) are referenced in the author entries and provide a rich source of further information on the artists. Two pictorial sections, one in color and one in black and white, are inserted in the body of the work and serve to show the variety of styles and media used by the artists of this region.

A useful index to artists either currently living and producing or those who materially influenced the course of art in Latin America and the Caribbean, this does not give in-depth coverage but does serve as a point of departure for research. A sound purchase, especially for academic libraries with strong programs in the studio and plastic arts.

Art in World History. 2v. By Mary Hollingsworth. 2004. 544p. glossary. illus. index. Sharpe, $199 (0-7656-8069-6). 709.

Art history reference sources tend to be chronological surveys, and this one, first published in Italy, is no exception. Content is arranged in 52 chapters, from "The Origins of Art" to "Modernism Revisited: Art and Architecture from 1945 to the Present Day." Intervening chapters cover topics such as "Buddhism, Taoism, and Confucianism: Art in China, 600–1368", "Gothic Cathedrals: Technology and Style", and "Artistic Freedom: Impressionism and Post- Impressionism." The highlight of the volumes is more than 1,300 illustrations, which occupy more than two-thirds of each page. Almost all in color, the illustrations have informative captions and are arranged in useful groupings that give a better overall sense of the art of a culture or period than isolated images would do. Maps and time lines serve to situate the art in time and place. Occasional sidebars discuss specific artists or works. Volume 2 concludes with a glossary and an "Index of Names and Places."

Although the goal of the set is never stated, there seems to be an effort to differentiate it from standard art history surveys by emphasizing art as an expression of culture. Comments about art as it reflects religious and political power or signals a cultural shift pop up frequently in the text. At the same time, although there are chapters on art in Africa, Asia, and Mesoamerica, the volumes are fairly conventional in their emphasis on Western Europe. In the chapter "Spain and the Catholic Empire: Art in the Spanish Dominions," *dominions* refers mainly to the Netherlands; there is just one brief paragraph and no illustrations on Spanish colonial art. The art of Oceania is treated only in terms of its influence on Western art.

Although readers will need to turn to large surveys such as Janson's *History of Art* (6th ed., Abrams, 2001) for more in-depth text and for bibliographic references, *Art in World History* offers an attractive introduction for general readers and students. It is recommended for public and undergraduate libraries.

African American Architects: A Biographical Dictionary, 1865–1945. Ed. by Dreck Spurlock Wilson. 2004. 550p. appendix. bibliogs. illus. index. Routledge, $95 (0-415- 92959-8). 720.

This alphabetically arranged, 168-entry biographical dictionary contains articles from 250 to 4,000 words in length on African American architects practicing in the late nineteenth and early to mid–twentieth centuries. All articles are internally cross-referenced and extended by photographs of the architects and the buildings they designed. Using the definition of the word *architect* to mean a person who has created a design and presented it visually such that it could be constructed, the 100 contributors have profiled both licensed and unlicensed individuals. Examples include Julian Francis Able (1881–1950), who designed the Free Library of Philadelphia; William Wilson Cooke (1871–1949), who designed small-town post offices throughout the Midwest; and David Augustus Williston (1868–1962), one of the first African American landscape designers. Biographical entries include a building list for each architect, identifying the client and building name, the address of the building at the time it was built, and the year in which it was built. Also here are entries for nine architectural programs and eight so called Negro Buildings designed for the most part by African American architects for one world's fair and seven southern regional fairs. The volume concludes with a general bibliography, an appendix listing buildings by state, and an accurate index.

The writing is generally clear and easy to read, though at times a little uneven. Most contributors are university or professionally affiliated, but some are relatives of the architects, and their articles tend to be less authoritative in tone. Despite this, there is nothing else comparable on the market, making *African American Architects* a sound purchase, especially for college and university libraries with architecture programs, though it is also intended for preservationists, architects, and historians.

The Billboard Encyclopedia of Classical Music. Ed. by Stanley Sadie. 2004. 480p. bibliogs. glossary. illus. index. Billboard, $29.95 (0-8230-7644-X). 781.6.

Designed for the intelligent music lover, this work combines depth of insight with a high degree of accessibility. Editor Sadie has been editor of the *New Grove Dictionary of Music and Musicians* (2d ed., Oxford, 2001) since 1970 and is a respected music critic.

Unlike most encyclopedias, this one is organized chronologically by period. After an introductory section on the foundations of music worldwide, there are chapters covering medieval, Renaissance, early and late baroque, classical, early and late Romantic, modern, and contemporary eras. Each chapter has these divisions: introduction (history and major events of the time and social and cultural context), personalities (biographies of key musical figures), styles and forms (new and developing), and instruments (invention, construction, role). Short entries marked by icons cover additional facts on six aspects of music: "Arts and Culture," "Inside the Music," "The Voice," "Performance," "Women in Music," and "Influences." Sidebars give more facts throughout. Other features are cross-referencing, a glossary of musical terms, bibliographies, a list of musical organizations, and an index. The few black-and- white illustrations are unremarkable.

The text of this work is a very slightly updated version of the *Billboard Illustrated Encyclopedia of Classical Music* (Watson-Guptill, 2000) but with a much lower level of visual appeal. The illustrated edition also has a listening guide for each chapter focusing on a specific work and a discography. These are missing from the work under review, although entries for personalities do list a recommended recording. Bibliographies are slightly different, but information is essentially the same and will be of great use to students of music, cultural history, and general history by period. Arrangement of the encyclopedia works very well, keeping relevant information together, and it is recommended for public, community college, and high-school libraries. Since both versions are available, it remains to choose one on the basis of price, weighing the value of the illustrations.

The Encyclopedia of Ancient Egyptian Architecture. Rev. ed. By Dieter Arnold. 2003. 274p. bibliogs. glossary. illus. maps. Princeton, $39.95 (0-691-11488-9). 720.9.

First published in 1994 and revised and updated for this translation, this comprehensive encyclopedia by a leading expert on Egyptian architecture provides an outstanding overview of the magnificent structures of ancient Egypt. The work contains 600 alphabetical entries ranging from two sentences to several pages, with each including a bibliography to facilitate

61

further study. More than 300 drawings (including plans and diagrams) and black-and-white photographs are provided. Cross-references appear in boldface throughout the text. Other special features include maps, a six-page chronological table, a very brief glossary, and a four-page select bibliography. Individual entries are provided for major Egyptian sites such as Djoser and monuments such as the tombs of the Valley of the Kings and the Ptolemaic temples of the Upper Nile. Building types, design, and construction are also examined in entries such as *Obelisk, Sandstone,* and *Ceiling construction.*

The Encyclopedia of Ancient Egyptian Architecture nicely complements the multivolume *Oxford Encyclopedia of Ancient Egypt* (Oxford, 2001), which covers the full range of ancient Egyptian topics. Given its reasonable price, the work is a valuable addition for academic and larger public libraries.

Encyclopedia of 20th-Century Architecture. 3v. Ed. by R. Stephen Sennott. 2003. 1,525p. bibliogs. illus. index. Fitzroy Dearborn, $495 (1-57958-243-5). 724.

Intended for the general public, students, and professionals, the *Encyclopedia of 20th-Century Architecture* contains more than 700 alphabetically arranged entries providing basic information on a variety of subjects. Articles range from 1,000 to 4,000 words.

Volume 1 has a list of entries and a separate list of entries arranged by theme. Themes include "Architects and Firms" (the largest category, with 267 entries); "Building Types" (52 entries); "Buildings and Sites" (172 entries); "Countries and Regions" (35 entries); "Materials and Building Technology" (36 entries); and others. Examples of topics include *Acoustics; Bank of China Tower; Concrete; Gas station; Israel; Paul, Bruno; Tent;* and *Vancouver, British Columbia, Canada.*

Articles on buildings include designer name(s), date of completion, and location and often describe design features, architectural themes and influences, and challenges in design. For example, the article on the AEG Turbine Factory touches on the somewhat contentious relationship between designer and engineer. Articles on architects zero in on the person's architectural career, describing major achievements, philosophy of design, and impact on the architectural community.

All articles are signed, and most end with a list of related topics as well as a list of suggested readings. The lack of Internet sites will disappoint some researchers. Articles on people often include a list of their selected works and publications.

Volume 3 provides a cumulative subject index with main entries listed in bold. The 600 mostly black-and-white illustrations usually show exterior shots of buildings. The lack of detailed illustrations highlighting specific design features forces readers to rely on text descriptions, which the general reader might find challenging.

The international coverage of not only architects and buildings but also building materials, locations, movements, and other architectural topics distinguishes this resource from reference tools such as the *Encyclopedia of Vernacular Architecture of the World* (Cambridge Univ., 1997) and the *International Dictionary of Architects and Architecture* (St. James, 1993). Recommended for large public libraries and academic libraries, especially those supporting architectural programs.

Encyclopedia of Sculpture. 3v. Ed. by Antonia Boström. 2003. 1,921p. bibliogs. illus. index. Fitzroy Dearborn, $375 (1-57958-248-6). 735.

Until now, reference material about sculpture could only be found in general art histories and encyclopedias. In this welcome addition to the literature of art history, sculpture finally gets its due. Just as a piece of sculpture challenges the viewer to look at a subject from several different perspectives (sometimes all at once), this comprehensive and well-organized work approaches its subject from a variety of viewpoints. Regional surveys and articles on styles and periods *(Minimalism, Modernism, Romanesque)*; materials *(Amber, Stone, Wood)*; forms *(Obelisk, Stela, Totem pole)*; techniques *(Metal casting, Pointing)*; and seminal sculptures *(Parthenon, Pietà)* join biographical information about sculptors and, in some cases, critical analysis of one or two of their works.

The more than 760 signed articles are alphabetically arranged, from one on modern Finnish sculptor Wäinö Aaltonen to one on several generations of the Baroque German Zürn family. A number of special features provide easy access to the content. In addition to a general index, there are also alphabetical and thematic lists of entries. Each article ends with carefully chosen suggestions for further reading, and many are accompanied by a black-and-white illustration. Entries on individual sculptors include lists of selected works and their years of completion. A list of contributors provides each one's credentials as well as a list of the articles written for this book. Cross-references abound, both in the index and the main text. A solid reference work appropriate for any large general reference collection as well as all art history collections.

Encyclopedia of American Folk Art. Ed. by Gerard C. Wertkin and Lee Kogan. bibliogs. illus. index. 2003. 612p. Routledge, $125 (0-415-92986-5). 745.

The editors state that this encyclopedia offers "quick and convenient access to a remarkably diverse body of information drawn from three centuries of American folk creativity"—and they are correct. They have chosen to use *folk art* as a composite term to include all the forms and fashions of often self-taught art, and not just the most traditional or historic art expressions. This means that, in addition to information on hundreds of folk artists (whether traditional, outsider, naive, or other), scholars, collectors, museum directors, and more are to be found among the 607 entries. Immigrants and native-born alike have tightly written biographies averaging one-half page in length, each with a short bibliography. Other entries cover types of art (e.g., *Jewish folk art, Native American folk art*); techniques *(Fraktur, Metalwork)*; museums *(New England Quilt Museum)*; religious practices *(Santería)*; and much more.

Black-and-white illustrations accompany some entries, with most of the examples in the 64 color-plate segments that appear in four groups throughout the book. Plates may include several pieces of art along with informative captions. One missing feature is references in the entry text to relevant plates, and vice versa—plate captions that refer readers to the appropriate entries. Plate 15 has two lovely examples of fireboards and there is an entry for *Fireboards and overmantels,* but neither refers to the other. Otherwise, the entries have extensive *see also* notes, as does the detailed index. There are also *see* entries, as in *Flat tulip artist* see *Daniel Otto.* In spite of the small font size throughout, the entries are very readable and engagingly written. The list of entries at the beginning is easy to scan and is a counterpoint to the index.

The editors give well-deserved praise to the 92 specialists who wrote the signed entries. They also guide readers to other valuable resources that predated and supplement this work. This encyclopedia will be useful to collectors, students, scholars, and experts. It is an excellent value for the cost and a recommended purchase for academic and large public libraries.

From Convent to Concert Hall: A Guide to Women Composers. Ed. by Martha Furman Schleifer and Sylvia Glickman. 2003. 403p. appendixes. bibliogs. glossary. illus. index. Greenwood, $75 (1-57356-411-7). 780.

Since recent years have seen an increase in the amount of scholarship devoted to this subject, there is a need for reference material to support the resulting courses of study. This carefully orchestrated work can play more than one part: it is both reference book, packed with a number of useful features; and textbook, even including a "Suggested Syllabus for a Fifteen-Week Semester with Three Class Hours per Week." The main theme is a historical survey of a representative group of some 150 women composers. Hildegard von Bingen, Clara Wieck Schumann, Cécile Chaminade, Nadia and Lili Boulanger, Laurie Anderson, and Mary Lou Williams are among them. After a prologue featuring abstracts of each of the succeeding chapters, there is a series of substantive chronological essays, beginning with the Middle Ages and the Renaissance and continuing on through to the twentieth century. Each chapter highlights the important women composers of each time period and often includes portraits or photographs of its subjects. A time line for the pertinent century (or centuries) follows, and each section ends with a bibliography, selected discography, and list of selected modern editions of scores. Appended material includes chronological and geographical lists of women composers, the suggested syllabus mentioned above, a glossary of musical terms, and a substantial general bibliography that includes selected online resources. A comprehensive index ensures easy access to the information about individual composers (whose names are printed in boldface type) in the text.

With its thoughtful organization, clearly written and carefully researched text, and numerous special features, this will be a welcome addition to any academic or large public library music reference collection.

The Harvard Dictionary of Music. 4th ed. Ed. by Don Michael Randel. 2003. 978p. bibliogs. illus. Harvard, $39.95 (0-674-01163-5). 780.

Reverting to its original title, *The Harvard Dictionary of Music* continues under editor Randel as a revision of his 1986 *The New Harvard Dictionary of Music*, so named at that time to reflect its significantly expanded scope from previous editions. The focus remains "the tradition of Western art music," with greater attention to world and popular music. Dozens of contributing scholars are listed in the front matter and denoted by initials at the end of entries.

Entries range from one or two words to multiple pages in length, defining or explicating terms for musical styles, instruments, performance marks, concepts, and works (e.g., *Blues, Consonance and dissonance, Koto, Largo, Moonlight Sonata, Percussion instruments, Suzuki method*). Black-and-white illustrations identify instruments, and staves and other forms of notation aid understanding of concepts (e.g., *Diminution, Mambo*). Many longer essays retain most of the text of the last edition, with brief updates to each section where appropriate. For example, *England* is enhanced by a listing of important British composers born in the twentieth century under the heading "History." Others have been substantially reworked or replaced (e.g., *Electro-acoustic music*). Many short entries have been completely revamped to reflect greater cultural importance or changing use or understanding of the terms. For example, *Reggae* now emphasizes the influence of Bob Marley. The content occasionally seems a bit behind the times, omitting terms like *MIDI* and *MP3* (though *Compact disc* is a new entry) and failing to mention significant technological advances in *Notation* and *Score* that enable new approaches to both representation and reproduction of musical ideas. Brief bibliographies accompany many of the articles, and these have been updated even if there were few major changes to the entry.

In comparison with other single-volume music references, such as the *Oxford Companion to Music* (2002) and *Baker's Dictionary of Music* (Gale, 1997), *Harvard* does not have biographical entries, is generally more scholarly in tone and content, and has many unique articles (e.g., *Boston dip waltz, Ecphonetic notation, Lombard rhythm*). Recommended for any comprehensive music reference collection.

Baker's Biographical Dictionary of Popular Musicians since 1990. 2v. 2003. 880p. appendix. bibliogs. glossary. illus. indexes. Schirmer, $195 (0-02-865799-3). 781.64.

Featuring 583 essays that vary in length from 500 to 2,000 words and have been written by critics, professors of popular culture, and experts on various genres of current music, *Baker's Biographical Dictionary of Popular Musicians since 1990* is a companion to the six-volume *Baker's Biographical Dictionary of Musicians: Centennial Edition* (2000). While the *Centennial Edition* focused on classical music, there is extensive coverage in the new set of contemporary rock, pop, country, hip-hop and R & B. Popular musicians from other genres are also treated, among them Danny Elfman, the Chieftains, Yo-Yo Ma, Wynton Marsalis, and Stephen Sondheim. The writing style is refreshing in its accessibility to a broad range of readers.

"Since 1990" means just that. Gladys Knight is omitted because she had little commercial success during the period, but the Beatles, who have not existed as a band since 1970, are included because of the release of their three *Anthology* CDs, the discovery of two unreleased songs, and the death of George Harrison. All entries include biographical information and an evaluation of the subject's career and style of music. Boxed sidebars called "Spotlight" describe songs, albums, or events that have been particularly significant to a genre or an artist; for example the Farm Aid concerts. The length of the entries reflects length of careers. All begin with birth dates and birthplace of the subject(s), genre, best-selling album since 1990, and a list of hit songs since 1990. Discographies are selective and include both pre- and post-1990 recordings. If there are other readings available on a subject, a bibliography is provided along with an official Web site. In cases of artists who are also actors, such as Ice Cube, there is also a selective filmography. The appendix is a collection of essays discussing grunge, rap, commercial radio, and the music industry since 1990. There is an index by genre in addition to a general index. More than 100 photographs illustrate the text.

Baker's Biographical Dictionary of Popular Musicians since 1990 is a worthwhile purchase for public, high-school and academic libraries.

Tin Pan Alley: An Encyclopedia of the Golden Age of American Song. By David A. Jasen. 2003. 475p. bibliog. illus. indexes. Routledge, $95 (0-415-93877-5). 782.42164.

Tin Pan Alley was a nickname given to an actual street in Manhattan (West Twenty-eighth Street between Broadway and Sixth Avenue) where many of the music publishers had their offices. Eventually, Tin Pan Alley became the generic term for publishers of popular American sheet music. These publishing businesses hired lyricists and composers to create popular songs and promoted these songs in their sheet-music form with attractive covers.

Jasen, an authority on ragtime and popular song, previously coauthored *Rags and Ragtime* (2d ed., Dover, 1989); *Recorded Ragtime, 1897–1958* (Archon, 1973); and *A Century of American Popular Music: 2,000 Best-Loved and Remembered Songs, 1899–1999* (Routledge, 2002). His latest work covers the history of Tin Pan Alley from its heyday in the 1880s to its demise in the 1950s. With more than 300 entries arranged in an A–Z format, the encyclopedia identifies composers, lyricists, publishers, singers, dancers, and bands. Illustrated with period photographs and sheet-music covers, entries include names, birth and death dates, and information ranging from a couple of sentences to several pages. Most of the entries are biographical; around a quarter of them treat genres, publishing companies, and more. A bibliography, a general index, and an index to songs are included. Entries on prominent composers and lyricists such as Irving Berlin, Richard Rodgers, and Jerome Kern include a complete listing of their published songs. The lists include the year and, if applicable, the show in which each song was performed.

Not only would *Tin Pan Alley* complement collections owning Jasen's other titles, it would be an excellent companion to *The Tin Pan Alley Song Encyclopedia* by Thomas Hischak [RBB Ja 1 & 15 03], which also includes information and commentary on more than 1,200 individual song titles from this era. Recommended for large music collections.

Performing Arts, Recreation

The Gorehound's Guide to the Splatter Films of the 1980s. By Scott Aaron Stine. 2003. 390p. illus. index. McFarland, paper, $32.50 (0-7864-1532-0). 016.79143.

Slasher Films: An International Filmography, 1960 through 2001. Kent Byron Armstrong. 2003. 366p. appendixes. illus. index. McFarland, $65 (0-7864-1462-6). 791.43.

Splatter film and its "half brother," the slasher, may appear synonymous to the uninitiated, but these volumes attempt to sort out what makes each genre unique.

Splatter films have been around about 40 years and still do not enjoy high status. The sequel to Stine's *The Gorehound's Guide to Splatter Films of the 1960s and 1970s* (McFarland, 2001) treats about 500 1980s titles, what Stine calls "the childhood days" of splatter films, which featured more special effects and more literalism. Most are U.S. productions, but a few European titles are covered.

Entries are listed alphabetically and range in length from a half page to two pages. Technical information includes director, crew, cast, length, release date, variance in titles, distributor, and distribution forms. Plot is described briefly, with extensive commentary and background providing most of the text. The author is a "reel" aficionado and strong in his opinions (e.g., "a disgusting, albeit riotously funny, splatter flick"). Readers should not expect objectivity; rather, they can count on passionate interest. Extensive cross-references help the reader find films listed with different titles. A list of sources for DVDs and videocassettes follows the film entries. The index is extensive. About 100 black-and-white photos from movie posters and film clips supplement the text.

According to Armstrong, author of *Slasher Films: An International Filmography, 1960–2001*, Alfred Hitchcock's 1960 film *Psycho* was the seminal slasher film. The prototype slasher film is defined as one that combines: an introductory murder or predictive event; a setting that does not inspire terror; visualized killings; a human or humanlike killer; systematic, thematic killing; and an unhappy or unresolved ending. Armstrong's well-developed introduction provides examples for each of these elements, and he uses the criteria to select more than 150 representative films, most of them U.S. made. The classics are found (e.g., *Scream, Texas Chainsaw Massacre*), but lesser-known films are also given good coverage.

Entries are arranged alphabetically by English title and vary in length from one to three pages. Information includes date, screenwriters, directors, film company, length, cast, and crew; a very detailed plot outline follows. A final paragraph gives the author's critique of the film's role in the genre. Writing is straightforward and generally objective. A few black-and-white photos provide a sense of the genre. Separate appendixes list slasher directors and screenwriters. The index is minimal.

These two titles overlap somewhat in coverage (both cover the *Friday the 13th* and *Halloween* series, for example), although Stine is much more opinionated. Both are recommended for libraries with relevant collections.

Coins and Currency: An Historical Encyclopedia. By Mary Ellen Snodgrass. 2003. 562p. bibliogs. glossary. illus. index. McFarland, $95 (0-7864-1450-2). 737.4.

Many books have been compiled on the coins and currency of the world, providing detailed accounts from individual countries to broad discussions of the currencies of the world. This encyclopedia has brought together some 299 terms, phrases, and names associated with coins and currency throughout the ages, from the Sumerian coin-shell money of 3,500 B.C.E. to the modern day euro. Hundreds of sources were consulted to provide a fascinating account of people, places, and terms that are associated with money.

Entries include *African money, Assay marks; Assignat; Bryan, William Jennings; Coins and currency in literature; Gold rush; Pieces of eight;* and *Wizard of Oz*. This last entry deals with the symbolism in L. Frank Baum's famous work about the furor over the gold standard that waged from 1880 to the end of the century. Since inscriptions that appear on coins provide some insight on the political, economic, and religious biases of the issuing countries, a respectable 26-page list of inscriptions is provided. Also, the interest in searching out wrecked treasure ships results in a list of shipwrecks from 70 B.C.E. to 1946, indicating the name of the ship and the cargo it was carrying.

The entries are well written for the general reader. The black-and-white photographs are adequate, and most entries have extensive *see also* references and a list of sources. A time line of coins and currency in history covers 3,500 B.C.E. to 2002. A brief glossary is included as well as a 20-page bibliography. The 27-page index covers in detail all material that is contained in the text. This is not a book for currency collectors who want to identify and price their collections but rather a general encyclopedia of information about the currencies of the world. It is a recommended resource for public and undergraduate libraries.

Encyclopedia of the Modern Olympic Movement. Ed. by John E. Findling and Kimberly D. Pelle. 2004. 602p. appendixes. bibliogs. illus. index. Greenwood, $75 (0-313-32278-3). 786.48.

In this, an Olympic year, the *Encyclopedia of the Modern Olympic Movement* is a timely offering. The text is edited by Findling, a professor of history at Indiana University Southeast, and Pelle, a counselor at the same institution. This work is an update of their *Historical Dictionary of the Modern Olympic Movement* (Greenwood, 1996) and features new material, including articles on the 2002 through 2010 games. As with the 1996 text, the purpose is to examine "the historical context in which the modern Olympic Games have taken place."

The volume focuses on the nonathletic facets of the games, including history, finances, and politics. The text contains 55 signed entries ranging from 2 to 14 pages in length. It is divided into two parts, "The Summer Games" and "The Winter Games," and articles are arranged chronologically in each section. The summer games portion begins with a chapter on the classical games and ends with an article on preparations for the 2008 games in Beijing. The section on the winter games commences with "Pre-Olympic Winter Games" and concludes with "Vancouver 2010." Each article ends with a thorough bibliographical essay. Access to articles is aided by a detailed index. In addition to the main text, there are several useful appendixes, among them an extensive general bibliographical essay that contains information on a range of Olympic Games resources, including archival collections, documentary films, and biographies.

The encyclopedia presents both the triumphs and debacles of the Olympics. For example, the text discusses Australia's "symbolic highlighting of Aborigines" at the Sydney games and the positive local economic effect of the 1984 games in Los Angeles. The text also explores the "gargantuan extravagances" of the Montreal games and the Salt Lake City bribery scandal.

The work will appeal to Olympics enthusiasts who are interested in a behind-the-scenes look at this great sports spectacle, and it is recommended for public and college libraries.

Bad Boys: The Actors of Film Noir. By Karen Burroughs Hannsberry. 2003. 780p. appendixes. bibliog. illus. index. McFarland, $75 (0-7864-1484-7). 791.43.

Film noir presents gritty stories and guilty viewing pleasure. About 90 male actors of classic film noir titles of the 1940s and 1950s are featured in this volume. The researcher will find the expected (James Cagey, Humphrey Bogart, Robert Mitchum), the less well known (Morris Carnovsky, Douglas Fowley), and actors who transcend the genre (Kirk Douglas, Alan Ladd). The author also wrote *Femme Noir: Bad Girls of Film* (McFarland, 1988). For the new volume, she chose actors who have played significant roles in several film noir releases, and viewed 240 films in order to describe the plots and characters accurately.

Most of the volume treats these "bad boys" in depth, in A to Z entries ranging from five to twelve pages in length. Personal life stories are intermingled with discussions of films. While the emphasis is on noir, some films outside the genre are discussed if they are seminal to the actor (e.g., the Andy Hardy series for Mickey Rooney). A filmography and bibliography conclude each entry. Black-and-white photos help the reader identify individual actors, some of whom, such as Jay Flippen and Gene Lockhart, may well be remembered more for their "mugs" than for their monikers. An additional 25 actors are given one-page treatments in the first appendix. Another appendix gives noteworthy lines, arranged by broad topic such as "Regarding Dames," "Sizing Up the Other Guy," and "Penetrating Put-downs" (e.g., Richard Widmark's line "I wouldn't give you the skin off a grape," from *Kiss of Death*). Following the general bibliography, an index lists titles, names, and awards.

Depth rather than breadth is the key to this enjoyable reference work, which will be welcomed by the film fan as well as the researcher and is recommended for larger film collections.

The Encyclopedia of American Independent Filmmaking. By Vincent LoBrutto. 2003. 566p. appendixes. bibliogs. illus. index. Greenwood, $74.95 (0-313-30199-9). 791.43.

Independent films have long held a certain cachet. This volume concentrates on the directors of U.S. films and the New York independent film scene as perceived by a film instructor.

Entries cover a few definitions (e.g., *Bolex camera, Deferred payments, Sexploitation films*); many directors (about 90 percent of the book's content); and a few film titles treated separately from their directors (e.g., *Pull My Daisy, Stand and Deliver*). Most entries are one to two pages long, with a few directors, such as Brian De Palma and George A. Romero, given four pages. The length of the article does not always correlate with the achievements of the director; for instance, the entry for Norman Mailer is almost as long as the one for David Lynch. Brief bibliographies follow a few of the entries. A few black-and-white photos supplement the text. Three appendixes complete the volume: "100 Significant Independent Films" (for which there are no criteria); winners of the Sundance and Independent Spirit Awards; and independent film distributor names (no address or other contact information). A bibliography and index follow.

Women and directors of color are underrepresented; the longest entry relative to women is *Women in prison films*. On the other hand, B movies (especially gore and porn) are overrepresented, while animation, documentaries, and children's films are barely mentioned or have outdated information. Actors and producers are rarely noted, and despite the book's title there is very little on the filmmaking process. Sundance and Slumdance festivals are covered, but other regional film festivals such as the Mill Valley festival are overlooked; indeed, an entry for film festivals would have been welcome. Better editing would have prevented misuse of the word *nadir* in the entry *Merchant-Ivory Productions*.

The work is valuable for coverage of obscure directors. However, it is not an exhaustive or evenhanded volume on the topic. Recommended to supplement collections with heavy film content.

The Encyclopedia of Hollywood Film Actors: From the Silent Era to 1965. By Barry Monush. 2003. 820p. bibliog. illus. Applause, $35 (1-55783-551-9). 791.43.

The first of a projected two-volume set, this encyclopedia provides biographical profiles of actors who worked in Hollywood between 1915 and 1965 (presumably the second volume will cover 1965 to the present). Author Monush, an associate editor of the annual publication *Screen World*, includes all Oscar-winning actors as well as performers who became prominent in film before the late 1960s, which is when, he notes, the demise of the studio star system occurred.

Entries are arranged in alphabetical order (Bud Abbott and Lou Costello to George Zucco), include vital statistics, and note any higher-education institution the actor attended. Narrative capsules of the actor's career are accompanied by black-and-white photographs obtained from *Screen World* archives. Monush has done extensive research to compile the biographies, and the entries convey his love of moviemaking. Did you know that Yul Brynner was a trapeze artist before he became "the King"? That the "Wicked Witch of the West," Margaret Hamilton, ran a nursery school before heading to Hollywood? That "Kojak" (Telly Savalas) was once a writer for the State Department? There are fun anecdotes included in every entry, and readers will learn new trivia each time they peruse the encyclopedia.

The capsules are followed by chronological listings of the actor's screen and stage work as well as credits for select television appearances. Data were compiled from a number of sources, and the *Encyclopedia* includes a bibliography of reference works that readers can use for additional research. There is no index.

Although there are other reference sources that include film actors, such as the *International Dictionary of Films and Filmmakers* (Saint James, 2000) and *The New Biographical Dictionary of Film* (Knopf, 2002), this is an item that academic libraries and specialized film libraries will want to add. It would also no doubt find an audience in public libraries.

The Encyclopedia of Orson Welles. By Chuck Berg and Tom Erskine. 2003. 462p. bibliog. illus. index. Facts On File, $60 (0-8160-4390-6); paper, $19.95 (0-8160-4391-4). 791.43.

This is the third and final entry on a single director in Facts On File's Great Filmmakers series. Welles created what many consider the finest film of all time, *Citizen Kane*. Readers of the book's entry on it may be surprised to learn that it was his first feature film, made when he was only 26! He was also responsible for that "most notorious of broadcasts" in 1938, the radio play of H. G. Wells' *The War of the Worlds*. And did you know that he wrote acclaimed high-school textbooks on Shakespeare?

Welles amassed many other directorial, acting, and writing credits in his lengthy career. Entries are arranged alphabetically, covering produced and unproduced films, plays, broadcasts, and scripts (*Compulsion, The Magnificent Ambersons, Time Runs*); people (John Barrymore, Rita Hayworth, Steven Spielberg); and topical entries (*Shakespeare by Welles, "Rosebud"*). Some of the text is highly detailed: *Macbeth* has more than seven pages, with casting and shooting background, scene-by-scene description and analysis, and critical response. The eight contributors write in a lively and engaging style, and entries are filled with fascinating facts. Black-and-white photos of key figures and films accompany many articles. A bibliography and index are included. The only thing readers may look for in vain is a filmography, or better yet, a list in time-line format detailing Welles' varied accomplishments in chronological order, perhaps divided by role as actor, director, etc. Most public and academic libraries will want to add this to the reference or circulating collection.

The Encyclopedia of War Movies: The Authoritative Guide to Movies about Wars of the Twentieth Century. By Robert Davenport. 2003. 452p. bibliog. illus. index. Facts On File, $75 (0-8160-4478-3). 791.43.

War is an important theme in American movies. Interestingly, one of the earliest films was the 1898 title *Tearing Down the Spanish Flag*, which quickly found an audience. However, this book contains American films dealing only with twentieth-century wars. It should also be noted that the selection is not exhaustive but reflects the author's own preferences. His background includes military and legal experience, and he was a technical advisor for *Pearl Harbor*.

More than 800 movies are covered, with entries generally ranging from one-sixth of a page to a couple of pages in length. Treatment seems a bit uneven (e.g., *Pearl Harbor* is given only a one-sentence plot summary, but more than 20 lines are devoted to describing the plot of the 1971 film *Murphy's War*). Beyond basic citation information, entries often include cast lists. Typically, one paragraph describes the plot, and another covers the actual battle or war effort. If the movie is based on a book, those details are given. About a quarter of the entries include interesting facts about the production, military service details of the actors and directors, famous quotes, awards, and technical or historical mistakes (e.g., visible sound equipment, continuity details, and date-specific factual errors). Sometimes the author notes the historical accuracy—or inaccuracy—of the film. About 50 black-and-white photos accompany the text.

A bibliography and index conclude the volume. The book would have benefited from having an index of movies listed according to the war being treated as well as a chronological listing.

The detailed information reflects the author's extensive knowledge and research. For this reason alone, the volume is a worthwhile addition to war movie literature. High-schoolers and adults will enjoy browsing this reference.

The Encyclopedia of Westerns. By Herb Fagen. 2003. 618p. appendixes. bibliog. illus. index. Facts On File, $75 (0-8160-4456-2). 791.43.

Western films endure even through the ebb and flow of their immediate popularity. This reference book covers more than 3,500 western films over the past 100 years. The author has tried to be as comprehensive as possible in listing feature films. He includes mainly sound productions and covers silent, serial, and TV films selectively. A few crossover titles, such as *Hud* and *Oklahoma!* show the Western influence.

Longtime western aficionado Fagen has written several books on this genre. Both Tom Selleck and Dale Robertson wrote prefaces for this volume, in support of westerns and their history.

A three-page introduction traces the history and main actors of western films. The body of the book consists of alphabetically arranged film titles. Each entry lists the credits. About half of the entries have only a sentence or two about the movie, but a few, such as the entries for *High Noon* and *Shane,* continue for two pages and include production notes, some plot summary and critical commentary, and quotes from critics, performers, and filmmakers. Series are cross-referenced. Writing is clear and usually positive. About 100 black-and-white captioned photos of actors and screen shots offer visual relief and information.

Five appendixes provide useful data: a one-page discussion and *A–Z* list of spaghetti westerns (noting date and director); a chronological list of western Oscar nominees and winners; a list of movies based on books; two supplementary chronological lists of silent and sound titles for which insufficient information or box office returns exist; and a selected bibliography. The index mainly cites names and film titles.

Though the book generally lacks depth, its broad base offers a good starting point for research on this genre. Recommended for film collections in academic and public libraries.

The Encyclopedia of Women in Radio, 1920–1960. By Leora M. Sies and Luther F. Sies. 2003. 407p. appendix. bibliog. indexes. McFarland, $95 (0-7864-1476-6). 791.44.

Icons such as Aunt Jemima and Betty Crocker had radio programs. Beginning on October 4, 1906, 50 women in different parts of the country played the role of Aunt Sammy to provide recipes, household hints, and even poetry from identical scripts prepared by the U.S. Department of Agriculture. Famous actresses such as Lucille Ball, Candice Bergen, Bette Davis, and Hattie McDaniel broadcast on radio. Even Eudora Welty had a place in the history of radio. Luther Sies, who documented radio history in *Encyclopedia of American Radio, 1920–1960* (McFarland, 2000), focuses here on women and the important if unappreciated role they played in that history.

The introduction provides an overview of the development of radio and the role of women in its evolution. The section on "How to Use This Book" is essential to understanding the citations. The encyclopedia itself consists of 10,500 entries covering all women performers, whether individuals or groups, through 1929; all women who had their own programs after 1929; and programs. The entries for individuals generally provide name, activity ("book reviewer," "violinist"), radio station and its location, and year or years. Some entries, such as that for "Happy Homemaker" Ida Bailey Allen, offer more detail. For programs, there are brief story descriptions, cast lists, and, in many cases, notes on time and day of broadcast, duration, and station. Nine informative essays cover topics such as *Comediennes, Gender discrimination,* and *Husband-and-wife talk shows.* The entries are followed by an appendix, "Broadcasters by Category"; an extensive bibliography; an index of programs; and an index of names. The two indexes do not distinguish main entries from mentions within entries.

The Encyclopedia of Women in Radio, 1920–1960 is a unique reference source that brings together information unavailable elsewhere or scattered throughout other works. This is a valuable tool for academic and large public libraries with collections on women's studies, journalism, broadcasting, entertainment, and radio.

Epic Films: Casts, Credits, and Commentary on over 350 Historical Spectacle Movies. 2d ed. By Gary Allen Smith. 2004. 312p. appendixes. bibliog. illus. index. McFarland, $49.95 (0-7864-1530-4). 791.43.

Epic films continue to delight and impress audiences. As early as 1907, the year of the first version of *Ben-Hur,* large-scale historical movies were being produced. Smith, a frequent film reviewer, describes 355 epics in this volume, starting with *Judith of Bethulia* (1914) and ending with the 2000 Oscar-winning *Gladiator.* This second edition has about 50 percent more entries, and all commentary is based on viewing rather than occasional recollection, as in the first edition.

Most of the films are from the U.S. and Italy. Smith limits his scope to "the period of time from the creation to the thirteenth century—from cavemen to the Crusades." Thus, the reader will not find *Gone with the Wind* in these pages. The work is not exhaustive; television productions are few and not as extensively treated. Although a few comic epics are included, such as *The Three Stooges Meet Hercules,* the Monty Python classics *Life of Brian* and *The Holy Grail* as well as Mel Brooks' *History of the World, Part 1* are omitted.

Smith's introduction provides an objective and encompassing history of epics, noting the interplay between film and TV. Each alphabetically arranged entry ranges from a quarter-page to two pages in length. The first paragraph lists the production credits (producer, director, crew, cast), followed by a plot summary. About a fifth of the entries give production history, editorial commentary, and snippets from movie reviews. Black-and-white photos complement the text on almost every page. Twenty other films are credited in the first appendix (with no explanation for why they are given this treatment), and 21 more epics that were not completed are listed in the second appendix. A bibliography and index complete the volume. It should be noted that the index of titles and names is incomplete and not always accurate. A chronological list of films, a list by country, and a list by topic (e.g., King Arthur, prehistoric, etc.) would have been useful.

Although the coverage is not complete, this volume provides a good introduction to the mainstream genre. Public, academic, and high-school libraries may consider this reference as a pleasant addition to their film collections.

Hollywood Musicals Nominated for Best Picture. By Frederick G. Vogel. 2003. 374p. appendixes. bibliog. illus. index. McFarland, $75 (0-7864-1290-9). 791.43.

Timing is everything. When Vogel began creating this work, there had not been a musical nominated for Best Picture since 1991's *Beauty and the Beast,* and so this reference book does not include the 2001 movie *Moulin Rouge,* which was both a musical and nominated for best picture. Nevertheless, the exclusion of that movie does not significantly distract from the stated purpose of the work, which is clearly indicated in the title. However, several other movies are also excluded, such as *Amadeus* (1984), *Red Shoes* (1948), *Love Affair* (1939), *The Bells of St. Mary's* (1945), *The Country Girl* (1954), and *Nashville* (1975), based on the author's criteria that a musical must have songs and music as a primary, integral part of the story.

Thirty-eight musicals from *The Broadway Melody* (1929) to *Beauty and the Beast* are described, summarized, and discussed, in entries of approximately ten pages. Each entry begins with production credits and then proceeds to background information about the production and cast. The majority of each entry consists of plot summary. Occasionally there is discussion of the influence of a movie on other movies and musicals.

Several appendixes follow the entries, including a list of Academy Award nominations and winners for Best Director, Best Picture, Best Song, Musical Scoring, and Best Actor/Actress. The bibliography pulls primarily from biographies and standard film and musical film works. Recommended for performing arts collections that have need of this specialized type of reference tool.

Short-Lived Television Series, 1948–1978: Thirty Years of More Than 1,000 Flops. By Wesley Hyatt. 2003. 318p. appendix. bibliog. illus. index. McFarland, paper, $39.95 (0-7864-1420-0). 791.45.

Hyatt, a television enthusiast, uses 1948 as the beginning point of his chronicle of TV shows that lasted a year or less, because that year included the first full nighttime (and some daytime) lineups for ABC, CBS, NBC, and DuMont (which folded in 1955). Programming practices remained fairly stable until 1978, when the push for ratings resulted in an unprecedented number of cancellations. Hyatt thought that documentation of more recent shows would be easier to locate, so he decided to focus on harder-to-find shows of earlier years. He also restricted his survey to regular season entertainment series: no news, documentaries, public affairs, sports, theatrical movie series, animation, or syndicated shows (i.e., those programs sold individually to stations rather than to networks). Variety shows and anthology series with no recurring cast members were also omitted.

Entries range from a few lines to a page in length. Each entry includes series genre, dates of airing, programs shown at the same time on other channels, major cast members, producers, directors, and sometimes writers. Longer entries describe the basic premise of each series and discuss the program's successes and failures. Most of the detailed information came from personal (and sometimes biased) interviews, though apparently many potential interviewees declined to talk about the shows they were associated with because of negative memories. A thorough index of names and titles concludes the work.

As the author correctly states, finding information about these early, short-lived television programs is difficult. Reading the "back-fill" stories of some of these programs gives them new life. Because of the specificity of the topic, this reference is probably most useful for those libraries having deep mass media communications collections.

The Oxford Encyclopedia of Theatre & Performance. 2v. Ed. by Dennis Kennedy. 2003. 1,559p. bibliogs. illus. index. Oxford, $275 (0-19-860174-3). 792.03.

This new encyclopedia from Oxford views theater and performance as "human expressions with large cultural significance." These expressions extend beyond traditional theater to include opera, film, dance, radio, and even circuses, rituals, and parades. The 4,300 alphabetically arranged entries span all time periods, starting with ancient Greek theater to the present, and are international and cross-cultural in scope. Entries range from a small paragraph to several pages; only the longer entries have brief bibliographies. There is, however, a general bibliography, divided up geographically and consisting of only monographs, at the end of volume 2.

Almost half (around 45 percent) of the subject matter consists of biographical entries on actors, playwrights, directors, designers, company managers, and critics (e.g., *Ferber, Edna; Ferron, Jacques*). Ten percent consists of city and regional entries (*Istanbul, Philadelphia*). The rest consists of concepts and theories (*Pornography and performance*); styles and movements (*Alternative theatre, Ballad opera*); historical themes (*Ghost*); organizations and institutions (*Czech National Theatre*); buildings and material elements (*Amphitheatre*); and media issues (*Cyber theatre*). A thematic table of contents divides entries into these eight categories, offering alternative access. There is also a "Selective Index of Dramatic Titles" that lists works and the entries in which they are mentioned (for example, *Rent* is discussed in the *Musical play* entry). This helps to compensate for the fact that there are no main entries on individual play titles. Additional features of the set include a list of the scholarly editors and contributors with brief biographical information, cross-references, occasional black-and-white illustrations, and a time line that situates key historical and cultural events with corresponding theater and performance events.

There are several reference theater books currently available that touch on some similar ground. Which one is the best depends on the features being sought. For example, *International Dictionary of Theatre* (St. James, 1992) offers better coverage of individual plays. The six-volume *World Encyclopedia of Contemporary Theatre* (Routledge, 1994) has even more detailed international coverage of current theater practice in other countries but lacks comparable ease of access. *Continuum Companion to Twentieth Century Theatre* (Continuum, 2002) is a less scholarly alternative for recent theater. Ultimately, although *The Cambridge Guide to Theatre* (rev. ed., Cambridge, 1995) remains the most comprehensive single-volume reference source and, at $50, is relatively cheap, *The Oxford Encyclopedia* is a solid set, recommended for academic and large libraries with strong theater collections.

African Americans in Sports. 2v. Ed. by David K. Wiggins. 2003. 440p. bibliogs. illus. indexes. Sharpe, $159 (0-7656-8055-6). 796.
Native Americans in Sports. 2v. Ed. by C. Richard King. 2004. 356p. bibliogs. illus. indexes. Sharpe, $159 (0-7656-8054-8). 796.

These sets feature alphabetically arranged articles on the history, influence, and accomplishments of African Americans and Native Americans in sports. In both titles, users will find meticulous research and historical perspectives on a wide variety of often underrepresented subjects.

Coverage in *African Americans in Sports* extends from the 1800s through 2002 and addresses athletics at both the national and international level. More than 400 articles have been written by almost 80 contributors, and while the majority are biographical, additional pieces address individual sports, teams, and organizations and associations. Thoughtful essays deal with social issues such as racial theories and civil rights. Biographical entries cover not only athletes but also coaches, managers, entrepreneurs, and sportswriters. Forty articles are devoted to women athletes. Basketball, baseball, boxing, football, and track-and-field all have multipage entries, while shorter articles address such activities as lacrosse, rodeo, bowling, and fencing. The Harlem Globetrotters have an entry, as does the Wake-Robin Club, an association founded in 1937 for African American women golfers. Additional articles address how African American athletes have been represented in such genres as autobiography and film.

Native Americans in Sports is a thorough look at the impact Native Americans have had on club, college, professional, and Olympic sports in the U.S. and Canada. Alphabetical entries provide detailed accounts of the lives and careers of individuals, teams, organizations, institutions, and specific sports, including traditional games of skill. Signed essays provide background and historical context for social issues such as racism, adaptation, and assimilation and also address contemporary controversies, such as mascots and gambling.

Some topics cover familiar ground. There are lengthy articles on Jim Thorpe, Will Rogers, and Tiger Woods (also found in the African American volume). However, lesser known figures, such as Fred Sasakamoose, the first full-blooded Indian to play in the National Hockey League, are also included. Women are well represented.

In both sets, occasional black-and-white archival photographs accompany the text. A list of entries by category, a general index, an index by sport, a general bibliography, and a chronology provide support. Public, academic, and secondary school libraries will want to offer these titles.

Baseball Players of the 1950s: A Biographical Dictionary of All 1,560 Major Leaguers. By Rich Marazzi and Len Fiorito. 2004. 450p. bibliog. illus. McFarland, $55 (0-7864-1281-X). 796.357.

For many, the 1950s were the golden age of baseball. The names DiMaggio, Newcombe, Mantle, Berra, Larsen, or Robinson (whether it is Brooks or Frank or Jackie) or "Teddy Ballgame" (Ted Williams) conjure up rose-tinted memories of a game played and watched with passion. Authors Marazzi and Fiorito have gathered biographical information on each and every ballplayer who played in the major leagues in the 1950s, even if their major league careers were short. Bill Abernathie, for example, made a single big league appearance in 1951. He then spent the rest of his baseball life in the minor leagues. After baseball, he became a sheriff's detective in California. Red Hardy, born in North Dakota, had two major league appearances out of the bullpen for the 1951 National League champion New York Giants. He later owned a jewelry store in Phoenix.

The length of the articles ranges from a very short paragraph to two pages depending on the length and strength of the player's professional career and the amount of information that the authors could gather. Statistics, the lifeblood of baseball, are included, but these are lifetime or career numbers, not year by year or team by team. Quotes and amusing anecdotes, as well as occasional black-and-white photographs, round out the biographies. The entries are in alphabetical order, and a general bibliography is included. There is no indexing.

The specificity and price make this a reference book for larger libraries, but if you love the game, you gotta have it.

A Biographical Dictionary of Major League Baseball Managers. By John C. Skipper. 2003. 370p. appendixes. bibliog. illus. index. McFarland, $45 (0-7864-1021-3). 796.357.

All libraries serving adolescent through adult populations will benefit from this focused reference work that covers managers in the major leagues of baseball—National Association of Professional Baseball Players, American League, Union League, Players League, American Association, Federal League, and National League, with the notable exception of the Negro Leagues—from 1871 on. In entries ranging from a few lines to two pages, biographical details on each manager include dates of birth and death, playing record, and managing record, including years, team(s), won-loss record(s), winning percentage(s), and final standing(s). A World Series record is included when applicable. The narrative on each manager provides well-written, insightful commentary on specific achievements both inside and outside baseball. The author's exhaustive work shows thorough research, with quotes from a large percentage of managers. One bit on George Tweedy Stallings reads "Stalling's short fuse was often lit when his pitchers became wild and put runners on base via walks. He died of heart disease nine years after he retired. Reportedly, when his health was deteriorating rapidly, a friend asked how he developed heart trouble. 'Oh, those bases on balls,' said Stallings."

Skipper (ironically, the author's name is also the generic nickname for a baseball manager, so destiny might be in play here) demonstrates a thorough grasp of manager skills, including scouting, strategy, pitcher management, authority control level, lefty-righty percentages, defensive signals, interpersonal relations, feud relationships (think Steinbrenner-Berra), trade savvy, oration skills, money management, and vision. Black-and-white pictures; appendixes of various types, including team-by-team manager chronologies; an index; and a strong bibliography complete this work, which is an obvious labor of love. Recommended for baseball history collections in public and academic libraries; beyond libraries, the wealth of general sporting knowledge in this work could be applied by a team manager of any sport at any level.

Encyclopedia of International Games. By Daniel Bell. 2003. 591p. appendixes. bibliog. index. McFarland, $75 (0-7864-1026-4). 796.

This is an extraordinary work from beginning to end. The author begins the preface by saying, "This book focuses on international multisport competitions held since 1896 that are based on the model of the modern Olympic Games." In addition to the Olympic Games, these include the Asian Games, the Firefighters World Games, the Goodwill Games, the Pan-American Games, the Special Olympics, and the World Dwarf Games, among more than 150 others.

Information is arranged alphabetically by game. Each entry includes a general description and a table showing host city and nation, dates, and numbers of participating nations, athletes, and sports for each year in which the particular games have been held. This is followed by a year-by-year summary listing the competing nations and the various sports and another table showing the medal counts. In some cases numbers are missing because information was not available. Whenever possible, the author identifies sports for women; it is interesting to watch this list grow as the text progresses through the Olympic Games sections. The work contains eight appendixes and a notes section along with a bibliography and index. The appendixes are quite detailed and include a great deal of easily accessible information. Games are listed by year, by nation, by host city, by number of participants, and by number of sports.

Though there are a number of reference sources on the Olympic Games, this volume captures information that is much more elusive. It would be a great addition to a public as well as an academic library and would be welcome by serious researchers and trivia buffs alike.

The International Motor Racing Guide: A Complete Reference from Formula One to NASCAR. By Peter Higham. 2003. 912p. bibliog. illus. David Bull, $49.95 (1-893618-20-X). 796.72.

Building on the success of the previous edition (*The Guinness Guide to International Motor Racing* [Motorbooks, 1995]), Higham's volume is an unrivaled reference work on motorcar racing at its upper echelons, from stock cars to the highly specialized machines of Formula 1 and the Indianapolis 500.

The first sections provide details on the history and rules of 20 different races, leagues, and championship series. Each section offers a year-by-year summary of top finishers, an overview of the season, and overall records for all drivers in each race they started in the league or series under consideration. The author has done a fine job of covering all the major American, European, and international series from Formula 3000 and ProCar up through Formula 1 and NASCAR. Effectively, this includes all major and many more minor established professional racing series and events.

In the section titled "Racing around the World," the author compiles information about every major racing venue. The section is organized by country, and for each venue, information about different configurations, changes to the course over time, and winners of major races are given. Also included are basic statistics of each course, Web addresses, and graphical depictions.

The last section of the volume is an alphabetical listing of drivers.

Higham's criteria for inclusion are quite broad and bring in many drivers who did no more than attempt to qualify for a major event. Each driver entry includes date and place of birth and a listing of starts within established major series along with the driver's record overall within that series. The very last page of the volume is a brief but helpful bibliography of works about racing, including titles of important magazines and media guides as well as books and a few Web sites.

This volume is highly recommended for any library serving fans who would like to have detailed information about the sport of motor racing. Public, high-school, and academic libraries will find it to be a fine addition to their collections.

Latino and African American Athletes Today: A Biographical Dictionary. Ed. by David L. Porter. 2004. 448p. bibliogs. illus. index. Greenwood, $85 (0-313-32048-9). 796.

Porter, the author of *African-American Sports Greats: A Biographical Dictionary* (Greenwood, 1995), has compiled and edited profiles of 174 African American and Latino athletes in 18 professional sports (primarily baseball, football, basketball, track and field, and boxing), written by contributors ranging from university students and educators to sports professionals and editors. This dictionary highlights notable individuals whose impact on the sport occurred after 1975 (and mostly after 1990). One of the inclusion criteria stipulates that the athlete must be living in the U.S. or a Latin American country.

The reference source is organized alphabetically by name of athlete. The entries are preceded by three lists of athletes included in the book and organized by name, heritage, and sport. A fourth list notes the 17 women who are covered. Each essay is two to four pages long, and some are accompanied by a black-and-white photo. The main focus of the entries is on sports biography—how the athlete grew up and became involved in sports, what have been the high and low points of his or her athletic career, and what impact the person has had on the sport. Private life is given little more than a sentence or two. A short list of electronic and print sources concludes each entry.

The entries are written clearly and matter- of-factly. Most importantly, they cover less well known athletes who have made a significant (if not always lasting) contribution to the sport they excel in, and they include some sports not often considered by sports reference sources (e.g., rodeo, speed skating, softball, and racing).

About one-quarter of the people covered in this book are also featured in comparable biographical essays in *Current Biography Yearbook* (Wilson), some of which were used as source material for the volume under review. There are several other reference titles that profile African American athletes, although Latino athletes are not as well covered. *Latino and African American Athletes Today* is suitable for high-school libraries and larger public libraries, where needed.

The Most Valuable Players in Baseball, 1931–2001. By Timm Boyle. 2003. 340p. appendixes. illus. index. McFarland, $45 (0-7864-1029-9). 796.357.

Boyle, a baseball historian and author of *Baseball's Best: The MVPs* (Contemporary, 1985) and *Total Fitness the NBA Way* (Harper, 2000), provides a biographical and historical trip through 70-plus years of baseball's greatest players.

Arranged chronologically, the book highlights the American and National League's most valuable players from 1931 to 2001. Boyle encapsulates the season, the league, and each player's lifetime statistics. Each entry includes the MVP's stats for the year, a colorful and personal summation of the season and the MVP's career, and a list of the top five vote getters for that year. Many entries include a photo.

Several appendixes list MVPs by position and team, highlight the career stats for each MVP, and provide the best marks achieved by MVPs during their season. For example, in 1936 Lou Gehrig had 167 runs, the league record. A unique feature in the appendix is "Missing MVPs." Prior to 1931, when the Baseball Writers Association of America took over the MVP awards, the award was irregular if it was given at all. Boyle fills in the gaps of these missing years with 40 MVPs and twice as many runners-up, all his own choices. Season statistics are included for each player selected. Some fictional winners include Ty Cobb in 1907, 1915, and 1918 and Babe Ruth from 1919 to 1921.

The index is extensive and includes names, schools, associations, stadiums, teams, leagues, family members, and general baseball terms. The preface and introduction provide a nice history of the MVP award and a synopsis of how the winners are selected.

Boyle's new book is more extensive and up-to-date than Donald Honig's *American League Most Valuable Players* (Bantam, 1989) and *National League Most Valuable Players* (Bantam, 1989) as well as Boyle's earlier work *Baseball's Best: The MVPs*. This is a must-have reference tool for baseball collections in public or school libraries, and academic libraries with strong ready-reference or sports programs should also consider it. A circulating copy would be useful as well.

Notable Sports Figures. 4v. Ed. by Dana Barnes. 2003. 1,903p. appendix. bibliogs. illus. indexes. Gale, $350 (0-7876-6628-9). 796.

This work attempts to cover all international, seminal sports figures from the nineteenth to the twenty-first century in all disciplines. More than 600 biographies cover not only athletes but also coaches, team executives, media figures, writers, and sportscasters. The criteria for selection included "first" achievements, impact on sport and then society, records set or broken, and involvement in controversial or newsworthy activities on or off the field.

Each entry is arranged alphabetically and contains a 1,000- to 2,500-word essay, contact information for the subject, and further readings, including Web sites. Sidebars provide chronologies of events in the lives of the subjects, lists of major awards and accomplishments, statistics, extracts from material such as magazine articles, and brief biographies of individuals who played significant roles in the sports figures' lives. Other valuable features are the three indexes: a geographic index, an occupational index, and cumulative subject index that provides access under team name, religion, awards, position played, and even diseases, such as HIV/AIDS.

Notable Sports Figures does not necessarily fill a void in biographical coverage of athletes when one considers the recent publication of several other sources, such as *Encyclopedia of North American Sports History* (2d ed., Facts On File, 2002) or *The Scribner Encyclopedia of American Lives: Sports Figures* (2002). Admittedly these two volumes are restricted to American or North American sports coverage, but after scanning the geographic index in *Notable Sports Figures*, it is quite evident that the emphasis is on American athletes. However, having all of the notables in one reference set will save the reference librarian time in searching for authoritative sources. *Notable Sports Figures* is recommended for high-school, public, and academic libraries where budget dollars will allow purchase.

Scholastic Visual Sports Encyclopedia. 2003. 224p. glossary. illus. index. Scholastic, $19.95 (0-439-31721-5). 796.

This encyclopedia for ages nine and up is designed to explain the rules and the equipment used for approximately 100 sports. It groups the sports into 14 sections such as "Track and Field," "Ball Sports," and "Motor Sports." The emphasis is upon the visual. Sections are color coded, and each begins with a page listing the sports included in the grouping. A graphic shows an athlete poised for action. The size of the chapters varies according to the number of events that qualify for inclusion.

Entries for individual sports range from one to four pages. The text is very brief, but detailed drawings help the reader understand the rules or finer points. Often an illustration is broken down so that each element of the jump, dive, or play is shown in the correct position. Many of these sports are part of either the summer or winter Olympics, and when there are differences in Olympic games and regular play, these are explained. Sidebars and boxes are used effectively to explain details, define terms, or show equipment.

The book is well organized, clearly written, and effectively illustrated. Though intended for a young audience, readers of all ages will enjoy browsing through it. School and public libraries should consider extra copies for circulation as well as reference. A similar title, *Sports: The Complete Visual Reference* (Firefly, 2000), covers more sports, including some not well known in the U.S.

Total Tennis: The Ultimate Tennis Encyclopedia. Ed. by Bud Collins. 2003. 938p. appendixes. illus. Sport Classic, $34.95 (0-9731443-4-3). 796.34203.

This third edition of Collins' unique perspective on the tennis world includes a wealth of information about a sport that has come in and out of the limelight over the last 20 years. Collins has loved tennis all his life, and tennis has been his life in his job as a sports journalist. He once again brings his significant credentials to this encyclopedic treatment of the professional and significant amateur players of tennis over the last century.

The first half of the volume is a year-by-year chronology noting the highlights for each year, starting in 1919 and stopping in 2002. Statistics for championship singles, doubles, and mixed-doubles winners in the major events are included. For a handful of players, Collins provides articles reprinted from magazines of the time.

Comprehensive statistics and a brief history for the major tournaments—the French Open, Wimbledon, the U.S. Open, and the Australian Open—are contained in the middle section of the encyclopedia along with a selection of color photographs. Similar information is provided on the Davis Cup, the Olympics, and other tournaments. A biographical section has entries for elite players and others who made a significant contribution to the game. Finally, there is statistical information for nearly 400 of the best players in tennis as chosen by Collins using a variety of criteria.

Whether a reader is interested in the articles on the players or the statistics, this is an excellent reference source on tennis. Recommended for most sports collections.

The Encyclopedia of Surfing. By Matt Warshaw. 2003. 774p. appendixes. bibliog. illus. Harcourt, $40 (0-15-100579-6). 797.3.

Warshaw is a former pro surfer, editor of *Surfer* magazine, and a journalist who has written several well-received trade titles about the sport. Here the author has compiled an exhaustive reference to the surfing world, organized into alphabetical entries.

The entries cover basic techniques ("goofy foot" and "regular foot" stances, for example) and gear; legendary surf breaks and competitions; the science of surfing (including explanations of how waves are measured); cultural references, such as major publications, films, and characters (the infamous Gidget earns a lengthy entry); famous surfers throughout history; and broader topics, such as *Drugs and surfing, Religion and surfing, Surf art,* and *Television and surfing,* that examine surfing's subculture and impact on larger society.

The extensive appendixes include a selected bibliography; selected surf contest results from 1954 through 2002; an exhaustive list of surf movies, videos, and DVDs as well as a list of surfing magazines around the world; and a selected surf music discography.

Warshaw's tone is both highly informed and personal. The entries define terms clearly and offer contextual analysis bolstered with quotes from various mainstream media sources. But Warshaw's profiles of individual surfers include some oddly subjective language. One official, for example, is described as a "fleshy, surf-erudite competition administrator," while legendary Laird Hamilton is the "brawny, blond master of tow-in surfing." The result is a unique resource that combines neatly categorized, rarely covered information with a lively, intimate view of the surfing world.

With surfing gaining prominence in the media, public and academic libraries will want to consider this one-of-a-kind resource. The reasonable price makes this accessible to those high-school libraries where materials on the subject are in demand.

Literature

The Columbia Guide to the Literatures of Eastern Europe since 1945. By Harold B. Segel. 2003. 641p. bibliogs. Columbia, $95 (0-231-11404-4). 809.

An increased awareness of the separate cultural identities of the states so long eclipsed by the Soviet Union has led to an interest in the literatures of these nations and the need for biographical and critical material to support this study. Columbia has published a timely resource that provides a wide range of information on almost 700 authors from Albania, the former East Germany, Serbia, Slovenia, and others, filling what would seem to be a considerable gap. In a random sample, 20 of the authors from this volume were checked in Gale's *Literature Resource Center* (LRC). Seven of the 20 had at least biographical information listed in LRC; the other 13 were not found.

Segel, professor emeritus from Columbia University, is solely responsible for this endeavor, from the selection of the authors to the text written about them. This provides an unusual consistency of tone and style and allows the author to precisely define and follow criteria for inclusion. The entries range in size from half a column to three pages and consist of biographical information, a list of works, works translated into English, and references to additional critical material. The longer entries contain critical commentary, and some include quotations from major pieces.

Segel has written a lengthy introduction that provides an overview of the literatures of the area and period covered, with a necessary emphasis on the influence of politics on art. Other useful features are a chronology of major political events of the period and region; a list of journals, newspapers, etc. from these countries; and a bibliography that consists of general works in English relating to this period and region. There is no standard index but rather a list of entrants by country of origin.

A clear typeface; white, nonreflecting paper; and wide inner margins contribute to this book's visual appeal. Its coverage provides access to information not easily found. This is an appropriate source for all academic and larger public libraries.

Critical Survey of Drama. 8v. 2d ed. Ed. by Carl Rollyson and Frank N. Magill. 2003. 4,558p. bibliogs. illus. indexes. Salem, $499 (1-58765-102-5). 809.2.

By now the format of Magill's *Critical Surveys* is a familiar one. Familiarity here doesn't breed contempt but rather an expectation of a solid reference work, carefully organized, up-to-date, and easy-to-use.

Combining material from the *Critical Survey of Drama: English Language Series* (rev. ed., 1994) and the *Critical Survey of Drama: Foreign Language Series* (1986) with a generous selection of new articles, these volumes offer 538 profiles spanning the ages and the continents. The 79 new articles include those on a number of playwrights whose work has been widely seen onstage during the last few years, among them Lee Blessing, Eric Bogosian, Rebecca Gilman, Spalding Gray, Tony Kushner, Alfred Uhry, and Paula Vogel. Some 88 articles have been updated to reflect changes in both the work and the lives of the subjects. Broadening the coverage to include writers from other parts of the world strengthens this work, and it lives up to the familiar line about all the world being a stage. Playwrights from all the major European nations are represented, as are those from the continents of Africa and Asia, the Caribbean region, and more.

As in other *Critical Surveys,* the signed articles are arranged alphabetically by dramatist and range in length from two or three to 10 or more pages. Each lists the author's principal dramatic works, other literary works, achievements, biography, a brief critical analysis, other major works, a bibliography, and a contributor byline. Of particular importance to anyone doing drama research, the dates of both first performance and first publication are provided for every play cited. The author profiles are followed by extended essays on a variety of topics, such as American regional theater, Restoration drama, Japanese drama, television drama, and acting styles. Additional resources include a general bibliography, a glossary of dramatic terms and movements, a list of major awards, a dramatic time line, and a chronological list of dramatists. Indexes include both geographical and categorized indexes of dramatists and a general subject index.

Among the notable features of this set are the pictures or photos of many of the entrants (very helpful for students' assignments) and the variety of appended material. High-school, public, and academic libraries will be well served by this well-crafted and carefully plotted resource.

Cyclopedia of World Authors. 5v. 4th ed. Ed. by Frank N. Magill and others. 2004. 3,432p. bibliogs. indexes. Salem, $404 (1-58765-122-X). 809.

These five volumes complement another of the publisher's sets, *Masterplots* (2d ed., 1996), since many of the authors whose work is represented there are included here. All the entries from the previous edition have been updated, and 349 new ones have been added. The alphabetically arranged articles consist of a characterization (such as "American short-story writer"); place and date of the subject's birth (and death); and, in some cases, identity ("Chinese American," "Christian"), followed by a list of principal works arranged by genre. A biographical essay provides a survey of the author's career. Brief lists of sources for further study complete each signed entry. Special features found in the last volume offer additional points of access: a time line arranged by the birth years of the authors listed; an author index listing all included authors, cross-referenced by pseudonyms or alternate names; and a "Geography and Identity Index" in which authors are listed under countries of origin and other categories, such as Christian, Jewish, African American/African descent, and gay or bisexual.

The focus here is on some 2,408 writers whose work is studied in high school and college in North America, and the resulting array spans the globe and the centuries. Not only are writers of fiction, poetry, and drama featured but also screenwriters, biographers, essayists, critics, historians, philosophers, and prominent figures in the social sciences, politics, and the sciences. The set encompasses Chinua Achebe, Francis Bacon, and Raymond Chandler, as well as Xenophon, Marguerite Yourcenar, and Paul Zindel. Outside of a general encyclopedia, where else can one find Edith and Jane Hamilton, Sinclair as well as Meriwether Lewis, and (on facing pages, no less), Helen and Henry Fielding? Averaging about 1,200 words in length, these articles will serve as quick and easy introductions for any reader (or reader's advisor). With a lineage extending back to 1958, this is one reference set that should continue to hold a place in high-school, college, and public library collections.

Encyclopedia of Literary Modernism. Ed. by Paul Poplawski. 2003. 516p. bibliogs. index. Greenwood, $100 (0-313-31017-3). 809.

While the main focus of this volume is English-language literary modernism from 1890 to 1939, the scope is actually much broader. The collected entries draw rich connections between literary modernism of this period and other disciplines, precursors and successors, and modernist writers in other languages. Main entries include people (Djuna Barnes, Samuel Beckett, Marcel Proust), disciplines *(Anthropology; Dance and literary modernism, 1890–1940; Film and modernism; Music)*, countries and cultures *(Africa and the South; Canada, French; Hispanic American modernismo; Russia)*, and movements and theoretical approaches *(Dada, Expressionism, Primitivism, Psychoanalysis)*. Literary modernist connections to World War I are covered in a nearly six-page entry, *The War*. There are separate entries for key works of James Joyce and for Stravinsky's *The Rite of Spring*, whose audacious premier is described with a verve unusual for a ready-reference encyclopedia.

The several hundred articles from nearly 70 academic contributors range from a few paragraphs *(Gruppo 63)* to some 15 pages for D. H. Lawrence and his work. Each entry is followed by a selected bibliography, with occasional annotations. A comprehensive index uses bold type to identify the main entry heading. Cross-references within and between entries also ease access. A selective bibliography of general works supplements the more specialized bibliographies at the end of each entry.

Encyclopedia of Literary Modernism will be most useful for academic libraries, but larger public and high-school libraries could benefit from having clearly presented ready-reference material on this very "influential artistic-cultural phenomenon" available in a single volume. The preface cites as valuable adjuncts to the current work Malcolm Bradbury and James McFarlane's classic essay collection *Modernism, 1890–1930* (reprint, Penguin, 1991) and *The Cambridge Companion to Modernism* (Cambridge, 1999), though it points out that neither was designed as a reference book.

Encyclopedia of World Writers: 19th and 20th Centuries. Ed. by Marie Josephine Diamond. 2003. 512p. bibliogs. index. Facts On File, $75 (0-8160-4675-1). 809.

Literature curricula from high school to college are including more writers from outside the British-American sphere. This volume, a companion to Facts On File's *Encyclopedia of British Writers: 19th and 20th Centuries* [RBB D 15 03], is edited by a professor of comparative literature at Rutgers University. It includes A–Z entries for approximately 300 African, Asian, Australian, Canadian, Caribbean, European, Latin American, and Middle Eastern authors of poetry, fiction, drama, essay, and autobiography. All of the writers in the book have had works anthologized in textbooks or have been studied in high-school literature courses. There are also articles on topics such as *Futurism* and *Magical realism*.

Author entries profile Margaret Atwood, Thomas Mann, Guy de Maupassant, Mishima Yukio, Octavio Paz, Wolo Soyinka, Rabindranath Tagore, and Leo Tolstoy, to name a few. Each entry contains a brief biography, critical analysis, a short (in some cases single item) list of major works in chronological order, and a bibliography of works about the author. These bibliographies are brief in order to encourage students to delve further into a particular author's work while not overwhelming them. Other features include an author time line that is simply a list of dates and authors included in this work, a list of the writers by geographical area, a selected bibliography of further readings not included at the end of each entry, and an extensive index.

There is considerable overlap with numerous other reference tools. Large literature series, such as the Wilson Authors Series and various publications from Gale and Salem Press, also cover world authors. *Encyclopedia of World Writers: 19th and 20th Centuries* is a worthwhile purchase for public, high-school, and undergraduate libraries seeking a compact, convenient introduction.

The Facts On File Dictionary of Classical and Biblical Allusions. By Martin H. Manser. 2004. 448p. index. Facts On File, $45 (0-8160-4868-1); Checkmark, paper, $18.95 (0-8160-4869-X). 809.

This dictionary is the latest effort by the author of, among other titles, *The Facts On File Dictionary of Foreign Words and Phrases* (2002) and *The Facts On File Dictionary of Proverbs* [RBB Mr 15 03], which are somewhat similar in format. As a companion volume to *The Facts On File Dictionary of Cultural and Historical Allusions* (2000), the new dictionary contains approximately 2,000 allusions drawn from the Bible, Greek and Roman mythology, and Norse mythology and includes some Egyptian and Celtic examples. All allusions predate 1,000 C.E. Each entry begins with the term (followed in some cases by a pronunciation guide), focuses on an explanation, and ends with an example. About half of the examples are from literature; others are sample constructions to illustrate common usage. Biblical allusions seem to outnumber other types, and all biblical quotations are taken from the King James Version.

The *Facts On File Dictionary of Classical, Biblical, and Literary Allusions* (1987) is broader in scope but has no examples as the present volume does. Focused content and alphabetical entry by allusion are strengths of this dictionary in comparison to *Allusions—Cultural, Literary, Biblical, and Historical: A Thematic Dictionary* (Gale, 1986). The latter's advantages include wider coverage, higher numbers of allusions, and access by theme. *Merriam-Webster's Dictionary of Allusions* (1999) and *The Oxford Dictionary of Allusions* (2001) contain more in-depth descriptions and extensive literary quotations illustrating each allusion but have many fewer classical and biblical allusions. *The Facts On File Dictionary of Classical and Biblical Allusions* is recommended for high-school and public libraries and academic libraries serving undergraduates.

Great World Writers: Twentieth Century. 13v. Ed. by Patrick M. O'Neil. 2003. 1,848p. bibliogs. glossary. illus. indexes. Marshall Cavendish, $459.95 (0-7614-7468-4). 809.

Conceived as a companion to *Great American Writers: Twentieth Century* (2002), this set surveys the lives and works of 93 distinguished non-American writers of the last century. In selecting them, an attempt has been made to balance the "claims of geography, culture, genre, and language." Authors from 42 countries are represented. About half are native speakers of English or chose to write in English, while the rest have been translated into English. Only about 20 are women. A partial selection includes Chinua Achebe, Isabel Allende, Italo Calvino, Joseph Conrad, Athol Fugard, Robert Graves, Doris Lessing, Yukio Mishima, V. S. Naipaul, Wole Soyinka, Dylan Thomas, J. R. R. Tolkien, Mario Vargas Llosa, and Virginia Woolf.

These are exciting volumes, intended to attract and hold the attention of young adults, even though some of the writers (Gao Xingjian, André Malraux, and Iris Murdoch, for instance) are far from mainstays of the high-school curriculum. The volumes are profusely illustrated with a roughly equal mix of photographs and imaginatively selected reproductions of largely unfamiliar paintings. Pages run the gamut of pastel colors, as well as white, while liberal use of varied text formats and headings facilitates browsing and quick access to key facts and resources. Each of the 10- to 25-page entries begins with a photographic portrait, vital statistics, identification, and significance. Each also has sections on the writer's life and work, a chronology of life highlights, a "Reader's Guide to Major Works," and a resource section that may include everything from books and films to Web sites and museums. Some entries include lists of film tie-ins and boxed features on a variety of topics. Each volume has its own index, while volume 13 includes a wealth of cumulative indexes, a glossary, and a list of Nobel Prize winners for literature.

Highly recommended for high-school and public libraries. Though the set is aimed at students, perusing these volumes is likely to turn on adult readers to some writers new to them.

Jewish Writers of the Twentieth Century. Ed. by Sorrel Kerbel and others. 2003. 695p. bibliogs. index. Fitzroy Dearborn, $125 (1-57958-313-X). 809.

Overviews of 314 writers of prose, fiction, poetry, and drama from all over the world are presented in this volume. A series of introductory essays covers "American-Jewish Literature," "British-Jewish Literature," "Hebrew Literature in the Twentieth Century," "Holocaust Writing," and "Yiddish

Writing in the Twentieth Century." The editors do not attempt to define "Jewish writing," and they accept "anyone who identified themselves as a Jew, or was perceived as such by others." This gave them a wide field for selection. Beginning with Theodore Herzl, the father of Zionism, who was also a dramatist, they chose an international group of writers, among them Anita Brookner, Nadine Gordimer, Franz Kafka, Primo Levi, Norman Mailer, Amos Oz, Boris Pasternak, and Marcel Proust.

The alphabetical entries are one to two pages long. They include a brief biography, a selected list of writings, a bibliography of selected critical works, and an essay about the writer's major works and style. The front of the book contains alphabetical and chronological lists of the writers covered. A title index of works included in the bibliographies and information about the 149 contributors appears at the end.

Although information about many of these authors is available in general encyclopedias and sources such as Gale's Dictionary of Literary Biography series, *Jewish Writers of the Twentieth Century* provides a focused context that explains how and why Jews have taken their places among the most important writers of the last century. It is a useful source for academic libraries, especially those supporting Jewish studies and comparative literature programs, and for large public libraries with an interested clientele.

Masterplots 2: Drama Series. 4v. Rev. ed. Ed. by Christian H. Moe. 2003. 1,824p. bibliogs. indexes. Salem, $404 (1-58765-116-5). 809.2.

Salem Press currently publishes 17 different sets of *Masterplots*. The parent set is the 12-volume *Masterplots* (2d ed., 1996), which considers more than 1,800 individual works of literature, including 400 plays. This current reference, an update to *Masterplots II: Drama Series* (1990), covers new territory. None of its 346 dramatic pieces are included in the 1996 parent set; 92 selections have never appeared in any *Masterplots* title.

Emphasis has been placed on twentieth-century works, and 20 selections are by authors born after 1950. Entries are restricted to works in English, but there is an international presence (South Africa, the Czech Republic, Nigeria, etc.). Plays are presented alphabetically by title, and each signed entry follows a similar format: headers listing title, author, plot type (genre), setting (time and locale), production and publication dates, and characters; essays providing a synopsis and discussion of themes, dramatic devices, and critical context; and sources for further reading. Entries average about 2,400 words.

Volume 4 has several indexes: title, author, and genre. The 45 genre categories include musicals, melodramas, comedies, and verse plays, to name a few. There are three additional reference aids. The first lists the 400 plays that appear in the 1996 revised second edition of *Masterplots*. The second provides a chronological listing of the selections that appear in this current work (only 6 predate 1900). The third will be of great interest to teachers and educators. It lists and briefly annotates 185 screen adaptations of works from the current edition and indicates their availability on video or DVD. Some, such as British TV productions from the 1950s, may be inaccessible, but others, such as *Amadeus, A Chorus Line,* and *Anne of the Thousand Days,* should be readily obtainable at local video stores.

This newest addition to a reference standard belongs in most public, academic, and secondary libraries. Hopefully, the days when *Masterplots* was routinely locked up in teachers-only, professional collections are long over, and this useful series is openly displayed and promoted. It serves as an effective tool to enhance student understanding of key literary works.

Timetables of World Literature. By George Thomas Kurian. 2003. 457p. bibliog. indexes. Facts On File, $65 (0-8160-4197-0). 809.

Timetables of World Literature is a chronicle of works of literature spanning seven periods in time: "The Classical Age (to A.D. 100)"; "The Middle Ages (100–1500)"; and the sixteenth through twentieth centuries. The chronology lists more than 12,000 titles and 9,800 authors and includes a variety of genres: novels, plays, poems, autobiographies and biographies, essays, meditations, romance, science fiction, mysteries, and history. Each of the seven sections into which the chronology is divided begins with a brief overview of the literature of the period followed by several short biographical summaries of the major writers. Following the biographies is a time line of historical events.

After the overview, each section lists births and deaths of notable authors and literary figures, literary events, such as the Pulitzer Prize and the Nobel Prize in literature, and important publications arranged alphabetically by language, then nationality. These lists are arranged by year, although the sections that cover the classical and medieval eras do not list every year of the relevant time periods. A brief bibliography and several helpful indexes follow the chronological portion of the work. A title index lists all the works by title, with the author's last name in parentheses. This is followed by an author index, a detailed genre index, and a language index.

This volume is a good resource for high-school, academic, or public libraries, especially where there is an emphasis on world literature.

Twayne Companion to Contemporary World Literature. 2v. Ed. by Pamela A. Genova. 2003. 1,685p. appendixes. illus. index. Twayne, $175 (0-8057-1700-5). 809.

The newest addition to the Twayne Companion to Literature series features 300 essays and 150 book reviews, mostly written since 1977, that are reprinted from the literary quarterly *World Literature Today* (WLT). The essays, ranging in length from 2 to 14 pages and sometimes accompanied by a black-and-white photograph, are arranged geographically by broad locale and then by individual country, where applicable. The eight main categories consist of general perspectives on world literature; the Arab world and the Middle East; Africa and the Caribbean; Asia; Latin America; Eastern Europe, Russia, and the Balkans; Northern Europe, and Western Europe. Asia and Western Europe are the most heavily represented regions, and North American and Canadian authors are excluded entirely.

All of the essays in the main section were reprinted from issues of WLT published between 1977 and 2001. Selections are intended to incorporate both influential and underrepresented writers and cultures to demonstrate "the dynamic systems of contemporary literature from across the globe." Following the main section of essays is appendix A, which has older essays reprinted from the 1989 special issue of WLT that featured a "best of" compilation from 1927 to 1977, when the quarterly was called *Books Abroad*. This is followed by appendix B, which features selected book reviews (six per year) from 1977 to 2001 from WLT. The index lists names, titles, and broad subjects, but given the geographical arrangement of the volumes and the often abstract nature of the essays, more detailed subject indexing would help ease the transition from critical anthology to reference tool.

Increased access to the WLT catalog of critical essays is a welcome thing, although indexing is also available in several humanities databases, and the book reviews are covered in book review indexes. Reference works covering world literature are scarce; the most similar thing in scope sitting on reference shelves is the five-volume *Encyclopedia of World Literature in the 20th Century* (St. James, 1999). In the *Encyclopedia* one can get an overview of the life and work of an author, for example, while in the *Twayne Companion* one might find an essay that analyzes his or her last novel and its relationship to nature. The sets complement one another, but the sophistication of *Twayne* probably makes it best suited for academic libraries.

The Beat Generation: A Gale Critical Companion. 3v. Ed. by Lynn M. Zott. 2003. bibliogs. illus. indexes. Gale, $325 (0-7876-7569-5). 810.9.

The second title in the Gale Critical Companion Collection follows *Harlem Renaissance* [RBB Ap 15 03]. The series focuses on literary movements or themes and offers organized, annotated collections of reprinted criticism. Volume 1 of *The Beat Generation* covers "Topics": an overview, the East and West Coast scenes, publishing, and the Beats' influence on the performing and visual arts. Volumes 2 and 3 are devoted to people and contain entries on 29 major literary figures associated with the Beat movement. In all three volumes, entries follow the same formula. An introduction to the topic or author and list of representative works is followed by a selection of primary sources (reprinted essays, journal entries, poems, newspaper accounts, etc.). Next is a section of general secondary essays on the topic or author. In some cases, a section on specific aspects of the topic or critical essays on specific titles follow. Each entry concludes with a list of annotated further reading culled from monographs and periodicals. The material is accompanied by 40 to 50 black-and-white images or sidebar graphics per volume.

Present in each volume are a chronology of key events and three indexes: author, title, and subject. The author index has cross-references to pseudonyms and to the other, seemingly endless stream of titles in the Gale literature series. All of the featured authors are major figures covered in other Gale series, but an effort to make this series unique is evidenced by the fact that only 15 percent of the critical essays reprinted here have appeared previously in other Gale publications.

William Lawlor's *The Beat Generation: A Bibliographic Teaching Guide* (Scarecrow/Salem, 1998) mines similar territory but offers only annotated bibliographies on the main Beat topics and people and is mostly aimed at teachers. Unlike the Gale set, it includes audio and visual material and (now largely outdated) Internet sites. The Gale set does a good job of spotlighting seminal Beat authors like Robert Duncan, Allen Ginsberg, Jack Kerouac, and Ken Kesey. One wonders at the omission of peripheral people like Charles Bukowski and Larry Eigner from the subject index, even if they aren't expected to be featured authors. Still, it is extremely useful to have all of this diverse material on the Beat Generation in one place, and the set is recommended for academic, high-school, and public libraries.

The Chronology of American Literature: America's Literary Achievements from the Colonial Era to Modern Times. Ed. by Daniel S. Burt. 2004. 805p. bibliogs. illus. indexes. Houghton, $40 (0-618-16821-4). 810.9.

This chronology includes more than 8,400 literary works by more than 5,000 writers. Sections for each year are grouped in five chapters by period, from 1582 to 1999. Within each year, entries are grouped by genre, such as diaries and other personal writings, fiction, essays, literary criticism and scholarship, nonfiction, poetry, and drama. Within each genre, authors are listed alphabetically, generally with birth and death dates and short descriptions of named works for the year. Each chapter has an introduction, averaging about four pages, that gives an overview of the major events of the period. Not surprisingly, increasing attention is given to more recent years. The last chapter, "Modernism and Postmodernism," treats the years 1950–99 and fills 245 pages, compared to the 86 pages of "The Colonial Period" (1582–1789). Interspersed through the text are black-and-white images, primarily of writers, and tables of events, such as births and deaths from the period, best-sellers, and literary awards and prizes. The author and title indexes are indispensable.

The volume's most immediate competitors are *Annals of American Literature, 1602–1983* (Oxford, 1986) and *A Chronological Outline of American Literature* (Greenwood, 1987). The indexing and descriptions of included titles, as well as narrative introductions, make *The Chronology of American Literature* preferable to both. These predecessors provide strictly titles and authors, and indexing does not get to the poem, story, or song level, the way it does in the newer volume. Neither provides the richness of detail present in *The Chronology of American Literature* that helps create a fuller sense of the context of literary development. In addition, *The Chronology of American Literature* includes the widest array of popular and little-studied authors. The year-by-year arrangement makes it a good complement to *The Oxford Companion to American Literature* (1995) or *The HarperCollins Reader's Encyclopedia of American Literature* (2002).

The Chronology of American Literature is easy to browse and, for book lovers, difficult to put down. Highly recommended for high-school, public, and academic libraries.

Encyclopedia of the Harlem Renaissance. By Aberjhani and Sandra L. West. 2003. 424p. appendixes. bibliogs. glossary. illus. index. maps. Facts On File, $65 (0-8160-4539-9). 810.9.

Although numerous reference works contain significant entries on the Harlem Renaissance, this is the first encyclopedia devoted to the movement. Entries are ordered alphabetically and cover famous names (Duke Ellington, Ralph Ellison, Zora Neale Hurston); influential organizations (National Association for the Advancement of Colored People, Universal Negro Improvement Association); popular black magazines and newspapers (*Amsterdam News, Chicago Defender, Pittsburgh Courier*); musicals (*Hot Chocolates, How Come?*); notable places ancillary to the awakening in Harlem (Chicago, Philadelphia, Washington, D.C.); and other topics (*Howard University, Patrons, Rent party*). Entries on nonblack people who had an effect on the time period, like Fiorella LaGuardia, illustrate the comprehensiveness of the volume.

Most entries are half a page, though some stretch over a few pages. The volume is liberally filled with photos and graphics that bring the time period to life. All entries are followed by a further reading list. Additionally, there is a compiled bibliography at the end of the book. Cross-references are plentiful and helpful. A brief (three-page) foreword, entitled "Race, Blackness, and Modernism during the Harlem Renaissance," provides a historical context and background for the entries, as does the introduction, "Black Phoenix Rising."

A "Glossary of Harlem Renaissance Slang" in appendix A defines terms such as *dogs* (feet) and *kicks* (shoes). Appendix B contains maps delineating subjects like African American population, states with laws banning interracial marriage, and train routes used to migrate northward. Even a somewhat detailed map of Harlem is provided. A chronology begins in 1619, when the first slaves came to Virginia, and continues up until the present day. Indexing is detailed but not comprehensive; the index entry *Talented Tenth*, for example, misses the references to "Talented Tenth" in the W. E. B. DuBois entry.

Overall, this is a fine resource—one could read it like a book, from cover to cover. Recommended for high-school, public, and academic libraries.

Hispanic Literature of the United States: A Comprehensive Reference. By Nicolás Kanellos. 2003. 314p. bibliogs. illus. indexes. Greenwood, $75 (1-57356-558-X). 810.9.

This work by Kanellos, professor of Hispanic and classical languages at the University of Houston, is a welcome addition to the numerous reference books on the literature of the diverse populations of the U.S. It is much more than a who's who of Hispanic literature.

Spain was the first nation to introduce a written European language to the mainland of what would become the U.S., and coverage begins with a detailed, readable overview of the records of Ponce de León's exploration of Florida in the early sixteenth century. The overview chapter ends with a bibliography for further reading. The chronology that follows begins in 1492 with the arrival of Columbus and traces the development of Hispanic literature and culture to 2002.

The bulk of the text is taken up by the chapter "Who's Who of Hispanic Authors of the United States," which consists of alphabetical entries, between 150 and 500 words in length, for more than 100 authors. Succeeding chapters discuss "Significant Trends, Movements, and Themes" (for example, the Nuyorican poets, indigenous writings, and immigration) and "Publishing Trends." This chapter is particularly enlightening as it discusses Spanish-language newspapers from all of the states with large Hispanic populations and the small presses that were significant in the careers of such luminaries as Sandra Cisneros and Ana Castillo. A chapter specifically detailing the history of Hispanic drama is also included.

Students, faculty, and collection development librarians will appreciate the list of "100 Essential Hispanic Literary Works" and the select bibliography. Title and subject indexes complete the work, which is recommended for public, high-school, and undergraduate collections.

Latino and Latina Writers. 2v. Ed. by Alan West-Duran. 2003. 1,072p. bibliogs. index. Scribner, $265 (0-684-31293-X). 810.9.

The latest offering from the Scribner Writers series showcases 57 writers. The set is introduced by five thematic essays engaging literature through the lens of feminist criticism; the historical development and emergence of Latino and Latina literature; approaches to a Latino autobiography; performance art and theater; and the impact of issues of identity, border crossing (in multiple senses of the term), and transculturation on the creation of a Latino literature. The rest of volume 1 contains 27 bio-bibliographical articles on Chicano and Chicana authors. Authors range from the well known (e.g., Sandra Cisneros, Rudolfo Anaya) to the lesser known (e.g., Tino Villanueva). Cuban and Cuban American, Puerto Rican, Dominican, and other authors round out volume 2, which also has an index offering access by title and author. Although the thematic essays range widely in scope, the authors selected for biocritical essays are primarily those who have written in English after 1960. The articles focusing on individual writers begin with a brief biography and continue by examining selected writings. Each article ends with a bibliography of major works, selected critical treatments of the author, and resources for further study. All articles are written by 55 scholars and writers who are involved in the study of Latino and Latina literature.

Other resources, such as Fitzroy Dearborn's *Encyclopedia of Latin American Literature* (1977) and Gale's *Hispanic Writers* (2d ed., 1999), focus primarily on authors from Spanish-speaking countries. The current volume is similar in style to Scribner's *Latin American Writers* (vols. 1–3, 1989; *Supplement 1*, 2002), which covers more than 200 Spanish- and Portuguese-speaking writers from the sixteenth century on. *Latino and Latina Writers* is recommended for public and academic libraries and for high-school libraries looking for substantive treatment.

The Oxford Encyclopedia of American Literature. 4v. Ed. by Jay Parini. 2004. 631p. bibliogs. illus. index. Oxford, $495 (0-19-515653-6). 810.

This encyclopedia brings together 350 signed, alphabetically arranged essays on American literature from the colonial period to the present. The essays, although written by scholars for a general readership, vary in both length (between 2 and 14 pages) and sophistication (some are appropriate only for the undergraduate level and above). The majority of well-known American authors in the canon are surveyed here, including favorites such as Faulkner, Frost, Hawthorne, Melville, Salinger, and Whitman. Author essays discuss both biographical and critical aspects of the writer and include a bibliography of major works, followed by a list of briefly annotated secondary sources. Forty-five of the entries are critical readings of notable texts that often get studied in the classroom, such as *The Bell Jar, The Sun Also Rises,* and *To Kill a Mockingbird.* Fifty-two of the essays are on literary movements like the Black Arts movement, literary periods such as the Harlem Renaissance, and themes such as detective fiction or war literature. All essays have a bibliography for further reading, and most essays are accompanied by one of 250 black-and-white illustrations. Where applicable, *see also* references are placed at the end of essays. Other features include a chronology starting with 1607 that juxtaposes select literary works with historical context; a topical outline; a directory of contributors; and a good index leading to both authors and titles.

The *Oxford* encyclopedia set does a wonderful job of covering American literature's core in depth but does not have a fully comprehensive range. In his preface, the editor notes that "in any work of this kind, exclusion is necessary," but that "every effort was made to include subjects who might interest high school and college students as well as the general reader." In particular, a number of important contemporary figures seem to be missing. For example, John Guare is mentioned only in relationship to Edward Albee's far-reaching influence, and Paul Auster and Stephen Millhauser are mentioned only in relationship to E. L. Doctorow's inspiration for younger writers. There is no mention of John Kennedy Toole at all.

When compared to other similar sources, *Oxford* is intrinsically better but lacks the same breadth. The *Encyclopedia of American Literature* (Facts On File, 2002), a three-volume set, offers broader coverage within 1,500 briefer entries but has ineffective cross-references and no cumulative index. A cheaper, single-volume option, the *Continuum Encyclopedia of American Literature* (2003), also has a better selection of contemporary American authors but an index that doesn't cover titles. The *Oxford* set is praiseworthy and recommended for most high-school, public, and academic libraries, though it needs to be used in conjunction with other, more comprehensive resources. It should be noted that supplements are promised in the preface, to take up additional authors as well as movements and texts.

Contemporary Gay American Poets and Playwrights: An A-to-Z Guide. Ed. by Emmanuel S. Nelson. 2003. 480p. bibliogs. index. Greenwood, $99.95 (0-313-32232-5). 812.

This handsome new guide to 62 gay male U.S. poets and playwrights complements Nelson's *Contemporary Gay American Novelists: A Bio-Bibliographical Critical Sourcebook* (Greenwood, 1993), and together these compilations complement the award-winning *Contemporary Lesbian Writers of the United States: A Bio-Bibliographical Critical Sourcebook* (Greenwood, 1993).

The poets and playwrights include well-known writers, such as Edward Albee, Allen Ginsberg, and James Merrill, but most are lesser known, especially in the broader world of literary studies. Some are no longer living (e.g., James Broughton, 1913–1999), but all are twentieth-century figures, many continuing into the twenty-first century. The contributors are mostly academics, but several are literary writers in their own right.

The articles, arranged in alphabetical order, vary in length from 4 to 16 pages. They have a uniform format: biography, major works and themes, critical reception, and bibliography (first works of the poet or playwright by genre, followed by works about him). Citations are standard, except that monograph citations don't include pagination. The volume concludes with a general bibliography, an index, and a list of contributors with brief biographical information. The index is limited almost entirely to names of persons and titles of works, with very few subject entries (among them, *AIDS, HIV,* and *Sadomasochism*).

This volume merits the same recommendation that RBB gave to Nelson's 1993 guide to novelists: "Nelson has done an excellent job in editing this book . . . which should be a welcome addition in all research libraries as well as other libraries where there is an interest in gay and lesbian culture." Many of these writers are not included in standard general literary reference sources, so this compilation's biographical, critical, thematic, and especially bibliographic information will be very helpful to students and scholars.

The Facts On File Companion to American Drama. Ed. by Jackson R. Bryer and Mary C. Hartig. 2003. 562p. appendixes. bibliogs. index. Facts On File, $71.50 (0-8160-4665-4). 812.

As stated in this volume's introduction, "American drama has often been regarded as the poor stepchild in the family of American literature." The introduction goes on to give an overview of American drama from its early beginnings in the 1700s to the present, while noting influential plays and playwrights. It also explains why American drama is neglected and why students and audiences remain "unaware of American drama 'before O'Neill'."

Most of the approximately 600 signed alphabetical entries cover major plays and playwrights. Others treat theater companies, theater movements, directors, and topics such as *Asian-American drama, Federal Theatre Project, Musical theater,* and *Off-Broadway.* Emphasis is on the twentieth century. Individual entries vary in length from half a page to about three pages. Biographical sketches of playwrights contain vital statistics and a brief amount of family information, with the bulk of the entry being about their works. Play entries contain a brief production history and a synopsis.

Most entries have a bibliography. There are two appendixes at the end of the volume. The first appendix lists winners of major drama prizes for the Pulitzer Prize, New York Drama Critics' Circle Award, Tony Award, and Obie Award. The second appendix is a lengthy general bibliography. There is also a detailed alphabetical index.

Despite its stepchild status, American drama is relatively well served by *The Cambridge Guide to Theatre* (rev. ed., 1995), *The Oxford Encyclopedia of Theatre and Performance* (2003), and Salem's *Critical Survey of Drama* (2d ed., 2003) and *Masterplots II: Drama Series* (rev. ed., 2003). The Facts On File volume is useful for its exclusively American focus. Written for a general audience, it is recommended for high-school, public, and academic libraries.

The Tennessee Williams Encyclopedia. Ed. by Philip C. Kolin. 2004. 350p. bibliogs. illus. index. Greenwood, $89.95 (0-313-32101-9). 812.

Here is a much-needed resource of a modern playwright who has contributed so much to stages and audiences around the world. The volume contains more than 150 entries, written by 56 scholars and arranged alphabetically, from playwright Edward Albee, who shared similar themes in his plays, to the play *You Touched Me!* Williams' only dramatic collaboration. The volume also provides a detailed preface about the book's format, followed by an alphabetical list of entries and a guide to related topics, arranged by broad categories, such as "Family and Early History," "Theater and Films," and "Works." A detailed chronology of Williams' key accomplishments and associations completes the front matter. A list of primary and secondary sources and a detailed index complete the book.

Though the encyclopedia covers biographical details and major figures in Williams' life, emphasis is on the plays. Play entries generally provide background information, plot summary, interpretation, and performance history, including adaptations, along with comparisons to other of Williams' works. For example, *Camino Real* is compared with *The Glass Menagerie* and *A Streetcar Named Desire.* The essays vary in length from one paragraph (such as for *Alpha Tau Omega,* his fraternity), to seven pages each on *The Glass Menagerie* and *A Streetcar Named Desire.* Each signed entry ends with a list of further reading suggestions.

The encyclopedia is an excellent resource for English and theater teachers and students. Though it is not comprehensive, it does provide the researcher with basic information on Williams' works and life. This is a worthwhile purchase for academic, large public, and some high-school libraries.

A Theodore Dreiser Encyclopedia. Ed. by Keith Newlin. 2003. 431p. bibliogs. index. Greenwood, $99.95 (0-313-31680-5). 813.

This encyclopedia provides undergraduate- and graduate-level students with a guide to Dreiser's 24 books, more than 870 magazine and newspaper articles, stories, poems, and essays. There are entries for each of his books and stories, selected articles, and other genres in which he wrote as well as for his major influences; people, places, and events in his life; and the literary and social contexts of his works.

Almost 70 academic contributors supplied the 279 entries, which are enumerated at the beginning of the encyclopedia, followed by a list of abbreviations and a chronology of Dreiser's life from his birth in 1871 to the formation of the International Theodore Dreiser Society in 1991. The entries vary in length from one paragraph on Stewart Barnes, a character in *The Bulwark,* to some that cover several pages, such as that for *A Hoosier*

Holiday, "the first 'automobile road book'." Each entry ends with a suggested reading list. The selected bibliography lists Dreiser's books, volumes in the University of Pennsylvania Dreiser Edition, and miscellaneous collections by him, followed by lists of biographical and critical secondary works.

This volume would be a worthwhile supplemental addition to academic libraries and to public libraries with extensive literature collections.

The Toni Morrison Encyclopedia. Ed. by Elizabeth Ann Beaulieu. 2003. 428p. bibliogs. index. Greenwood, $89.95 (0-313-31699-6). 813.

This encyclopedia covers Morrison's works, characters, locations, themes (e.g., *Children*), and general topics (e.g., *Oprah's Book Club*). The alphabetically arranged entries are the work of 52 contributors. Also included is a 14-page selected bibliography citing Morrison's novels, essays, stories, and interviews, as well as criticism on Morrison's works selected from books and articles. Typically, articles on themes, general topics, and works span several pages, while entries on characters and locations range from one sentence to one paragraph. A list of references concludes many, but not all, entries.

Entries on Morrison's works usually provide a plot summary followed by a review of major themes within the work. For example, the entry for *The Bluest Eye* includes a discussion of racism and black female identity. Theme coverage is broad and should be useful for students. For example, the six-page article titled *Migration* discusses migration in the novels *The Bluest Eye, Sula, Song of Solomon, Tar Baby, Beloved, Jazz,* and *Paradise* and ends with a list of further readings. Other examples of theme headings include *Hunger, Masculinity, Sex/Sexuality,* and *Trickster.* Although a general index is included, a separate theme index might further assist readers.

The Toni Morrison Encyclopedia makes a nice supplement to resources such as Gale's *Contemporary Authors* and *Masterplots II: African American Literature* (Salem, 1994) as well as circulating items such as *Critical Essays on Toni Morrison* (G. K. Hall, 1988). Intended for the scholar and the general reader, some articles may prove challenging for high-schoolers. Suitable for academic and public libraries.

The World of Toni Morrison: A Guide to Characters and Places in Her Novels. By Gloria Grant Roberson. 2003. 262p. appendix. bibliog. index. Greenwood, $49.95 (0-313-32380-1). 813.

Morrison is universally recognized as an exceptional writer. Winner of the National Book Critics Circle Award in 1977, the Pulitzer Prize in 1988, and the Nobel Prize in 1994, she writes rich, complex novels replete with references to myth, history, culture, and religion. For many readers, the nuances and depth of these references are not fully realized because of a lack of familiarity. This book will remedy that lack.

More than 800 entries, arranged alphabetically and ranging from six words (*Windemere*) to 53 lines (*Dead, Macon III*), identify the historical, cultural, biblical, and mythological framework of *The Bluest Eye, Sula, Song of Solomon, Tar Baby, Beloved, Jazz,* and *Paradise*. Although most of the entries are for fictional characters and places, approximately 10 percent describe actual persons, places, or events, such as Saint Augustine, Abraham Lincoln, Cincinnati (Ohio), Kentucky wonder beans, and Mary Jane candy. Each entry includes an abbreviation for the appropriate novel and page references that point the reader to the relevant pages in the novel. There is also an appendix that lists the entries alphabetically by book.

This easy-to-use, clearly written reference resource will be valuable for public libraries that serve book discussion groups and provide homework help for book reports. Academic libraries will find it useful for assisting students and researchers who are interested in the works of Morrison. *The Toni Morrison Encyclopedia* [RBB O 15 03] also has entries for fictional characters and locales but provides, in addition, synopses of Morrison's works as well as entries for her general themes and for various aspects of her career. The two titles are complementary.

Asian American Short Story Writers: An A-to-Z Guide. Ed. by Guiyou Huang. 2003. 359p. bibliogs. index. Greenwood, $94.95 (0-313-32229-5). 818.

Covering 49 Asian American writers, each entry in this volume includes sections titled "Biography," "Major Works and Themes," "Critical Reception," and "Bibliography." The bibliography lists studies of and works by the author—novels, poetry collections, interviews, and, of course, short story collections. Studies include book reviews and journal articles.

Most articles are three to five pages long, with the most text devoted to themes and critical reception. For example, the article on Ha Jin is five and one-half pages and includes a two-paragraph biography, a one-page bibliography, a two-and-one-half-page overview of Jin's three short story collections, and a one-and-one- half-page survey of critiques and awards.

Each entry is signed. Associate professors and Ph.D. candidates comprise the majority of the 30 contributors. Other than the fact that they reside in the U.S. or Canada, the criteria for selecting the authors who are covered are unclear. Of the 25 female and 24 male writers, 2 were born in the nineteenth century—Sui Sin Far and Winnifred Eaton. The youngest is Evelyn Lau (1971–). Editor Huang, currently chairs the English Department at Kurtzdown University of Pennsylvania. Huang's prior editing experience includes a work on Asian American poets and another on Asian American autobiographers.

Students should find this resource easy-to-use. One can utilize the table of contents, thumb through the alphabetically arranged articles, or use the index. Additional features include an introductory 19-page essay on the Asian American short story examining the works of Sui Sin Far, Hisaye Yamamoto, and Oscar Peñaranda. Following the entries, a bibliography provides a list of anthologies, secondary sources, and relevant periodicals.

The reference source *Asian American Literature: Reviews and Criticism of Works by American Writers of Asian Descent* (Gale, 1999) is similar but covers a smaller number of short story writers. Recommended for high-school, public, and academic libraries.

The Oxford Companion to Mark Twain. By Gregg Camfield. 2003. 767p. bibliog. illus. index. Oxford, $75 (0-19-510710-1). 818.

The scope of this resource is broad. Arranged alphabetically, entries cover writings, major characters, individuals, organizations, and a large number of general topics affiliated in some way with Samuel Clemens, or Mark Twain. Topical entry headings include *Cities, Death, Food, Science, Sex and sexuality,* and many others. A handful of "feature essays" are the contributions of noted scholars or well- known writers, such as Nat Hentoff on *Censorship* and Arthur Miller on *Performance*. More than 40 black-and-white illustrations depict items such as Clemens' pilot certificate and political cartoons.

Lengths of entries range from a single paragraph to several pages, often providing detailed descriptions and criticisms. Many articles contain material derived from primary sources such as letters and speeches. For example, the article *Work habits* includes quotes from five letters, an excerpt from Clemens' autobiography, and two sentences from one of his notebooks. Entries for writings avoid chapter-by-chapter summaries and instead follow Clemens' writing process mixed with a discussion of themes and meanings. The inclusion of down-to-earth practicalities such as volumes sold provides an added perspective.

The tone of this resource is scholarly yet entertaining. Numerous cross-references provide easy access to related articles. Occasional complex terminology will challenge some high-school students and adults. A thematic list of entries, bibliography, index, and chronology of Clemens' works are also included.

There is some duplication with *Mark Twain A to Z: The Essential Reference to His Life and Writings* (Facts On File, 1995), which has nearly 1,300 entries and more than 130 illustrations. Another similar resource is *The Mark Twain Encyclopedia* (Garland, 1993). However, the high use of primary sources as well as broad topics makes *The Oxford Companion to Mark Twain* a nice addition, suitable for both public and academic libraries.

The Age of Milton: An Encyclopedia of Major 17th-Century British and American Authors. Ed. by Alan Hager. 2004. 392p. bibliogs. index. Greenwood, $99.95 (0-313-31008-4). 820.9.

This encyclopedia provides 79 entries detailing the works and lives of innovators of the intellectually fervent late Renaissance–early Enlightenment period. *Authors* is defined broadly to include composers and scientists as well as diarists, novelists, playwrights, poets, essayists, and philosophers. Though most are British or American, some European writers and artists "who significantly influenced British and American literary culture" are included. Alphabetical entries average three to five pages, with longer ones devoted to major figures like Thomas Hobbes, John Milton, and William Shakespeare. Each entry is consistently divided into "Biography," "Major Works and Themes," "Critical Reception" (including both contemporary and later reactions over the centuries), and "Bibliography." Most bibliographies are about half a page long and are subdivided into "Works by" and "Studies of" sections. Cross-references are included.

Recognizable names abound, including some whose entries may surprise. For example, Oliver Cromwell is included on the basis of his numerous letters, compiled and edited by historian Thomas Carlyle 200 years after his death. Fourteen female authors appear, including Aphra Behn, "the first recognized professional woman writer in English," and Mary Rowlandson, author of "the first book by an Anglo-American woman." Artists such as Rembrandt, Reubens, and Van Dyck are included for the influence exerted by their work on the writers and thinkers of the period, although the connection is not always made clear.

The contributing authors of the entries are mostly professors or Ph.D. candidates and display cogent, informative, and lively writing. The volume ends with a "List of Authors by Birth Year" and a "Selected General Bibliography." Overall, this is a useful guide to the writing and thinking of seventeenth-century American and British authors, suitable for academic and large public libraries.

The Continuum Encyclopedia of British Literature. Ed. by Steven R. Sefarin and Valerie Grosvenor Myer. 2003. 1,184p. appendixes. bibliogs. index. Continuum, $175 (0-8264-1456-7). 820.

Intended to complement Continuum's *Encyclopedia of American Literature* (1999), this compendium covers "literature that is by definition British in scope or origin, including the literatures written in English from the colonial to the postcolonial experience in Africa, Australia, Canada, the Caribbean, India, and New Zealand." However, it does not provide separate articles on authors from these areas unless their nationality is British. The team of more than 200 contributors includes academics from a variety of countries as well as such distinguished authors as Peter Barnes and Claire Tomalin.

Most of the encyclopedia's 1,700 entries are devoted to writers. The only title entries are for early works by unknown authors, for example, *Ancrene Wisse* and *Beowulf*. The 69 topical articles provide lengthy historical overviews of specific genres, themes, literary periods, and geographical areas. Among these are *Caribbean literature in English, Feminism, Old English,* and *War and literature*. With the exception of brief author entries of approximately 300 words or less, articles are signed and include bibliographical references.

Coverage of newer authors such as Iain Banks, Roddy Doyle, J. K. Rowling, and Zadie Smith is commendably generous, but some entries for living authors lack currency. For example, the articles on Fleur Adcock, Brian Aldiss, and Paul Theroux mention none of their publications from the past decade. Moreover, the editors' policy regarding British nationality limits treatment of many notable writers from Commonwealth countries (such as Booker Prize winners Peter Carey, J. M. Coetzee, and Thomas Keneally) to brief mentions in the survey articles.

Fortunately, the volume has a detailed index, which is invaluable for locating information on authors not accorded separate entries and cross-references from pseudonyms and variant names. Supplementary material includes a chronological chart noting historical and literary highlights, lists of monarchs and poets laureate, and lists of literary prizewinners.

With more than 7,000 entries, the sixth edition of *The Oxford Companion to English Literature* (2000) provides more comprehensive coverage of English-language literatures. On the other hand, *Continuum* frequently offers greater depth because its entries are generally longer. For example, the *Continuum* article on playwright David Hare is five times longer than the one in the *Oxford Companion*. In spite of its flaws, this work will be a useful addition to public and academic libraries. However, its steep price may prohibit its purchase by the smaller libraries that would benefit the most from its contents.

Encyclopedia of British Writers: 19th and 20th Century. 2v. Ed. by Christine L. Krueger and others. 2003. 880p. bibliogs. indexes. Facts On File, $150 (0-8160-4670-0). 820.9.

More than 800 British writers of the last two centuries are profiled in concise entries in these two volumes. Both volumes begin with introductory essays by the general editors and continue with author time lines, alphabetically arranged entries, selected bibliographies, and indexes. Each article sets its subject in context, and entries on authors awarded "major" status also include brief critical analyses of one or more individual works. In addition to the entries on individual writers, each volume also includes articles on key literary terms or movements: for example, in the nineteenth-century volume there are short essays on romanticism and the Oxford and Pre-Raphaelite movements, and in the twentieth-century volume there are pieces on imagism, the Bloomsbury Group, and the Theater of the Absurd. Articles are often enhanced with suggestions for further reading.

Entrants include poets, essayists, playwrights, and novelists. The range of authors represented is wide and embraces not only the familiar names found in literature survey classes, such as James Joyce, D. H. Lawrence, G. B. Shaw, and Anthony Trollope, but many "popular" authors like Agatha Christie, Ian Fleming, and Rafael Sabatini. Children's authors are also given their due, with articles on J. M. Barrie, A. A. Milne, Beatrix Potter, and J. K. Rowling, to name a few. Although most of those included count one of the British Isles as their birthplace, there are many representatives from countries that are part of the British Commonwealth, among them Margaret Atwood, J. M. Coetzee, Michael Ondaatje, and Salman Rushdie. Current literary stars like Martin Amis, Roddy Doyle, Ian McEwan, and Zadie Smith are also included.

The writing is clear and straightforward, and each article presents an overview of the life and works of its subject. Both the suggestions for further reading and the selected bibliographies feature fairly recent, easily available titles. Libraries serving high-school and college students will find this a useful source, as will readers' advisors or anyone looking for a quick course on the last two centuries of Brit lit.

Modern British Women Writers: An A-to-Z Guide. Ed. by Vicki K. Janik and Del Ivan Janik. 2003. 428p. bibliogs. index. Greenwood, $94.95 (0-313-31030-0). 820.9.

Most of the 58 women included here were born in England or were from countries formerly part of the British Empire or Commonwealth. All were active in the twentieth century, and many are still writing. Each signed entry includes an overview of the subject, an analysis of her work, an assessment of the critical response to it, and a bibliography including primary and secondary sources. A sizable selected bibliography completes the work.

Although the selection of writers is limited by time period and geography, there is still considerable variety in the range of writers included. Contemporary playwrights like Caryl Churchill, Pam Gems, and Timberlake Wertenbaker are here as well as classic mystery writers Agatha Christie, P. D. James and Dorothy Sayers. Prolific writers (and sisters) A. S. Byatt and Margaret Drabble are profiled, as are writers whose work has been lately "rediscovered," like Barbara Pym and Jean Rhys. Current "literary" favorites Anita Brookner, Penelope Fitzgerald, and Elizabeth Jane Howard are among the entrants, as are several women writers of color (India's Attia Hosain and Kamala Markandaya and Nigeria's Buchi Emecheta). Poets as various as Edith Sitwell and Stevie Smith have found "a room of their own" here, and Bloomsbury is also "in the house," represented by Virginia Woolf and Vita Sackville-West. This useful handbook should find a place in libraries serving high-school students and undergraduates as well as the general public.

South Asian Novelists in English: An A-to-Z Guide. Ed. by Jaina C. Sanga. 2003. 308p. bibliogs. index. Greenwood, $89.95 (0-313-31885-9). 820.9.

This volume provides summaries of 53 novelists who write in English and have achieved various levels of acclaim. Most of the writers were born in Bangladesh, India, Pakistan, or Sri Lanka.

Arranged by the novelist's last name, each article contains four sections: biography, "Major Works and Themes," "Critical Reception," and bibliography. For example, the three-page entry for Adib Khan includes a three-paragraph biography highlighting events such as place of birth, education, and current place of employment. "Major Works and Themes" is limited to Khan's three novels. Excerpts from book reviews and references to book awards make up "Critical Reception." References in the bibliography fall under two categories: works, including formats in addition to novels, and studies, consisting mostly of book reviews. Entries on writers with international prominence, such as Salman Rushdie, rely less on book reviews and more on scholarly articles and books. Several article bibliographies cite Internet sources. Unfortunately, a few author bibliographies included article citations without page numbers.

Each entry is signed by one of 41 contributors, mostly faculty members and Ph.D. candidates based in the U. S., although some international contributors are included. A two-page general bibliography inventories notable anthologies, secondary sources, and a list of 10 periodical titles of interest (e.g., *Indian Writing Today*). A combined author, subject, and title index is provided.

Similar information is included in broader literary reference resources. Of the first 25 writers in *South Asian Novelists in English,* 21 are covered in the online version of Gale's *Contemporary Authors.* However, a single-volume compilation of English-writing South Asian novelists is a convenient research tool and should also prove useful in collection development. Suitable for large public libraries and academic libraries.

World Writers in English. 2v. Ed. by Jay Parini. 2003. 782p. bibliogs. index. Scribner, $265 (0-684-31289-1). 820.9.

British language and art forms were sown in countries as different as Canada and India with, as the introduction notes, "marvelous results for anyone interested in literature in English." Part of the Scribner Writers series, *World Writers in English* contains biographical and critical essays exploring the lives and works of 40 authors, among them Nigeria's Chinua Achebe, Hong Kong's Timothy Mo, and India's Salman Rushdie. Some of the writers, such as Margaret Atwood and J. M. Coetzee, are probably familiar to the general reader; others, such as Agha Shahid Ali and Jack Mapanje, are less well known. The set supports a burgeoning interest on campuses in the contributions of nations other than the U.K., Ireland, or the U.S. to literature in English.

The essays, typical for the Scribner Writers series, are by noted scholars. They provide a detailed biographical sketch of the author and place his or her works in the context of that life and of the post- colonial cultures most tend to belong to. For example, black South African writer Alex La Guma's entry discusses his political activist career, which colored his writing and the resultant depictions of South Africa in those writings. Useful though much of this is, other important contributions to research come in the extensive bibliographies that follow each entry, detailing both the author's works and a selection of other critical and biographical studies.

If there is one criticism to be leveled at this set, it is that there are only 40 authors included. Yet this is a significant step in English literature reference works and, as such, is an essential addition to any general or academic reference collection.

The Oxford Companion to Chaucer. Ed. by Douglas Gray. 2004. 526p. bibliogs. maps. Oxford, $95 (0-19-811765-5). 821.1.

Like many of the volumes in the Oxford Companion series, this work is an invaluable guide—in this case, to the life, times, and work of Geoffrey Chaucer, the Middle English poet who gave us *The Canterbury Tales* and *Troilus and Criseyde.*

The stated goal of this work is to "help readers and students in the understandinzg" of the poet's works. It does so through more than 2,000 alphabetically listed entries on the life, family, friends, works, characters, and sources of Chaucer. Beyond this, there are some contextual entries dealing with other contemporaneous European writers, Chaucer's verse, and his prevalent themes and topics.

The entry on *The Wife of Bath's Prologue and Tale* demonstrates the volume's utility for both general reader and specialist. It opens with an analysis of the *Prologue* ("a confessional monologue") and follows with an overview of both the *Prologue* and the *Tale.* For literary scholars, there are also some manuscript notes ("the first contribution in Fragment III"). For those interested in learning more, there is a cross-referenced entry from *Fragments* to the entry on *The Canterbury Tales* that details the 10 extant fragments of the Ellesmere manuscript. The entry on the *Ellesmere Manuscript* tells us that this is "the most famous and most elegant" of the surviving manuscripts—of which there are relatively many, attesting to the popularity of the *Tales.*

Each entry usually has a brief (and in the case of the works, selective) list of further reading. The volume begins with a list of "the most substantial topical entries" (for example, *Clothes, London, Rhetoric*), a chronology, and maps and ends with an extensive bibliography. For all students of Chaucer, this is a worthy addition to their libraries. Academic and large public libraries will want to have it.

The Brontës A to Z: The Essential Reference to Their Lives and Work. By Lisa Paddock and Carl Rollyson. 2003. 252p. appendix. bibliog. illus. index. map. Facts On File, $65 (0-8160-4302-7). 823.

In more than 500 entries, this offering from the acclaimed and popular Literary A to Z series covers every aspect of the lives of the Brontës. In their introduction, the authors note that interest in the Brontës continues to grow, thanks to "intense scholarly study and—in some cases—nearly cultlike devotion."

Alphabetically arranged, the volume includes synopses of the Brontës' writings, their publishing history, and critical reception; entries for all characters, both major and minor; historical events and people who influenced the lives and writings; real and fictional settings; and family members, friends, publishers, and even pets. There are also entries for notable Brontë biographers and scholars. The entries vary in length from 17 pages of plot summary and analysis (with photographs from film versions) for *Wuthering Heights,* to a few lines for Naomi Brocklehurst, founder of the infamous Lowood School in Charlotte Brontë's *Jane Eyre.* Other features include a map of Brontë country; a detailed chronology; a categorical appendix that lists entries under headings such as "Brontë Authorities" and "Publishers, Publications, and Organizations"; and a bibliography.

This volume is a good introduction to readers unfamiliar with the Brontës as well as a worthwhile resource for scholars and fans. It would be a valuable addition to high-school, public, and academic libraries.

A Mary Shelley Encyclopedia. By Lucy Morrison and Staci Stone. 2003. 539p. appendixes. bibliog. index. Greenwood, $94.95 (0-313- 30159-X). 823.

Mary Shelley is famous as, first, the author of *Frankenstein* and, second, as the wife of a famous poet and daughter of a famous novelist and philosopher. Due in no small part to *Frankenstein*'s place on high- school and college reading lists, her other works have been reprinted in recent years. This has resulted in a reassessment and an emergence of Shelley from the shadows of her great work and her family. Exploring these other works leaves one with a sense of an incredible life story and intellect that *Frankenstein* barely revealed.

This encyclopedia provides readers of Shelley's works with a context—it offers information on her family, friends, residences, and more, as well as entries on her works, characters, influences, and themes. It boasts in the introduction of containing "textual footnotes to nearly all aspects of Shelley and her works." For example, the entry *Prometheus* mentions the Greek mythological figure but also the uses the myth was put to by Percy Bysshe Shelley (in, for example, *Prometheus Unbound,* 1820) and the reinvention of the myth by Mary in her most famous novel (subtitled *or, The Modern Prometheus*).

The entries are the short type one expects of an encyclopedia, fully cross-referenced (in bold type) and factual. The design is somewhat confusing, especially in entries where there is a lot of cross-referencing; also, one is left wondering about the need for the two appendixes of quotes used by Shelley. The comprehensive bibliography of works referenced in the encyclopedia entries makes for a very useful glimpse of Shelley, her works, the influences, and scholarship. This volume is recommended for academic and large public libraries.

The Oxford Companion to Italian Literature. Ed. by Peter Hainsworth and David Robey. 2003. 644p. bibliogs. maps. Oxford, $75 (0-19-818332-1). 850.9.

Oxford *Companions* to English, French, and German literature are now joined by one that aims to present the whole of Italian literature, from the early thirteenth century to the present.

Not surprisingly, ample space is afforded to important authors, such as Giovanni Boccaccio, Dante Alighieri, and Francesco Petrarch, from the thirteenth and fourteenth centuries, to Umberto Eco and Luigi Pirandello, from the twentieth. These are matched by shorter entries on minor, yet significant, figures, including Carlo Collodi, author of the much-loved children's story *Pinocchio.* Important literary works appear under their English title when extremely well known as such (e.g., Dante's *Divine Comedy,* not *Divina Commedia*). Otherwise, one must know the Italian (e.g., Pirandello's *Sei personaggi in cerca d'autore,* not *Six Characters in Search of an Author*). Literary genres and movements are presented along with entries on *Literary theory, Semiotics,* and *Textual criticism.* The importance of literary magazines and publishers is covered, including individual entries on specific literary journals such as *Il Ponte* and publishing houses such as Rizzoli. Entries treat Italian literature written in Latin and various dialects as well as the influence of classical and patristic writings on Italian literature. The social and political contexts in which Italian literature has developed are covered in some detail, with entries on important cities, historical events, and political philosophies.

The nearly 2,400 entries are alphabetically arranged and were written by a team of international Italianists. Only the lengthier entries include supplemental bibliographies and usually provide no more than one or two references. The prefatory matter includes a nice introduction not only to the *Companion* itself but also to Italian literature.

Two other recent reference works deserve mention. The *Dictionary of Italian Literature* (rev. ed., Greenwood, 1996) contains 362 entries, the majority of which are devoted to authors. The essays are far lengthier and provide substantial supplemental bibliographies. *The Feminist Encyclopedia of Italian Literature* (Greenwood, 1997) is not, as the title might suggest, an encyclopedia of Italian women writers. Rather, it examines the Italian literary tradition in a feminist perspective. *The Oxford Companion to Italian Literature* is the most comprehensive reference tool for Italian literature in English, the brevity of most entries notwithstanding. Recommended for academic and large public library collections.

Encyclopedia of Latin American Theater. Ed. by Eladio Cortés and Mirta Barrea-Marlys. 2003. 514p. bibliogs. index. Greenwood, $125 (0-313-29041-5). 862.009.

Intended as an introduction to Latin American theater for English-speaking users, this resource covers 20 countries, with some smaller countries omitted (e.g., St. Kitts, St. Lucia).

Arrangement is by country. Each country section contains an introductory survey essay followed by *A–Z* biographical and topical entries. Essay length varies (e.g., 4 pages for Panama, 20 pages for Puerto Rico). Articles trace theater developments from pre-Columbian times to the present, with emphasis on the nineteenth and twentieth centuries. Each essay includes a bibliography. Although the volume is intended for English speakers, many bibliographies cite mostly Spanish-language resources. For example, of the 31 citations in the bibliography for Mexico, 26 refer to Spanish-language titles.

The *A–Z* sections contain mostly author entries. Each entry provides a short profile centered on theater experience; a list of works arranged chronologically (English translations accompany many Spanish titles); and, in most cases, a selected bibliography of works about the playwright. Topical entries are few. Examples include *Independent theaters* in Uruguay and *Theatrical institutions and festivals* in Venezuela.

Additional features include articles on Chicano and Nuyorican theater, a 15-page overview article on Latin American theater, and a general bibliography. A list of entries is included in the front, and an index to names, theater schools, institutions, and companies, but not play titles, rounds out the volume.

Some of the writers covered here might be hard to find in other resources. Still, libraries that own *The Encyclopedia of Latin American Literature* (Fitzroy Dearborn, 1997) or *The Cambridge History of Latin American Literature* (1996) may decide against purchasing this specialized resource. For larger public and academic libraries.

The Cervantes Encyclopedia. 2v. By Howard Mancing. 2004. 863p. bibliogs. index. Greenwood, $149.95 (0-313-30695-8). 863.

Mancing, a widely published scholar whose work primarily covers sixteenth- and seventeenth-century Spanish literature, has produced an encyclopedia focused solely on Cervantes. There are two other Cervantes encyclopedias, but both are in Spanish.

The Cervantes Encyclopedia endeavors to put Cervantes and his works into, as Mancing states in the introduction, "a series of contexts: historical, cultural, personal, literary, critical, textual and intertextual." All the characters from all of Cervantes' works are identified, as are all the historic figures, whether associated with Cervantes or alluded to in his works. In addition, religious and mythological allusions, important episodes from *Don Quixote*, major influences by and on Cervantes, and some aspects of modern scholarship are covered in a single *A–Z* order. Particular attention is paid to subsequent literature inspired in some way by Cervantes, with entries for Woody Allen, Jane Austen, and Paul Auster, to give just a few examples.

As Mancing is the sole author, there is a near-perfect level of consistency in how the articles are written and how the overall work is structured. There are some slightly peculiar rules as to how the information is arranged, but all is clearly laid out in the introduction. Fictional characters like Sancho Panza are alphabetized by first name, while real people are listed last name, first name. Many of the articles have bibliographies, and though the emphasis is on English-language sources, a number of the cited items are in Spanish. A chronology of events in Cervantes' life precedes the entries, and there are a selected bibliography and a lengthy index at the end of the second volume. The slick cover can give the superficial impression that this is a high-school rather than academic source, but in fact it is quite scholarly. For academic and large public libraries where there is an interest in Cervantes or Spanish literature in general, this is a fine choice.

Geography, Biography

Biographical Dictionary of Modern World Leaders: 1992 to the Present. By John C. Fredriksen. 2003. 566p. bibliogs. illus. index. Facts On File, $65 (0-8160-4723-5). 909.82.

This entry in the Facts On File Library of World History series covers heads of state as well as a few other prominent leaders, such as Gerry Adams and Kofi Annan, from 190 countries. The author, whose previous works include *America's Military Adversaries: From Colonial Times to the Present* (ABC-CLIO, 2001) and *American Military Leaders: From Colonial Times to the Present* (ABC-CLIO, 1999), has again written conscientious biographies for the secondary-school level and up.

The 400 entries are arranged alphabetically by person's name. All of the entrants were either in power as of 1992 or have risen to power since then. Essay length is between 700 and 1,500 words. The biographies discuss the personal and political forces that shaped these men and women, note the challenges they have faced, and assess their strengths and weaknesses as leaders. Direct quotations are incorporated, and some photographs are provided. The text is clear and enlightening. The bibliographic references at the end of each entry may not be readily available, especially in the case of leaders of smaller countries.

An index by country quickly identifies who has been included. The general index connects other people and events; for example, the index entry for September 11, 2001, leads to information related to more than 30 countries and their leaders' reactions. Pronunciation aids for names that are unfamiliar to English speakers might have been useful.

This book is highly recommended for high-school, public, and academic library collections as a thorough and accessible work for understanding leadership, national policies, and foreign relations.

Encyclopedia of Islam and the Muslim World. 2v. Ed. by Richard C. Martin. 2003. 823p. bibliogs. glossary. illus. index. maps. Macmillan, $265 (0-02-865603-2). 909.

The reference literature for Islam has long consisted of either a densely academic, multivolume encyclopedia or several, often specialized, single-volume works with brief definitions. Happily, there is now a reference work falling between these two extremes. The *Encyclopedia of Islam and the Muslim World* is a scholarly work "about Islamic cultures, religion, history, politics, and the like as well as the people who have identified with Islam over the past fourteen centuries."

A team of international scholars is responsible for the 515 entries, which are arranged alphabetically and range from 200 to 5,000 words in length. Many include some sort of illustration and end with helpful *see also* references and excellent supplemental bibliographies. A useful index completes the set. Coverage includes the religious dimensions of Islam as well as the development of the tradition in various parts of the world (e.g., Africa, South Asia, U.S.). Cultural issues of importance to the history of Islam (e.g., architecture, calligraphy, language) are also treated. Entries such as *Political organization* and *Political thought* demonstrate the historical completeness for which the encyclopedia strives, tracing developments from the life of the Prophet to the present day. Even topics of contemporary interest include a historical perspective. The entry for *Jihad* describes the many meanings of the term, including its contemporary association with violence, and how the concept has developed historically. The treatment of secularization in the Muslim world includes a comparison to historical events in the West, thereby helping the reader to understand that it cannot be understood solely from a Western perspective. Finally, the biographical entries include important figures from the religious, cultural, and political history of the Muslim world.

The *Oxford Encyclopedia of the Modern Islamic World* (1995) is close in spirit and size (four volumes) to this new work, but its coverage includes far less historical figures and events. The *Encyclopedia of Islam and the Muslim World*, on the other hand, "seeks to contextualize contemporary Islam within the longer history of Islam." As such, it can easily serve as a standard reference source with its scholarly, yet accessible, content. Highly recommend for academic and large public libraries.

Encyclopedia of the Crusades. By Alfred J. Andrea. 2003. 356p. bibliogs. illus. index. maps. Greenwood, $75 (0-313-31659-7). 909.07.

Andrea, professor emeritus of medieval history at the University of Vermont, wants the reader to learn about the classic era of the Crusades (ca. 1095/1096–1291 C.E.) through factual sources, not "romantic histories." Thus he compiled this work and wrote it in a "readable and enjoyable" manner for his intended audience of high-school students, undergraduates, and the general public. There are more than 200 entries, each one between approximately 10 lines and four pages in length. Some entries one would expect to find, such as *Children's Crusade* and *Richard I the Lionheart.* However, the author has also expanded the field to encompass, for example, the recent focus in academia on gender studies by including several entries dealing with women.

The introduction gives the entries some historical context and defines the term *crusade* for the reader. The entries are in alphabetical order and include cross-references in bold type to other entries in the book. Many entries also include suggested readings, both primary sources and historical studies. At the end of the work, the author has included a chronology of important dates and events, a "Basic Crusade Library" of further readings in bibliographic essay style, and a general index. Entries are enhanced by 100 photos and six maps.

Although it is impossible to write a detailed history of the Crusades in a mere 356 pages, Andrea has done a fine job of capturing the spirit of the time and has written a concise, enjoyable work. He also managed to present an inclusive history that covers women, as well as members of the Islamic world, "treated not as victims but rather as full-fledged actors." This encyclopedia is recommended for high-school, undergraduate, and public libraries.

Global History: Cultural Encounters from Antiquity to the Present. 4v. Ed. by David W. Del Testa. 2004. 734p. bibliogs. glossaries. illus. index. maps. M. E. Sharpe, $325 (0-7656-8043-2). 909.

Global History covers significant cultural encounters from 5,000 B.C.E. to the present. Each volume encompasses a specific time period with articles chronologically arranged. In total, the set contains 80 articles representing important instances of cross-cultural contacts, for example, "China's Contact with Southeast Asia" (200 B.C.E.–1433 C.E) or "The Great Revolt of Palestinian Arabs" (1936–39). In selecting topics, the editor looked for examples of interaction "that produced meaningful, appreciable historical exchange on a global level." Many of the articles focus on historical events or particular civilizations, but some treat recent social and technological developments, such as AIDS and satellite broadcasting.

Each volume has an introduction that provides some background and also briefly discusses historiographical approaches to the pertinent era. The articles, varying in length from three or four to 15 pages, are divided into four sections, which offer an introduction to major themes of the exchange, historical background on the civilizations or societies involved or on the events leading up to it, a description of the actual exchange, and an analysis of the significance of the exchange or related developments. Finally, a primary source document is appended. Text in each article is augmented by a time line, a sidebar detailing key steps in the exchange, cross-references, and a four- to 10-item bibliography. The articles are further enhanced by a photograph and a large map illustrating some aspect of the exchange being discussed. Each volume ends with a cumulative time line, glossary, cumulative bibliography, and comprehensive set index. In addition, volume 4 cumulates the glossaries and bibliographies.

The articles are clearly written and engaging enough to hold the attention of most readers from high school up. *Global History*'s cross-cultural approach differentiates it from standard world history reference sources, and it is recommended for high-school, public, and college libraries.

Atlas of the World's Deserts. By Nathaniel Harris. 2003. 192p. bibliog. glossary. illus. index. maps. Fitzroy Dearborn, $125 (1-57958-310-5). 910.

Deserts are beautiful places, even when unforgiving of those who do not respect their nature. This is an attractive book, written for the nonspecialist, that portrays that nature with a wealth of simple maps, lovely photographs, and considerable basic introductory information. Topical chapters, each dealing with some general characteristic such as physical geography, plants, or animals, are interspersed with atlas sections on the deserts of Africa, Asia, the Americas, and Australia and the Poles (the arid "cold deserts" of the Arctic and Antarctica). Each major desert area is described by a location map, a larger desert map, a sentence or two about specific areas identified on the map, a fact file, and illustrations of some unique attributes. The deserts are not always easy to find on the small location maps.

This is both a browsing book and beginning reference book for the topics included. For the most part, the information and layout of the book are handsomely integrated. Many of the numerous sidebars include illustrations, but there are several (for example, the one describing the moloch in the chapter "Creatures of the Desert") that would have benefited from accompanying photographs.

The author concludes by discussing the exploitation of deserts and their resources and some environmental issues surrounding desertification. He ends on a somewhat hopeful note stating it is too early to tell what will happen because of climate change and the desertification process. A glossary, bibliography of books and Web sites arranged by chapter, and index complete the volume. The book is recommended for high-school, public, and undergraduate libraries, although the price will make it out of reach for some.

Biography for Beginners: World Explorers. Ed. by Laurie Lanzen Harris. 2003. 598p. appendixes. glossary. illus. indexes. maps. Favorable Impressions, P.O. Box 69018, Pleasant Ridge, MI 48960, $55 (1-931360-20-0). 910.

This volume contains 102 entries, arranged in alphabetical order, on people who have broadened our knowledge of the world and is a follow-up to *Biography for Beginners: Presidents of the United States* (Omnigraphics, 1998). Black-and- white maps, as well as black-and-white drawings and photographs, appear on nearly every two-page spread. The text is written at a fourth-grade reading level, and the entries are geared toward students "in grades two through five who are studying world explorers for the first time." The text should be very appealing to the early reader, with short, easy-to-read sentences.

Explorer is defined here "as someone from the past 2,500 years... who left his or her native land and traveled to an area that was unknown to them." Subjects include traditional explorers as well as scientists, astronauts, and mapmakers. There are also summary entries on specific groups whose collective contributions are important to the history of discovery, such as the Phoenicians and the Vikings. Each entry begins with a heading listing the explorer's name, birth and death dates, nationality, and a brief description of the individual's importance to the history of exploration. Certain entries conclude with a list of Internet sites with more information. Some readers may find it confusing that within the articles both cross-references and terms appearing in the glossary are indicated by bold type.

Individuals covered range from Hanno of Carthage (c. 500 B.C.E.) to Mae Jemison. Also profiled are Alexander the Great, Kit Carson, Leif Eriksson, and Amerigo Vespucci. The text concludes with a glossary, time line, subject index, and indexes by nationality of explorer and area of exploration. One note: although the text uses the terms *Indian* and *Native American* interchangeably, indicating the term *Indian* is not a pejorative, some readers and communities may feel otherwise. This title would be a useful addition in elementary- school libraries as well as in public libraries.

Exploring Polar Frontiers: A Historical Encyclopedia. 2v. By William James Mills. 2003. 797p. bibliogs. glossary. illus. index. maps. ABC-CLIO, $185 (1-57607-422-6). 910.

Interest in the Arctic and the Antarctic has grown with the increased coverage of global warming and its effect on sea levels, the popularity of the *Endurance* saga, and the burgeoning interest in adventure travel. Recent titles such as *Antarctica: An Encyclopedia from Abbott Ice Shelf to Zooplankton* (Firefly, 2002) and *Antarctica and the Arctic: The Complete Encyclopedia* (Firefly, 2001) have provided some information about polar exploration. This excellent encyclopedia, written by the librarian at the Scott Polar Research Institute, concentrates entirely on the history of polar exploration and will be welcomed by both scholars and the general public.

More than 500 entries cover people, places, expeditions, ships, countries, and subjects from 325 B.C.E. to the present, with the majority of coverage in the twentieth century. Examples of subject entries include *Inuit contributions to polar exploration, Magnetic poles, Sledges and sleds, Surveying and mapping, Whaling and Antarctic exploration,* and *Women explorers.* Entries range in length from a single paragraph to eight pages.

The entries are accompanied by more than 160 illustrations, 20 maps, and 22 tables. Each entry has references and suggestions for further reading.

There is a chronological polar time line that lists polar expeditions by region, a 135-word glossary of technical terms (such as the different forms of ice and types of vessels), abbreviations and acronyms, an extensive bibliography, and an index. Unfortunately, the index is structured so that the entries for explorers and ships are not where many readers will look for them. For example, Roald Amundsen (the first man to reach the South Pole) is listed under *N* (Norwegian explorers) but not under *A* (Amundsen). There is, however, an alphabetical listing of all entries in the front matter as well as lists of entries in chronological order and by broad category.

Indexing aside, this is an excellent and thorough resource for anyone interested in the history of polar exploration. It is highly recommended for academic and public libraries where there is interest in the Arctic and Antarctic.

The Kingfisher Geography Encyclopedia. By Clive Gifford. 2003. 488p. glossary. index. illus. maps. Kingfisher, $39.95 (0-7534-5591-9). 910.

This book is directed to students in grades four through eight. Its most exciting feature is the superior illustrations, which take up about 50 percent of the page space. Chapter 1, "The Physical Earth," "describes how the planet was formed and then shaped by the forces of nature, by water and ice, by wind and volcanoes." It also explores how people's lives are influenced by climate and geography. Photos, charts, maps, and graphs are used to explain mountains, rivers, atmosphere, and more. Other articles cover the human impact on the earth.

In the main body of the encyclopedia, the world is divided by continent and subdivided by country. Helpful subdivisions are provided as needed. For example, the general U.S. section is followed by articles on the Eastern U.S., the Midwest and the Great Lakes, the South, the Western U.S., and Alaska and Hawaii. Articles vary from half a page (Bermuda, Gabon) to five (Germany) or six pages (India).

Each entry for a country includes text about its geography, industries and products, people, history and government, and what makes it unique or interesting. Each also has a picture of its flag, a physical map, a map locating it in the region, captioned photographs, and a summary of facts on area, population, capital city and its population, main languages, main religions, currency, main exports, and type of government. The book ends with a ready-reference section in which world maps and charts explore topics such as biomes, winds and ocean currents, time zones, religions, and communications.

This appealing book promises to spark the interest of users. Unfortunately, there is no key to the colors used in the physical maps of the countries (one can make a good guess), nor are there any sources or dates for statistics that are used. They are characterized only as "up-to-the-minute." Nevertheless, the book is recommended for school and public libraries needing a convenient, up-to-date geography encyclopedia for children.

Literature of Travel and Exploration: An Encyclopedia. 3v. Ed. by Jennifer Speake. 2003. 1,479p. bibliogs. illus. indexes. Fitzroy Dearborn, $375 (1-57958-247-8). 910.4.

Literature of Travel and Exploration is intended to be "a reference tool for teachers, researchers, and students looking for a starting point in what has become a rapidly evolving academic discipline." It includes more than 600 alphabetically arranged articles on topics from antiquity to the present, including countries or regions *(Great Lakes and Saint Lawrence River, Haiti)*; cities *(London, Venice)*; travel routes *(Crusades, Silk Route)*; individuals (Herodatus, Thor Heyerdahl, Jan Morris); types of narratives *(Buccaneer narratives, Missionary narratives, Undersea exploration)*; artifacts of travel writing *(Diaries, Guidebooks, Postcards)*; and types of transportation *(Dogsleds, Sailing Ships)*. About 300 scholars worldwide contributed the signed articles.

General or topical encyclopedias provide overviews of travel-rated topics and suggestions for further reading, often recent secondary, scholarly sources, but *Literature of Travel and Exploration* leads readers to the individuals who wrote about their travels and lists editions of their writing—primarily, but not always, in English—and, when appropriate, repositories of relevant manuscripts. Articles are between 1,000 and 5,000 words in length. Bibliographies contain as many references as appropriate, from 3 items for *Logbooks* to almost 60 for *Volcanology*. Not all items are readily accessible, such as the two references, both in Swedish, for *Balloons and airships*. Most bibliographies do not include recent secondary sources, although some include biographies.

Many articles have black-and-white reproductions from primary sources. The set includes alphabetic and thematic lists of entries and an index that identifies subjects within articles. A separate "Booklist Index" locates works discussed within the entries.

This is a rich and inspiring introduction to primary sources for undergraduate and advanced high-school students and an excellent source for further research for graduate students and other scholars. Unique in scope and purpose, it complements two other resources of narrower focus, *Trade, Travel, and Exploration in the Middle Ages: An Encyclopedia* (Garland, 2000) and *Encyclopedia of Exploration to 1800: A Comprehensive Reference Guide to the History and Literature of Exploration, Travel, and Colonization from the Earliest Times to the Year 1800* (Hordern, 2003). It is highly recommended for college and university collections and large public libraries.

Indian Placenames in America: Volume 1: Cities, Towns, and Villages. By Sandy Nestor. 2003. 240p. bibliog. index. McFarland, $45 (0-7864-1654-8). 917.3.

Nestor does an admirable job of reviewing the Indian-language sources for the names of American cities, towns, and villages. The text, divided by state, presents each name along with county or parish and population based on the 2000 U.S. census. The body of each entry contains a history of the naming averaging 15 lines. Entries cover alternate meanings and spellings, for example, variants of the town of Tehama, California, and of the Potawatomie nation. The bibliography contains extensive listings of books, media articles, and archival materials but little guidance regarding Internet sites. The index lists only place-names.

Nestor's writing style intrigues the reader to examine minutiae of American history, such as the effects on aboriginal cultures of railroads, European diseases, missionaries, outposts, mining, crafts, and trade in hides and whiskey. Commentary names tribes and their leaders, settlers, and dates and places of significant events, such as immigration over the Oregon Trail and the emergence of the weaving trade in Chimayo, New Mexico. Faults of the book are few but worth mentioning. The author fails to explain criteria for inclusion and to account for the absence of such familiar places as Miami, Florida, and Pontiac, Michigan. The indexing of important people, tribes, and events, such as Lewis and Clark, the Narragansett, and King Philip's War, would increase the value of the work for a wider range of users. Despite these omissions, the book is a useful, easy-to-use aid for the historian, genealogist, student, teacher, and librarian seeking precise data.

United States Counties. By Mark Dunn and Mary Dunn. 2003. 464p. appendixes. index. McFarland, $95 (0-7864-1515-0). 917.3.

Arranged state-by-state and providing brief entries on each U.S. county, this is an interesting, somewhat-flawed, but, in the end, useful title. It is a compilation of facts about county population, land area, prominent geographical features, name origin, history, products and industries, famous and infamous residents, and more. A brief discussion of county governance in each state precedes the listing of counties.

For all the volume's breadth, details are sometimes lacking. For example, Blue Earth County, Minnesota, is described as having been named for the Blue Earth River. However, in checking *County Name Origins of the United States* (McFarland, 2001), the reader would learn that Blue Earth was the closest English translation for the Sisseton Indian term for the water that emerged from the blue-green clay in the region. More in-depth demographic data can easily be found in *Counties USA* (2d ed., Omnigraphics, 2003) or *County and City Extra: Special Decennial Census Edition* (Bernan, 2002). Better agriculture data can be found in the *Yearbook of Agriculture*. But the Dunns have created a unique compilation from information that is scattered across many separate resources.

Appendixes at the back of the book list the boroughs of Alaska, which is the only state in the union to have no counties (or parishes, as they are known in Louisiana), and the independent cities of the U.S. that are not part of nearby counties. Virginia has 40 of these entities. No bibliography is provided, so users will not learn what materials were consulted in the writing of this text. In addition, there is not a single map to assist in locating where the counties exist within each state. But in spite of what has been left out, *United States Counties* succeeds because it collects a large amount of information into one convenient spot. It is a good title for small or medium-sized libraries that cannot afford numerous titles to cover the subject matter as well as for comprehensive geography collections.

★**African American Lives.** Ed. by Henry Louis Gates Jr. and Evelyn Brooks Higginbotham. 2004. 1,025p. bibliogs. illus. index. Oxford, $55 (0-19-516024-X). 920.

More than 600 black Americans who have made a distinctive imprint on American society and culture are profiled in this reference source. Edited by two widely published and respected Harvard scholars—cultural critic Gates and historian Higginbotham—and written by a broad selection of scholars, this volume is intended as a forerunner to an eight- volume encyclopedia entitled *African American National Biography,* which is scheduled to be published in 2006; it will contain biographies of 6,000 notable African Americans.

The alphabetically arranged biographical entries are well written and focus on the subject's contributions to both the subculture and history of black Americans, as well as the person's effect on the general history and culture of the U.S. The entries highlight the lives of both well-known (e.g., George Washington Carver, W. E. B. DuBois, Dizzy Gillespie, Martin Luther King) and lesser-known African Americans (e.g., Olympic rower Anita DeFrantz, rodeo entertainer Bill Pickett, nursing administrator and activist Mabel Doyle Keaton Staupers), and they represent many cultural, political, and scholarly fields of interest. Averaging one to three pages in length and sometimes complemented by a small black-and-white photo or artwork reproduction, entries include the person's dates of birth and death and conclude with a very short list of further reading, obituary references where applicable, and an author byline.

The entries are accurate and clearly written and confront controversy directly and fairly. For example, the essay on O. J. Simpson impartially discusses his guilt or innocence in the murder of his former wife and how this controversy has overshadowed the football player's gridiron accomplishments, and the entry on Amira Baraka discusses the poet's controversial views of American whites and Jews in the context of his contributions to American poetry.

African American Lives is an excellent complement to Gates' one-volume encyclopedia *Africana: The Encyclopedia of the African and African American Experience* (Basic, 1999) because it provides authoritative biographical detail about important black Americans as opposed to the latter's more general focus on the interrelationships between the African culture and American history. *African American Lives* also provides adult readers with more comprehensive biographical information than what is found in the eight-volume *African American Encyclopedia* (2d ed., Marshall Cavendish, 2001), which is intended for high-school and lower-level college students.

Relatively inexpensive, *African American Lives* offers accessible and authoritative biographical and critical information on a well-selected representative group of influential black Americans. It also offers all libraries a glimpse into what promises to be a major publishing event in 2006—the publication of a multivolume biographical encyclopedia on African Americans. *African American Lives* is highly recommended for most academic and public libraries, as well as some high- school libraries.

African-American Social Leaders and Activists. By Jack Rummel. 2003. 246p. bibliogs. illus. indexes. Facts On File, $44 (0-8160-4840-1). 920.

Part of Facts On File's A to Z of African Americans series, this volume deals with African American social reformers and political activists from the eighteenth century up to the present. Its intended audience is high-school students, undergraduates, and the general public. The author includes 164 profiles, each one between one and three pages long, with Martin Luther King Jr.'s entry the longest at almost four pages. Other entries include Joseph Cinque, Jesse Jackson, Rosa Parks, and Sojourner Truth. Rummel has written other biographical works, such as *Langston Hughes* (Chelsea, 1988) and *Malcolm X* (Chelsea, 1989).

The book begins with an introduction that provides historical context. The actual articles are listed in alphabetical order and include cross-references to other individuals profiled in the book. Fifty black- and-white photographs accompany the text. After each entry the author provides a list of further readings, and he has also included a general bibliography at the end of the work. There is a general index as well as one that lists individuals by year of birth and another by their main activities, such as abolition and education.

In clear, concise language, the author manages to write entries that strike a good balance between the personal and the public, briefly sketching backgrounds before delving into accomplishments and professional activities. One minor flaw is the fact that so many of the "further readings" listed after each entry are Web based; at least one Web site we checked was already out of date and inaccessible. This book is recommended for high-school, undergraduate, and public libraries. Although there are other works that discuss reformers from a particular era, no other work covers this 200-year span.

Distinguished Asian American Political and Governmental Leaders. Don T. Nakanishi and Ellen D. Wu. 2003. 229p. appendixes. bibliogs. illus. index. Greenwood, $69.95 (1-57356- 325-0). 920.

Heightened political participation by Asian Americans since World War II is noteworthy when one considers the disenfranchisement of early Chinese and Japanese immigrants to the U.S. This book is an alphabetical compilation of biographies of 96 Asian Americans who are elected officials, political activists, judges, and major political appointees active from 1950 until the present. Leaders were chosen to show diversity of electoral and nonelectoral forms of political participation and representation. Among them are U.S. Secretary of Labor Elaine Chao, Judge Lance Ito, and Minnesota state senator Satveer Chaudhary.

Each entry includes a photo plus basic biographical data, followed by an essay outlining the person's early years, education, and career highlights. Bibliographic sources are listed, although in some cases the lists contain only information obtained from the biographee or his or her Web page. Appendixes include a table arranged by date of birth and another listing the individuals by type of position, such as governor or activist. The index is adequate, although the bold type used to indicate main entries is a little hard to distinguish. The book's appearance could have been improved with a better quality of paper and sharper photos.

About half of the persons in this volume are also included in Greenwood's *Distinguished Asian Americans: A Biographical Dictionary* (1999). Still others are covered in *Notable Asian Americans* (Gale, 1995). *Distinguished Asian American Political and Governmental Leaders* is recommended for those public and undergraduate libraries that do not hold comparable titles or that serve large Asian American populations.

Extraordinary Asian Americans and Pacific Islanders. Rev. ed. By Susan Sinnott. 2003. 288p. bibliog. illus. index. Children's Press, $39 (0-516-22655-X); paper, $16.95 (0-516-29355-9). 920.
Extraordinary People in the Movies. By Judy L. Hasday. 2003. 288p. bibliog. illus. index. Children's Press, $39 (0-516-22348-8); paper, $16.95 (0-516-27857-6). 791.43.

Each of these titles, part of the Extraordinary People series for upper-elementary- and middle-school readers, offers short biographies of outstanding individuals, historical as well as contemporary. As in any assemblage of this type, readers may question the exclusion or inclusion of certain personalities. However, the authors have succeeded in providing a range of nationalities, occupations, age groups, and gender. In addition to the biographical content, a few brief essay-type articles appear in each title, covering related topics and issues such as "Internment Camp Inmates," "Vietnamese Boat People," "Can Oscar Become Color-Blind?" and "Evolution of the Motion Picture."

The format of each volume is the same, with biographical entries arranged chronologically by the biographee's birth date and topical entries interspersed among the biographies. Entries average four pages and feature short sentences, an explanation of unfamiliar words within the text, easily read fonts, and lots of white space. Each biography begins with a photograph of the subject, birth and death dates, and occupation or brief description. The table of contents consists of thumbnail photos with the same information. Each title also has an index and short bibliography with most copyrights in the 1990s. Titles in both bibliographies include many above the level of the targeted audience. *Extraordinary People in the Movies* also includes a list of organizations and Web sites and "Mentionables," a listing of additional people with single-paragraph biographies.

The biographies do not contain much in-depth information. Those in *Extraordinary People in the Movies* are little more than a recitation of the subject's childhood, marriage(s), film credits, and awards. *Extraordinary Asian Americans and Pacific Islanders* offers a bit more on the subject's background, education, and influence on society. Because of its scope, biographees in this title include politicians, authors, entertainers, athletes, etc. Information in the themed articles is also quite superficial but might serve to spark the reader's interest to look further.

The intended audience will enjoy browsing through these volumes but will not find much useful information apart from trivia. These will not replace more in-depth biographical resources but could serve as a jumping-off point for further research.

The Houghton Mifflin Dictionary of Biography. 2003. 1,661p. Houghton, $48 (0-618-25210-X). 920.02.

This new biographical dictionary has a complicated genealogy. It is derived from *Chambers Biographical Dictionary*, the American edition of which was published by Cambridge University Press until 1993 (Cambridge published its own *Cambridge Biographical Dictionary* in 1998). The sixth edition of *Chambers* was published in the U.S. in 1997. *The Houghton Mifflin Dictionary of Biography* is based on the seventh, 2002 edition of *Chambers* but "updated, expanded, and Americanized."

The dictionary's more than 18,000 entries include year of birth and death, a brief descriptive phrase ("English statesman," "French cyclist"), and a paragraph of biography. Some entries, such as those for George Eliot and William James, cite a source or two. Three hundred individuals, among them Menachem Begin, Winston Churchill, Thomas Edison, and Hannibal, are treated in special-feature boxes. These featured entries are generally longer than other entries, have more extensive lists of sources, and often include a quote. All entries are cross-referenced. For the most part, information seems to be current through 2001.

Both the *Chambers Biographical Dictionary* and *The Cambridge Biographical Dictionary* have a British slant, and *Houghton Mifflin* still has plenty of entries for Commonwealth cricketers. But readers will also find Lance Armstrong, Mia Hamm, Mark McGwire, and Serena Williams and Venus Williams. Also here are Russell Crowe, Frank Gehry, Rudy Giuliani, Mohammad Khatami, Kim Jong Il, Don King, Pervaiz Musharraff, Gwyneth Paltrow, and Vladimir Putin. None of these individuals appear in *The Cambridge Biographical Dictionary*, *Houghton Mifflin*'s closest competitor. Among the handful of other one-volume biographical encyclopedias, *Merriam-Webster's Biographical Encyclopedia* (rev. ed., 1995) is the largest (30,000 entries) and has many Americans who are not found elsewhere, but it does not cover living persons. *Encyclopedia of Biography* (St. Martin's, 1996) has illustrations but offers just 10,000 entries. *The Houghton Mifflin Dictionary of Biography* is now the most current one-volume biographical dictionary and is recommended for high-school, public, and academic libraries.

Notable Caribbeans and Caribbean Americans: A Biographical Dictionary. By Serafín Méndez-Méndez and Gail A. Cuneo. 2003. 465p. appendixes. bibliogs. illus. index. Greenwood, $74.95 (0-313-31443-8). 920.0729.

Filling a unique niche in reference collections, these two- to three-page biographical sketches are arranged alphabetically and cover 167 Caribbeans from all walks of life, including politicians, artists, scientists, and athletes. Every entry includes references and suggested readings, and appendixes cross-reference the entries according to profession and island of origin. Entrants include Harry Belafonte, Fidel Castro, Hector Hyppolite, and V. S. Naipaul. The editors sought a balance between historical (José Martí, Toussaint L'Ouverture, Jean Rhys) and contemporary (Jamaica Kincaid, Geraldo Rivera, Sammy Sosa) figures.

Some prominent Caribbeans, such as Faustin Soulouque and François Duvalier, were not included. As stated in the introduction, the volume presents individuals "who have distinguished themselves" and "enriched their islands." The intention may have been to include only those who made a positive contribution, but this does not make for a definitive reference tool. Also excluded are people about whom information is readily available, for example, Colin Powell. However, the biographies that are included are useful, and this volume will be a good addition to high-school, public, and undergraduate reference collections.

Scholastic Book of Outstanding Americans: Profiles of More Than 450 Famous and Infamous Figures in U.S. History. By Sheila Keenan. 2003. 256p. bibliog. glossary. illus. index. Scholastic, $19.95 (0-439-28358-2). 920.073.

It may say something about American society that the first and last entries in this upper-elementary- and middle-school-level reference book are for two highly respected sports figures, Hank Aaron and Babe Didrikson Zaharias. In general, though, the profiles are an eclectic assortment, a mix of historical and contemporary people who made their names in a field or profession. Some individuals, such as George Washington, Martin Luther King Jr., or Toni Morrison, are given full-page entries. Most share a page with another person. People who are generally associated together, such as Abbot and Costello, Lewis and Clark, the Marx Brothers, or Rodgers and Hammerstein, are profiled as a team. There is good balance between the historical and contemporary entries. There is also a good mix of cultural backgrounds and professions. Despite the word *infamous* in the subtitle, most entries are for Americans who made positive contributions to society.

The entries, arranged in alphabetical order, are short capsules that provide quick identification. Most begin with a picture or photograph, often in color, and dates. Cross-references are made within the article by placing names in bold type. A glossary, a bibliography of books and Web sites, and an index serve as reference aids.

In a book of this kind, there are always quibbles about who has been included and who has been left out, but overall the choices represent the best in their fields. Although no entry is detailed enough for reports, this book is a good starting point. The price is affordable for all libraries serving the targeted audience.

Dictionary of American Family Names. 3v. Ed. by Patrick Hanks. 2003. 2,816p. bibliogs. Oxford, $295 (0-19-508137-4). 929.4.

This hefty set purports to outline the etymology of 70,000 American family surnames. The introduction claims that more than 85 percent of Americans will be able to locate their family name in these volumes. The population sample for compiling this resource was 88.7 million, roughly one-third of all U.S. inhabitants. Names are ordered alphabetically across the three volumes, with each entry containing the frequency of the name's occurrence, etymology, languages, spelling variants, typology (identifying when the name denotes a place, occupation, status, or forebear), regions in which the name appears, and cross-references. The entries are clear and lucid, without reliance on confusing abbreviations or symbols.

As the helpful general introduction indicates, the *Dictionary* is intended only to be a starting point for etymological or genealogical research. This introduction also has brief but informative sections about names in specific regions or time periods (ancient Rome, for example), and hereditary, patronymic, habitational, topographic, and seasonal names. A second introductory section, "Surnames, Forenames, and Correlations: Some Facts and Figures," explains the survey population as well as the normalization and presentation of the data. A third opening segment, "Introductions to Surnames of Particular Languages and Cultures," is particularly helpful in its specificity, providing information on surname history in regions ranging from the British Isles to East Asia, in addition to chronicling immigration patterns. Anyone can benefit from this information, whether they find their actual family name here or not. Each one of these introductory chapters contains its own bibliography, though it should be noted that many of the sources listed in the regional sections are not in English.

The introductory chapters provide more than 100 pages of helpful advice for researchers both using these volumes as well as going beyond them for further investigation. Additionally, clear structure and layout make this work a great source for lightning-quick reference into the origins of one's family name. The *Dictionary of American Family Names* is a useful tool for both the beginning and advanced researcher and is recommended for academic and large public libraries.

Dictionary of Pseudonyms: 11,000 Assumed Names and Their Origins. 4th ed. By Adrian Room. 2004. 522p. appendix. bibliog. glossary. McFarland, $75 (0-7864-1658-0). 929.4.

Containing more than 2,000 new entries since the third edition, published in 1998, this work now includes 11,000 names and a new introduction. The book is arranged alphabetically by pseudonym. The entries contain the year of birth and death, the birth name, and annotations ranging in length from a few words to half a page. Several entries contain very useful bibliographic citations to books and journal articles.

The widely diverse entries range from the pop singer Meat Loaf (Marvin Lee Aday) to the great Jewish scholar known as both Rambam and Maimonides (Moses ben Maimon). Unlike many other pseudonym dictionaries, such as the *Hawthorn Dictionary of Pseudonyms* (Hawthorn, 1971), *Pseudonyms and Personal Nicknames* (Scarecrow, 1972), and the *Dictionary of Literary Pseudonyms* (ALA, 1995), which contain minimal or no annotations, this volume includes many annotations and also provides much broader international and historical coverage. In addition, the introductory essay provides an excellent historical overview, and a unique glossary defines literary and linguistic terms related to pseudonymy. One limitation: the volume does not include separate entries for birth names, although a couple of the previously listed titles do include cross-references. Despite this limitation, this work is an excellent reference source for this frequently discussed topic. Recommended for public and academic libraries.

History

American History Online. 2004. [Online database]. Facts On File, call for pricing [http://www.factsonfile.com]. (Last accessed April 22, 2004).
World History Online. 2004. [Online database]. Facts On File, call for pricing [http://www.factsonfile.com]. (Last accessed April 22, 2004).

American History Online (AHO) and *World History Online* (WHO) are new history databases offered by Facts On File.

AHO contains the complete full text of the Facts On File resources *The Encyclopedia of American History* (2003), the *Encyclopedia of Battles in North America* (2000), and the database *Landmark Documents in American History* (2003), as well as volumes from the American Political Biographies series, the American Profiles series, and the American Biographies series.

WHO contains numerous Facts On File resources, including the complete full text of 18 encyclopedias such as the *Encyclopedia of Terrorism* (2002), as well as other resources such as the *Dictionary of Wars: Revised Edition* (1999). Both databases also contain selected text from additional resources (e.g., *Encyclopedia of the World's Nations* [2002]).

In addition to basic and advanced search, users of either database can select from six different content categories. In AHO, these categories are Biographies, Subject Entries, Primary Sources, Timeline, Maps and Charts, and Image Gallery. Selecting a category displays more search options. For example, after picking Biographies, users can browse or search biographies by occupation, subject, or time period. Although browse and search options are many, some individual selections tend to be very broad. For example, AHO's subject headings include Cold War, Exploration, and Science and Technology. In place of the Image Gallery, WHO offers Curriculum Content Standards which provides access through a browsable list of National World History Content Standards and Benchmarks.

Basic search defaults to full-text searching, automatic word stemming, and the AND operator (phrases need quotes). Users should get results, often many results, which are ranked by relevancy. Sadly, search tips are not obvious. The Advanced Search screen consists of four text-entry boxes enabling a search of all the words, the exact phrase, at least one of the words, and without particular words. Each text box can be limited to either full text or title/heading. Plus, searches can be limited to one or more content categories. Photos, drawings, maps, and other illustrations can be enlarged in a separate window. Editor-selected Internet sites are arranged by subject (e.g., Religion), and listings include title of Web page, sponsoring entity, URL, and a single-sentence description.

Entry length and content vary, depending on the source. For example, AHO's four biographical entries on Franklin Roosevelt range from just under 700 words to more than 7,500 words. Each article can include links within the article text, as well as related links arranged on article sidebars. In some cases, linking is inconsistent. For example, one WHO article on Saddam Hussein had no links on the words *Baath, Iraq,* or *Kurds*, while another article did. Some articles have been updated to reflect recent developments but still retain an old publication date.

The content and simple search interface favor younger users. Libraries should also consider Gale's *History Resource Center: US* (2000) and *History Resource Center: The Modern World* (2001), which provide access to a wider variety of material. AHO and WHO are suitable for secondary schools and large public libraries. They are two of six history databases offered by Facts On File; the History Database Center search interface enables users to search simultaneously across multiple databases and is available automatically to subscribers to two or more of the publisher's online history resources.

Eighteenth Century Collections Online. [Internet database]. Gale, pricing on request [http://www.gale.com/ EighteenthCentury/index.htm]. (Last accessed September 5, 2003).

Eighteenth Century Collections Online (ECCO), called "the most ambitious single digitization project ever undertaken, with nearly 150,000 English-language titles . . . published between 1701 and 1800," will contain more than "33 million pages of material . . . printed in the United Kingdom, along with thousands of important works from the Americas" when completed. It is based upon Gale imprint Primary Source Microfilm's *Eighteenth Century Collection,* itself an ongoing microfilm project based on *The English Short Title Catalog* that includes the holdings of the British Library and 1,500 others worldwide. The ability to conduct full-text searches within these works will be ECCO's prime selling point and prove a boon for bleary-eyed researchers who would otherwise be forced to scan the works for a fleeting word or two. At the time of last access, only the History and Geography collection is online, with other disciplines to be loaded between November 2003 and May 2004.

The search interface is quite intuitive, offering Basic Search, Advanced Search, Browse Authors, and Browse Works. The latter two are basic A–Z listings. The Basic Search screen has a text box where search terms are entered. Terms may include phrases (using quotation marks) and Boolean and wildcard operators. The searcher selects from a drop-down menu to limit the search to Keyword, Author, Title, or Full Text. One can also limit by a range of years.

The Advanced Search offers multiple text boxes, each with drop-down menus limiting the search terms to those categories listed above as well as Front Matter, Main Text, Indexes, Publisher, and Place of Publication. Each text box may then be combined with *and, or,* and *not* operators from yet another drop-down menu as well the ability to set a Fuzzy Search Level. The latter option takes into consideration variations of spelling and may be set to None, Low, Medium, or High.

The results list allows one to view full citations to works as well as their eTable of Contents (a clickable listing of contents in a book) and, for some, a List of Illustrations. Most important, one can click on the title itself and retrieve an image of the title page and proceed through the entire work page by page. A print icon allows one to reformat the page for printing within a browser or as a PDF file.

Full records include a hyperlinked listing of page numbers where the search terms entered can be found. Clicking on each page link loads an image of the page with the search term highlighted—a blessing considering some of the text may be difficult to read (not any fault of Gale's, which employed excellent scanning methods, but because of the original typeface). Each record also has a Search This Work button, which allows one to enter terms (including the ability to do a fuzzy search) and retrieve results within the work.

The wealth of works available in the collection will interest researchers in a variety of disciplines. Ultimately, legal material from Parliament will be included, and of course the literary works included will be formidable. Groundbreaking though it may be, only larger academic libraries with a clientele interested in works of this specific period will likely be able to justify the expense.

Encyclopedia of American Studies. [Internet database]. Grolier, pricing from $490 [http://go.grolier.com]. (Last accessed September 5, 2003).

The *Encyclopedia of American Studies* is the latest addition to *Grolier Online*. The print version, containing 660 entries that examine various cultural phenomena within the academic American studies context, appeared in four volumes in 2001. The American Studies Association, under whose sponsorship the encyclopedia was published, continues to work on developing and expanding the database. There are 17 new articles that do not appear in the print set, including *Business cycles, Reality TV,* and *World Trade Center.* Plans are to update the database annually.

Searching requires few steps and little guesswork. Users can conduct a search of the entire text or article titles, with Full Text being the default. Advanced Search offers more ways to refine a search by combining up to three terms but otherwise is not much different from Full Text searching using Boolean operators and wildcards. Other search options are browsing a list of biographical entries or entry headings or browsing within broad subject categories such as "Arts and Literature" and "Gender and Family." All of these options are available on every page.

We did a Full Text search of *'Columbian Exposition'* (using single quotes as instructed by Help) and retrieved 15 results, with the most relevant—*World's fairs and expositions*—listed first. Results lists display article titles along with the first few lines of text. Navigation through longer articles is facilitated by tables of contents. Many articles are accompanied by thumbnails of illustrations and maps as well as links to the article bibliography, related articles, and relevant Web sites from the Grolier Internet Index.

In addition to the encyclopedia content, the database offers a Curriculum feature and Related Sites. The Curriculum feature lists programs in American studies in the U.S. and elsewhere, along with links if they are available. The related Web sites are organized under five categories: "American Studies Association," "Associations and Centers Worldwide," "Interdisciplinary Sources," "Primary Sources for American Studies," and "Columbia American History Online." This last resource, which offers e-seminars for students and teachers of American history, is also accessible from an icon in the frame at the bottom of every page but requires a separate subscription. Also in the bottom frame are links to dictionaries, an atlas, and a text box for searching across all of the databases that comprise a library's Grolier Online subscription package.

We like this database for its clean look and straightforward searching. On all but the splash page the user has to scroll down to the bottom of the page to access the Help utility, but this is a minor inconvenience. Academic and public libraries will want to consider subscribing even if they already have the print version—perhaps not so much for the value-added features like Web links but because of the muscle provided by integrating *Encyclopedia of American Studies* with other Grolier Online databases, particularly *Encyclopedia Americana*. Like several other Grolier Online offerings, the *Encyclopedia of American Studies* is available in an ADA-compliant, text-only version.

ProQuest Historical Newspapers. [Internet database]. ProQuest, pricing on request [http://www.proquest.com/products/pt- product-HistNews.shtml]. (Last accessed September 5, 2003).

Databases can be habit forming, and now, with additions and improvements, *ProQuest Historical Newspapers* (PHN) may become an addiction for researchers. PHN is a large undertaking beginning with the digitization of the *New York Times* from 1851 to 2000, which includes 3.4 million pages and 25 million articles. ProQuest has added to this huge searchable database the *Wall Street Journal* (1889–1985), the *Washington Post* (1877–1987), and the *Christian Science Monitor* (1908–1990). Currently, portions of the *Los Angeles Times* (1881–1994) are being loaded. It and the *Chicago Tribune* (1847– 1922) should be complete by the end of 2004.

The search software is unique to PHN. The default is the Basic search (full text and citation), with the choice of specific paper and date range. A new More Search Options allows a basic search by article type, author, and a sort results. These options may discourage users from using the Advanced search.

The options are more numerous in the Advanced search. It allows searches of citation and article text, article text, citation and abstract, title, author, and article type. The article type can limit by birth or legal notice, display or classified ad, real estate transaction, marriage, obituary, weather, photo stand-alone, review, front page (perfect for searching birthdays), and even lottery numbers. Additional features include the current search at the end of the results list; the choice of 10, 20, or 30 citations on a page; and citations listed with the earliest or latest first. The default for these last two features would be different if the reviewer could choose.

As librarians have discovered, the wealth of information available in PHN is amazing: an advertisement for a *Milton Bradley* puzzle from 1898, a photo of Rosa Parks being fingerprinted in 1956, a miscellaneous news item from 1867 about the murder of a young woman pushed from a carriage after an abortion, and an article on the stock market crash on October 23, 1929. Adjacent to this front-page news is a headline "College Sports Tainted by Bounties." The more times change, the more they remain the same.

The major criticism of the current version of PHN is the inability to find a word or phrase in an article after a full-text search. The CONTROL+F feature or the highlighting of the word or words would be perfect. Researchers will discover that searching for a specific word or phrase in a long article or through numerous classified ads or obituaries is like looking for a needle in a historical haystack. Ads and obituaries are numbered, but according to PHN, "they are there for zoning purposes and have nothing to do with placement of the page."

Printing continues to be a problem. Even with pages of instructions, librarians and patrons still have difficulty in getting a good print copy of a section of an article or an advertisement. Two other criticisms will be hard to fix: some issues have poor reproduction and some photos and articles are blocked by copyright restrictions. One improvement since earlier reviews is the citation on the top of complete articles. Citations are lacking from the second page of an article and from ads and a portion of a page.

Help screens are available, but some include information on searching all ProQuest databases, which is confusing to the novice. There is a good "Quick Print Guide" (seven pages), which could be helpful to users. The guide provides searching tips but admits that "you cannot search for daily stock quotes with a high degree of reliability."

ProQuest is to be commended for embarking on, adding to, and improving this major project, which provides fascinating primary sources to researchers. We get what we pay for, and the magnitude of information included in PHN means that it is not inexpensive. Certainly, it is a recommended purchase for public, high-school, and academic libraries that can afford it.

Encyclopedia of the Lewis and Clark Expedition. By Elin Woodger and Brandon Toropov. 2003. 438p. appendixes. bibliogs. illus. index. maps. Facts On File, $65 (0-8160-4781-2). 917.804.

This encyclopedia attempts to cover every aspect of Lewis and Clark's transcontinental journey, including the plants, animals, people, and places they encountered. Entries are alphabetical and range from topics like dogs to Indian guides to navigation to *Sex during the expedition*. Each entry includes extensive cross-references and is followed by sources for further reading, many of which are available on the Web. Adding variety are the numerous illustrations and images, which aid in visualizing the events, people, and places of the famous expedition. Portraits of the two men are included, and some painted scenes show more than any written entry could—an Indian chief trying to rub the blackness off of York, Clark's slave, for example. Not to be overlooked are the myriad maps tracing the circuitous routes of the expedition. Many of these are included in a helpful 22-page chronology at the start of the volume; the rest are in an appendix.

The encyclopedia also includes an introduction (with cross-references) that distills the entire undertaking down to less than 10 pages. A list of Native American tribes encountered and a useful 16-page bibliography are also provided. The bibliography contains books, journal articles, and Web sites and is divided into sections such as "Biographical Information"; "Campsites, Route, and Trails"; and "Journals and Letters." A list of entries by subject further aids the user. Overall, this is an excellent resource, clearly organized and well written. A user can dip into it at any point and begin an education in one of the most intriguing and extraordinary achievements in American history. Recommended for high-school, public, and undergraduate libraries.

Exploring Ancient Civilizations. 11v. 2003. 880p. bibliogs. glossaries. illus. indexes. maps. Marshall Cavendish, $329.95 (0-7614-7456-0). 930.

Containing 249 cross-referenced articles, this alphabetically organized encyclopedia designed for grades five and up covers the time period between 6,500 B.C.E. and 500 C.E., the span beginning with the development of writing and agriculture and concluding with the fall of the Roman Empire. The accessibly written entries fall into several thematic areas: civilizations and peoples (*Angles and Saxons, Mesopotamia*); biographies of both historical and legendary figures (*Ashoka, Xerxes, Zeus*); places (*Acropolis, Jerusalem*); philosophy and religion (*Confucianism, Roman mythology*); and writings (*Dead Sea Scrolls, Ramayana*). There are also entries that are not culturally specific, among them *Architecture, Farming,* and *Weights and measures*. Each of the lavishly illustrated articles, which run two to eight pages, contains at least one boxed sidebar giving information either on items of particular interest included in the subject under discussion, biographical information on people who do not have separate entries, or quotations from contemporary sources.

Color coding on both the tops of the pages and in the lower corners indicates to which of seven geographical areas the subject pertains. Clearly reproduced color photos, reproductions, and maps enhance the readable text. The table of contents for the full set is in the first volume, which also includes a thematic table of contents. The final volume contains a comprehensive index and glossary, a detailed time line, bibliography, lists of resources for younger readers and for further study, and several thematic indexes.

This set will remind librarians of Grolier's *Ancient Civilizations* (2000), which also presents A–Z topics in multiple highly illustrated volumes for grades six and up. The Grolier set has perhaps half as many entries, but entries are often longer. Grolier has a comprehensive index in each volume; Marshall Cavendish has separate volume indexing in addition to the useful multiple indexes in volume 11. Both sets are accessible, attractive, informative, and recommended for school and public library collections, but libraries may not need both, especially in an era of tight budgets.

Handbook to Life in Ancient Egypt. Rev. ed. By Rosalie David. 2003. 417p. bibliogs. illus. index. maps. Facts On File, $50 (0-8160-5034-1). 932.

David (professor of Egyptology, University of Manchester, England), surveys Egypt from predynastic times through the arrival of Islam, concentrating on the period before the establishment of the Ptolemies as the ruling dynasty. The chapters are thematic, covering Egyptology and archaeology, history, geography, society and government, religion, funerary customs and beliefs, architecture and building, written evidence, the military, foreign trade and transport, economy and industry, and everyday life.

David has added material based on the many discoveries since the 1998 edition. In the chapter "Egyptology, Archaeology, and Scientific Mummy Studies in Egypt," which is new, she discusses the application of modern scientific techniques, including medical diagnosis, to mummies. All the techniques are described briefly but clearly. There is a section on the Schistosoiasis Research Project, which may be the most far-reaching chronological study of a disease ever undertaken. Mummies are being tested for evidence of the disease, which is still a danger to modern Egyptians. Among other changes are a brief section on pets added to the chapter on everyday life and a rewritten section on temples to reflect new thinking about the different temple types. The section on Tomb KV5 has been rewritten and moved to the new chapter on archaeology. However, much of the text remains the same as in the earlier edition.

The format of the book has not changed. Besides an extensive bibliography, with more up-to-date citations, each chapter has suggested readings, some of which may be available in larger public libraries. The text is liberally illustrated with photographs, line drawings, and excellent maps.

Less scholarly than *The Oxford Encyclopedia of Ancient Egypt* (2000), the new edition of *Handbook to Life in Ancient Egypt* is recommended for high-school and public libraries; lower-division undergraduates and adults looking for quick information should find it useful as well.

Encyclopedia of Barbarian Europe: Society in Transformation. By Michael Frassetto. 2003. 419p. bibliogs. illus. indexes. ABC-CLIO, $95 (1-57607-263-0). 940.1.

In this encyclopedia, the phrase *barbarian Europe* is used in place of what was once designated the Dark Ages. Current research, reflected in abundance in this work, shows that the latter term was an erroneous euphemism—rather, the period of European history that roughly begins with the fall of the western Roman Empire and ends with the fall of the Carolingians should be seen as one of transition, when the seeds of the modern nation-state were sown.

In more than 200 entries, Frassetto, a medieval scholar, delves into the research that places barbarian Europe in this new context. From the standard references such as Charlemagne and the Battle of Poitiers to the less familiar (but no less important) Judith (mother of Charles the Bald) and Witenagemot (general council of the Anglo-Saxon kings), this work addresses the idea of transition in an informative, easy-to-read manner. There is a special focus on the roles played by women and on the social and cultural context of this period. For example, there are entries for *Education and learning* and *Family*.

The work opens with an essay on the historiography of the time period showing how current scholarship has encouraged the new perspective. This is followed by a historical overview of the years under consideration. A detailed chronology takes the reader from 305 C.E. (the retirement of Emperors Diocletian and Maximian) to 1,000 C.E. (the writing of *Beowulf*). Each entry is cross-referenced and has a list of further readings. A worthy bibliography also draws out some of the themes of the work.

This is an excellent addition to reference collections. Although some of the same topics are covered in reference sources on the Middle Ages, this is the only volume that focuses entirely on the barbarian period. It is recommended for public and academic libraries.

Encyclopedia of the Renaissance and the Reformation. Rev. ed. Ed. by Jennifer Speake and Thomas G. Bergin. 2004. 550p. bibliogs. illus. index. Facts On File, $75 (0-8160-5451-7). 940.2.

This revised edition of *Encyclopedia of the Renaissance* (1987) has approximately 2,100 entries, 200 of which are new. Length ranges from a paragraph to two pages, with diverse entries such as *Erasmus, Desiderius; Libraries;* and *Spanish Inquisition*. The fact that the scope has been widened to encompass the Reformation means that many articles have been expanded. Other revisions reflect recent scholarship with enhanced coverage of, for example, literacy, families, and the role of women. Editors Speake, a prolific reference book editor, and Bergin, a Yale University professor now deceased, were also responsible for the first edition.

The articles are in alphabetical order and include cross-references to other entries. Many entries contain suggestions for further reading, and the editors have also included a general bibliography. In the previous edition, the general bibliography listed primary as well as secondary sources. This time around, however, the bibliography contains only secondary sources, and emphasis is placed mostly on recent scholarship. Primary sources aren't completely ignored but are discussed only within the entries. The encyclopedia has an index of historical persons and a chronology of events from 1300 to 1620. Also included are 100 black-and-white images as well as a section of beautifully printed artworks, about half of which were in the previous edition.

Facts On File has delivered another valuable general encyclopedia for the novice scholar. There are, however, some changes that could enhance this work. Though there is an entry for *Reformation*, there is none for *Renaissance*. Although it can be argued that the entire book is a description of the Renaissance period, it would have been helpful to have a general entry on the topic. The decision not to include primary documents in the bibliography is unfortunate, as it assumes the reader will know where to look to find these materials. Nonetheless, this will be a welcome addition to high-school, undergraduate, and public libraries.

The Greenhaven Encyclopedia of the Middle Ages. By Thomas Streissguth. 2003. 332p. appendix. bibliog. illus. index. Greenhaven, $74.95 (0-7377-0793-3). 940.1.

Several works on the Middle Ages have been published for middle-school and high-school students in the last few years, including *Medieval World* (Grolier, 2001), *The Middle Ages: An Encyclopedia for Students* (Scribner, 1996), and *Middle Ages Reference Library* (UXL, 2001). The Greenhaven volume provides another option for the high-school level. It is not going to satisfy information requests for obscure figures or events or provide in-depth analysis, but it does hit the major events, themes, and individuals. Unlike some of the other works mentioned here, the focus is almost entirely European. Except for a few entries dealing with the Islamic world, this is not the book to buy for a global perspective.

Approximately 520 entries are followed by an appendix that lists rulers, leaders, and popes. A four-page chronology, six-page bibliography, and index round out the text. The bibliography contains fairly academic materials, including some key older texts, as well as a brief list of Web sites. The majority of the entries cover individuals such as Dante Aligheri; Jan van Eyck, the Flemish artist; Joan of Arc; and John Lackland, the rival and brother of Richard I the Lion-Hearted; and groups such as *Franciscans, Habsburg dynasty,* and *Mercenaries*. Examples of topical subjects include *Excommunication, Hunting,* and *Serfs,* but neither education nor women warrant a separate entry of their own, instead being referenced in the index. Among events that are included are *Black Death; Crécy, battle of;* and *Great Schism*. None of the entries are very long, generally ranging from a paragraph to a page and a half. The longest entry, *Crusades,* is three pages.

In these days of tight budgets, a work that provides a decent overview of a complex subject is always welcome. This title is appropriate for high-school libraries and public libraries that could use a convenient, single-volume resource on the topic.

The Oxford Dictionary of the Renaissance. By Gordon Campbell. 2003. 862p. appendixes. bibliogs. illus. Oxford, $150 (0-19-860175-1). 940.2.

Most of the 4,000 entries in this volume were written by Campbell, professor of Renaissance literature at the University of Leicester, with assistance from an advisory board of university professors in the U.S. and England. The *Dictionary* covers 1415 (the Battle of Agincourt) to 1618 (the beginning of the Thirty Years' War), with flexibility to include some earlier and later topics.

Geographical scope includes "countries whose cultures were touched in significant measure by the revival of classical learning," especially those underrepresented in English-language sources. More than half of the entries are biographical. Other topics include law, theology, and science as well as art, literature, and music. Many involve Italy, but France and Spain are also well represented, and there is content related to Portugal, Denmark, and Germany. Some longer entries are international in scope. For example,

Artillery encompasses Turkey, England, Italy, France, Spain, and Scotland. Most entries are one or two paragraphs in length, but broader topics (e.g., *Medici villas, Wars of religion*) are one to two pages long. Entries frequently end with two or three bibliographic references, including abbreviations for the 37 historical and biographical sources listed at the beginning of the volume. The text is supported by 100 black-and-white illustrations, a thematic index, and several appendixes, including a table of ruling houses.

The *Encyclopedia of the Renaissance* (Scribner, 1999) contains 1,200 articles ranging from one-half to nearly 50 pages in length. The *Oxford Dictionary* has significantly more (if generally much shorter) entries; in our sample of 86 entries, 30 were not found in the *Encyclopedia of the Renaissance* index. Among those unique to Oxford are the artistic terms *Arabesque* and *Grisaille* and the doctrine of *Ubiquitarianism*. Oxford is especially strong in *Gardens*, with entries for eight specific regions (e.g., *Bohemian and Moravian gardens, Scottish gardens*).

The *Oxford Dictionary of the Renaissance* is recommended for public and academic libraries, especially those not owning the larger Scribner set or desiring strong coverage of the Renaissance.

The Renaissance: An Encyclopedia for Students. 4v. Ed. by Paul F. Grendler. 2003. 970p. bibliog. illus. index. maps. Scribner, $395 (0-684-31281-6). 940.2.

For those libraries that purchased the critically acclaimed *Encyclopedia of the Renaissance* (Scribner, 1999) but found that the students were intimidated by the scholarly multivolume set, here is a rewritten and condensed version for the middle- to high-school audience. This version, like the original, is edited by Grendler and published in association with the Renaissance Society of America. Comparisons between the two sets are inevitable, with the scaled-down version having about 460 entries in 4 volumes as opposed to the original set having more than 1,700 in 6 volumes. The student set has 60 color plates, and the original set has 48 plates.

The Renaissance: An Encyclopedia for Students has a straightforward, alphabetical subject organization. The entries cover people, places, events, concepts, works of art and literature, and scientific achievements from around 1350 to 1620. Examples of people who are covered are Fra Angelico, Francis Bacon, Hernán Cortés, Henry VIII, Martin Luther, Teresa of Ávila, and William Shakespeare. Other entries cover *Art in Italy, Books and Manuscripts, Childhood, Clothing, Humanism, Peasants' War, Science, Venice*, and *Witchcraft*, to cite just a few. Cross-references are included at the end of each article, and length ranges from one paragraph to two pages at the longest. A comprehensive index at the end of each of the four volumes references both entries in the specific volume and the whole set. A six-page collection of suggested resources includes Web sites.

Among the special features are short definitions in the margins of words that might be difficult for the intended audience, a time line of major events, and a genealogy of ruling European families. Illustrations throughout the set and four sets of thematic color plates add to the set's appeal. The color plates relate to the themes of "Art and Architecture," "Daily Life," "The Renaissance City," and "New Frontiers."

Grolier's *Renaissance* (2002) has approximately half the number of entries, uses color throughout, and is designed for a slightly younger group (grades 5 through 10). The Scribner set is an excellent adaptation from the original for a new audience. It is recommended for school and public libraries.

The Encyclopedia of Ireland. Ed. by Brian Lalor. 2003. 1,218p. illus. indexes. Yale, $65 (0-300-09442-6). 941.5003.

This massive volume contains more than 5,000 entries by more than 900 contributors from more than 100 universities. The breadth of the work is one of its strongest features. Subjects from history, political science, science, literature, art, architecture, economics, and more receive coverage. The more than 700 illustrations are beautiful, mostly in color, and add an important dimension. The preface explains that this is one of the rare attempts to provide unitary coverage of both the Republic of Ireland and Northern Ireland. Considering as a whole these two territories whose history and culture are so intertwined makes this an extremely useful volume.

One of the unique features of this book is the references from English to Irish. For example, under *Cattle raid*, the user is referred to *Táin bó*, which is the Irish term. Other notable articles include *Diaspora, Environment*, and *Travellers, or the travelling people*. Each county in Ireland and Northern Ireland receives an entry complete with a map. Famous figures from historical times to the present are well represented, from Méabh, legendary queen of Connacht, to Grace O'Malley, sea captain and pirate, to Mary Robinson, first woman president of Ireland. A subject and a general index serve as finding aids, as do the numerous cross-references. We found some dead links; for example, several entries refer the reader to *Missionary activity*, which does not exist. There are no bibliographies or lists of further readings.

The Encyclopedia of Ireland is an important resource on many levels. It is well written, beautifully illustrated, and massive in both physical size and content. More comprehensive than *The Encyclopedia of Ireland: An A–Z Guide to Its People, Places, History, and Culture* (Oxford, 2000), it is a recommended purchase for public and academic library reference collections.

Encyclopedia of the Victorian Era. 4v. Ed. by James Eli Adams and others. 2004. 1,632p. appendixes. bibliogs. illus. index. maps. Grolier, $499 (0-7172-5860-2). 941.08.

Designed with a broad audience in mind, this interdisciplinary encyclopedia edited by Adams (associate professor of English, Cornell) and two experienced reference book editors is "intended to provide sweeping coverage of the social, political, and intellectual landscape of the British-dominated world during the years of the reign of Queen Victoria, 1837–1901." Though the emphasis is British, coverage extends to places around the globe where Victorian culture made a mark. Thus, the discussion in *Agriculture* is not confined to Britain but also considers India and America.

More than 620 alphabetically arranged entries vary in length from 500 to 4,000 words and cover topics such as *Child labor, Crimean War, Domestic workers, East India Company, Electricity, Gardens and garden design, Gothic revival, Music halls, Race and racism, Railways*, and *Sanitation*. The preface explains that, since biographical information is generally so easy to find, subject-based essays were favored over biographies in the selection of topics, but some individuals are included because they were "inarguably important" or because they "represented a tendency." Approximately one-third of the entries are biographical, covering Alexander Graham Bell, Julia Margaret Cameron, Lewis Carroll, Charles Darwin, Karl Marx, and others. Among the Americans who are included are Horatio Alger, Susan B. Anthony, John James Audubon, and P. T. Barnum.

The 350 black-and-white illustrations are generally well chosen. Further reading lists attached to entries include primary as well as secondary material and some Web pages, many from the Victorian Web [http://www.victorianweb.org]. Appendixes provide an undated map of the British Isles (a map of Victorian London would have been a nice addition), selected primary documents, and selected Web resources. *See also* references facilitate access, as does a "Synoptic Table of Contents" that classifies entry headings under broad topics such as "Biographies" and "Sexuality and Gender." The index is quite detailed. For example, under *diseases and epidemics*, in addition to the main entry, there are 37 other page references, from *Boer War* to *worldwide smallpox outbreak (1871–73)*, along with *see also* references to *cholera* and *venereal disease*.

Though a few contributors employ academic jargon, writing is very accessible on the whole. Adding to the set's readability is the strong emphasis on matters of daily life. Entries such as *Cabs and omnibuses, Governesses, Hair, Lighting*, and *London Season* provide value for fans of Victorian fiction, as well as for students and researchers. The encyclopedia is recommended for academic and large public libraries.

Queen Victoria: A Biographical Companion. By Helen Rappaport. 2003. 465p. bibliogs. illus. index. ABC-CLIO, $55 (1-85109-355-9). 941.081.

By virtue of her length of reign, her place in a rapidly changing world, and her character, Alexandrina Victoire was a remarkable ruler. Her reign of more than 50 years during one of the glory periods of British history remains a subject of fascination and interest.

Almost 120 entries cover Victoria's extended family and close friends, members of her household, private secretaries, personal interests, prime ministers, "pet hates" and obsessions, and homes. Also covered are various topics and political events that marked and help define the Victorian era. Examples include *Brown, John; Jack the Ripper; Koh-I-Noor diamond; Racial and religious prejudice; Smoking*; and, of course, her beloved husband, Prince Albert. Each entry is a minimum of two pages, with most being four to five pages long. Related entries and further readings are listed at the end of each. An extensive bibliography of primary and secondary sources includes many of the excellent biographies that have been written about Queen Victoria.

The intent of this and other volumes in the ABC-CLIO Biographical Companions series is to focus more on the person and his or her place in the world than on larger world events. It is recommended for high-school, public, and academic libraries that can afford to purchase narrowly focused works.

Reader's Guide to British History. 2v. Ed. by David Loades. 2003. 1,620p. bibliogs. indexes. Fitzroy Dearborn, $295 (1-57958-242-7). 941.

There are not many works of historiography that cover the complete secondary historical literature of a country or topic, but Fitzroy Dearborn's series of reader's guides are outstanding works that introduce students and librarians to these important titles. The *Reader's Guide to British History* is the newest in this series, and the depth and breadth of the titles included are overwhelming. The aim of the set is to introduce the reader to the most informative works of secondary scholarship on a wide range of political, social, economic, biographical, and religious topics in the history of the British Isles. More than 1,000 topics are covered in essays that range from a minimum of 1,000 words to 3,000 words in length. Major topics such as the "American Colonies," "Architecture," "Monarchy," and "National Identities" are divided into three, four, or five separate essays so that the topic can be covered in depth. The chronological range is from prehistoric times to the present government of Tony Blair.

Each topic is covered in an essay that opens with a bibliographic list of the secondary titles included (anywhere from 6 to 20 of the most important and influential works), an overview of the topic and the related scholarship, and then a brief discussion and evaluation of each of the titles. The books and ideas in them are compared to one another and to the earlier scholarship on the subject. *See also* references refer the reader to related essays. The contributors are professors of history, lecturers in history, or editors of historical journals in the British Isles, the Commonwealth countries, or the U.S.

The essays are preceded by an alphabetical list of entries and a thematic list of entries. The thematic list is very helpful to students looking for information about a specific time period, because they will see both people and events that relate directly to that period. At the end of the work is a complete list of all the books and articles discussed, along with a general index of subjects, people, events, and places mentioned in the essays.

This set is an important guide to British history for undergraduate and graduate students doing historical research and for librarians looking to develop their collections in British history. It is highly recommended for all academic libraries and large public libraries.

Austria-Hungary & the Successor States: A Reference Guide from the Renaissance to the Present. By Eric Roman. 2003. 688p. appendixes. bibliog. illus. index. maps. Facts On File, $85 (0-8160- 4537-2). 943.
Great Britain: A Reference Guide from the Renaissance to the Present. By Richard S. Tompson. 2003. 552p. appendixes. bibliog. illus. index. maps. Facts On File, $85 (0-8160-4474-0). 941.

These volumes are part of Facts On File's European Nations series, which is aimed predominantly at a high-school and college- student audience and provides concise country-based surveys of European history. The reference guides contain a broad array of political, cultural, social, and other content, and their arrangement facilitates browsing for the casual reader.

The volume on Austria and Hungary "traces the history of the Austrian Empire from its beginnings to its dissolution and then the history of the successor states of a separate Austria and Hungary, as well as the new states of Czechoslovakia and Yugoslavia, to the present day." The history of each state is discussed in chapters that make up more than 50 percent of the volume. Information is current through 2002. Following the historical chapters is a 200- page "Historical Dictionary A–Z" with more than 160 entries for people, places, and events. Entries range from a paragraph or two to more than five pages for *Anti-Semitism in the successor states.* A series of chronologies, a list of rulers and statesmen, a section of more than 20 maps, and a very selective bibliography round out the book.

The volume on Great Britain has a similar structure. Eight chapters provide narrative on British history from pre-1399 to the twenty-first century. The 329-page historical dictionary covers a surprising breadth of content, with entries for British politicians, artists, writers, legal terms, governmental acts, architecture, geography, and more. Additionally, the dictionary includes references to Great Britain's involvement in Africa, India, and Ireland. A chronology is followed by four appendixes: "Maps," "Genealogies," "English Sovereigns from 899," and "United Kingdom Prime Ministers from 1721." The bibliography is much more substantial than that in the Austria-Hungary volume. The contents of each volume are complemented by black-and-white photographs and illustrations.

Although not inexpensive for one-volume reference books, these titles are worthy additions to most university and public library collections because they contain such expansive material in compact form.

Cassell's Dictionary of Modern German History. By Tim Kirk. 2003. 480p. appendixes. bibliog. index. maps. Cassell; dist. by Sterling, $39.95 (0-304-34772-8). 943.

First published in Great Britain, this dictionary, authored by University of Newcastle professor Kirk, aims to outline the progress of Germany from a disparate group of duchies and fiefdoms in the eighteenth and nineteenth centuries through the world-shaping events of the two world wars to the reunited nation it is today. Major political movements; key events; important economic, cultural, and social elements; and major figures in "modern" German history are covered in more than 1,800 entries. The nominal starting point chronologically for the book is about 1700, though the most emphasis is given to the twentieth century. Seminal topics like the Holocaust and World War I or II are covered in about a full page, while others, like the peace of Utrecht or Berchtesgaden (Hitler's "Eagle's Nest" retreat), take up only a sentence or short paragraph.

Although entries are generally short, as expected in a dictionary, cross-references are plentiful and helpful, keeping the interested user thumbing from entry to entry to fill in knowledge gaps. The back of the volume contains six black-and-white maps of Germany at pivotal stages in history. There is an extremely helpful 35-page chronology, ranging from the siege of Vienna by Turks in 1683 to an arson attack on a Dusseldorf synagogue in 2000. The appendixes also contain extensive lists of political leaders, emperors, kings, heads of state, chancellors, and cabinet members as well as election results (Reichstag and Bundestag). Finally, a subject index and a further reading section, 10 pages each, are provided. The subject index is in list form, with major categories such as "Geography," "Nazi Germany," and "Political and economic history" listed. The further reading section is in narrative format, making it difficult to utilize at a quick glance.

This is a very handy and comprehensive resource presented with overall clarity and insight. It is recommended for academic and large public libraries.

Medieval Italy: An Encyclopedia. 2v. Ed. by Christopher Kleinhenz. 2003. 1,290p. appendix. bibliogs. illus. index. maps. Routledge, $295 (0-415-93929-1). 945.

This new resource is volume 9 in the Routledge Encyclopedias of the Middle Ages, a series that began in 1993 and is intended for both the specialist and nonspecialist. The scope ranges from the late Roman Empire to the end of the fourteenth century. This comprehensive work contains 970 entries alphabetically arranged and varying in length from 100 to 10,000 words. The approach is interdisciplinary, with entries focusing on anything from major artists and cultural movements to particular cities and monuments. Longer entries are subdivided into sections, enabling quick scanning. For example, the entry on *Black Death* contains the subheadings "The Onset of the Plague," "Medieval Medical Explanations," and "Social Consequences."

Each entry is followed by cross-references and a bibliography. The bibliographies may contain references to primary materials, translations, secondary sources, and critical studies. In the case of a major figure like Dante, the bibliography is a full two pages long. Because a choice was made to use familiar names as entry headings, looking up Dante under his last name, Alighieri, yields no *see* reference redirecting one to *D*, which is where his entry is actually located (though there is such a *see* reference in the index). The volumes are sprinkled with illustrations and photographs. Three maps at the beginning of volume 1 roughly show the myriad political changes Italy went through in this time period, including the vast array of republics and patriarchates that emerged in the mid-1300s. Of course, as the introduction points out, "Italy" in this period refers more to a geographical entity than a political one, since Italy did not become a nation until the latter half of the nineteenth century. The appendix consists of a five-page list of popes and rulers, including Roman and Byzantine emperors; kings of the Visigoths, Vandals, Ostrogoths, and Lombards;

the Carolingian Dynasty; and Norman, Aragonese, Angevin, and Hohenstaufen leaders. This is helpful for getting a quick idea of who was in charge at what time.

Overall the encyclopedia is well written, broad in its scope, and expansive in its coverage. It is recommended for academic libraries and large public libraries.

Encyclopedia of Russian History. 4v. Ed. by James R. Millar. 2004. 1,828p. bibliogs. illus. index. Macmillan, $475 (0-02-865693-8). 947.

A scholarly resource accessible to a general audience, the *Encyclopedia of Russian History* provides more than 1,500 entries encompassing more than 1,000 years of Russian history, from the formation of Kievan Rus in the mid-ninth century to the present- day Russian Federation. A seven-member editorial board of Russian scholars headed by editor-in-chief Millar (Director of the Institute for European, Russian, and Eurasian Studies, George Washington University) oversaw topic selection. All entries are signed by one of more than 500 contributors.

Entries are arranged alphabetically. To access them, users can scan the article title list in volume 1 or use the cumulative subject index in volume 4. Bold type in the index designates main entries. Volume 1 also provides a list of article titles arranged by one of 21 general topics, such as "Agriculture," "Government," "Religion," and "Science and Technology."

Types of entries include those for people, places, events, and other subjects of historical interest. Entries on individuals include czars (Nicholas I), military leaders (Georgy Zhukov), presidents (Vladimir Putin), writers (Alexander Pushkin), and others (Yelena Bonner, Yuri Gargarin, Anna Pavlova, Grigory Potemkin, Grigory Rasputin). Examples of nonbiographical article titles include *Boyar, Great Northern War, Liberal Democratic Party, Motion pictures, Ruble, Space program, Ukraine and Ukrainians,* and *Yalta Conference.* Entry length ranges from 250 to 5,000 words. Among the longest are *Cold War, Communist Party of the Soviet Union,* and *October Revolution.* Each entry offers a list of *see also* references and a bibliography with citations that point to English-language materials, mostly scholarly books. Also included are journal articles and, rarely, Web sites. Some 285 black-and-white photographs accompany the text, and each volume also contains an eight-page section of color plates. For the most part, illustration quality is excellent. However, readers looking for maps, chronologies, and dynastic charts will find only a handful, all of them embedded in entries.

With 2,300 entries, the 483-page *Encyclopedia of Russian History: From the Christianization of Kiev to the Break-Up of the U.S.S.R.* (ABC- CLIO, 1993) is older and lacks the depth of the newer set. As a historical resource to the largest nation on Earth, the *Encyclopedia of Russian History* is highly recommended for most academic libraries and large public libraries.

Facts about China. Ed. by Xiao-Bin Ji. 2003. 751p. appendix. index. Wilson, $105 (0-8242-0961-3). 951.

No general library catering to students or adults should be without accurate, up-to-date reference tools about the world's most populous country. *Facts about China* is meant "to serve as a reference guide for readers who are just beginning to learn about China." A brief introduction orients readers with some general ideas about China and common difficulties in learning about it, such as naming patterns and uncertain dates.

In nine chapters of 20 to 50 pages, different authorities cover "Geography and Climate," "Peoples and Languages," "Systems of Thought and Belief," and "Health and Medicine," among other broad topics. Each is clearly presented and extensively subdivided and concludes with a list of key, mostly book, research resources. Today's beginning researcher would likely welcome Internet and video resources as well. Tables and charts accompany several sections. Part 2 is a 200-page chronology of key dates and events. Part 3 is an *A–Z* of several hundred one- to two-paragraph entries on topics, from *Academia Sinica* to *Zuo Zongtang.* Part 4 provides 50 pages of information about traveling to China, including things to know and places to go. An appendix gives a conversion chart for Pinyin to Wade-Giles and a rather inadequate map of modern China (showing only six Chinese cities and no rivers) and its neighboring countries. A far more detailed map, or several, would have been helpful. The detailed, 82-page index gives separate entries for, and fails to cross-reference, the identical Yangtze (Yangzi) and Chang Jiang rivers. The "Geography and Climate" section consistently and confusingly cites the Chang Jiang River as China's longest, greatest river and fails to identify it with the Yangtze.

Despite relatively minor inadequacies, the wealth of well-organized information in *Facts about China* will make it useful even to those who are not new to the study of China. Recommended for public, academic, and high-school libraries.

World Eras: Volume 10: West African Kingdoms, 500–1590. By Pierre-Damien Mvuyekure. 2003. 385p. bibliogs. glossary. illus. index. maps. Gale, $120 (0-7876-6047-7). 966.

Patterned after the American Decades and American Eras reference series, this is the tenth volume in World Eras, a cross-disciplinary series that provides an overview from a global perspective with a strong emphasis on daily life and social history. Each volume covers a civilization for a specific period, e.g., European Renaissance and Reformation or Imperial China, and shows its interaction with the rest of the world at the time. Several of the contributors to the present volume are African history specialists.

The first chapter is a 73-page comparative chronology, almost by year, showing events outside West Africa. The format of the subsequent chapters is the same: well-documented chronology, overview, topics, sources, and significant people. The chapters cover "Geography"; "The Arts"; "Communication, Transportation, and Exploration"; "Social Class System and the Economy"; "Politics, Law, and the Military"; "Leisure, Recreation, and Daily Life"; "The Family and Social Trends"; "Religion and Philosophy"; and "Science, Technology, and Health."

The text is enriched throughout by many illustrations, such as maps and photos, and sidebar primary sources, including documents. The illustrations are usually clear, although some of the gray-shaded maps are too small. The influence of Islam on the history and culture of the region is very apparent. The work concludes with a glossary, general references, and an accurate, three- column, 10-page index.

Although this apparently unique resource is aimed at high- school students, it would also be useful in undergraduate and larger public libraries.

Encyclopedia of Cuba: People, History, Culture. 2v. Ed. by Luis Martinez-Fernandez and others. 2003. 688p. appendixes. bibliogs. illus. index. maps. Greenwood, $175 (1-57356-334-X). 972.91.

The editors intend this work to be a nonpoliticized look at Cuban people, politics, history, and culture. Some 80 contributors write honestly and objectively of the varied viewpoints of Cuban citizens and expatriates.

The encyclopedia is not arranged in strict alphabetical order. Instead, there are 12 topical chapters, among them "Geography, Environment, and Urbanization"; "History and Government: The Revolutionary Period (1959–)"; "Popular Culture and Religion"; and "Cuban Diaspora." Within each chapter the entries are in alphabetical order and vary in length from one paragraph to several pages. Most are about 250 words. Examples include *Baseball, Cattle ranching, Gays and lesbians, Little Havana, Radio Marti, Revolution of 1933,* and *Secada, Jon.* Each entry is signed and has a list for further reading. Cross-references are in bold print. There are many black-and-white pictures throughout, and volume 1 offers 8 pages of color pictures. Maps and charts appear in appropriate places.

The 15 appendixes include a political chronology, several primary source documents (most are texts of laws), and a list of presidents from 1868 to the present. An extensive index and bibliography can be found in volume 2. At the front of each volume is an alphabetical list of entries with their page numbers. The topical arrangement lends itself to a few problems with access, although the index and other finding tools minimize those difficulties. Because the entries are not in strict alphabetical order, the reader has to use the index or the list of entries to find the cross-referenced articles.

The articles themselves are fascinating, written to be accessible to a wide range of readers. This excellent introduction to a colorful and important nation is recommended for high-school, public, and academic libraries.

★**American Decades Primary Sources.** 10v. Ed. by Cynthia Rose. 2003. bibliogs. illus. indexes. Gale, $855 (0-7876-6587-8). 973.91.

Aimed at the high-school and undergraduate levels, but definitely accessible to middle-schoolers, this set is a treasure trove of more than 2,000 primary sources on U.S. history and culture represented by more than 75 types of sources, such as architectural drawings, graphs, letters, magazine articles, memoirs, reports, Supreme Court decisions, speeches, and literary works. Each volume focuses on one decade of the twentieth century. Readers will find materials related to the Gibson Girl, the Triangle Shirtwaist Factory fire, antilynching campaigns, the Tuskegee syphilis experiment, the Eames chair, penicillin, *The Power of Positive Thinking, The Smothers Brothers Comedy Hour,* the *Apollo 11* lunar landing mission, the American Indian movement, *Roe* v. *Wade*, the Apple IIc computer, *Jane Fonda's Workout Book*, *Angels in America*, the Million Man March, and the Ebola virus—and this is just a glimmer.

The volumes are consistently arranged. An introductory section that provides excellent ideas and materials for lesson plans is followed by 12 subject-specific sections, for example, "The Arts," "Education," "Law and Justice," and "Lifestyles and Social Trends." Each of these 12 sections begins with its own table of contents and a chronology that is related to the subject for the relevant decade. Arranged chronologically within each section, each of the approximately 200 primary sources per volume includes a brief essay offering historical background and context, sidebars, illustrations (themselves often primary sources), key facts, a synopsis, and further resources. The consistency of the 12 section subjects throughout the set allows a patron to follow a thread, such as civil rights or medical advances, across the twentieth century. Each volume concludes with a list of general resources (books and Web sites), a primary source type index, and general volume index.

Given the sheer physical size of the set (it weighs in at 51 pounds), an electronic version—or, better yet, its incorporation into one of Gale's current databases, such as *History Resource Center: U.S.*—is desirable. However, although electronic search capabilities would certainly speed access to a particular document, the presentation of information in print form offers opportunities for serendipitous browsing—and learning—not yet duplicated in the online world.

This resource is excellent as a companion to the *American Decades* (Gale, 1996–2000) set or as a stand-alone. Even if a library had access to all of the books, periodicals, and other items used as sources, they would lack the surrounding context and the added features, not to mention the convenience. Secondary school libraries in states with curriculum standards that require access to primary resources should place this on their priority purchase lists if they can afford it. Undergraduate and public libraries supporting historical research should also consider purchase.

American Presidents: Year by Year. 3v. By Lyle Emerson Nelson. 2003. 734p. illus. index. M. E. Sharpe, $225 (0-7656- 8046-7). 973.

In this set chronicling the lives of the U.S. presidents from George Washington to the election of George W. Bush, volume 1 covers 1732–1860, volume 2 covers 1861–1932, and volume 3 covers 1933–2000. The author has compiled a unique reference work by showing a "vertical and a horizontal view of future and former presidents at the same time."

Each year starts with a one- to two-page summary of the sitting president's activities, followed by an entry on each living predecessor and/or successor. For example, in 1799, the third year of John Adams' presidency, George Washington died. Thomas Jefferson, as vice president, was plotting his own election to the executive office; James Monroe became governor of Virginia; John Quincy Adams was U.S. minister to Prussia; and 17-year-old Martin Van Buren was studying law. In 1992, the year George H. W. Bush lost his bid for a second term, former president Richard M. Nixon criticized Bush's foreign aid policy, Gerald R. Ford spoke at the Republican National Convention, Jimmy Carter addressed the Democratic National Convention, and Ronald Reagan entertained Mikhail and Raisa Gorbachev at his California ranch. Future president Bill Clinton won the presidency with only a 43 percent popular vote, and George W. Bush was running the Texas Rangers baseball team.

The master index, repeated in each volume, helps pull together information on each president. Black-and-white illustrations are scattered throughout.

Filled with personal, political, and professional details, the set not only provides valuable reference information but also is interesting to read. It is hoped that the author will continue this chronicle into the future. This resource would be an excellent addition to an academic or public library.

American Presidents in World History. 5v. 2003. bibliogs. glossaries. illus. indexes. Greenwood, $200 (0-313-32564-2). 973.

Arranged chronologically from George Washington to George W. Bush, this set for grades five and up proffers a unique view of U.S. and world history. Instead of the usual biography or administration highlights, it examines each president's actions and policies from a global perspective.

Entries average 13 pages in length. For each entry, a fact file covers date and place of birth, political party, vice president(s) and secretary(ies) of state during his term(s), years as president, and date of death (where applicable). The narrative section begins with biographical background on each man and his election to the presidency. The easy-to-follow text then proceeds to discuss the foreign relations challenges he faced and his role as a leader. Light is shed on often dense, seldom explained treaties and diplomatic maneuvers, considering world history as it affected U.S. decision making. The entry for George W. Bush ends with the possibility of war in Iraq.

Sidebars provide additional information on the presidents and other important figures as well as issues and events in the U.S. and elsewhere. Each volume includes a glossary, bibliography, and index. Definitions for terms and phrases are also found in parentheses within the text. The short bibliographies list both books and Web sites. Many of the books are university press titles, which will not serve as further readings for the intended audience. Illustrations are in black and white.

With its unique emphasis on foreign relations, *American Presidents in World History* is a wonderful supplement to reference sources such as UXL's *The Complete American Presidents Sourcebook* (2001) and Grolier's *The Presidents* (1996) as well as U.S. history textbooks for grades five and up. Recommended for school and public libraries.

The Civil War. 10v. 2004. bibliog. glossary. illus. index. maps. Grolier, $309 (0-7172-5883-1). 973.7.

This set, intended for students in grades five through nine, features detailed, multipage articles that address significant individuals, battles, events, and conditions of the American Civil War. The alphabetically arranged entries, written by a team of editors, feature fairly sophisticated vocabulary and presume that readers have a basic understanding of contemporary historic, social, and political scenarios. *See also* references direct researchers to related entries. A common glossary, full-set index, and further reading list (print materials and Web sites) complete each volume.

What makes this resource noteworthy is the breadth of coverage. There are the expected offerings: biographical entries on both Union and Confederate generals, politicians, and activists; detailed accounts of fortifications, battles, and campaigns; and descriptions of various lifestyles, Northern and Southern, rural and urban. Standard research topics are included: *Abolition, Ku Klux Klan, Pacifism, Plantation life, Slavery,* and so on. There are also entries on each state and its course throughout the conflict. The roles women played are addressed not only in the entry *Women and the war effort* but also *Home front* and *Nurses and nursing* and in biographies for Belle Boyd, Dorothea Dix, Harriet Beecher Stowe, and Mary Edwards Walker, to name a few. There are entries on authors, musicians, artists and illustrators, photographers, and newspaper reporters. Underreported stories are covered, such as the sinking of the *Sultana* steamship and Native American participation in the war. Finally, there are a number of topics sure to catch the interest of browsers, such as *Espionage and counterespionage, Mascots,* and *Smugglers and piracy.*

The double-column text is accompanied by boxed inserts containing primary source material (eyewitness accounts, excerpts from letters and diaries, contemporary newspaper reports, etc.). Colorful graphics appear on every page and include archival photographs, political cartoons, maps, broadsides, and other vintage illustrations.

Most middle-school collections should already own UXL's five- volume set, *The American Civil War* (2000). Another standard is the one-volume *Civil War and Reconstruction: A Student Companion* (Oxford, 2001). The current offering is an appealing and accessible choice for school and public libraries that want to provide updated and expanded coverage.

Conspiracy Theories in American History: An Encyclopedia. 2v. Ed. by Peter Knight. 2003. 925p. bibliogs. illus. index. ABC-CLIO, $185 (1-57607-812-4). 973.

"Conspiracy theories (and, from time to time, actual conspiracies) have played a vital role in shaping the course of American history." So states the editor of this set, which is the work of more than 123 contributors. It is intended as "a serious and comprehensive summary of all the major events, ideas, and figures of U.S. conspiracy thinking."

The set begins with "Conspiracy Theories in America: A Historical Overview" and "Making Sense of Conspiracy Theories," two excellent articles that provide background and understanding of the subject. This material is followed by more than 300 entries for both actual and imagined conspiracies. Examples of theories include the extremely well known as well as the somewhat obscure. As might be expected, the entry on the John F. Kennedy assassination is the longest, covering 15 pages. Among other entries are *AIDS, Cattle mutilations, Oklahoma City bombing, Pearl Harbor,*

Tobacco industry, UFOs, and *Whitewater.* The theories are arranged alphabetically and include *see also* references and brief bibliographies of related works. Appropriate Web sites are also listed for some.

Section 3 contains approximately 100 extracts from primary source documents, arranged chronologically from Cotton Mather's *Wonders of the Invisible World* (1692) to *Lawton et al. v. Republic of Iraq* (2003). A headnote explains the context of each.

This is a fascinating reference set that presents intriguing (albeit sometimes far-fetched) theories. Examining these theories, one can see how almost any event or idea can be viewed as a conspiracy, actual or imagined. This would be an excellent addition to academic and large public libraries.

Encyclopedia of African-American Politics. By Robert C. Smith. 2003. 418p. bibliogs. illus. index. Facts On File, $85 (0-8160-4475-9). 973.

Politics has always been a prime component of the history of African Americans in the U.S. Seeking to clarify the issues in African American politics, this volume will be useful for students as a handy source of information as well as a starting point for further research.

The 462 entries cover events, people, laws, government policies, court cases, and concepts, such as *Affirmative action*; *Chisholm, Shirley*; *Civil Rights Act of 1964*; *Culture of poverty*; *Globalization*; *Kwanza*; *Lynching*; *Plessy v. Ferguson*; and *Slavery in Western thought*. Occasional black- and-white illustrations enhance understanding of the topics discussed. Most entries are one or two pages, with the longest (*Affirmative action*) being seven pages. Each entry concludes with a list of resources for further reading. The book also includes eight "Documentary Sources in the Study of African-American Politics," an 11- page bibliography, and a detailed index.

Though there is considerable overlap with other reference tools on African Americans, this volume's emphasis on the purely political aspects of topics such as the abolitionist and civil rights movements and historically black colleges and universities, as well as the dynamic between African Americans and concepts such as capitalism and leadership, make it unique. For public and academic libraries that need materials with this perspective, it will be a welcome addition to the reference collection.

★Encyclopedia of the Great Depression. 2v. Ed. by Robert S. McElvaine. 2003. 1,134p. bibliogs. illus. index. Macmillan, $265 (0-02-865686-5). 973.91.

Frequent modern references to the Depression and New Deal programs make this new work particularly welcome. It "provides an overview of the severe economic slump that impoverished countless Americans" and transformed U.S. government, business, and social programs. More than 500 alphabetically arranged articles focus on topics in politics, economics, religion, science, art, and literature, ranging from *Abraham Lincoln Brigade* to *Wright, Richard*. Articles are from 300 to 5,000 words in length. The number and variety of photographs illustrate the time period very well and make the work especially attractive. Editor McElvaine, of Millsaps College, has written or edited several other Depression-related books.

Entries are signed and include useful bibliographies (but few Internet sites). The encyclopedia is especially strong in social history topics and pays particular attention to issues related to gender and race. There is some repetition (both *Class* and *Caste and class* and both *Strikes* and *Sit-down strikes*). Nearly half of the articles are biographies, covering individuals such as James Agee, Busby Berkeley, Felix Frankfurt, J. Edgar Hoover, Jesse Owens, Diego Rivera, Walter Ruether, and Mae West, to name just a few. Cross-references are plentiful. For example, *Communication and the press* has references to *Advertising in the Great Depression*, *Communications Act of 1934*, *Federal Communications Commission (FCC)*, *Hollywood and the Film Industry*, and *Radio*. However, *Tennessee Valley Authority (TVA)* has no cross-reference to *Rural Electrification Administration (REA)*. An A–Z list of articles, a list of the 270 contributors with their academic affiliations and the entries for which they are responsible, and an outline that groups entry headings under broad topics precede the encyclopedia portion of the text. A time line and an index constitute the back matter.

This set covers a time period of great popular interest, emphasized in high-school and college courses. *The Encyclopedia of the Great Depression and the New Deal* (Sharpe, 2001) takes a different approach, offering thematic essays and a selection of primary documents in addition to entries that are arranged in several parts instead of in a single alphabet. It is appropriate for public and academic libraries. *Depression America* (Grolier, 2001) is designed expressly for high- school students and takes a thematic and highly visual approach. *Encyclopedia of the Great Depression* is an attractive and accessible resource that will be a valuable addition to most high-school, college, and public library collections.

Life & Times in 20th-Century America. 5v. 2003. bibliogs. illus. indexes. Greenwood, $200 (0-313-32570-7). 973.91.

Intended for students at the sixth to eighth grade reading levels, this set examines twentieth-century U.S. history through the lens of the social conditions of the time. Each volume covers a 20-year span—*Becoming a Modern Nation: 1900–1920*; *Boom Times, Hard Times: 1921–1940*; *Hot and Cold Wars: 1941–1960*; *Troubled Times at Home: 1961–1980*; and *Promise and Change: 1981–2000*. The volumes each begin with an engagingly written overview of the period that includes a time line of key events and is followed by nine chapters, a bibliography, and a volume index. The nine chapters cover family life; social and political attitudes; education; the economy; work; religion; health, science, and technology; leisure, sports, and entertainment; and fashions and fads. Each is complemented by photographs, charts, illustrations, sidebars, fact boxes, and excerpts from primary documents. Terms and phrases are defined in parentheses within the text. The parallel construction of the volumes allows a reader to trace a particular topic, such as education, through the century. It also encourages patrons to compare and contrast how people and events influenced a topic.

The set meets its goal of reaching patrons reading at a grade six to eight level. However, the 20-year grouping is somewhat artificial. While there is a bibliography in each volume, there are neither footnotes nor endnotes, nor is there a cumulative set index. The simplification of some details occasionally leads to a convoluted, hard-to-grasp sentence structure. Better editing might have caught minor errors, such as a mismatch between the colors and key code in a population chart showing "Rural vs. Urban Population" in volume 1; mention of Nancy Drew and the Hardy Boys in the 1900– 1920 volume instead of the 1921–1940 volume; and spelling of the name of German foreign secretary as Arthur Zimmerman instead of Zimmermann.

The set is appropriate for school and public libraries. In some states, it would tie in more with the high-school than the middle- school curriculum.

The Mexican American Experience: An Encyclopedia. By Matt S. Meier and Margo Gutierrez. 2004. 456p. bibliogs. illus. index. Greenwood, $79.95 (0-313-31643-0). 973.

By 2010—based on statistics of the 2000 census—it is predicted that persons of Mexican ancestry will be the largest minority group in the U.S. With this in mind, the authors, as a means of promoting a better understanding, present an abundance of facts and figures related to *Mexicanos*, from the 1848 Treaty of Guadalupe to the present day, with emphasis on the Southwestern region of the U.S. More than 800 entries encompass labor issues (*Boycott, grape*); legislation (*Box Bill, 1926*); religion (*Guadalupe, Virgin of*); historical events (*Taos Rebellion, 1846–1847*); organizations (*English Only movement*); and discrimination (*Bloody Christmas, 1951*) as well as such luminaries as singer Joan Baez, activist Eleuterio Escabar, golfer Nancy López, poet Ricardo Sánchez, and revolutionary Pancho Villa. All entries are listed by category in the "Guide to Selected Related Entries." The preface is a lesson in itself as it defines and explains often misused and confused terms such as *Californio, Tejano, Nuevomexicano, Chicano, Mexican American, raza, Mexicano, Hispano,* and *Latino*. Articles range in length from a short paragraph to more than a full page and provide cross-references and further readings.

Although noteworthy for the information provided, this volume is not without flaws. A random sampling of the bibliographical information offered for further reading found locating many of the cited materials difficult, and the few illustrations fail to capture attention. Because of pertinence to the Southwest, this source would be recommended for inclusion in collections in public libraries and high schools in that region. Public and school libraries in other regions might consider it if there are strong curricular needs.

Political Corruption in America: An Encyclopedia of Scandals, Power, and Greed. By Mark Grossman. 2003. 466p. appendixes. bibliogs. illus. index. ABC-CLIO, $85 (1-57607-060-3). 973.

In this resource, political corruption is defined as "the dishonest use of a position of elected power to gain a monetary advantage." Therefore, other types of scandals, such as sexual misconduct, are not included. However, some notable exceptions are covered, for example, Watergate and the Iran-Contra Affair. The majority of the more than 250 entries are devoted to people, such as mayors of big cities, governors, senators, representatives, presidents, and other government officials. Additional types of headings cover court cases, names of scandals (e.g., *Swartwout-Hoyt Scandal*), legislative acts (e.g., *Hatch Act*), and other miscellaneous topics (e.g., *Honoraria*). Content focuses primarily on the nineteenth and twentieth centuries.

Articles average about two pages in length, and most include a reference list. Many articles contain lengthy quotations, thereby adding a second voice to the topic under discussion. The author presents complex issues clearly. For example, the two-page article on Whitewater outlines key events in chronological order from 1978 up to the final Whitewater report, issued in March 2002. Numerous illustrations accompany the articles, including many political cartoons, which adds a touch of humor.

Eight appendixes demonstrate the attention to detail evident throughout this volume. For example, appendix 3, "Independent Counsel Investigations, 1979–1999," lists not only names and results but also the costs of the investigations. Other appendixes cover government cases of censure, expulsion, and impeachment. A chronology lists events related to political corruption from 1635 to 2003. A 21-page bibliography cites resources by format (e.g., books, government documents). We found no references to Internet sites.

Ethics in U.S. Government: An Encyclopedia of Investigations, Scandals, Reforms, and Legislation (Greenwood, 2001) covers primarily the post–World War II period. *The New Encyclopedia of American Scandal* (Facts On File, 2001) is much broader in scope. Many entries in *Political Corruption in America* are not in *The New Encyclopedia of American Scandal*. *Political Corruption in America* should be useful in most academic, high-school, and public libraries.

Student Almanac of African American History. 2v. 2003. bibliog. illus. index. maps. Greenwood, $80 (0-313-32596-0). 973.
Student Almanac of Native American History. 2v. 2003. bibliog. glossary. illus. index. maps. Greenwood, $80 (0-313-32599-5). 970.

These attractive almanacs use essentially the same format to provide information on topics of interest to users in middle school and up. Each volume contains about four chapters that are arranged in chronological sequence and take the user from the earliest to the present time. Each chapter provides a survey of the topic; for example, "Unwilling Immigrants: Slavery in Colonial America, 1492–1763" informs the user about the nature of slavery, how it came to the Americas, and how it changed as it was codified under law until the American Revolution. These surveys are brief, covering a great deal of information in a simplified manner. They are accompanied by alphabetically arranged entries that provide slightly more detail on specific people, events, and terms. Throughout the volumes are sidebars jammed with lengthy quotes from primary source materials like diaries, poetry, period magazines, and newspapers. Charts and maps (without scale or a compass rose) and small black-and-white photographs add interest and provide additional information. There is also a time line that helps orient users.

Each volume has a glossary; a short bibliography of books on general topics; a list of media, CD-ROMs, and Web sites; and a short list of books on more specific topics like history, folklore, and fiction. Each volume reprints the entire index so users can refer to information contained in both volumes of the set. Unfortunately, the index does not list photographs or sidebar material. The overall arrangement of these almanacs makes them slightly more difficult to use for quick sound bites of information than UXL's *African American Almanac* and *Native North American Almanac* (both 1994), but they will be a welcome addition to school and public libraries where there is a need for additional information about African and Native Americans.

Women during the Civil War: An Encyclopedia. By Judith E. Harper. 2003. 472p. bibliogs. glossary. illus. index. Routledge, $95 (0-415-93723-X). 973.7.

The Civil War was the seminal point for so much of what America is today, and women played an important part. This unique encyclopedia brings together information on individual women, ethnic groups, occupations, issues, and even women soldiers.

The encyclopedia is designed for scholars and students who need information on women both individually and collectively. The 128 entries range in size from several paragraphs to several pages. Each provides cross-references where appropriate and a selected readings list. A number of black-and-white photographs accompany the text. The work concludes with an extensive bibliography and an index with the main entries in bold type.

The individuals covered include the famous, such as Dorothea Dix, Sojourner Truth, and Harriet Tubman, and less-well-known women, some of whom disguised their sex and served in the army, such as Sarah Rosetta Wakeman. The entry *Military women* provides insights on how they got away with the deception and why they decided to enlist. Of course the more traditional activities such as sewing uniforms and flags are included, as are tasks of taking on farming, running businesses, and holding the family together. The problems of women doctors who were not allowed to heal the wounded; nurses who fought with surgeons over patient care; the ambiguity of what to do with the former slaves after they were freed; and a host of other issues are all examined in some depth.

This work is an important reference resource for most libraries. The bibliography would make an excellent checklist for collection development. Although the biographies are useful, the essays helping to place women in a Civil War context are even more significant. A necessary acquisition for public and academic libraries with collections on the Civil War, social movements such as abolition, and women's studies.

Broadway: Its History, People, and Places: An Encyclopedia. 2d ed. By Ken Bloom. 2003. 679p. illus. index. Routledge, $95 (0-415- 93704-3). 974.7.

Broadway is the only reference book dedicated to the "history, people, and places" of the Great White Way. Articles on Broadway history include *Billboard, Critics, Dramatists Guild, Federal Theatre Project, Poster,* and *Tony Award*. People include important composers, choreographers, critics, producers, directors, playwrights, and performers (e.g., *De Mille, Agnes; Kern, Jerome; Merman, Ethel; Simon, Neil*). Biographies run from a few paragraphs to six or more pages. Places include theaters and other establishments such as restaurants, which may or may not be extant. For each theater there is a very detailed chronological history of shows, as well as information about owners, financing, and current status. This is not the place to look up information about a show, since there are few entries by show title. Most shows are covered within the articles on various theaters and retrievable through the index.

There are some odd omissions. The entry for *Cats,* the longest- running show ever on Broadway, does not give opening and closing dates. There is an article on the history of burlesque, but not on the musical. There are no individual articles on people who some might say merit them (Elia Kazan, Bernadette Peters), though their names are indexed on many pages. There is no general history or time line of Broadway trends and events. A category index would have been useful to see headings for entries for theaters, composers, etc. at a glance.

Black-and-white photos and illustrations grace many of the entries, often replacing those in the first edition. It is clear that many articles have been revised to include more recent facts or productions. Some have been greatly expanded (e.g., *Kaufman and Hart; Prince, Harold*), and there are also new entries, such as those on individual critics. The biggest strength of this work for reference is found in the histories of the theaters themselves. Libraries with strong theater collections will want to add it.

Subject Index

AFRICA
African Folklore: An Encyclopedia. 48
World Eras: Volume 10: West African Kingdoms, 500-1590. 87

AFRICAN AMERICANS
African American Architects. 61
African American Lives. 80
African American Social Leaders and Activists. 80
African Americans at War: An Encyclopedia. 42
African Americans in Science, Math, and Invention. 49
African Americans in Sports. 66
African Americans in the Military. 42
African-American Political Leaders. 42
African-American Religious Leaders. 25
Encyclopedia of African-American Politics. 89
Encyclopedia of the Harlem Renaissance. 72
The Greenwood Encyclopedia of African American Civil Rights: From Emancipation to the Twenty-First Century. 35
Harlem Renaissance (Web). 17
Latino and African American Athletes Today: A Biographical Dictionary. 68
Student Almanac of African American History. 90

ANIMALS
Encyclopedia of the Aquatic World. 52
Firefly Encyclopedia of Birds. 53
Grzimek's Animal Life Encyclopedia: v.1: Lower Metazoans and Lesser Deuterostomes. 53
Grzimek's Animal Life Encyclopedia: v.12-16: Mammals. 53
Grzimek's Animal Life Encyclopedia: v.2: Protostomes. 53
Grzimek's Animal Life Encyclopedia: v.3: Insects. 53
Grzimek's Animal Life Encyclopedia: v.4-5: Fishes. 53
Grzimek's Animal Life Encyclopedia: v.6: Amphibians. 53
Grzimek's Animal Life Encyclopedia: v.7: Reptiles. 53
The Kennel Club's Illustrated Breed Standards: The Official Guide to Registered Breeds. 60
National Geographic Reference Atlas to the Birds of North America. 53
World of Animals: Birds. 54

ARCHITECTURE
African American Architects. 61
Encyclopedia of 20th-Century Architecture. 62
The Encyclopedia of Ancient Egyptian Architecture. 61

ART
Art in World History. 61
Encyclopedia of American Folk Art. 62
Encyclopedia of Sculpture. 62

ASIAN AMERICANS
Asian American Short Story Writers: An A-to-Z Guide. 74
Distinguished Asian American Business Leaders. 40
Distinguished Asian American Political and Governmental Leaders. 80
Extraordinary Asian Americans and Pacific Islanders. 80

ASTRONOMY
The Cambridge Guide to the Solar System. 50
Firefly Atlas of the Universe. 50

ATLASES
Atlas and Dictionary Update, 2004. 5
Atlas of the World's Deserts. 78
Children's Atlas Roundup. 6

AVIATION
Pioneer Aviators of the World: A Biographical Dictionary of the First Pilots of 100 Countries. 59

BASEBALL
Baseball Players of the 1950s: A Biographical Dictionary of All 1,560 Major Leaguers. 67
A Biographical Dictionary of Major League Baseball Managers. 67
The Most Valuable Players in Baseball, 1931-2001. 68

BIOETHICS
Encyclopedia of Bioethics. 24

BIOGRAPHY, GENERAL
The Houghton Mifflin Dictionary of Biography. 81
Scholastic Book of Outstanding Americans: Profiles of More Than 450 Famous and Infamous Figures in U.S. History. 81

BIRDS
Firefly Encyclopedia of Birds. 53
National Geographic Reference Atlas to the Birds of North America. 53
World of Animals: Birds. 54

BUDDHISM
Dictionary of Buddhism. 28
Encyclopedia of Buddhism. 28

BUSINESS
The Basic Business Library. 21
Business and Industry. 39
Distinguished Asian American Business Leaders. 40
Encyclopedia of American Business. 40

CAREERS
Career Discovery Encyclopedia. 39
Ferguson's Career Guidance Center. 37

CARIBBEAN
Latin America and Caribbean Artists of the Modern Era: A Biographical Dictionary of More than 12,700 Persons. 61
Notable Caribbeans and Caribbean Americans: A Biographical Dictionary. 81

CHILDREN
Encyclopedia of Children and Childhood in History and Society. 31

CHINA
Facts about China. 87

CHRISTIANITY
Biographical Dictionary of Evangelicals. 26
The Encyclopedia of Protestantism. 26
Jesus in History, Thought, and Culture. 26
Men and Women of the Bible: A Reader's Guide. 26

CIVIL WAR
The Civil War. 88
Women during the Civil War: An Encyclopedia. 90

COINS
Coins and Currency. 64

COLONIALISM
Colonialism: An International Social, Cultural, and Political Encyclopedia. 36

COMMUNICATION
Encyclopedia of International Media and Communications. 29
Propaganda and Mass Persuasion: A Historical Encyclopedia. 29

COMMUNITY
Encyclopedia of Community: From the Village to the Virtual World. 34

COMPUTERS
A to Z Computer Science. 21
When There's TMTT (Web). 20

CONFUCIANISM
RoutledgeCurzon Encyclopedia of Confucianism. 25

COUNTIES
United States Counties. 79

CRIME AND CRIMINAL JUSTICE
The Dictionary of Crime Terms. 45
The Encyclopedia of High-Tech Crime and Crime-Fighting. 45
Encyclopedia of Murder and Violent Crime. 45
The FBI Encyclopedia. 44

CUBA
Encyclopedia of Cuba: People, History, Culture. 87

CULTURES
Peoples of North America. 32
How People Live. 33

DATABASES
American History Online. 82
Classical Music Library. 60
CQ Researcher en Español. 40
Eighteenth Century Collections Online. 82
Enciclopedia estudiantil hallazgos. 14
Enciclopedá universal en español. 14
Encyclopaedia Britannica Online. 1
Encyclopedia Americana Online. 2
Encyclopedia of American Studies. 82
Ferguson's Career Guidance Center. 37
Gale Virtual Reference Library. 12
Grolier Multimedia Encyclopedia. 3
HQ Online. 37
The New Book of Knowledge Online. 3
Nueva enciclopedia cumbre en línea. 14
Oxford Scholarship Online. 12
Proquest Historical Newspapers. 83
Reference Universe. 21
Salud para todos. 54
World Book Online Reference Center. 4
World History Online. 82

DEATH
Encyclopedia of Forensic Science. 44
The Encyclopedia of Suicide. 44
Handbook of Death and Dying. 33

DICTIONARIES
Atlas and Dictionary Update, 2004. 5
Cut Me Some Slang (Web). 16
The Facts On File Encyclopedia of Word and Phrase Origins. 48
Garner's Modern American Usage. 48
Merriam-Webster's Collegiate Dictionary. 13
Talking Terrorism: A Dictionary of the Loaded Language of Political Violence. 29

DINOSAURS
Dinosaur: The Complete Guide to Dinosaurs. 51
The Dinosaur Atlas. 51
Scholastic Dinosaurs A to Z: The Ultimate Dinosaur Encyclopedia. 52

ECONOMICS
The American Economy: A Historical Encyclopedia. 38
Distinguished Women Economists. 38
The Oxford Encyclopedia of Economic History. 38

EDUCATION
Directory of Distance Learning Opportunities: K-12. 45
Education and Technology: an Encyclopedia. 45
Encyclopedia of Distributed Learning. 46

ENCYCLOPEDIAS
Grolier Multimedia Encyclopedia. 3
Enciclopedia estudiantil hallazgos. 14
Enciclopedia universal en español. 14
Encyclopaedia Britannica. 1
Encyclopaedia Britannica Online. 1
Encyclopedia Americana. 2
Encyclopedia Americana Online. 2
Grolier Student Encyclopedia. 24
The New Book of Knowledge. 3
The New Book of Knowledge Online. 3
Nueva enciclopedia cumbre en línea. 14
Spanish-Language Online Encyclopedias. 14
World Book Encyclopedia. 4
World Book Online Reference Center. 4

ENGLAND
Encyclopedia of the Victorian Era. 85
Great Britain: A Reference Guide from the Renaissance to the Present. 86
Queen Victoria: A Biographical Companion. 85
Reader's Guide to British History. 86

ENVIRONMENT
The Atlas of U.S. and Canadian Environmental History. 30
The Encyclopedia of Human Ecology. 55
Encyclopedia of World Environmental History. 30
Indigenous Peoples and Environmental Issues: An Encyclopedia. 30
Pollution A to Z. 45

EXPLORATION
Biography for Beginners: World Explorers. 78
Exploring Polar Frontiers: A Historical Encyclopedia. 78
Literature of Travel and Exploration. 79

FASHION
Fashion, Costume, and Culture: Clothing,

Headwear, Body Decoration, and Footwear through the Ages. 46
Fashion, Turn to the Left (Web). 16

FICTION
Crime Fiction IV: A Comprehensive Bibliography, 1749-2000. 22

FILM
Bad Boys: The Actors of Film Noir. 64
The Encyclopedia of American Independent Filmmaking. 64
The Encyclopedia of Hollywood Film Actors: From the Silent Era to 1965. 64
The Encyclopedia of Orson Wells. 65
The Encyclopedia of War Movies. 65
The Encyclopedia of Westerns. 65
Epic Films: Casts, Credits, and Commentary on over 350 Historical Spectacle Movies. 66
Extraordinary People in the Movies. 80
Film Noir Guide. 22
The Gorehound's Guide to the Splatter Films of the 1980s. 63
Hollywood Musicals Nominated for Best Picture. 66
Korean War Filmography. 22
Slasher Films: An International Filmography, 1960 through 2001. 63

FINANCE
Encyclopedia of Retirement and Finance. 32

FOLKLORE
African Folklore: An Encyclopedia. 48
The Encyclopedia of Celtic Mythology and Folklore. 29

FOOD
The American History Cookbook. 60

GARDENING
The American Horticultural Society Encyclopedia of Gardening. 59
The American Rose Society Encyclopedia of Roses. 59
Flora: A Gardener's Encyclopedia. 59

GAY AND LESBIAN STUDIES
Contemporary Gay American Poets and Playwrights: An A-to-Z Guide. 73
Encyclopedia of Lesbian, Bisexual, and Transgendered History. 33

GEOGRAPHY
Cassell's Dictionary of Modern German History. 86
The Kingfisher Geography Encyclopedia. 79

GOVERNMENT AND POLITICS
American Presidential Campaigns and Elections. 35
Biographical Dictionary of Modern World Leaders: 1992 to the Present. 77
Distinguished Asian American Political and Governmental Leaders. 80
Encyclopedia of African-American Politics. 89
Encyclopedia of American Foreign Policy. 36
Encyclopedia of American Religion and Politics. 35
Encyclopedia of Constitutional Amendments, Proposed Amendments, and Amending Issues, 1789-2002. 40
Encyclopedia of Presidential Campaigns, Slogans, Issues, and Platforms. 36
Encyclopedia of Public Administration and Public Policy. 34
Encyclopedia of the Central Intelligence Agency. 37
Major Acts of Congress. 41

No, Not Those Primaries (Web). 19
Political Corruption in America: An Encyclopedia of Scandals, Power, and Greed. 89
Presidents, Vice Presidents, Cabinet Members, Supreme Court Justices, 1789-2003. 42
The United States Executive Branch: A Biographical Directory of Heads of State and Cabinet Officials. 42
United States Gubernatorial Elections, 1776-1860. 36

HARLEM RENAISSANCE
Encyclopedia of the Harlem Renaissance. 72
Harlem Renaissance (Web). 17

HEALTH AND MEDICINE
Consumer Health Information Source Book. 22
Directory of Drug & Alcohol Residential Rehabilitation Facilities. 43
Encyclopedia of Alzheimer's Disease. 56
The Encyclopedia of Arthritis. 57
The Encyclopedia of Autoimmune Diseases. 57
The Encyclopedia of Complementary and Alternative Medicine. 56
The Encyclopedia of Deafness and Hearing Disorders. 58
Encyclopedia of Folk Medicine: Old World and New World Traditions. 56
Encyclopedia of Health Care Management. 43
The Encyclopedia of HIV and AIDS. 57
The Encyclopedia of Infectious Diseases. 57
The Encyclopedia of Nutrition and Good Health. 55
The Encyclopedia of Parkinson's Disease. 57
The Encyclopedia of Sexually Transmitted Diseases. 58
The Encyclopedia of Work-Related Illnesses, Injuries, and Health Issues. 58
Human Diseases and Conditions, Supplement 2: Infectious Diseases. 58
Rx for Consumer Health Reference: One-Volume Medical Encyclopedias. 13
Salud para todos. 54
Statistical Handbook of Infectious Diseases. 56
The Medical Library Association Guide to Searching and Finding Health Information on the Web. 23
The Merck Manual of Medical Information: Home Edition. 55
World of Epidemics: A Cultural Chronology of Disease from Prehistory to the Era of SARS. 56

HINDUISM
Handbook of Hindu Mythology. 28
Hinduism (Web). 17

HISPANIC AMERICANS
Hispanic Literature of the United States. 72
Latina and Latino Voices in Literature. 23
Latino and Latina Writers. 72
The Mexican American Experience: An Encyclopedia. 89

HISTORY, AMERICAN
American Decades Primary Sources. 87
American History Online. 82
American Presidents in World History. 88
American Presidents: Year by Year. 88
Conspiracy Theories in American History. 88
Encyclopedia of American Military History. 43
Encyclopedia of the Great Depression. 89
Encyclopedia of the Lewis and Clark Expedition. 83
Life & Times in 20th-Century America. 89
United States History. 23

HISTORY, ANCIENT
Ancient Europe, 8,000 B.C.-A.D. 1,000. 10
Exploring Ancient Civilizations. 83
Handbook to Life in Ancient Egypt. 84

HISTORY, WORLD
Austria-Hungary & Word Successor States: A Reference Guide from the Renaissance to the Present. 86
Dictionary of Historic Documents. 22
Encyclopedia of Barbarian Europe: Society in Transformation. 84
Encyclopedia of the Crusades. 78
Encyclopedia of the Romantic Era, 1760-1850. 60
Europe, 1450 to 1789. 12
Global History: Cultural Encounters from Antiquity to the Present. 78
Industrial Revolution: Almanac. 38
Industrial Revolution: Biographies. 38
Industrial Revolution: Primary Sources. 38
A World History of Tax Rebellions. 39
World History Online. 82

HOLIDAYS
Encyclopedia of Christmas and New Year's Celebrations. 46
The Halloween Encyclopedia. 47
Holiday Symbols and Customs. 47
Religious Holidays and Calendars. 50
United State Holidays and Observances: By Date, Jurisdiction, and Subject, Fully Indexed. 47
World Book's Celebrations and Rituals around the World. 47

HUMAN RIGHTS
The Wilson Chronology of Human Rights. 35

IMMIGRATION
The Newest Americans. 31

IRELAND
The Encyclopedia of Ireland. 85

ISLAM
Encyclopedia of Islam and the Muslim World. 77
The Oxford Dictionary of Islam. 28

ITALY
Medieval Italy: An Encyclopedia. 86
The Oxford Companion to Italian Literature. 76

JAPAN
Dictionary of the Modern Politics of Japan. 34

LABOR
Historical Encyclopedia of American Labor. 39
Work in America: An Encyclopedia of History, Policy, and Society. 37

LATIN AMERICA
Encyclopedia of Latin American Theater. 77
Latin America and Caribbean Artists of the Modern Era: A Biographical Dictionary of More than 12,700 Persons. 61

LAW
Great American Judges: An Encyclopedia. 41
Landmark Legislation, 1774-2002. 41
U.S. Laws, Acts, and Treaties. 41
Women and the Law. 41

LIBRARY SCIENCE
International Encyclopedia of Information and Library Science. 21

LITERATURE, AMERICAN
Asian American Short Story Writers: An A-to-Z Guide. 74
The Beat Generation: A Gale Critical Companion. 71
The Chronology of American Literature: America's Literary Achievements from the Colonial Era to Modern Times. 72
Contemporary Gay American Poets and Playwrights: An A-to-Z Guide. 73
The Facts On File Companion to American Drama. 73
Hispanic Literature of the United States. 72
Latina and Latino Voices in Literature. 23
Latino and Latina Writers. 72
The Oxford Companion to Mark Twain. 74
The Tennessee Williams Encyclopedia. 73
A Theodore Dreiser Encyclopedia. 73
The Toni Morrison Encyclopedia. 74
The World of Toni Morrison: A Guide to Characters and Places in Her Novels. 74

LITERATURE, BRITISH
The Age of Milton: An Encyclopedia of Major 17th-Century British and American Authors. 74
The Brontes A to Z: The Essential Reference to Their Lives and Work. 76
The Continuum Encyclopedia of British Literature. 75
Encyclopedia of British Writers. 75
A Mary Shelley Encyclopedia. 76
Modern British Women Writers: An A-to-Z Guide. 75
The Oxford Companion to Chaucer. 76

LITERATURE, WORLD
Another Look At . . . World Authors, 1995-2000. 5
The Cervantes Encyclopedia. 77
The Columbia Guide to the Literature of Eastern Europe since 1945. 69
Critical Survey of Drama. 69
Cyclopedia of World Authors. 69
Encyclopedia of Literary Modernism. 70
Encyclopedia of World Writers. 70
The Facts On File Dictionary of Classical and Biblical Allusions. 70
Great World Writers: Twentieth Century. 70
Jewish Writers of the Twentieth Century. 70
Masterplots 2: Drama Series. 71
The Oxford Companion to Italian Literature. 76
South Asian Novelists in English: An A-to-Z Guide. 75
Timetables of World Literature. 71
Today in Literature (Web). 19
Twayne Companion to Contemporary World Literature. 71
World Writers in English. 76

MEN'S STUDIES
American Masculinities: A Historical Encyclopedia. 31
Men and Masculinities: A Social, Cultural, and Historical Encyclopedia. 31

MIDDLE AGES
Dictionary of the Middle Ages. 11
Encyclopedia of the Crusades. 78
The Greenhaven Encyclopedia of the Middle Ages. 84
Medieval Italy: An Encyclopedia. 86

MUSIC
Baker's Biographical Dictionary of Popular Musicians since 1990. 63
The Billboard Encyclopedia of Classical Music. 61
Classical Music Library. 60
From Convent to Concert Hall: A Guide to

Women Composers. 62
The Harvard Dictionary of Music. 62
Tin Pan Alley: An Encyclopedia of the Golden Age of American Song. 63

MYTHOLOGY
The Encyclopedia of Celtic Mythology and Folklore. 29
The Facts on File Encyclopedia of Mythology and Legend. 27
Greek and Roman Mythology A to Z. 27
Norse Mythology A to Z. 27
The Oxford Dictionary of Classical Myth and Religion. 27

NAMES
Dictionary of American Family Names. 81
Dictionary of Pseudonyms: 11,000 Assumed Names and Their Origins. 81
Indian Placenames in America: Volume 1: Cities, Towns, and Villages. 79
Naming Pains (Web). 18
Native American Names

NATIVE AMERICANS
Native Americans in Sports. 66
Student Almanac of Native American History. 90

PARANORMAL
The Gale Encyclopedia of the Unusual and Unexplained. 24
The New Encyclopedia of the Occult. 24

PHYSICS
A to Z of Physicists. 50
Building Blocks of Matter. 50

PLANTS
Botanica North America: The Illustrated Guide to our Native Plants, Their Botany, History and the Way They Have Shaped Our World. 52
Flora: A Gardener's Encyclopedia. 59

POPULATION
Ancestry in America: A Comparative City-by-City Guide to over 200 Ethnic Backgrounds—with Rankings. 30
Encyclopedia of Population. 30
Profiles of America: Facts, Figures & Statistics for Every Populated Place. 34

PRESIDENTS
American Presidential Campaigns and Elections. 35
American Presidents in World History. 88
American Presidents: Year by Year. 88
Encyclopedia of Presidential Campaigns, Slogans, Issues, and Platforms. 36
Presidents, Vice Presidents, Cabinet Members, Supreme Court Justices, 1789-2003. 42
The United States Executive Branch: A Biographical Directory of Heads of State and Cabinet Officials. 42

QUOTATIONS
The Oxford Dictionary of Modern Quotations. 24
The Oxford Dictionary of Phrase, Saying, and Quotation. 24

RADIO
The Encyclopedia of Women in Radio. 65
Museum of Broadcast Communications Encyclopedia of Radio. 46

RELIGION
African-American Religious Leaders. 25
Biographical Dictionary of Evangelicals. 26
Dictionary of Buddhism. 28
Encyclopedia of American Religion and Politics. 35
The Encyclopedia of Angels. 26
Encyclopedia of Buddhism. 28
The Encyclopedia of Protestantism. 26
Encyclopedia of Religion and War. 27
Encyclopedia of Religious Freedom. 35
Encyclopedia of Science and Religion. 27
Handbook of Hindu Mythology. 28
Hinduism (Web). 17
Jesus in History, Thought, and Culture. 26
Men and Women of the Bible: A Reader's Guide. 26
The Oxford Dictionary of Classical Myth and Religion. 27
The Oxford Dictionary of Islam. 28
Religion and American Cultures: An Encyclopedia of Traditions. 25
Religious Holidays and Calendars. 50
RoutledgeCurzon Encyclopedia of Confucianism. 25

RENAISSANCE
Encyclopedia of the Renaissance and the Reformation. 84
The Oxford Dictionary of the Renaissance. 84
The Renaissance: An Encyclopedia for Students. 85

RUSSIA
Encyclopedia of Russian History. 87

SCIENCE
The American Heritage Children's Science Dictionary. 48
Biology Resources in the Electronic Age. 23
Building Blocks of Matter. 50
The Cambridge Guide to the Solar System. 50
Encyclopedia of Air. 51
Encyclopedia of Life Sciences. 52
Encyclopedia of Science and Religion. 27
Encyclopedia of Water. 51
The Facts On File Marine Science Handbook. 49
The Facts On File Geometry Handbook. 49
Firefly Atlas of the Universe. 50
How It Works: Science and Technology. 55
The New Encyclopedia of Science. 48
Top 10 Science Reference Sources for under $100. 8
Water: Science and Issues. 51

SCIENCE HISTORY
The Oxford Companion to the History of Modern Science. 49
Science in the Enlightenment: An Encyclopedia. 49

SCIENTISTS
A to Z of Computer Scientists. 21
A to Z of Marine Scientists. 51
A to Z of Physicists. 50
A to Z of Scientists in Weather and Climate. 51
African Americans in Science, Math, and Invention. 49

SPANISH LANGUAGE
CQ Researcher en Español. 40

Enciclopeidia estudiantil hallazgos. 14
Enciclopeidia universal en español. 14
Nueva enciclopedia cumbre en línea. 14
Reference Books in Spanish for Children and Adolescents. 7
Salud para todos. 54
Spanish-Language Online Encyclopedias. 14

SPORTS
A Biographical Dictionary of Major League Baseball Managers. 67
African Americans in Sports. 66
Baseball Players of the 1950s: A Biographical Dictionary of All 1,560 Major Leaguers. 67
Baseball Statistics (Web). 15
Encyclopedia of International Games. 67
Encyclopedia of the Modern Olympic Movement. 64
The Encyclopedia of Surfing. 69
The International Motor Racing Guide: A Complete Reference from Formula One to NASCAR. 67
Latino and African American Athletes Today: A Biographical Dictionary. 68
The Most Valuable Players in Baseball, 1931-2001. 68
Native Americans in Sports. 66
Notable Sports Figures. 68
Scholastic Visual Sports Encyclopedia. 68
Total Tennis: The Ultimate Tennis Encyclopedia. 68

STYLE MANUALS
The Chicago Manual of Style. 10

TECHNOLOGY
Exploring Technology. 54
How It Works: Science and Technology. 55
How Stuff Works (Web). 18
Illustrated Dictionary of Automobile Body Styles. 58
It Came from Outer Space: Everyday Products and Ideas from the Space Program. 55

TELEVISION
Short-Lived Television Series, 1948-1978: Thirty Years of More than 1,000 Flops. 66

TERRORISM
Encyclopedia of Terrorism. 29
The Grey House Homeland Security Directory. 44
Talking Terrorism: A Dictionary of the Loaded Language of Political Violence. 29

THEATER
Broadway: Its History, People, and Places: An Encyclopedia. 90
Encyclopedia of Latin American Theater. 77
The Oxford Encyclopedia of Theatre & Performance. 66

WARFARE
African Americans at War: An Encyclopedia. 42
African Americans in the Military. 42
Amazons to Fighter Pilots: A Biographical Dictionary of Military Women. 43
Dictionary of Military Terms: A Guide to the Language of Warfare and Military Institutions. 43
Encyclopedia of American Military History. 43
Encyclopedia of Modern Ethnic Conflicts. 32
Encyclopedia of Religion and War. 27

WATER
Encyclopedia of Water. 51
Water: Science and Issues. 51

WOMEN'S STUDIES
A History of Women in the United States. 12
Amazons to Fighter Pilots: A Biographical Dictionary of Military Women. 43
Distinguished Women Economists. 38
The Encyclopedia of Women in Radio. 65
Encyclopedia of Women in the American West. 32
From Convent to Concert Hall: A Guide to Women Composers. 62
The Greenwood Encyclopedia of Women's Issues Worldwide. 32
Women and the Law. 41
Women during the Civil War: An Encyclopedia. 90

YOUTH REFERENCE
The American Heritage Children's Science Dictionary. 48
Biography for Beginners: World Explorers. 78
Business and Industry. 39
Career Discovery Encyclopedia. 39
Children's Atlas Roundup. 6
The Civil War. 88
Dinosaur: The Complete Guide to Dinosaurs. 51
The Dinosaur Atlas. 51
Enciclopedia estudiantil hallazgos. 14
Encyclopedia of Life Sciences. 52
Encyclopedia of the Aquatic World. 52
Exploring Ancient Civilizations. 83
Exploring Technology. 54
Extraordinary Asian Americans and Pacific Islanders. 80
Extraordinary People in the Movies. 80
Fashion, Costume, and Culture: Clothing, Headwear, Body Decoration, and Footwear through the Ages. 46
Great World Writers: Twentieth Century. 70
Greek and Roman Mythology A to Z. 27
The Greenhaven Encyclopedia of the Middle Ages. 84
Grolier Student Encyclopedia. 24
How It Works: Science and Technology. 55
How People Live. 33
Industrial Revolution: Almanac. 38
Industrial Revolution: Biographies. 38
Industrial Revolution: Primary Sources. 38
The Kingfisher Geography Encyclopedia. 79
Life & Times in 20th-Century America. 89
The New Book of Knowledge. 3
The New Book of Knowledge Online. 3
The Newest Americans. 31
Norse Mythology A to Z. 27
Peoples of North America. 32
Reference Books in Spanish for Children and Adolescents. 7
The Renaissance: An Encyclopedia for Students. 85
Scholastic Book of Outstanding Americans: Profiles of More Than 450 Famous and Infamous Figures in U.S. History. 81
Scholastic Dinosaurs A to Z: The Ultimate Dinosaur Encyclopedia. 52
Scholastic Visual Sports Encyclopedia. 68
Student Almanac of African American History. 90
Student Almanac of Native American History. 90
Twenty Best Bets for Student Researchers. 9
World Book's Celebrations and Rituals around the World. 47

Title Index

A to Z of Computer Scientists. 21
A to Z of Marine Scientists. 51
A to Z of Physicists. 50
A to Z of Scientists in Weather and Climate. 51
African American Architects. 61
African American Lives. 80
African American Social Leaders and Activists. 80
African Americans at War: An Encyclopedia. 42
African Americans in Science, Math, and Invention. 49
African Americans in Sports. 66
African Americans in the Military. 42
African Folklore: An Encyclopedia. 48
African-American Political Leaders. 42
African-American Religious Leaders. 25
Age of Milton: An Encyclopedia of Major 17th-Century British and American Authors. 74
Amazons to Fighter Pilots: A Biographical Dictionary of Military Women. 43
American Decades Primary Sources. 87
American Economy: A Historical Encyclopedia. 38
American Heritage Children's Science Dictionary. 48
American History Cookbook. 60
American History Online. 82
American Horticultural Society Encyclopedia of Gardening. 59
American Masculinities: A Historical Encyclopedia. 31
American Presidential Campaigns and Elections. 35
American Presidents in World History. 88
American Presidents: Year by Year. 88
American Rose Society Encyclopedia of Roses. 59
Ancestry in America: A Comparative City-by-City Guide to over 200 Ethnic Backgrounds—with Rankings. 30
Ancient Europe, 8,000 B.C.-A.D. 1,000. 10
Another Look At . . . World Authors, 1995-2000. 5
Art in World History. 61
Asian American Short Story Writers: An A-to-Z Guide. 74
Atlas and Dictionary Update, 2004. 5
Atlas of the World's Deserts. 78
Atlas of U.S. and Canadian Environmental History. 30
Austria-Hungary & Word Successor States: A Reference Guide from the Renaissance to the Present. 86

Bad Boys: The Actors of Film Noir. 64
Baker's Biographical Dictionary of Popular Musicians since 1990. 63
Baseball Players of the 1950s: A Biographical Dictionary of All 1,560 Major Leaguers. 67
Baseball Statistics (Web). 15
Basic Business Library. 21
Beat Generation: A Gale Critical Companion. 71
Billboard Encyclopedia of Classical Music. 61
Biographical Dictionary of Evangelicals. 26
Biographical Dictionary of Major League Baseball Managers. 67
Biographical Dictionary of Modern World Leaders: 1992 to the Present. 77
Biography for Beginners: World Explorers. 78

Biology Resources in the Electronic Age. 23
Botanica North America: The Illustrated Guide to our Native Plants, Their Botany, History and the Way They Have Shaped Our World. 52
Broadway: Its History, People, and Places: An Encyclopedia. 90
Brontes A to Z: Essential Reference to Their Lives and Work. 76
Building Blocks of Matter. 50
Business and Industry. 39

Cambridge Guide to the Solar System. 50
Career Discovery Encyclopedia. 39
Cassell's Dictionary of Modern German History. 86
Cervantes Encyclopedia. 77
Chicago Manual of Style. 10
Children's Atlas Roundup. 6
Chronology of American Literature: America's Literary Achievements from the Colonial Era to Modern Times. 72
Civil War. 88
Classical Music Library. 60
Coins and Currency. 64
Colonialism: An International Social, Cultural, and Political Encyclopedia. 36
Columbia Guide to the Literature of Eastern Europe since 1945. 69
Conspiracy Theories in American History. 88
Consumer Health Information Source Book. 22
Contemporary Gay American Poets and Playwrights: An A-to-Z Guide. 73
Continuum Encyclopedia of British Literature. 75
CQ Researcher en Español. 40
Crime Fiction IV: A Comprehensive Bibliography, 1749-2000. 22
Critical Survey of Drama. 69
Cut Me Some Slang (Web). 16
Cyclopedia of World Authors. 69

Dictionary of American Family Names. 81
Dictionary of Buddhism. 28
Dictionary of Crime Terms. 45
Dictionary of Historic Documents. 22
Dictionary of Military Terms: A Guide to the Language of Warfare and Military Institutions. 43
Dictionary of Pseudonyms: 11,000 Assumed Names and Their Origins. 81
Dictionary of the Middle Ages. 11
Dictionary of the Modern Politics of Japan. 34
Dinosaur Atlas. 51
Dinosaur: The Complete Guide to Dinosaurs. 51
Directory of Distance Learning Opportunities: K-12. 45
Directory of Drug & Alcohol Residential Rehabilitation Facilities. 43
Distinguished Asian American Business Leaders. 40
Distinguished Asian American Political and Governmental Leaders. 80
Distinguished Women Economists. 38

Education and Technology: an Encyclopedia. 45
Eighteenth Century Collections Online. 82
Enciclopedia estudiantil hallazgos. 14
Enciclopedia universal en español. 14

Encyclopaedia Britannica. 1
Encyclopaedia Britannica Online. 1
Encyclopedia Americana. 2
Encyclopedia Americana Online. 2
Encyclopedia of 20th-Century Architecture. 62
Encyclopedia of African-American Politics. 89
Encyclopedia of Air. 51
Encyclopedia of Alzheimer's Disease. 56
Encyclopedia of American Business. 40
Encyclopedia of American Folk Art. 62
Encyclopedia of American Foreign Policy. 36
Encyclopedia of American Independent Filmmaking. 64
Encyclopedia of American Military History. 43
Encyclopedia of American Religion and Politics. 35
Encyclopaedia of American Studies. 82
Encyclopedia of Ancient Egyptian Architecture. 61
Encyclopedia of Angels. 26
Encyclopedia of Arthritis. 57
Encyclopedia of Autoimmune Diseases. 57
Encyclopedia of Barbarian Europe: Society in Transformation. 84
Encyclopedia of Bioethics. 24
Encyclopedia of British Writers. 75
Encyclopedia of Buddhism. 28
Encyclopedia of Celtic Mythology and Folklore. 29
Encyclopedia of Children and Childhood in History and Society. 31
Encyclopedia of Christmas and New Year's Celebrations. 46
Encyclopedia of Community: From the Village to the Virtual World. 34
Encyclopedia of Complementary and Alternative Medicine. 56
Encyclopedia of Constitutional Amendments, Proposed Amendments, and Amending Issues, 1789-2002. 40
Encyclopedia of Cuba: People, History, Culture. 87
Encyclopedia of Deafness and Hearing Disorders. 58
Encyclopedia of Distributed Learning. 46
Encyclopedia of Folk Medicine: Old World and New World Traditions. 56
Encyclopedia of Forensic Science. 44
Encyclopedia of Health Care Management. 43
Encyclopedia of High-Tech Crime and Crime-Fighting. 45
Encyclopedia of HIV and AIDS. 57
Encyclopedia of Hollywood Film Actors: From the Silent Era to 1965. 64
Encyclopedia of Human Ecology. 55
Encyclopedia of Infectious Diseases. 57
Encyclopedia of International Games. 67
Encyclopedia of International Media and Communications. 29
Encyclopedia of Ireland. 85
Encyclopedia of Islam and the Muslim World. 77
Encyclopedia of Latin American Theater. 77
Encyclopedia of Lesbian, Bisexual, and Transgendered History. 33
Encyclopedia of Life Sciences. 52
Encyclopedia of Literary Modernism. 70
Encyclopedia of Modern Ethnic Conflicts. 32
Encyclopedia of Murder and Violent Crime. 45
Encyclopedia of Nutrition and Good Health. 55
Encyclopedia of Orson Wells. 65
Encyclopedia of Parkinson's Disease. 57

Encyclopedia of Population. 30
Encyclopedia of Presidential Campaigns, Slogans, Issues, and Platforms. 36
Encyclopedia of Protestantism. 26
Encyclopedia of Public Administation and Public Policy. 34
Encyclopedia of Religion and War. 27
Encyclopedia of Religious Freedom. 35
Encyclopedia of Retirement and Finance. 32
Encyclopedia of Russian History. 87
Encyclopedia of Science and Religion. 27
Encyclopedia of Sculpture. 62
Encyclopedia of Sexually Transmitted Diseases. 58
Encyclopedia of Suicide. 44
Encyclopedia of Surfing. 69
Encyclopedia of Terrorism. 29
Encyclopedia of the Aquatic World. 52
Encyclopedia of the Central Intelligence Agency. 37
Encyclopedia of the Crusades. 78
Encyclopedia of the Great Depression. 89
Encyclopedia of the Harlem Renaissance. 72
Encyclopedia of the Lewis and Clark Expedition. 83
Encyclopedia of the Modern Olympic Movement. 64
Encyclopedia of the Renaissance and the Reformation. 84
Encyclopedia of the Romantic Era, 1760-1850. 60
Encyclopedia of the Victorian Era. 85
Encyclopedia of War Movies. 65
Encyclopedia of Water. 51
Encyclopedia of Westerns. 65
Encyclopedia of Women in Radio. 65
Encyclopedia of Women in the American West. 32
Encyclopedia of Work-Related Illnesses, Injuries, and Health Issues. 58
Encyclopedia of World Environmental History. 30
Encyclopedia of World Writers. 70
Epic Films: Casts, Credits, and Commentary on over 350 Historical Spectacle Movies. 66
Europe, 1450 to 1789. 12
Exploring Ancient Civilizations. 83
Exploring Polar Frontiers: A Historical Encyclopedia. 78
Exploring Technology. 54
Extraordinary Asian Americans and Pacific Islanders. 80
Extraordinary People in the Movies. 80

Facts about China. 87
Facts On File Marine Science Handbook. 49
Facts On File Companion to American Drama. 73
Facts On File Dictionary of Classical and Biblical Allusions. 70
Facts on File Encyclopedia of Mythology and Legend. 27
Facts On File Encyclopedia of Word and Phrase Origins. 48
Facts On File Geometry Handbook. 49
Fashion, Costume, and Culture: Clothing, Headwear, Body Decoration, and Footwear through the Ages. 46
Fashion, Turn to the Left (Web). 16
FBI Encyclopedia. 44
Ferguson's Career Guidance Center. 37
Film Noir Guide. 22
Firefly Atlas of the Universe. 50
Firefly Encyclopedia of Birds. 53
Flora: A Gardener's Encyclopedia. 59

From Convent to Concert Hall: A Guide to Women Composers. 62

Gale Encyclopedia of the Unusual and Unexplained. 24
Gale Virtual Reference Library. 12
Garner's Modern American Usage. 48
Global History: Cultural Encounters from Antiquity to the Present. 78
Gorehound's Guide to the Splatter Films of the 1980s. 63
Great American Judges: An Encyclopedia. 41
Great Britain: A Reference Guide from the Renaissance to the Present. 86
Great World Writers: Twentieth Century. 70
Greek and Roman Mythology A to Z. 27
Greenhaven Encyclopedia of the Middle Ages. 84
Greenwood Encyclopedia of African American Civil Rights: From Emancipation to the Twenty-First Century. 35
Greenwood Encyclopedia of Women's Issues Worldwide. 32
Grey House Homeland Security Directory. 44
Grolier Multimedia Encyclopedia. 3
Grolier Student Encyclopedia. 24
Grzimek's Animal Life Encyclopedia: v.1: Lower Metazoans and Lesser Deuterostomes. 53
Grzimek's Animal Life Encyclopedia: v.12-16: Mammals. 53
Grzimek's Animal Life Encyclopedia: v.2: Protostomes. 53
Grzimek's Animal Life Encyclopedia: v.3: Insects. 53
Grzimek's Animal Life Encyclopedia: v.4-5: Fishes. 53
Grzimek's Animal Life Encyclopedia: v.6: Amphibians. 53
Grzimek's Animal Life Encyclopedia: v.7: Reptiles. 53

Halloween Encyclopedia. 47
Handbook of Death and Dying. 33
Handbook of Hindu Mythology. 28
Handbook to Life in Ancient Egypt. 84
Harlem Renaissance (Web). 17
Harvard Dictionary of Music. 62
Hinduism (Web). 17
Hispanic Literature of the United States. 72
Historical Encyclopedia of American Labor. 39
History of Women in the United States. 12
Holiday Symbols and Customs. 47
Hollywood Musicals Nominated for Best Picture. 66
Houghton Mifflin Dictionary of Biography. 81
How It Works: Science and Technology. 55
How People Live. 33
How Stuff Works (Web). 18
HQ Online. 37
Human Diseases and Conditions, Supplement 2: Infectious Diseases. 58

Illustrated Dictionary of Automobile Body Styles. 58
Indian Placenames in America: Volume 1: Cities, Towns, and Villages. 79
Indigenous Peoples and Environmental Issues: An Encyclopedia. 30
Industrial Revolution: Almanac. 38
Industrial Revolution: Biographies. 38
Industrial Revolution: Primary Sources. 38
International Encyclopedia of Information and Library Science. 21
International Motor Racing Guide: A Complete Reference from Formula One to NASCAR. 67
It Came from Outer Space: Everyday Products and Ideas from the Space Program. 55

Jesus in History, Thought, and Culture. 26
Jewish Writers of the Twentieth Century. 70

Kennel Club's Illustrated Breed Standards: Official Guide to Registered Breeds. 60
Kingfisher Geography Encyclopedia. 79
Korean War Filmography. 22

Landmark Legislation, 1774-2002. 41
Latin America and Caribbean Artists of the Modern Era: A Biographical Dictionary of More than 12,700 Persons. 61
Latina and Latino Voices in Literature. 23
Latino and African American Athletes Today: A Biographical Dictionary. 68
Latino and Latina Writers. 72
Life & Times in 20th-Century America. 89
Literature of Travel and Exploration. 79

Major Acts of Congress. 41
Mary Shelley Encyclopedia. 76
Masterplots 2: Drama Series. 71
Medical Library Association Guide to Searching and Finding Health Information on the Web. 23
Medieval Italy: An Encyclopedia. 86
Men and Masculinities: A Social, Cultural, and Historical Encyclopedia. 31
Men and Women of the Bible: A Reader's Guide. 26
Merck Manual of Medical Information: Home Edition. 55
Merriam-Webster's Collegiate Dictionary. 13
Mexican American Experience: An Encyclopedia. 89
Modern British Women Writers: An A-to-Z Guide. 75
Most Valuable Players in Baseball, 1931-2001. 68
Museum of Broadcast Communications Encyclopedia of Radio. 46

Naming Pains (Web). 18
National Geographic Reference Atlas to the Birds of North America. 53
Native Americans in Sports. 66
New Book of Knowledge. 3
New Book of Knowledge Online. 3
New Encyclopedia of Science. 48
New Encyclopedia of the Occult. 24
Newest Americans. 31
No, Not Those Primaries (Web). 19
Norse Mythology A to Z. 27
Notable Caribbeans and Caribbean Americans: A Biographical Dictionary. 81
Notable Sports Figures. 68
Nueva enciclopedia cumbre en linea. 14

Oxford Companion to Chaucer. 76
Oxford Companion to Italian Literature. 76
Oxford Companion to Mark Twain. 74
Oxford Companion to the History of Modern Science. 49
Oxford Dictionary of Classical Myth and Religion. 27
Oxford Dictionary of Islam. 28
Oxford Dictionary of Modern Quotations. 24
Oxford Dictionary of Phrase, Saying, and Quotation. 24
Oxford Dictionary of the Renaissance. 84
Oxford Encyclopedia of Economic History. 38
Oxford Encyclopedia of Theatre & Performance. 66
Oxford Scholarship Online. 12

Peoples of North America. 32
Pioneer Aviators of the World: A Biographical Dictionary of the First Pilots of 100 Countries. 59
Political Corruption in America: An Encyclopedia of Scandals, Power, and Greed. 89
Pollution A to Z. 45
Presidents, Vice Presidents, Cabinet Members, Supreme Court Justices, 1789-2003. 42
Profiles of America: Facts, Figures & Statistics for Every Populated Place. 34
Propaganda and Mass Persuasion: A Historical Encyclopedia. 29
Proquest Historical Newspapers. 83

Queen Victoria: A Biographical Companion. 85

Reader's Guide to British History. 86
Reference Books in Spanish for Children and Adolescents. 7
Reference Universe. 21
Religion and American Cultures: An Encyclopedia of Traditions. 25
Religious Holidays and Calendars. 50
Renaissance: An Encyclopedia for Students. 85
RoutledgeCurzon Encyclopedia of Confucianism. 25
Rx for Consumer Health Reference: One-Volume Medical Encyclopedias. 13

Salud para todos. 54
Scholastic Book of Outstanding Americans: Profiles of More Than 450 Famous and Infamous Figures in U.S. History. 81
Scholastic Dinosaurs A to Z: The Ultimate Dinosaur Encyclopedia. 52
Scholastic Visual Sports Encyclopedia. 68
Science in the Enlightenment: An Encyclopedia. 49
Short-Lived Television Series, 1948-1978: Thirty Years of More than 1,000 Flops. 66
Slasher Films: An International Filmography, 1960 through 2001. 63
South Asian Novelists in English: An A-to-Z Guide. 75
Spanish-Language Online Encyclopedias. 14
Statistical Handbook of Infectious Diseases. 56
Student Almanac of African American History. 90
Student Almanac of Native American History. 90

Talking Terrorism: A Dictionary of the Loaded Language of Political Violence. 29
Tennessee Williams Encyclopedia. 73
Theodore Dreiser Encyclopedia. 73
Timetables of World Literature. 71
Tin Pan Alley: An Encyclopedia of the Golden Age of American Song. 63
Today in Literature (Web). 19
Toni Morrison Encyclopedia. 74
Top 10 Science Reference Sources for under $100. 8
Total Tennis: The Ultimate Tennis Encyclopedia. 68
Twayne Companion to Contemporary World Literature. 71
Twenty Best Bets for Student Researchers. 9

U.S. Laws, Acts, and Treaties. 41
United State Holidays and Observances: By Date, Jurisdiction, and Subject, Fully Indexed. 47
United States Counties. 79
United States Executive Branch: A Biographical Directory of Heads of State and Cabinet Officials. 42
United States Gubernatorial Elections, 1776-1860. 36
United States History. 23

Water: Science and Issues. 51
When There's TMTT (Web). 20
Wilson Chronology of Human Rights. 35
Women and the Law. 41
Women during the Civil War: An Encyclopedia. 90
Work in America: An Encyclopedia of History, Policy, and Society. 37
World Book Encyclopedia. 4
World Book Online Reference Center. 4
World Book's Celebrations and Rituals around the World. 47
World Eras: Volume 10: West African Kingdoms, 500-1590. 87
World History of Tax Rebellions. 39
World History Online. 82
World of Animals: Birds. 54
World of Epidemics: A Cultural Chronology of Disease from Prehistory to the Era of SARS. 56
World of Toni Morrison: A Guide to Characters and Places in Her Novels. 74
World Writers in English. 76